Brian + Ronda
Christmas
1994

GOLF COURSES
OF THE PGA TOUR
Second Edition

PHOTOGRAPHS BY
JOHN JOHNSON,
PGA TOUR PHOTOGRAPHERS,
AND OTHERS

MAPS BY ELIZABETH PEPER

HARRY N. ABRAMS, INC., PUBLISHERS
A GOLF MAGAZINE BOOK

GOLF COURSES
OF THE PGA TOUR

Second Edition

BY GEORGE PEPER
EDITOR-IN-CHIEF, GOLF MAGAZINE

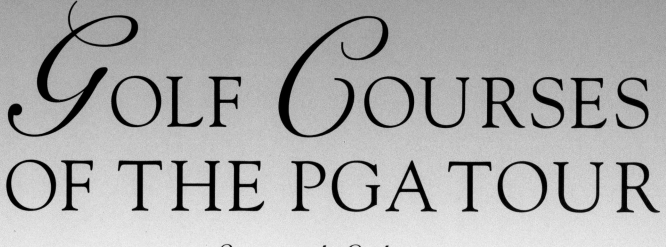

Table of Contents

Project Director: Margaret L. Kaplan
Designers: Robert McKee and Tania Garcia
Photo Editor: John K. Crowley

Library of Congress Cataloging-in-Publication Data
Peper, George.
Golf courses of the PGA Tour/ by George Peper;
foreword by Deane R. Beman; photographs by John Johnson;
maps by Elizabeth Peper. — 2nd ed.
p. cm.
"A Golf magazine book."
Includes index.
ISBN 0-8109-3380-2
1. Golf courses — United States. 2. PGA Tour.
I. Title.
GV975.P465 1994
796. '352'06' 873 — dc20   94–4099

Printed and bound in Japan

ENDPAPERS: Augusta National Golf Club, 16th hole
HALF TITLE PAGE: TPC at Sawgrass, 8th hole
TITLE PAGES: Pebble Beach Golf Links, 7th hole
CONTENTS PAGES:Doral Country Club, 18th hole
COPYRIGHT AND FOREWORD: Oakwood Country Club, 3rd hole

FOREWORD

*by Deane R. Beman
Commissioner,
PGA Tour, 1974-1994*

One of the wonderful experiences the PGA Tour offers its players and fans is the chance to see some of the magnificent golf courses that dot the North American landscape. Each course has its own characteristics—from the green strips of fairway that carve through western desert to the towering Northern fir trees, the rugged California coast to the Florida lagoons. Some courses can be charming, others frightening—but each presents a challenge, and each lies in wait for an annual visit by the best players in the world.

Thanks to the efforts of George Peper, we were able to share these venues with you a few years ago in the original edition of *Golf Courses of the PGA Tour*. Now we're pleased to include many new tournament sites—and even a couple of new tournaments—in this completely revised and updated edition.

George's evocative text is illustrated with hundreds of new color photographs and maps to help you enhance your knowledge of the courses and gain appreciation both for the men who have designed them and the men who have conquered them. It's an ideal companion to help you follow the weekend golf telecasts.

So sit back and imagine it is Sunday morning. You can hear the crash of the Pacific and feel the mist on your skin on the 18th tee at Pebble Beach. Or think about your two-stroke lead as you approach the treacherous island 17th hole at the Tournament Players Club at Sawgrass. Walk the fairways in the footsteps of Ben Hogan, Sam Snead, Arnold Palmer, and Jack Nicklaus as they forge their magnificent careers. It's all here— the history, beauty, and excitement of the PGA Tour.

LA COSTA COUNTRY CLUB

Nobody gets invited to this tournament—they invite themselves by winning a tournament on the previous year's Tour. It's the smallest field of the year, but man for man, it's also the strongest.

It's been that way since 1953, when the total purse was $35,000 and first prize was $10,000—paid in silver dollars. In those days, $10,000 was a princely sum, about the same as the total Ben Hogan collected that year for winning the Masters, U.S. Open, and British Open.

Not the least of the attractions for the pros is that everyone who arrives a winner also goes home a winner. Since the average field is roughly two dozen players, there's no 36-hole cut and every entrant is guaranteed a hefty check. In 1994, Rocco Mediate finished 16 strokes behind winner Phil Mickelson, but still collected $18,500.

This is also the only event of the year in which players from the PGA Tour and Senior Tour compete simultaneously. Since 1984, the winners from the previous year's Senior circuit have gathered at La Costa each January to determine their own champion of champions. In 1993, both Tours played from the same tees because in 1992 Raymond Floyd had achieved an unprecedented double, winning tournaments on both the regular and Senior PGA Tours. Thus, Floyd competed simultaneously for both purses (but won neither).

For the players' wives, a week at the Mercedes Championships is the hottest invitation of the year, since La Costa is as renowned for its facials, massages, and herbal wraps as for its tees, fairways, and greens. Some guests stay here for a week and never realize there's a golf course outside.

The fact is, there are two of them, and the course the pros play is a composite using the best holes from each. When

6th and 7th holes

10th hole

the Tournament of Champions (as it was known until 1994) arrived here in 1969 after a long run in Las Vegas at the Desert Inn Country Club, the pros expected the shorter La Costa to be easier, but they hadn't figured on the five-inch rough. Jack Nicklaus was the most notable victim, taking an 80 in the first round as Gary Player won on a score of 284, four under par.

The first four holes are relatively tame, but at the fifth tee the pros confront a 446-yard par four that is the toughest assignment on the course. A stream runs down the left side of the landing area, then cuts diagonally across the fairway at about the 300-yard mark. The green is the smallest on the course and is bunkered to the left and back. Even the strongest players need long irons—and straight ones—to get home.

The sibling to that hole is number ten, a 450-yard par four, where water again crosses the fairway. In this case, the hazard does not come into play off the tee, but with lengthy bunkers on the left and several large trees on the right, the drive is nonetheless one of the most difficult in town.

La Costa's finish—holes 15 through 18—is called The Last Mile, and when the prevailing north wind is up it can feel like ten miles.

The 15th is the easiest of the four. A classic short dogleg par four, it is played from an elevated tee and the drive should be shaded to the right to avoid a large sycamore protecting the left corner of the dogleg. The approach is a short iron, but it's not an easy shot, particularly when played into the teeth of the wind. Five bunkers surround this elevated green.

Reading Rough
BY LANNY WADKINS

La Costa would be a relatively easy course were it not for one factor—deep, dense rough. The thick grass is on everyone's mind during every hole of the Tournament of Champions.

Ninety-nine percent of the lies in the fairway can be played the same way, but in the rough no two lies are alike. Indeed, the most important aspect of playing from the rough is being able to read the lie and choose the shot that offers the best promise of success.

Remember a couple of rules. If the ball is sitting in deep rough, you won't be able to hit it as far as you would from the fairway; but if the ball is sitting cleanly in light or moderate rough, you'll likely hit a "flyer," a spinless shot that can travel as much as 30 yards farther than a shot hit with the same club from a fairway lie. In either case you'd almost never use the same club for, say, a 170-yard shot from the rough that you'd use for a 170-yard shot from the fairway.

Bermudagrass usually is more tangly than bent or rye rough. Lies in which the rough grows against the direction of the shot are more difficult than those in which the grass grows with the shot. And remember that, unless you have a very clean lie, you'll have almost no chance of maneuvering the ball from left-to-right or right-to-left or of applying any backspin to the shot.

Lanny Wadkins is a back-to-back winner (1982–83) of the Mercedes Championships.

18th hole

There is no sand to worry about from the tee at 16, but pine trees on the inside corner of this left-to-right dogleg have proved nettlesome to many a competitor. This hole has also been the scene of two rules controversies. In 1982 Ron Streck suffered a two-stroke penalty after brushing aside some tree limbs while attempting to play his approach shot. A television viewer called in, cited Streck's infraction of the rule that prohibits improving one's lie, and instead of winning the tournament, Streck finished in a four-way tie for second. A decade later, Paul Azinger's ball moved as he was preparing to play a pitch shot to this green. A discussion ensued as to

whether or not he had addressed the ball, and the ruling was that he had, incurring a penalty which moved him out of contention going into the final round.

The 17th hole at La Costa is consistently one of the most difficult par fives on the Tour and one of the few that the pros do not play in an average of less than five strokes. The reasons are its length—569 yards into the prevailing wind—and the nearly 200-yard-long lake that hugs the right side of the fairway, plaguing both the second and third shots. Pros seldom write the number 7 on their cards, but this hole produces a couple of dozen each year.

A good tee shot is important on 18, where the long approach must be played to an elevated, well-bunkered, severely sloping green. The traditional Sunday pin placement—front-right—puts a premium on yardage calculation because the bunker fronting the right side of the green catches many underclubbed shots.

Gene Littler won the Tournament three times in succession from 1955 through 1957, and since then an odds-defying four players have defended their titles successfully—but what a foursome they are: Jack Nicklaus (1963–64), Arnold Palmer (1965–66), Tom Watson (1979–80), and Lanny Wadkins (1982–83).

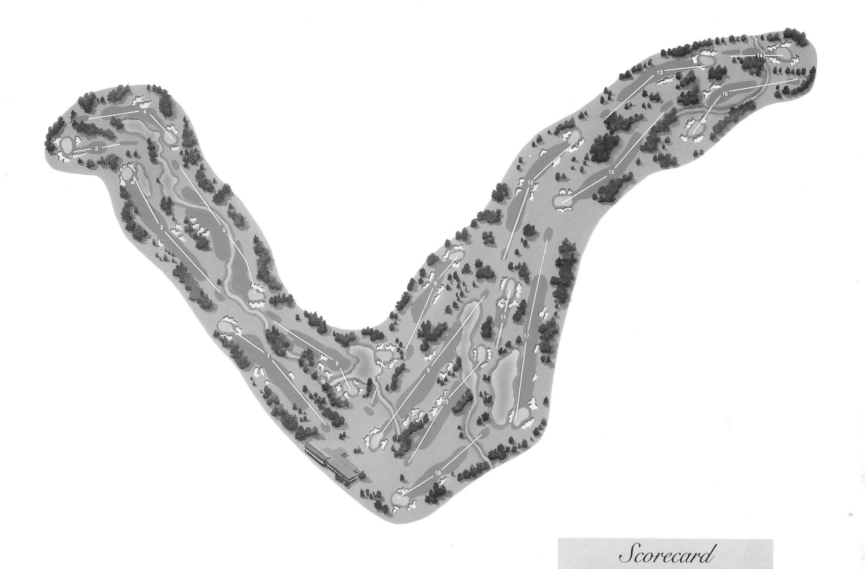

18th hole

Scorecard

Hole	Yards	Par	PGA Tour Avg. Score
1	412	4	4.025
2	526	5	4.773
3	187	3	3.039
4	386	4	3.993
5	446	4	4.245
6	365	4	3.970
7	188	3	2.997
8	398	4	3.974
9	538	5	4.786
OUT	3446	36	35.802
10	450	4	4.147
11	180	3	2.912
12	541	5	4.707
13	410	4	3.964
14	204	3	3.025
15	378	4	3.954
16	423	4	4.108
17	569	5	4.959
18	421	4	4.043
IN	3576	36	35.819
TOTAL	7022	72	71.621

WAIALAE COUNTRY CLUB

17th hole

United Airlines Hawaiian Open

awaii's nickname is Paradise, and the same word could be applied to Waialae. When the pros make their annual boondoggle to Oahu, they know they'll be playing a course where the greens are perfect, the par fives are reachable with irons, and birdies are as plentiful as coconuts.

Waialae is the work of Seth Raynor, protégé of C. B. Macdonald, the St. Andrews–trained gentleman golfer whose autocratic personality and daunting designs spearheaded the growth of golf in turn-of-the-century America. Raynor visited Hawaii and drew up the plans in November of 1926, but he never saw his vision take shape, for in February of the following year he died.

His design prevailed, however, incorporating several ideas from Macdonald's American courses and from the original Scottish links. At the first hole, for example, Raynor plotted a short par five whose doglegging fairway and severely front-bunkered green recalled the "Road Hole" at St. Andrews, often called the toughest par four in the world.

At 6,975 yards, Waialae is one of the shortest par 72s on the Tour. Its four par fives—the first, ninth, 13th, and 18th holes—are particularly vulnerable, averaging barely 530 yards. But these holes are the key to the excitement at the Hawaiian Open. Witness the performance of Bruce Lietzke, who scored three eagles in a single round. Or Andy Bean, who won the 1980 event with a record score of 22-under-par 266 by playing the par fives in 13 under par. Or Hale Irwin, who bettered Bean's total by one a year later when he eagled the final hole. Or the ultimate example, Isao Aoki, who in 1983 holed one of the most electrifying shots of all time, a 128-yard wedge that bounced into the 72nd hole for an eagle that gave him a

4th hole

To Gamble or Not to Gamble

BY MARK O'MEARA

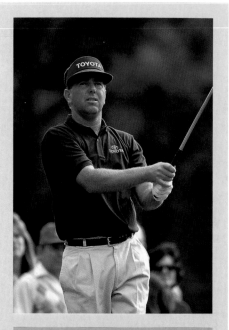

On a course with four reachable par fives, such as Waialae, you're continually asked to decide whether to go for the green in two strokes. The question, of course, is whether the reward is worth the risk.

If there's not much trouble—no out of bounds, water, or penal bunkering—you usually have nothing to lose by giving it a shot, but if hazards of any kind lurk near the green, think carefully. Remember that by laying up and wedging onto the green you'll still have a chance for birdie and a good chance for par, whereas a lengthy second shot, while introducing the possibility of a 3, also leaves you open to a 6 or more.

If you decide to give it a go, the most important point is to take plenty of club. Choose your weapon based not on the total distance you hit the club but on your "carrying" distance, the length the club flies the ball, which on the longer clubs can be 20 yards or so less than the total distance. If, however, you decide to lay up, then truly lay up. Keep the ball back in an area where you'll be able to take a full swing at your third shot instead of having to finesse a wedge shot. With a full swing you'll be able to apply more backspin for maximum control.

Mark O'Meara won the 1985 Hawaiian Open.

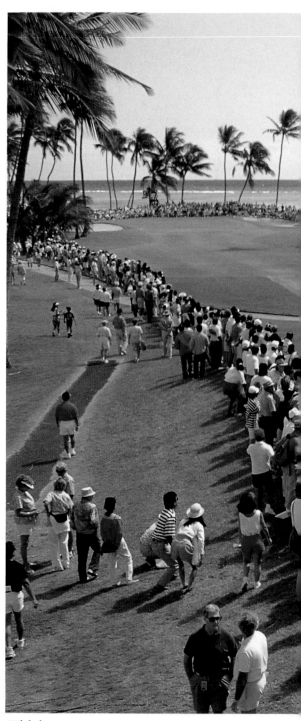

11th hole

13th hole

one-stroke victory. Short on yardage, the Waialae fives are long on drama.

Besides, they are not quite as short as they look. Golf at Waialae means golf in wind—constant, swirling, gusting, confounding wind. About 80 percent of the time it is a tradewind from the northeast, but occasionally a Kona wind from the opposite direction will arrive. Still, since the par fives point in four different direc-

tions, neither condition offers an advantage. On a given day, a Tour player might reach one green with a 5-iron, one with a 2-iron, one with a 3-wood, and one not at all.

Wind is an even greater factor on the par threes. The 196-yard fourth hole is called Apiki, the Hawaiian word for "tricky." Its elongated, two-level green, bunkered on both sides, is the most elu-

sive target on the course and is made more difficult because the hole normally plays upwind. Club selection varies from a 3-wood to a 5-iron.

Its sister, the 182-yard seventh, also plays into the wind and also is surrounded by sand. The elevated green on this hole is patterned after the sixth at C.B. Macdonald's most famous project, the National Golf Links in Southampton,

New York. In 1992, as part of a major rejuvenation of the course, architect Desmond Muirhead added mounding at the rear of the green, easing the viewing for spectators while complicating the assignment for the players.

The same refurbishing program has added difficulty to about a third of the holes through tighter bunkering in the driving areas. At the par-four 12th hole,

7th hole

Hole	Yards	Par	PGA Tour Avg. Score
1	539	5	4.582
2	362	4	4.107
3	410	4	4.097
4	196	3	3.231
5	478	4	4.132
6	435	4	4.240
7	182	3	3.124
8	402	4	4.007
9	513	5	4.541
OUT	3517	36	36.061
10	355	4	3.984
11	181	3	3.028
12	446	4	4.110
13	508	5	4.439
14	412	4	4.095
15	398	4	4.143
16	419	4	4.111
17	187	3	3.051
18	552	5	4.549
IN	3458	36	35.510
TOTAL	6975	72	71.571

sun. Two-time champions Hubert Green, Lanny Wadkins, and Corey Pavin will admit that some of their hottest putting has occurred on Oahu.

But the truth is that everything grows well on this island. The Waialae course is an arboretum with dozens of different species of trees and flowering shrubs in bloom year-round. Many of them have names as colorful as their blossoms: bauhinia, Chinese fan palm, graveyard plumeria, monkey pod, madre de coco, false kamani, wili-wili, Madagascar olive, be-still, tuckeroo, and cow-itch.

Although it did not become an official PGA Tour event until 1965, the Hawaiian Open goes back to 1928, when the inaugural was won by Wild Bill Mehlhorn; other notable champions have included Gene Sarazen, Craig Wood, and Cary Middlecoff. Ted Makalena, a home-grown pro and the best Hawaiian golfer in history, won the event five consecutive years. During World War II, the tournament was played at other courses because Waialae's fairways were strung with

the green was repositioned, bringing a lake into play on the second shot.

If you like watching the pros sink mammoth putts, check out the midwinter telecast of this event. The greens at

Waialae are among the fastest and smoothest in the world. Although grown with bermudagrass, not associated with slick, true putting, the Tifdwarf bermuda surfaces at Waialae benefit from constant

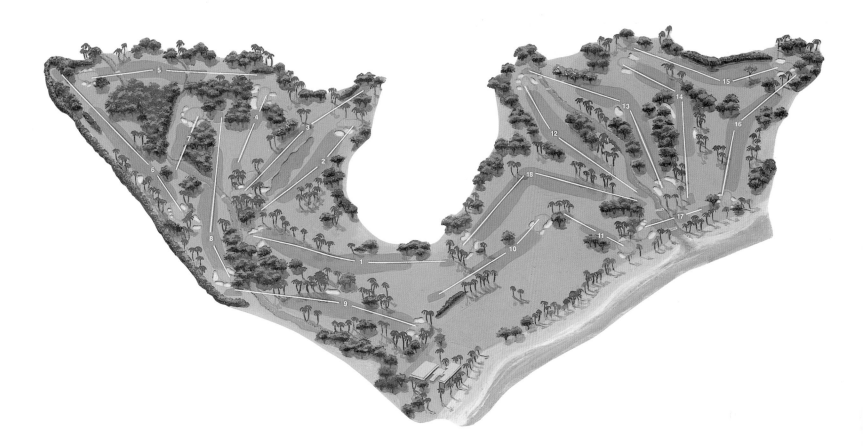

barbed wire to prevent landings by Japanese aircraft. No damage was done to the course during the bombing of Pearl Harbor, but near a bunker on the first hole, Private Prewitt (Montgomery Clift) was "shot" during the filming of *From Here to Eternity*.

Waialae is one club that had nothing to fear in 1990 when the Shoal Creek racial controversy prompted the PGA Tour to investigate membership practices at its venues. This club is a model of multiethnic harmony, with about half the membership Caucasian and the rest a mixture of Japanese, Chinese, Hawaiian, Korean, black, East Indian, and Filipino.

It is fitting, therefore, that on this course Isao Aoki became the first Japanese player to win an American Tour event. And it is further appropriate on this serene, democratic island that the man who took the impact of Aoki's miraculous closing eagle, Jack Renner, came back a year later and beat the field for his own day in the Hawaiian sun.

9th hole

STARR PASS GOLF CLUB

TUCSON NATIONAL GOLF CLUB

It all started with a crap game. Back in the 1940s, Leo Diegel, the pro at the El Rio Country Club, convinced then PGA Commissioner Fred Corcoran that Tucson was a big enough town to take on a professional Tour event. At about the same time, the old El Paso Open was going broke, so in January of 1945 the Tucson Open was inserted in El Paso's January time slot, the third stop on the winter Tour.

There was only one problem—no purse. This was in the days before corporate sponsors. Ah, but this was also the Wild West, where men took things into their own hands. So Diegel set up a makeshift casino in the El Rio clubhouse, drafted a few of the better-known gamblers in town to deal blackjack, ran a Calcutta, and coaxed the locals into high-stake crap games.

The gamble paid off. A half century later, the Northern Telecom Open is going strong. Today, it is one of the ten oldest events on the PGA Tour—and producing some of the Tour's youngest winners. In 1990, University of Arizona All-American Robert Gamez accepted a sponsor's exemption and cruised to a four-stroke victory, the first player since Ben Crenshaw in 1973 to win in his first start on the Tour. A year later, 20-year-old Phil Mickelson, while still a junior at Arizona State, became the youngest amateur ever to win a Tour event when he sank an eight-foot birdie putt on the 72nd hole to edge Tom

Purtzer and Bob Tway. Then, in 1992, Lee Janzen, a third-year pro, emerged from a logjam of players on the final day to post his first professional win, presaging a victory one year later in the U.S. Open.

Two courses are used for this event, Starr Pass Golf Club and Tucson National Golf Club. Starr Pass, originally the TPC at StarPass, was designed in 1986 by Bob Cupp and Craig Stadler, an architect and a player who share the conviction that a golf course lives and dies on the challenge of its putting greens. Consequently, the greens at Starr Pass

are fast and heavily contoured, several of them with more than one tier.

One of the most difficult holes on the course is the very first, a downhill dogleg that winds 439 yards while sloping left toward the virtually unplayable desert. The green has three tiers, and when the pin is in front or back, extreme accuracy is required of the approach. A similar assignment awaits at the close of the nine, where a 437-yarder doglegs left and downhill, this time to a shallow green bunkered in front and back.

The center of excitement on this course is unquestionably number 14, a

Tucson National, 9th hole

Northern Telecom Open, Arizona

Tucson National, 18th hole

Starr Pass, 7th hole

Starr Pass, 14th hole

Starr Pass, 3rd hole

Starr Pass, 16th hole

Striking from the Desert Floor
BY LEE JANZEN

When you're playing a course in the Arizona desert, be prepared to hit a few shots from tight, sandy lies.

The good news is that these lies usually look more forbidding than they actually are. What you need is precise, clean contact, and that means a compact, controlled swing.

In setting up to the ball, do yourself a favor and grind your spikes well into the sand—this will help ensure good balance and footing. Grip down on your club a little bit, too, to compensate for the lowered stance and to enhance control.

I try to play these shots with relatively little leg action and a more sweeping swing than usual, to ensure that I contact the ball before the sand. The worst mistake is to throw your arms and club at the ball, to hit at it rather than swing through it. So take one club more than you would from the fairway, and give it a smooth, patient swing.

Lee Janzen's victory in the 1992 Northern Telecom Open was his first PGA Tour win.

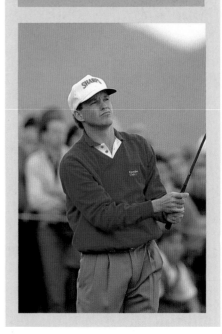

506-yard par five where those who hope to reach the green in two must play their lengthy second shots across a deep canyon. The alternative is to lay up and then wedge to the undulating green guarded by two bunkers. On Sunday in 1991, Phil Mickelson failed to carry the canyon and posted a triple-bogey 8 before recovering for his victory.

Two of the last four holes on the course are strong par threes. Number 15 plays a deceptive 199 yards to a green set at eye level that narrows from front to back, and the 203-yard 17th features an enormous three-tiered green where the assignment is to find the correct tier with your tee shot or bring plenty of imagination and touch to your first putt.

The longest par four on the course is the 454-yard 18th. Bunkers protect the right side of this green, so the ideal approach is from the left. But the player who hits his drive in that direction will have to carry a trio of large and deep fairway bunkers. Meanwhile, the right side of the fairway is lined by a rising slope and is slightly rippled to offer irregular lies.

The Orange and Gold nines at Tucson National are part of a 27-hole complex which, along with the Tucson National Golf Resort, underwent a major refurbishment in 1990. In contrast to Starr Pass, which like most modern desert layouts was carved out of the arid sand and scrub as a target course, Tucson is an expansive course, designed in 1960 before the days of land and water restriction.

It is longer than Starr Pass but its wide, lush fairways leave plenty of room to swing, and encourage aggressive play. Johnny Miller holds the course record here, a 61 back in the days when Miller

Starr Pass, 18th hole

seemed to win every time he stepped near a cactus. Miller also shares the tournament record of 263—25 under par.

One hole at Tucson National that virtually every player subdues is the second, a 495-yard par five that in 1992 ranked as the single easiest hole on the PGA Tour.

But most players will feel some intimidation on the tee at number nine. A lake runs down the right side of this rightward dogleg, a 440-yard uphiller that requires strength as well as accuracy.

It is followed by another lengthy, watery dogleg. The tenth, which is played as a par five by amateurs, presents a tee shot similar to that at the 18th hole at Doral, with trees to the right and a lake on the left. The hole winds 456 yards from right to left around the lake before culminating at an elevated, well-bunkered green. The same lake reappears on 18 and makes the home hole the toughest on the course. The tee shot on this 465-yard brute must be long, but also must be left to avoid the lake. Then it's a long iron to the severely sloped green flanked by bunkers. This is one of the two or three most difficult finishing holes on the Tour.

Scorecard

	Starr Pass					Tucson National		
Hole	Yards	Par	PGA Tour Avg. Score		Hole	Yards	Par	PGA Tour Avg. Score
1	439	4	4.086		1	410	4	3.995
2	427	4	4.047		2	495	5	4.375
3	502	5	4.591		3	377	4	3.838
4	437	4	4.273		4	170	3	3.019
5	155	3	2.996		5	395	4	3.863
6	350	4	3.984		6	426	4	3.864
7	197	3	3.142		7	202	3	3.042
8	543	5	4.848		8	528	5	4.635
9	437	4	4.094		9	440	4	4.178
OUT	3487	36	36.061		OUT	3443	36	34.809
10	380	4	3.944		10	456	4	4.331
11	522	5	4.612		11	515	5	4.797
12	430	4	4.266		12	182	3	2.994
13	396	4	4.050		13	406	4	3.951
14	506	5	4.894		14	405	4	3.891
15	199	3	3.094		15	663	5	4.759
16	433	4	4.040		16	427	4	3.982
17	203	3	3.123		17	186	3	2.990
18	454	4	4.085		18	465	4	4.304
IN	3523	36	36.108		IN	3705	36	35.999
TOTAL	7010	72	72.169		TOTAL	7148	72	70.808

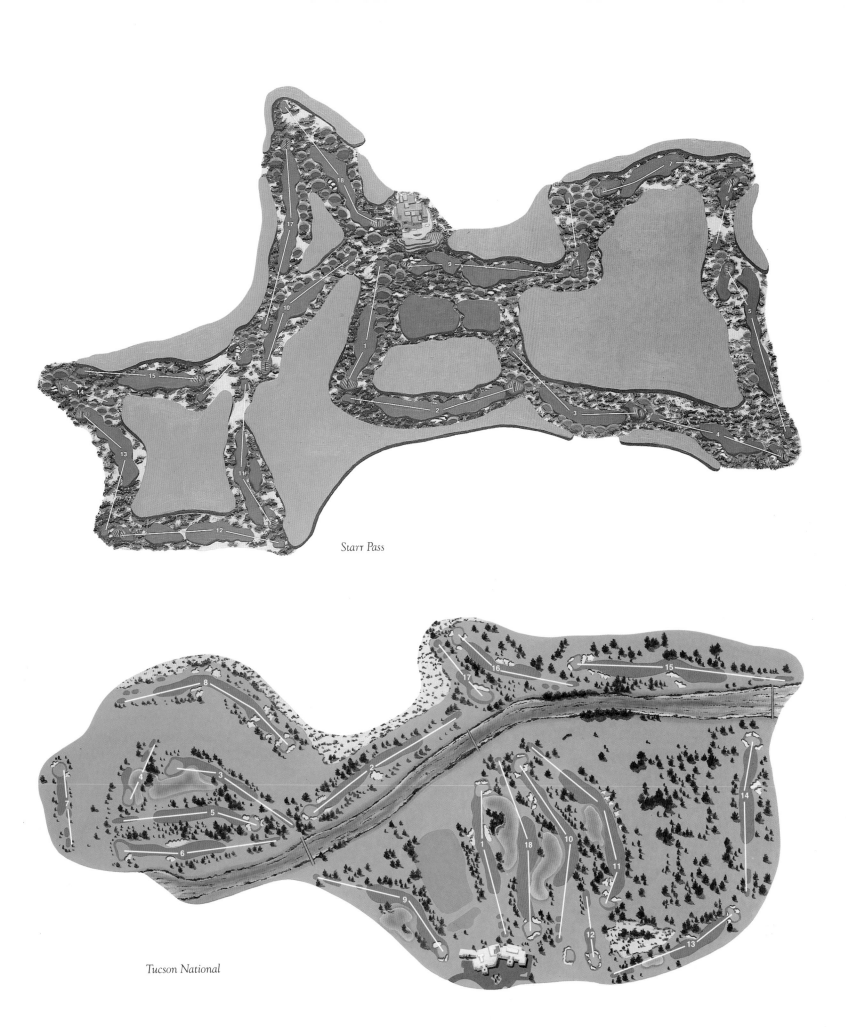

Starr Pass

Tucson National

TPC OF SCOTTSDALE

12th hole

Phoenix Open, Arizona

*I*f the PGA Tour were a beauty contest, the TPC of Scottsdale would have no chance at first prize—but it would be a lock for Miss Congeniality. No course is more popular with the pros than this one.

In contrast to the first generation of Tournament Players Courses—a succession of "target golf" tests characterized by ribbon-thin fairways, grasping hazards, and severely contoured greens—this is an open, amiable, friendly course with room to hit, room to miss it.

Completed in 1986, it is the work of Tom Weiskopf and Jay Morrish, along with player consultants Jim Colbert and Howard Twitty. They were commissioned by the City of Scottsdale to fashion a rare animal—a championship/ municipal course—that would test the best players in the world while encouraging a swift pace of play from the thousands of amateurs who would annually assault it. Working with dead-flat, barren desert, the architects excavated and sculpted a million cubic yards of dirt, created two sizable lakes, an enormous practice area, and 18 playable, pliable holes.

Shouldering mounds and faux dunes aid visibility for spectators while simultaneously acting as guard rails for errant shots. Some fairways move upwind, some down, some are straight, others bend one way or the other. The greens are contoured but not severely sloped, and virtually all of them can be reached with bounce-on approaches. "Hopefully, long wild hitters, short straight hitters, left-to-right players, right-to-left players, and good putters will each find an equal number of holes that favor their games," says Morrish.

One hole that favors only long straight hitters is number 11, a brute of a four that stretches 469 yards—400 of them along a lake—and culminates at a raised green. Perhaps even tougher is the 14th, playing

444 yards into the wind and through a corridor surrounded by desert.

The course's most memorable hole is the 15th, a par five in the mold of the famed 13th at Augusta National, with water lining the entire left side of the hole and then surrounding the green to create an island. The green is eminently reachable in two, but so is the water.

A Weiskopf/Morrish trademark is the drivable par four, and at Scottsdale it makes a dramatic appearance at number 17, a hole of 332 yards to an ample, open green. Birdies are not uncommon here, but neither are double-bogeys, for a large bunker haunts the left side of the fairway and water guards the left of the green.

At number 18, the key shot is the drive, which must clear 200 yards of water. Fred Couples found double trouble here in 1988. Leading the tournament by a stroke with one hole to go, he pulled his tee shot into the water and had to scramble for a bogey 5 to tie Sandy Lyle. The third hole of sudden death brought them back to the 18th

Scorecard

Hole	Yards	Par	PGA Tour Avg. Score
1	410	4	3.948
2	416	4	3.991
3	554	5	4.727
4	150	3	2.906
5	453	4	4.101
6	389	4	4.025
7	215	3	3.134
8	470	4	4.084
9	415	4	4.007
OUT	3472	35	34.923
10	403	4	4.027
11	469	4	4.117
12	195	3	3.163
13	576	5	4.585
14	444	4	4.157
15	501	5	4.657
16	162	3	3.005
17	332	4	3.801
18	438	4	4.051
IN	3520	36	35.563
TOTAL	6992	71	70.486

18th hole

16th hole

The Low Road
BY MARK CALCAVECCHIA

One of the charms of the TPC of Scottsdale is the fact that it gives players alternate routes to many greens. In contrast to many TPC courses, you don't have to play darts with high shots all day long. At Scottsdale, many of the greens may be reached with bounce-on approaches. In this sense, it's a bit like playing on a British links course.

When you face one of these shots, let the club do most of the work for you. Don't try to hit a low running shot with a pitching wedge. Take at least an 8-iron, and don't be afraid to go to as long a club as a 5-iron. Some players like to vary the clubs for this shot, but I'd recommend you pick a favorite middle or short iron and play most of your running shots with it.

It's important to play this shot in your mind before trying it for real. Make your best guess at where to land the ball so that it will roll safely to the hole, being sure to play the "break" of the intervening terrain as well as the green. The bump-and-run is rarely a straight shot.

As far as technique, think of this as an extended chip shot. Grip down on the club, play from a slightly open stance, and make a controlled arm swing with minimal lower-body movement. Keep your wrist action quiet, too—the best way to regulate distance on this shot is by varying the length of your backswing.

As a two-time victor in the Phoenix Open (1989, 1992), Mark Calcavecchia is in elite company.

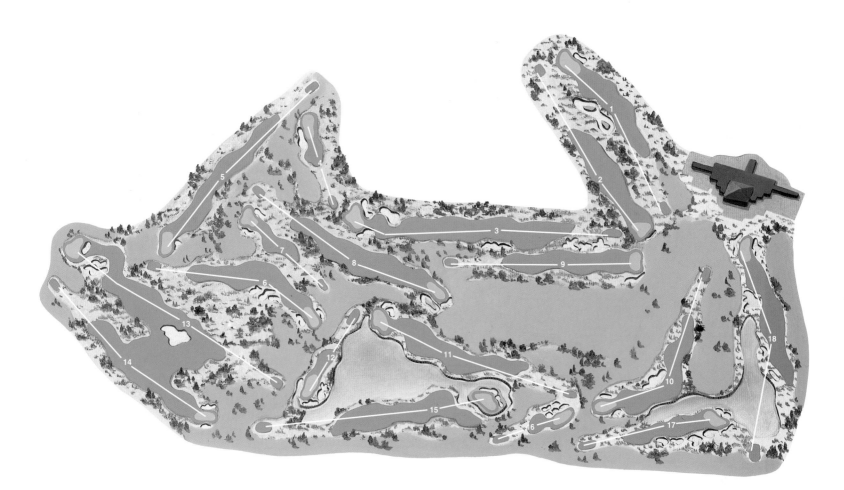

tee, where Couples again yanked his ball into the lake. Lyle bogeyed the hole but won the tournament as Couples could manage only a 6.

Two of the first six Phoenix Opens played here were won by Mark Calcavecchia. In 1989 he set a course record of 21 under (263). His victory in 1992 came on a score one stroke higher, but it surely was an immensely welcome victory. Four months earlier, at the Ryder Cup

Matches on Kiawah Island, South Carolina, he had suffered the worst humiliation of his career. Four holes up with four holes to go in his singles match against Colin Montgomerie, he fell into one of the most horrendous collapses in the history of golf—triple-bogey, bogey, triple-bogey, bogey—to tie. Although America eventually edged Europe by a half point, Calcavecchia was devastated. It seemed he might never recover. But at

Phoenix he did, opening the tournament with a hole-in-one at the fourth on Thursday and charging home on Sunday with a 63 that blew away the field.

As a multiple Phoenix Open champion, Calcavecchia joined an elite group that includes Byron Nelson, Ben Hogan, Jimmy Demaret, Lloyd Mangrum, Gene Littler, Arnold Palmer, and Johnny Miller in a tournament whose history goes back more than 60 years.

PEBBLE BEACH GOLF LINKS

POPPY HILLS GOLF COURSE

SPYGLASS HILL GOLF COURSE

It has been called "the greatest show in golf." Certainly, the AT&T Pebble Beach National Pro-Am has a few attractions P.T. Barnum would have killed for. Consider the dramatis personae, a box-office cast that in any year may include Clint Eastwood, Jack Lemmon, Bill Murray, Michael Keaton, Craig T. Nelson, Joe Pesci, and Don Johnson, not to mention star athletes Orel Hershiser, Joe Montana, Mark McGwire, and Roger Clemens. Now consider the stage set—California's Monterey Peninsula—a backdrop of scenic splendor beyond the imagination of all but the ultimate Producer. Finally, bring in a hundred or so of the finest professional golfers in the world and ask them to beat each others' brains out while simultaneously battling some of the worst wind and wetness Mother Nature can muster. Now that's entertainment!

Bing Crosby originated this event, which carried his name until 1985. A member and several-time champion of Lakeside Country Club near Los Angeles, Crosby got the idea of staging a pro-am for Lakeside members as a chance to get the average hacks together with a few of the pros. That was back in 1937, when Bing owned a home on the golf course at Rancho Santa Fe, and it was there that the first "Crosby Clambake" was held, with Sam Snead the inaugural champion. As Bing handed him the winner's check of $500, the legendarily tight-fisted Snead is reputed to have said, "Thank

you very much, Mr. Crosby, but if you don't mind, I'd rather have cash."

The tournament stayed at Rancho Santa Fe for five years before it was discontinued during World War II. By the time it reappeared in 1947, Crosby was a

Pebble Beach, 12th hole

member of the Cypress Point Golf Club. A group of locals from Monterey urged him to move the Clambake to the Peninsula, and so he did, spreading play over Cypress, Pebble Beach Golf Links, and the Monterey Peninsula Country Club. The Bing Crosby Pebble Beach National Pro-Am remained on those three until 1967, when Spyglass Hill Golf Club took the place of Monterey. Then,

in 1991, after a racial controversy surrounding the PGA Championship at Shoal Creek in Birmingham, Alabama, spurred an inquiry into the membership policies of all PGA Tour sites, Poppy Hills Golf Club replaced Cypress Point, which

opted to discontinue hosting the tournament.

But the show goes on late each January, amid weather conditions that discriminate equally against all who play. "Crosby weather" (now "AT&T weather") is an expression that conjures images associated less with golf than with Green Bay Packers football. In 1981, the rain was so hard and so constant that the

Pebble Beach, 9th hole

tournament didn't start until Saturday. In windy 1990, play was suspended on Saturday because the ball would not stay still long enough on the greens for players to putt. Bob Gilder, tied for the lead at 137 after two rounds, got caught in the worst of the blow, shot 85, and missed the third-round cut. Ed Dougherty 14-putted one hole—yes, 14-putted the 17th at Cypress Point. Years ago, Johnny Weissmuller, once the world's greatest swimmer, walked off his rain-soaked pro-am round and declared, "I've never been so wet in my life." And in 1962, it actually snowed. But there has never been a chance that the event would relocate to Palm Springs or San Diego. As Crosby observed one year, "Playing this tournament anywhere else would be like asking Sir Laurence Olivier to play Richard III in a bowling alley."

This event was the first to be played over more than one course, and it was also the first of the big celebrity pro-ams. Under its unique format an amateur teams up with the same professional for three straight days, playing one round on each of the three courses. After the third round, a cut is made of both the professionals and the pro-am teams, and the survivors return to Pebble Beach on Sunday for both the pro-am and individual pro championships. The record for a pro-am team is 42 under par, established in 1992 by Greg Norman and his fellow Australian, business magnate Kerry Packer.

An invitation to the AT&T is a major status symbol. Only 180 amateurs play each year, but the tournament annually receives hundreds more requests. For decades, Crosby selected the lucky group, rotating in a contingent of 50 or so newcomers each year. After Bing's death his son Nathaniel, the 1981 U.S. Amateur Champion, took over the bittersweet chore of saying "yes" to a few and "no" to the majority. Today, it is more or less a committee decision by Nathaniel and his fellow members of the AT&T Pebble Beach Golf Foundation.

Maury Luxford, for many years the tournament chairman and official starter, claimed he was once approached in the men's room of the Los Angeles Airport by a stranger who had recognized him. "I've got $25,000 in my pocket," the man said, "and if you can get me into the Crosby, it's yours."

The offer was declined, but certain amateurs are granted entry every year. These are the core celebrities from the worlds of entertainment and athletics, along with a smattering of politicians and corporate kingpins. All that is required of them is a relatively high entrance fee ($4,000) and a relatively low handicap (21 or less).

The fact is, however, that a few of the big names also have big handicaps. Raymond Floyd, a good friend and frequent pro-am partner to Clint Eastwood, an 18 handicapper, claims he can count on one hand the number of holes where Dirty Harry helped the team. And Jack Lemmon, although claiming to have a

Spyglass Hill, 1st hole

Spyglass Hill, 4th hole

handicap in the neighborhood of 15, has been known to use that many strokes on a single hole. Despite a quarter-century of trying, he has never made the cut.

One year Lemmon splashed at the ball nine times before reaching the 18th green at Pebble Beach. As he lined up his lengthy putt for a 10, he asked his caddie, "Which way does this break?"

"Who cares?" replied the caddie.

Then there's the classic story of Lemmon and the dog, an episode that epitomizes the terror that consumes amateurs in the AT&T. On one tee, Lemmon was preparing to hit his drive when out of the gallery tore a big, scruffy mutt. It ran straight through Lemmon's legs and disappeared into the crowd on the other side of the tee. Without batting an eye, Lemmon played a fine tee shot.

Jimmy Demaret was doing color commentary on television at the time,

and after Lemmon's round he went up to Jack.

"That was really remarkable, Jack. That dog ran right between your legs and you didn't let it disturb you at all."

Lemmon gave Demaret a look of absolute incredulity and said, "You mean, that was a *real* dog?"

In recent years the star of the tournament has been comic actor Bill Murray. In 1993, he led the gallery at Pebble's 17th tee in an impromptu group wave to the Met Life blimp, then danced a brief polka with a septuagenarian spectator in the bunker just left of the 18th green before stepping up and holing a 40-foot putt. Although traditionalists claim that such antics are detrimental to the game, Murray has become the undisputed clown prince of Pebble Beach, and the galleries love him.

A subtle caste system prevails with regard to the three groups of pro-am

teams rotating among the courses. The "A" group plays Poppy Hills and Spyglass Hill on the first two days of the tournament and finishes at Pebble on Saturday, when national television covers only that course. It is ego-bruising for a celebrity or top pro to discover that his Saturday round is at Poppy or Spyglass.

There are some pros and amateurs, in fact, who would just as soon avoid Spyglass altogether. In the view of many players, it is simply too hard.

"Pebble Beach makes you want to play golf," says Jack Nicklaus, a three-time AT&T champion. "Spyglass Hill makes you want to go fishing."

Jim Murray, the demon columnist for the *Los Angeles Times*, once wrote:

If it were human, Spyglass would have a knife in its teeth, a patch on its eye, a ring in its ear, tobacco in its beard, and a

Spyglass Hill, 15th hole

blunderbuss in its hands. It's a privateer plundering the golfing main, an amphibious creature, half ocean, half forest. You play through seals to squirrels, sand dunes to pine cones, pounding surf to mast-high firs. It's a 300-acre unplayable lie.

And Lee Trevino put it as only he can: "They ought to hang the man who designed this course," he said. "Ray Charles could have done better."

The man who designed Spyglass is Robert Trent Jones, dean of American golf course architects and the most prolific practitioner in the history of his profession. He envisioned the course as his crowning achievement, an opportunity to blend the sea, the dunes, and the forest into an exhilarating 18-hole package.

To his eternal credit, he used restraint. In the past Jones had been accused of bulldozing courses to death, but at Spyglass he left the best land—the dunes area of holes two through five— essentially untouched as a sort of Pine Valley on the Pacific.

The golfer descends to that seaside area via the first hole, a mammoth par five that winds 600 yards in a gentle leftward turn. Generally played into the ocean breeze, this is one of the toughest starting holes on the Tour. It is a formidable place to have to make a 5, whether your name is Jack Lemmon or Jack Nicklaus.

The next four holes weave through the sand dunes: the 350-yard second surging uphill, followed by the picturesque par-three third, played straight at the windy sea. Number four, one of the finest and most natural mid-length par fours anywhere, demands accurate placement of both the tee shot and the approach. Miss either one even slightly and you'll find yourself in unraked sand or, worse yet, ice plant.

Ice plant is the vilest flora in golf. The feeling at impact with this rubbery succulent is about the same as when hitting a 1-iron out of a pile of Reeboks. Simply moving the ball is an achievement, getting it to the fairway a miracle, and approximating your target an accident. Back in the 1953 Crosby, Porky Oliver

Spyglass Hill, 7th hole

hit his ball into this stuff, then swung at it 14 times before getting free.

After another windy par three at number five, the course meanders back uphill, where it stays for the rest of the round, threading through thick stands of Monterey pines. The best-known hole on the back nine is the 12th, a downhill par three that Jones modeled after the famous Redan Hole at North Berwick in Scotland. With the canted green wedged between water left and a steep, bunkered rise on the right, accuracy is vital.

The 14th is a rare double-dogleg par five with water in front of the green, a relatively easy par for the pros but a tough birdie. And the longest, toughest four on the course—and probably the tournament—is number 16, a 465-yard dogleg right with trees lining the fairway on both sides. Long hitters such as John Daly and Fred Couples fly the trees and cut the dogleg, leaving short irons uphill to the green, but the Tour's mere mortals will go at this with a careful drive and a hopeful long iron.

Tall trees encroach on the last two holes as well, both par fours. The fact is, you're not out of the woods on this

course until you pull out of the parking lot.

When AT&T officials were forced to drop Cypress Point as a tournament venue, they knew they had a tough act to follow. One of the most revered courses—and likely the most charming—in the game (currently ranked second in the world by *GOLF Magazine*), Cypress has been called the Sistine Chapel of Golf. For 43 years it brought great pleasure—and great pain—to those who assaulted it in tournament play, particularly at its famed 16th hole, a 231-yard shot across a chasm of rocks and pounding surf.

Now, however, it is but a memory for AT&T participants. In place of that 70-year-old course came a mere four-year-old. In place of a highly exclusive enclave of 250 members came a public facility owned by the Northern California Golf Association. In place of a course measuring just 6506 yards came a course of the same par weighing in at 6865 yards, longer than either Spyglass or Pebble.

Poppy Hills is the creation of Robert Trent Jones, Jr., namesake and younger son of Spyglass's designer. Although Jones the younger displays a distinctive,

Poppy Hills, 2nd hole

imaginative, and sometimes quirky style of his own, certain aspects of Poppy Hills recall his father's philosophy—notably an affection for bigness.

The greens needed to be large to accommodate heavy play (the course actually sees more rounds per year than Pebble Beach), but these average between 6,000 and 7,000 square feet—that's more than twice the size of those at Pebble, where the largest target is barely 3,800.

Jones also put plenty of slope into his surfaces. Indeed, the whole feeling at Poppy is one of movement—slopes, hills, ravines, knolls, and plenty of doglegs right and left. It is an angular, assertive, and strong course—and in its first year as an AT&T site, it jarred many of the pros. Dave Stockton called it "the only course I've ever played that even had a double dogleg in the men's room," and three-time AT&T Champion Johnny Miller said, "There's no way I can play it with-

out three-putting at least four greens." Its severest critics christened it "Poopy Hills."

Others were more positive. In his first competitive round on the course, Rocco Mediate aced the 210-yard 15th hole with a 5-iron and shot 67 en route to a tie for fourth place. "I like the course a lot," he said. "It's very challenging." And The King himself had at least faint praise for Poppy. "There are a couple of mounds on greens that are a problem," said Arnold Palmer, "but overall I kind of enjoyed it."

Jones and his NCGA associates knew from the outset that changes would be needed, but they had made a pact not to alter the course for four years, lest they set a pattern for quick fixes and knee-jerk reaction. However, once having heard the comments from the AT&T players, they began to make a few refinements.

The hardest hole on the course had been number three, a 406-yard par four

(exacting an average of nearly 4.5 strokes from the pros) where left-side bunkering had forced tee shots to hug the right, where the fairway falls off into nasty underbrush. Two of the severest pot bunkers were removed, giving some more breathing room.

Two more bunkers were removed at the fourth hole, a double dogleg par five that had been too severe for most average players. At the par-three sixth hole, the player's line of sight into the green has been improved by the removal of a high "nose" of turf on a bunker fronting the green. And at number nine, a strong, rolling par five of 557 yards, the fairway was better defined through the lowering of a hump that rose between two bunkers in the landing area.

Poppy Hills does share one eccentricity with Cypress Point—back-to-back par fives (there are five on the course, along with five par threes). In Poppy's case,

Poppy Hills, 9th hole

however, they're on separate nines, as the ninth is followed by 515-yard number ten, an up-and-downhiller to a green guarded by a pond. It is one of the prettiest holes on the course, and can be one of the toughest. The first time Dan Forsman played it, he took a 9. Forsman needed to birdie the last three holes that day to break 80.

Following a lengthy three at number 11, it's another five at the 12th. The original design here featured a sea of bunkers in the tee-shot landing area, the crook of a sharp rightward dogleg. The sand deterred good players from trying to cut the corner. Now, about 60 percent of the sand is gone, encouraging more boldness.

Another right-angle dogleg must be negotiated at the 14th, a par four of 417 yards, but the toughest hole on the back may be the 16th, a rightward-bending 439 yards to a tightly bunkered green. After a relatively tame par three at 17,

the course finishes in character with a double-doglegging par five, uphill 500 yards to a mammoth, fiercely sloped green.

Gradually, the pros have begun to overcome their wistfulness for Cypress Point and have begun to accept Poppy Hills for what it is, a course that asks for a lot but rewards those who can conquer it. Whereas low rounds were always the rule at Cypress, any player who betters 70 at Poppy Hills will make major gains on the rest of the field.

Spyglass Hill and Poppy Hills are fine golf courses and they seem to be gaining in popularity with the pros. But they will never be Pebble Beach. Indeed, perhaps no other test of golf—on or off the Tour—can match Pebble, the consensus pick of many authorities as the finest course in the world.

The man who made it possible was Samuel F. B. Morse, namesake and

nephew of the inventor of the telegraph. Morse was a visionary and conservationist who in 1919 obtained financing for a group of investors to purchase 5,300 acres which became known as the Del Monte Properties. The land included a rustic lodge which became the focal point for the development of the Pebble Beach Golf Links.

Golf at this time was in its infancy in America and Morse, although a sportsman, was not a golfer. But he sensed the investment potential of golf course real estate, and he knew he had some very valuable property. At the same time, as a devoted environmentalist, he could envision the role a course could play in preserving the natural beauty of the spectacular coastline he and his associates had acquired.

When it came time to entrust the design of Pebble Beach, Morse made an unorthodox but inspired decision, nam-

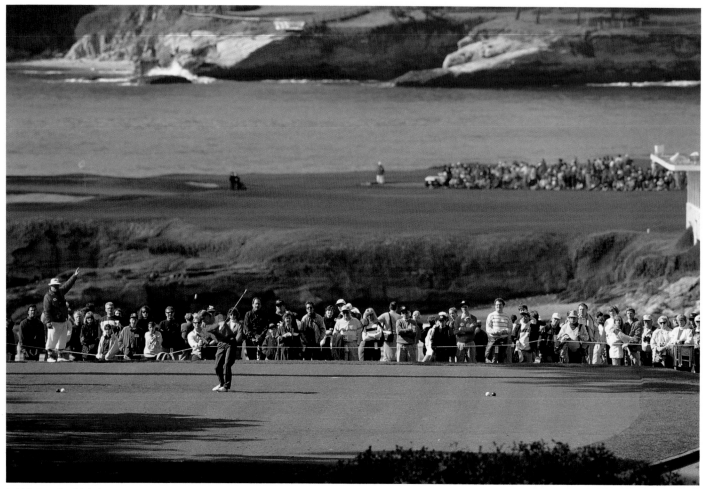

Pebble Beach, 5th hole

ing Douglas Grant and Jack Neville. Neither man had ever designed a golf course, but both knew a thing or two about how to play the game— each was a California State Amateur Champion. Morse reasoned that anyone who could play that well had to be able to design a course. In this case, he was right.

Over the last three quarters of a century, numerous refinements have taken place—most notably by Chandler Egan prior to the 1929 U.S. Amateur (he converted the 18th hole from a par four to a par five) and by Jack Nicklaus prior to the 1992 U.S. Open—but today Pebble Beach remains essentially the same spectacular layout that Grant and Neville originally unveiled.

Some have argued that the first five holes of the course lack the character of the last 13. From a scenic standpoint, that is inarguable. But all five are

nonetheless solid tests of shotmaking, beginning with the slender first, an opening dogleg with out-of-bounds on both sides. The 502-yard second, with its second shot over a barranca shaded on the left side by an enormous tree, is a classic gambler's five.

Number three may seem a relatively simple dogleg left until the drive is pushed or hooked. In either case, the ensuing shot to the small, angled, tightly bunkered green suddenly becomes difficult. The fourth hole is nearly fifty yards shorter than any other par four at Pebble, but bunkers to the left and sea cliffs hard by the right call for a careful tee shot, then a surgically accurate short iron to a green that is the smallest and one of the most severely contoured on the course. As for the fifth hole, a tunnel of trees makes this uphill 166-yard shot claustrophobically daunting. Five also features a

climate-controlled green. As part of the preparations for the 1992 U.S. Open, rubber tubing was installed a foot below the surface of the green. Today, warm water is pumped in, keeping the green thawed on cold mornings and encouraging good growth of grass.

Lee Trevino contends, "If you're five over when you get to the sixth hole at Pebble, it's a good time to commit suicide." At the sixth tee begins a stretch of the most beautiful and testing holes in the world.

The easiest of them may be the first. Halfway to the green of this 516-yard par five, the fairway swoops dramatically upward, leaving a sheer drop off the cliff into Stillwater Cove on the right. A good drive leaves a blind second shot up that hill. It also leaves most golfers wondering whether they can possibly hit a ball high enough and hard enough to reach the top and, if so, whether that ball can possibly stay on the shelf. The pros play the hole as a drive, then a long iron or wood onto or near the green. Into a stiff wind off the Pacific, make that two long irons or woods.

The tiny seventh is the shortest hole on any major championship course, and yard for yard it also may be the hardest. On a mild day it's merely a crisp wedge to the dot of a green embraced by rock, sand, and sea. But catch it during a hard blow, and you will have to summon the straightest, bravest mid-iron of your life. Eddie Merrins, "The Little Pro" from Bel-Air Country Club in Los Angeles, aced this hole during one blustery Clambake—with a 3-iron. And one year Sam Snead was so intimidated by it that he *putted* down the dirt path to the green. In the windblown final round of the '92 U.S. Open, Tom Kite missed the green with a 6-iron, then holed-out a 50-foot chip for a birdie 2 that launched him to a two-stroke victory.

Number eight signals the start of the most breathtaking trilogy of par-four holes anywhere in golf. It begins with a blind uphill tee shot that must be aimed at a distant chimney. One may strike the ball 300 yards down the left edge of the fairway, but no more than 200 down the right, as the sea cliff cuts diagonally across the fairway, creating a chasm that must be jumped with the second shot (or circumvented with the second and third). The 200-yard carry to this small, severely pitched green is well recorded as Jack Nicklaus's favorite second shot in golf.

The hardest hole on the front nine is arguably the last one, a brawling 464-yard par four that plays downhill while falling left to right toward the ever-menacing cliffs. Those who seek to avoid the perils of the right may find equally severe trouble in the thick rough and bunkers on the left. The green sits on the brink of a precipice. Occasionally, even a putt has been known to fall off the edge and onto the beach below. In the 1963 Clambake, Dale Douglass took a 19 here. Yes, 19.

Only slightly less difficult is the tenth, another long (426-yard) tightrope walk along the cliffs of doom. Again, the green hugs the edge. This time, though, it is partly cradled in sand. Jack Nicklaus won the 1972 U.S. Open despite hitting the beach twice and making 6 on this hole in the final round.

The next six holes weave along the upland part of the course. Eleven is a short par four but it plays uphill to a narrow, angled green cinched by sand. Twelve is a 202-yard par three that can be a full fairway wood into the wind and even more difficult downwind, since its green is notoriously hard to hold. Thirteen plays slightly uphill to a tightly bunkered green, with some of the fastest-sliding putts on the course.

But the most feared green is at 14. On this lengthy par five, even the pros coddle and coax their drives and second shots around the clockwise dogleg in order to leave a fighting chance of playing a wedge or short iron that will hit and hold the two-tiered putting surface, which is fronted on its high left side by a deep, steep-faced bunker. Once on the green, the battle has just begun. Back in the 1978 PGA Championship, Danny Edwards six-putted this one.

Holes 15 and 16 are two doglegs where the tee shot is everything. The 15th calls

Pebble Beach, 6th hole

Pebble Beach, 8th hole

for a draw (hit it straight and you'll be bouncing down Monterey's 17-Mile Drive). At 16 the preferred shot is a quiet fade around a pair of deep bunkers. Eucalyptus trees crowd the green here, so only a well-placed tee shot will allow an unobstructed approach. Jack Nicklaus's 1972 victory here came courtesy of Johnny Miller, who, appearing on television for the very first time as a professional, shanked his approach shot and made bogey, allowing Jack to win by one.

Nicklaus has had more success than anyone at Pebble, the course he has always called his favorite. Jack won a U.S. Amateur, a U.S. Open (the first—and probably the last—player to take both titles on the same course), and also won three AT&T titles when it was still known as The Crosby.

At least some of Nicklaus's good fortune has occurred at the par-three 17th. It was at this 209-yard hole during the 1972 U.S. Open that he stung a 1-iron into a stiff wind and hit the flagstick, leaving a tap-in putt for the birdie that clinched the title. But it was at this hole also that Nicklaus saw his chances for a second U.S. Open at Pebble drift away. Anyone who follows golf knows that the 17th hole at Pebble Beach was the site of Tom Watson's miracle chip from heavy rough at the back left of the green.

At the time, Watson and Nicklaus were tied for the lead in the 1982 Open, with Jack safe in the clubhouse. When Watson's tee shot strayed into six-inch-high rough, Jack's chances for a record fifth Open title looked excellent. But Watson got some luck—the ball settled into a good lie.

"Get it close," said Watson's caddie to his boss.

"I'm not going to get it close," said Tom. "I'm going to sink it."

And he did, flipping the ball over the fringe and down the bank of the hard green into the back of the hole, one of the most electrifying strokes in the history of championship golf. It gave Watson a one-stroke edge and the adrenaline to birdie 18 for a two-stroke victory.

Pebble Beach, 7th hole

The best of this magnificent course is saved for last. By almost unanimous agreement, the 18th at Pebble has no parallel as a finishing hole. Curved gracefully along 548 yards of the rockbound coast, it is as demanding as it is beautiful, as exciting as it is treacherous. The ideal tee shot bites off a bit of the water, while avoiding a pair of bunkers to the right and a pair of pines in the center of the fairway. The second shot must be banged down the right center, ideally leaving a full wedge to the small, firm green. On every one of the three shots, water is in mind even more than it is in view.

If there is such a thing as horses for courses, it is true for this event, as "Monterey Mark" O'Meara has won four titles in seven years (1985, 1989, 1990, 1992). "I guess I owe a lot to Pebble Beach," he says. "I wish this course were private. Then I could buy a membership."

Happily, Pebble Beach is a public course. Although it has been owned by two different Japanese conglomerates during the last few years, and at one point there were rumors that memberships would be sold at a cost of well into six figures, that is not currently a threat. Anyone may play Pebble—anyone, that is, with the requisite time and money. At last count, the cost of the green fee and cart was $250, and the duration of the average round was close to five hours. But people from all over the world happily pay the price and endure the traffic. As well they should.

Pebble Beach, 9th hole

Pebble Beach, 10th hole

Scorecard

Pebble Beach			
Hole	Yards	Par	PGA Tour Avg. Score
1	373	4	4.042
2	502	5	4.558
3	388	4	3.986
4	327	4	3.889
5	166	3	3.059
6	516	5	4.734
7	107	3	3.062
8	431	4	4.225
9	464	4	4.338
OUT	3274	36	35.893
10	426	4	4.299
11	384	4	3.951
12	202	3	3.160
13	392	4	4.006
14	565	5	5.126
15	397	4	4.012
16	402	4	4.033
17	209	3	3.015
18	548	5	4.968
IN	3525	36	36.570
TOTAL	6799	72	72.463

Spyglass Hill			
Hole	Yards	Par	PGA Tour Avg. Score
1	600	5	4.992
2	350	4	4.124
3	150	3	2.990
4	365	4	4.113
5	180	3	3.167
6	415	4	4.304
7	515	5	4.747
8	395	4	4.419
9	425	4	4.282
OUT	3395	36	37.138
10	400	4	4.163
11	520	5	4.734
12	180	3	3.002
13	440	4	4.184
14	555	5	5.022
15	130	3	3.029
16	465	4	4.415
17	320	4	4.031
18	405	4	4.239
IN	3415	36	36.819
TOTAL	6810	72	73.957

Poppy Hills			
Hole	Yards	Par	PGA Tour Avg. Score
1	413	4	4.268
2	162	3	2.981
3	406	4	4.305
4	560	5	5.041
5	426	4	4.166
6	181	3	3.144
7	388	4	4.028
8	390	4	4.139
9	557	5	4.635
OUT	3483	36	36.707
10	515	5	4.833
11	214	3	3.190
12	531	5	4.859
13	393	4	4.196
14	417	4	4.020
15	210	3	3.139
16	439	4	4.283
17	163	3	3.068
18	500	5	4.766
IN	3382	36	36.354
TOTAL	6865	72	73.061

Pebble Beach, 18th hole

Pitching from the Rough

BY TOM WATSON

Probably the one shot of my career that will be most remembered was the short pitch that I holed from heavy rough to the right of the 71st green in the 1982 U.S. Open at Pebble Beach. When playing such a shot, I use a sand wedge and hit the ball much the same way I would a sand shot. I open both my stance and clubface. I take the club up abruptly and away from my body on the backswing by hinging my wrists, to avoid as much grass as possible on the takeaway. On the forward swing I slide the club under the ball with the clubface held firmly open by the last three fingers of my left hand. I can even hit slightly behind the ball, as if it were in the sand, with good results. Remember that the ball will tend to run farther out of rough than from a regular lie.

Tom Watson won back-to-back victories in the AT&T Pebble Beach National Pro-Am (1977, 1978) as well as the 1982 U.S. Open at Pebble Beach.

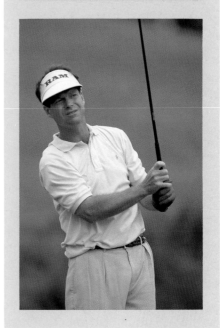

47

RIVIERA COUNTRY CLUB

n 1992, Fred Couples and Davis Love dominated the PGA Tour, each winning well over a million dollars. But on only one occasion did the two titans go head to head—in a sudden-death playoff at Riviera. And why not—after all, for eight decades this has been the golf course of the stars.

Not golf stars, real stars—the likes of Elizabeth Taylor and Gregory Peck, Spencer Tracy and Katharine Hepburn, and virtually every golf-addicted entertainer from W. C. Fields to Glen Campbell.

In 1925, the members of the Los Angeles Athletic Club decided to expand their facilities to include golf. They approached George C. Thomas, the Philadelphia aristocrat cum autocrat who, when he wasn't cultivating roses or breeding English setters, was an imaginative genius at golf course architecture. Thomas had transplanted to Southern California and designed the Bel-Air and Los Angeles Country Club courses, two layouts that impressed the principals at the LAAC. So they summoned him to their chosen site, a 240-acre tract in the center of the Santa Monica Canyon.

Thomas stood on a precipice and surveyed the expanse of tangled brush, cactus, eucalyptus, pines, oaks, and sycamores, all scattered across a deep riverbed. After a time he offered the club fathers his opinion: He could build them a golf course, but it would not be much of a layout because of the limitations imposed by the poor terrain. Still, he supposed, it would be "good enough for the Los Angeles Athletic Club."

Such arrogance did not sit well with the fathers, who informed Thomas that even the best course would be none too good for the LAAC. They may also have hinted that the project was beyond Thomas's capabilities, for the architect thrust himself into the job, offering his services without pay.

However, no other expense was spared in the construction of the Riviera Country Club. A crew of more than 200

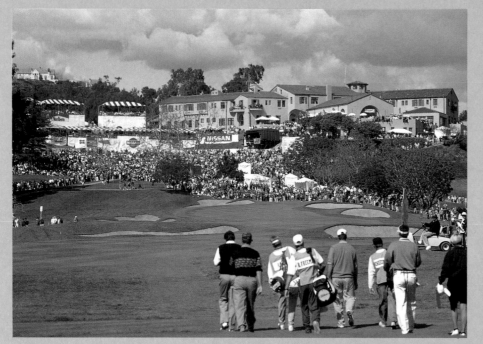

9th hole

18th hole

men hacked through the canyon for 18 months, installing 100,000 feet of pipe, trucking in topsoil from the San Fernando Valley, sowing 19,000 pounds of grass seed, and depositing 1,350 tons of beach sand. Dozens of trees were cut down and dozens more were planted. In those days the cost of constructing an 18-hole layout ran roughly $100,000. The bill for Riviera came to over $650,000, making it, as nearly as anyone could determine, the most expensive golf course in the world.

But the money was well spent. Almost immediately the National Golf Foundation ranked Riviera third on a list of the world's top ten, behind Pine Valley in New Jersey and Pinehurst Number 2 in the sandhills of North Carolina. Today, despite nearly 70 years and the blossoming of thousands of formidable golf courses worldwide, Riviera retains its position in the upper ranks of the world's greatest courses.

At Riviera, Thomas unveiled a collection of architectural gambits that grabbed the golf fraternity by its knickers. Among the innovations were a doughnut-shaped green with a pot bunker at its center, a par four with two

Putting Cross-Handed
BY FRED COUPLES

A few years ago I switched from a conventional putting grip to one with my left hand lower than my right. What ensued were the most productive seasons of my career, including my second victory at Los Angeles.

I didn't switch out of desperation—I was always a pretty decent putter, but ever since my college days I'd fiddled with a cross-handed grip. It just seemed to feel better on the practice green. Now I know it not only feels good, it works. If you're having trouble with your putting, I recommend that you give it a try.

For one thing, it will help you to align yourself squarely. With your left hand below your right, your shoulders will be level and you'll find it easy to align yourself parallel to your target line. This will promote a straight-back/straight-through stroke that flows smoothly through impact and starts the ball smack on your intended path.

To set the grip properly, stand square to the target and let your left arm hang down until it is just below your right.

Grip the putter with your left hand, and then apply your right hand, tucking it up next to your left forearm. Then make a swing with no hand or wrist movement— just hit the ball with a pendulum stroke. Practice this for a while, and see if you don't start to feel more confidence in your putting.

Fred Couples is a two-time (1990, 1992) Nissan Los Angeles Open champion.

1st hole

9th hole

alternative fairways, and a green half-barricaded by a grass mound the size of a diner. He also molded the final green into the base of a huge natural amphitheater, likely the first execution of what the PGA Tour calls Stadium Golf.

On opening day in June of 1927, no one broke or equaled par on Riviera. In fact, after six months the best score anyone had squeezed from it was a 73, two over par. Then one of the club's glitterati, Douglas Fairbanks, posted a $1,000 purse for a medal tournament. The event attracted a strong and talented field, and Willie Hunter, the likable Scot who had won the 1921 British Amateur, did the deed with a 69.

Riviera has confounded and delighted both pros and amateurs ever since. Tom Watson, a two-time L.A. Open champion, says, "Riviera is the type of course

that makes you want to shoot your very best." And you will have to. In 1984, when the PGA Tour first issued statistics on the toughest holes on the Tour, Riviera had eight of those holes, more than any other course.

It begins literally on the edge of a cliff, the first tee hard by the clubhouse and overlooking the entire property 75 feet below. The opening hole is a short but tight and ingeniously bunkered par five, giving the high-handicap player a good chance at par while tempting the stronger player to go for birdie or even eagle.

The Tour players count on that birdie because the next three holes all are among the toughest. The second is a members' par five which is converted on tournament week into a 460-yard par four for the pros. It usually plays into a

quartering wind and always plays into a narrow green.

Number three heads 434 yards dead into the wind. Here the green is relatively deep but also slender and guarded by gaping bunkers on both sides.

One of the largest bunkers on the course protects the entry on the par-three fourth, forcing an all-carry tee shot of 238 yards. Ben Hogan, never a man given to lavish praise, once called this "the greatest par three in America."

The doughnut green is at number six. Although the little pot bunker in the center gets all the talk, more sand in front and behind the green makes club selection harrowing on this 170-yard shot. In 1987, T. C. Chen made an ace here during round three. As things turned out, he needed it, as his final score of 275 tied Ben Crenshaw and Chen won

6th hole

the tournament in sudden death, his only victory on the Tour.

Number eight is the hole where Thomas offered alternative fairways. However, one of them has since been eliminated, with the result that this hole calls for the straightest drive on the course.

The par-35 front nine at Riviera is generally regarded as about a half shot tougher than the par-36 back, a notion that adds wonder to the fact that in 1991 Andrew Magee blazed to the turn in 28 strokes.

Number 10 at Riviera is one of golf's great short par fours, 311 yards of compressed architectural guile. With a slight tailwind, the Tour players can easily drive this green, but few of them try. The tiny, angled target is fiercely sloped, with a dif-

ficult bunker at its rear. Most pros would rather approach it with a crisp 90-yard wedge than gamble on getting an easy shot around the green.

One reason for that caution is kikuyu-grass, an African weed which grows in extreme density throughout the course. When cut to a low height it is perhaps the perfect fairway grass, perching the ball high atop its stiff leaves. But in the fringe and rough, where the height of the grass can be four or more inches, kikuyu grabs at the landing ball and swallows it deep into its tendrils, making crisp impact impossible. Faced with such lies, and chipping to Riviera's small, hard greens, even the pros can look like monkeys.

Dozens of eucalyptus trees make play difficult on the 413-yard 12th hole where

the approach is across a broad barranca which, although usually dry, plays as a water hazard. But the real killer here is a sycamore just to the left of the green, said to have caught more stray rubber than any guard rail on the L.A. Freeway.

Big numbers are common at the 13th, a right-to-left dogleg where out-of-bounds lurks down the entire left side of the hole. In 1991, Riviera began a major refurbishing program that brought a new tee to this hole, moving it closer to the out-of-bounds and increasing the bend in the fairway.

Two years later, the club undertook an even more ambitious project when it converted all 18 of its greens from poa annua to creeping bentgrass. Ben Crenshaw and his architect partner Bill Coore supervised the project, which required Riviera

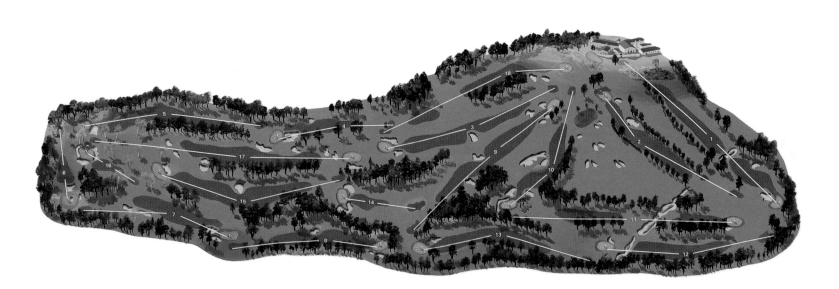

members to use temporary greens for six months. Crenshaw's goal was to maintain the contours of George Thomas's design while increasing the overall size of the greens by about 14 percent. One green which desperately needed enlarging was that of the 16th hole, where the surface—2,300 square feet—was less than half the size of the average putting green. Even on a par three of only 168 yards, that's an extremely small target.

Riviera's 18th has been called 447 yards of heartbreak. The tee shot is blind to a plateau fairway that banks and doglegs gracefully to the right, like a turn at Indy. A drive to the left will leave a "shank" lie, with the ball below the feet. On the right the terrain is level, but a row of overhanging trees blocks a direct shot to the green. The most unforgiving spot on the course may be the steep bank to the left of the green, particularly when the pin is also cut on that side. The resulting shot can be as short as ten feet, but with a sharp slope, the snatching kikuyu, and a green like waxed marble, most players— Tour pros included—will not get up and down.

Directly behind the 18th green is the majestic Riviera clubhouse, constructed in 1925 with meticulous care to please the most glamorous membership in golf. Among its early members were Mary Pickford, Basil Rathbone, W.C. Fields, Spencer Tracy, Katharine Hepburn,

Leslie Howard, Adolphe Menjou, Johnny Weissmuller, Burt Lancaster, Gregory Peck, Dean Martin, and Jerry Lewis.

In the thirties, a Mr. and Mrs. Taylor from England became equestrian members of the club. Their 11-year-old daughter worked out daily on her horse Hal over the steeplechase course, for she had been selected after a five-year search to play the lead in an MGM feature called *National Velvet*. Her name was Elizabeth.

More recently, the star system at Riviera has included Peter Falk, James Garner, Peter Graves, Robert Wagner, Don Rickles, and Glen Campbell, the last-named of whom for several years was the official host of the L.A. Open.

Many movies have been shot here, including *Follow the Sun*, starring Glenn Ford. Indeed, much of the true story behind *Follow the Sun* took place at Riviera, for it is the saga of Ben Hogan, who won two L.A. Opens and a U.S. Open on the course in a span of 18 months.

It was also at Riviera, in 1962, that Jack Nicklaus won his first check as a professional. Yet this is one of the few courses on the Tour where the Golden Bear never notched a victory. He may actually have come closest not in a Los Angeles Open but in the PGA Championship Riviera hosted in 1983. With a 66 in the final round Nicklaus charged to a second-place finish, one short of victor Hal Sutton.

Scorecard

Hole	Yards	Par	PGA Tour Avg. Score
1	501	5	4.544
2	460	4	4.307
3	434	4	4.080
4	238	3	3.229
5	426	4	4.044
6	170	3	2.999
7	406	4	4.053
8	368	4	3.970
9	418	4	4.088
OUT	3421	35	35.314
10	311	4	3.848
11	561	5	4.856
12	413	4	4.138
13	420	4	4.084
14	180	3	3.024
15	447	4	4.252
16	168	3	2.988
17	578	5	4.861
18	447	4	4.213
IN	3525	36	36.264
TOTAL	6946	71	71.578

However, virtually every other prominent player of the last half century has found the winner's circle here, including Hogan (3 times), Sam Snead (2), Byron Nelson, Jimmy Demaret, Lloyd Mangrum (4), Arnold Palmer (3), Billy Casper (2), Johnny Miller, Hale Irwin, Lanny Wadkins (2), Tom Watson (2), and Fred Couples (2), a list that reaffirms Riviera's stature as the golf course of the stars.

PALMER COURSE/PGA WEST

TAMARISK COUNTRY CLUB

LA QUINTA COUNTRY CLUB

INDIAN WELLS COUNTRY CLUB

BERMUDA DUNES COUNTRY CLUB

California is the ritziest, glitziest state in the Union. Palm Springs is the ritziest, glitziest part of California. And the fairways of Palm Springs are the ritziest, glitziest acreage in the world.

The businessmen who gather here each winter could pool their assets and pay off the national debt. Instead, they play golf. For four straight days they play golf in the desert, matching chips, quips, and stock tips with an array of actors, athletes, politicians, and the pros competing for a million-dollar purse in the Bob Hope Chrysler Classic, the ritziest, glitziest tournament on the PGA Tour. As the host puts it, "This is the only event in the world where guys can get money out of the desert without drilling for oil."

Bermuda Dunes, 18th hole

Palmer Course, 9th hole

The pro-am entry fee is several thousand dollars, but it buys a lot—the four days of golf take place over four lush courses and in the company of four different Tour pros. (On Sunday, the low 70 pros go it alone in the final round of this 90-hole event.)

It's worked that way since 1960, when the event first known as the Palm Springs Golf Classic was won by Arnold Palmer with a score of 338. Arnie went on to win this tournament a record five times, the last of them in 1973, his final victory on the regular PGA Tour.

Twenty years later, Palmer remains a major presence in the desert through one of his designs, the Palmer Course at PGA West, which in 1988 replaced Eldorado Country Club as one of the five sites over which this tournament is contested. (Two courses—La Quinta and Tamarisk—are used in alternate years; the Palmer Course, Bermuda Dunes, and Indian Wells all are played each year, taking turns as the host club and venue for the final round.)

The Palmer Course, one of a quintet of layouts at the PGA West Resort, is the kinder, gentler brother of Pete Dye's satanic Stadium Course. Back in 1986, the Stadium took a turn as the Hope host—but it exited the same year after the pros moaned that it was humiliatingly difficult. Interestingly, the amateurs, playing from tees well forward, found the Stadium the easiest of the Hope courses that year, although one man who suffered was late House Speaker Thomas P. "Tip" O'Neill, immortalized on national television for his dozen or so fruitless swipes in the San Andreas Fault, a cavernous bunker bordering the 16th green.

At 6,901 yards, the Palmer Course, while not as savage as the Stadium, is clearly the toughest of the Hope venues, with a rating from the back tees of 70.454. The back nine begins with the hole known as "Monster," a 455-yard par four that doglegs slightly left around the edge of a lake. It annually ranks among the most difficult holes on the PGA Tour. Only slightly less testing is the 13th,

Palmer Course, 17th hole

Palmer Course, 15th hole

another lengthy four (446 yards) where both the tee shot and approach must avoid water on the right and bunkers to the left.

As a tournament player Palmer had a penchant for daring, dramatic finishes, and the same is true of his namesake course. The 16th, nicknamed Double Cross, doglegs sharply right, calling for carries over a canal on both the drive and second shot. Number 17 is a mere 131 yards but its narrow strip of green—barely ten paces wide—is bordered by water on the left and the rocky feet of the Santa Rosa Mountains on the right. Furthermore, the hole plays from a tee elevated 75 feet, so its tiny target appears even more elusive.

Palmer's final hole is the perfect place to cap a charge, a reachable par five that dares its assailants to go for broke. Although a relatively short 532 yards, it is lined by water down the entire left side and anyone hoping to get home in two will have to defy that water on the long approach. In 1993, under perfect conditions, four players shot 63's on the Palmer Course, and then Tom Kite topped them all, carding five birdies and an eagle in his last nine holes—29 strokes—for a 62 and a five-stroke victory. For the five rounds, Kite posted a total of 325—35 under par and an average score of 65 per day—that broke the previous tournament record by four strokes.

Tamarisk, one of the first Palm Springs courses, was carved out of the desert in 1952 by William P. "Billy" Bell, the cad-diemaster who apprenticed as a construc-tion superintendent for George C.

Thomas and then rose to become the most prolific golf course architect in the West. Bell took 200 acres of barren land dotted with a few thirsty creosote bushes and fashioned what is today a lush oasis, its holes lined with lakes and ponds (the first water hazards in Palm Springs) and clad with more than 8,000 trees. A few years ago, architect Ron Fream oversaw a redesign which updated the bunkering and added mounding that has enhanced both the strategic quality and the difficul-ty of this course. Still, if you want to start your day with a birdie, this is the place to come. Indeed, dozens of eagles are made each year and the PGA Tour field averages 4.183 strokes on Tamarisk's 482-yard par-five opener, making it statis-tically the easiest of the nearly 1,000 holes on the PGA Tour.

Bermuda Dunes, 8th hole

On comparatively short courses, such as those we play at the Bob Hope Chrysler Classic, we find ourselves facing approach shots of under 100 yards. That means playing lots of wedge shots, and many of those wedges are half and three-quarter wedges.

Amateurs tend to have trouble with these shots, and I think the reason has to do with poor rhythm. Somewhere in midswing, they seem to get nervous and rush the shot. They don't trust their swings, and I suspect that's because they rarely practice these shots.

Actually, half and three-quarter wedges aren't that difficult. They're merely abbreviated swings, where your arms swing back to the nine or ten o'clock position instead of 11 or 12. The longer you swing the club back, the farther the ball will go. Don't make any other changes, particularly on the follow-through, where it's important to make a full, unabbreviated finish. But most of all, steal some time and devote an hour or so of practice exclusively to these shots. It'll give you a big edge on many of your fellow players.

John Cook is the 1992 Bob Hope Chrysler Classic champion.

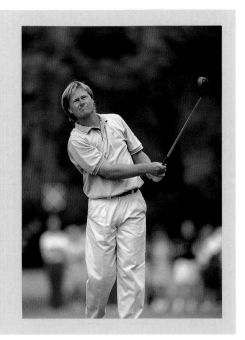

Seven lakes add to the beauty and challenge of the La Quinta course, where the toughest hole is surprisingly but unquestionably a par three, the 200-yard 12th. The boomerang-shaped pond, well short of the hole, doesn't bother the pros, but the rolling green and large flanking bunkers do. When the pin is up front, in the narrow neck between those bunkers, this hole taxes the pros for more 4's than 3's.

The shortest of the Hope courses—indeed the shortest course on the PGA Tour—is Indian Wells. At just 6478 yards it is nearly 200 yards shorter than any other par-72 layout the pros play. Bert Yancey shot 61 here 20 years ago, and it seems likely that a sub-60 number will occur here in the near future. The course culminates in the manner of the Palmer Course, with a short (501 yards) and dramatic par five whose green is bordered on the right by an elongated bunker and on the left by a five-level cascading waterfall, added by architect Ted Robinson in 1985. But none of that bothered Mark O'Meara. He double-eagled the hole in 1992, en route to a tie for the lead at the end of 90 holes, only to lose in a five-way playoff.

Bermuda Dunes is another oasis in the desert, its rolling, palm-lined fairways forming a straightforward challenge with no tricks or unnecessary punishments. The number-one handicap hole is the fifth, a par four of 432 yards. Bunkers on the left put pressure on the drive, and the approach must negotiate more sand on both sides of the green.

Water comes into play at four holes, most notably at the par-four tenth, a dog-leg left where a big draw will be rewarded but a big fade will be punished by the lake on the right of the fairway.

Bermuda Dunes's 18th is another drama-producing finisher, a reachable but menacing par five with out-of-bounds on the left and a lake that reaches out to grab any approach that strays to the right of the long, narrow green.

Palmer Course, 18th hole

Bermuda Dunes

Hole	Yards	Par	PGA Tour Avg. Score
1	538	5	4.580
2	418	4	3.872
3	377	4	3.823
4	209	3	3.013
5	432	4	3.951
6	368	4	3.821
7	176	3	2.945
8	540	5	4.628
9	389	4	3.860
OUT	3447	36	34.493
10	414	4	3.965
11	382	4	3.894
12	160	3	2.857
13	564	5	4.769
14	385	4	3.907
15	399	4	3.990
16	451	4	4.012
17	212	3	3.127
18	513	5	4.513
IN	3480	36	35.034
TOTAL	6927	72	69.527

Indian Wells

Hole	Yards	Par	PGA Tour Avg. Score
1	388	4	3.936
2	355	4	3.833
3	382	4	3.968
4	162	3	3.013
5	517	5	4.467
6	140	3	2.726
7	338	4	3.899
8	515	5	4.582
9	398	4	3.954
OUT	3195	36	34.378
10	446	4	4.169
11	398	4	4.086
12	343	4	3.724
13	197	3	3.041
14	483	5	4.450
15	163	3	2.883
16	354	4	3.791
17	398	4	3.983
18	501	5	4.563
IN	3283	36	34.690
TOTAL	6478	72	69.068

Palmer Course/PGA West

Hole	Yards	Par	PGA Tour Avg. Score
1	427	4	4.084
2	512	5	4.580
3	180	3	2.929
4	395	4	3.958
5	207	3	3.070
6	560	5	4.608
7	439	4	4.042
8	358	4	3.758
9	456	4	4.187
OUT	3534	36	35.216
10	455	4	4.304
11	512	5	4.481
12	201	3	3.055
13	446	4	4.074
14	571	5	4.824
15	155	3	2.981
16	364	4	3.949
17	131	3	2.943
18	532	5	4.627
IN	3367	36	35.238
TOTAL	6901	72	70.454

La Quinta

Hole	Yards	Par	PGA Tour Avg. Score
1	382	4	3.855
2	433	4	4.136
3	186	3	2.972
4	397	4	4.020
5	498	5	4.531
6	521	5	4.417
7	174	3	2.941
8	391	4	3.992
9	391	4	3.875
OUT	3373	36	34.739
10	389	4	4.039
11	526	5	4.637
12	200	3	3.171
13	508	5	4.543
14	436	4	4.097
15	194	3	3.034
16	411	4	3.930
17	419	4	4.058
18	396	4	3.855
IN	3479	36	35.364
TOTAL	6852	72	70.103

Tamarisk

Hole	Yards	Par	PGA Tour Avg. Score
1	482	5	4.183
2	171	3	2.905
3	443	4	4.063
4	509	5	4.595
5	199	3	3.056
6	375	4	3.833
7	331	4	3.794
8	393	4	3.857
9	439	4	3.944
OUT	3342	36	34.230
10	407	4	3.976
11	191	3	2.905
12	550	5	4.738
13	417	4	3.833
14	225	3	3.024
15	423	4	4.048
16	404	4	3.968
17	395	4	3.794
18	527	5	4.389
IN	3539	36	34.675
TOTAL	6881	72	68.905

Four of Arnold Palmer's five Hope victories occurred in years when the host course was Bermuda Dunes, twice in playoffs and the last time on a closing birdie to edge his nemesis, Jack Nicklaus.

BD's reputation for producing drama has continued, as sudden-death playoffs have occurred each of the last four times it was the host course. Surely, the most electrifying of them came in 1992, after

John Cook, Rick Fehr, Tom Kite, Mark O'Meara, and Gene Sauers all finished the 90 holes at 336, 24 under par. Cook won on the fourth playoff hole over Sauers with a chip-in eagle, having

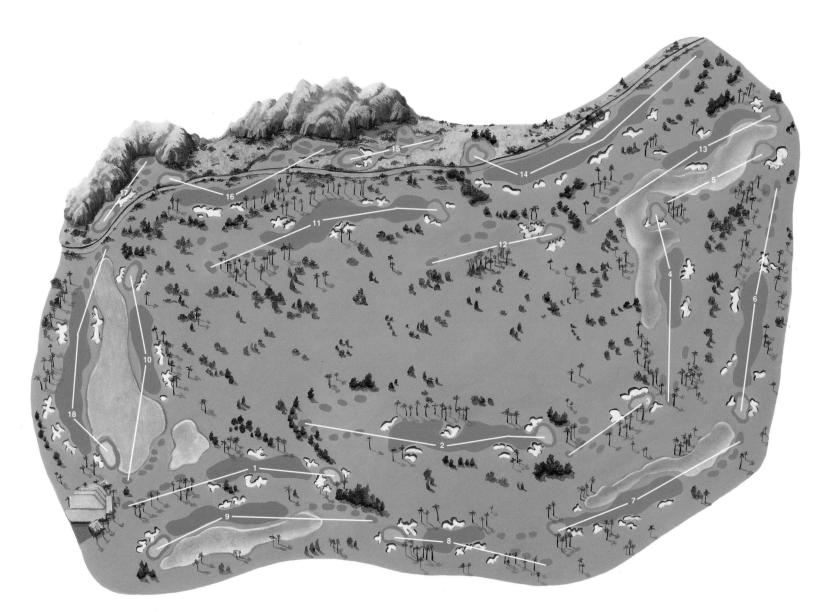

Palmer Course/PGA West

played the four holes of sudden death in birdie, birdie, birdie, eagle.

One might think that a 90-hole event would tend to separate the scores at the top, and yet recently the Hope has produced playoff finishes more frequently than any event on the Tour—seven in the past 12 years. Bob Hope and his tournament committees are proud of that statistic, as they are of a more important number—the 23 million dollars that the Bob Hope Chrysler Classic has raised for charity, by far the largest contribution of any event on the PGA Tour.

Palmer Course, 11th hole

TORREY PINES GOLF CLUB

eneath the buttoned-down, neatly pressed surface of the PGA Tour lurks a potential for lunacy, an ability to produce situations so goofy and preposterous, not even Ripley would believe them. Among these tales from the dark side, perhaps none is more bizarre than the story of the Walrus and the towel.

In 1987, Craig Stadler was disqualified at San Diego because he had used a towel to keep his pants dry while kneeling to play a shot from under a tree. The infraction, for "building a stance" (a violation of Rule 13-3), occurred during round three but was not discovered until Sunday, when the shot was shown on the Saturday highlights segment leading into the final day's telecast on NBC. Viewers called in to report the violation, and Stadler, who finished the tournament and would have tied for second place, missed out on a check for $36,000.

Stadler's story is but one of a series of sagas from the tournament in San Diego, where the Tour's penchant for the perverse seems to surface with uncommon regularity. After all, this is the event where in 1954 a local boy named Gene Littler outplayed a field full of pros and won the tournament as an amateur; where in 1975 Bruce Devlin took six swings at a ball in a water hazard; and where—at the same hole—David Edwards once holed-out a driver from the fairway for a double eagle.

San Diego is where Pete Brown made up six strokes in the final round to become the second black man to win a PGA Tour event; where Ray Floyd blew two playoffs by missing the same baffling putt; where Jack Nicklaus charged home on Sunday with five birdies and two eagles—and lost—and where a roly-poly, gum-chewing kid named Greg Twiggs took his only Tour title. At this tournament, not even the famous San Diego

South Course, 13th hole

fair weather has been normal. In 1992, one round was canceled, not for rain, sleet, snow, or hail but because of pea soup fog.

On most days, however, the courses of the Buick Invitational of California are sun-drenched and in play for all. Set along a row of cliffs at the edge of the Pacific Ocean, Torrey Pines North and South constitute one of the finest municipal golf facilities in the world. Fifty-one weeks out of the year, they are operated by the city of San Diego for the enjoyment of the public. One week each winter, they host the PGA Tour.

Few courses in America, and perhaps no muni course, can boast a more spectacular natural setting. The ocean is in view from many of the holes and in play on a couple of them, where the fairways cling to the ledges of a steep canyon that drops 300 feet to the sea. Most of the trees on the course are the starkly beautiful Torrey pines for which the club is named, an ancient variety of long-needle fir that is native only to San Diego and the Channel Islands off Santa Barbara.

Both courses were designed during the early fifties by William P. "Billy" Bell, a protégé of George C. Thomas, the famed architect of the Bel-Air and Los Angeles Country Club courses. Bell died before he could see completion of his work, but his son, William F. Bell, oversaw the construction.

Par for both courses is 72, but the South is over 400 yards longer and plays roughly one and one-half strokes tougher than the North. The pros spread over both courses on Thursday and Friday of the tournament; after the cut, the competition is restricted to the South Course.

Wind is a major factor here, particularly in the afternoon, when it gusts through the canyons and lengthens the holes that play toward the sea. The greens are not fast, but their breaks are subtle and often confounding. Raymond Floyd, when asked about the most unforgettable putt of his career, recalled not one but two putts at Torrey Pines.

Playing Low Shots
BY PHIL MICKELSON

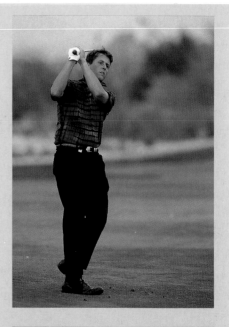

When a golf course is named after a tree, you can usually expect to play some unorthodox shots. Craig Stadler is the most famous, but virtually all of us who've played Torrey Pines have been forced, at one time or another, to hit a shot under, over, around, or through the trees.

When you have to play a low shot—whether under a tree or not—keep a couple of things in mind. First, your lie. If you're in heavy rough, you'll have to hit down hard on the ball, and that will create a lofted shot. If you're in light, fluffy rough, you may have a flyer lie which tends to produce high shots. The best lie for a low shot is actually hardpan, but from the fairway it's not hard to keep the ball low. Next, visualize the shot you want to play—see the trajectory, and match that trajectory to a club. If you have to hit under a tree branch, take at least one club less lofted than the club you visualized.

Whatever club you choose, grip down a bit, and play the ball a couple of inches in back of its usual position in your stance. Then, take the club back low to the ground, stretching your arms outward as you move the club back straight from the ball. The backswing should be compact—three-quarters your usual length—and on the downswing both your body and your club should drive laterally through the ball rather than upward. To hit low, finish low.

One final tip when you have to low-bridge a tree branch: Keep your swing easy—don't hit a full shot. With a soft impact you won't generate the full loft of the club in your hand.

Phil Mickelson's first victory as a professional was the 1993 Buick Invitational of California.

South Course, 3rd hole

North Course, 7th hole

"The first was in 1975, on the first hole of a sudden-death playoff [number 15 of the South Course] with J.C. Snead and Bobby Nichols," said Floyd. "I hit a putt that I was convinced was going in the hole—no way I was going to miss. I went to get it, and then it just lipped out. It was the most amazing thing I'd ever seen. In fact, for a long time after that, I actually had nightmares about it. I kept seeing it in my mind, over and over.

"Then, unbelievably, the same thing happened—on the same hole and under the same circumstances—in 1981 when I was in a playoff with Bruce Lietzke and Tom Jenkins. As had been the case six

years earlier, they both missed their birdie putts. I hit mine, and it was breaking right into the center of the hole again. Then, just at the lip, it swerved away and missed." Floyd lost both of those playoffs, and still scratches his head every time he thinks about that 15th green.

One player who has sweet memories of the South Course is Johnny Miller, who has a special fondness for hole number four. When he won the tournament in 1982, Miller birdied it four days in a row, an achievement which becomes even more remarkable when one considers that this is a 453-yard uphill par four that runs along the cliff. When a drive or

approach tumbles off that cliff it is still playable, but the prognosis for recovery is grim. Imagine having to hit a 9-iron off a sidewalk to the roof of a skyscraper across the street, and you get a feel for the assignment. One player who doesn't have fond memories here is Payne Stewart, who in 1993 took a triple-bogey 7 after incurring a two-stroke penalty for an illegal drop from a cart path. The incident cost Stewart the lead—and eventually the tournament.

The hardest hole on the course is number seven. Another 453-yard four, it doglegs right and plays into the prevailing wind off the Pacific. As if that wasn't

North Course, 6th hole

tough enough, a greenside bunker was added and the existing bunkers on the hole were enlarged during course renovations in 1988.

On the inward path, the hole that looms large is the 12th. Its 468 yards play uphill and into the wind. Tall trees and four-inch rough line both sides of the fairway, a bunker on the right catches fades that fade too much, and another one a bit farther down the fairway snags draws that draw too much. A ball in either of them almost inevitably means a shot lost on the way to the sand-flanked green.

Number 15, where Floyd had his double trouble, is an excellent short four of

356 yards. Originally a straight hole, it is now a slight dogleg left for the pros, thanks to a tee added in 1973 that tacked 50 yards onto the hole. The smart drive is shaded to the right to avoid a large eucalyptus tree on the left side of the fairway. Number 17 is the type of hole that gives even the straightest hitters pause. The canyons gape on the left while a large bunker and a fence of trees await on the right.

Each of the four nines at Torrey Pines ends with a reachable par five, but the most dramatic is number 18 on the South Course, where invariably the tournament is won or lost. The key to this hole is the elongated pond which was added to the

left-front of the green in 1968. In that year, Tom Weiskopf sank a 25-foot eagle putt from off the green to edge Al Geiberger by a stroke. Since then the hole has produced a collection of dramatic finishes that rival any on the Tour. The pond became known as Devlin's Billabong in the final round of 1975 after the Australian played six shots from its near shore in an attempt to blast his ball onto the green. Only three strokes off the lead when he first hit the hazard, Devlin toppled into a tie for 30th. Today, a plaque marks his watery grave.

This tournament has been a fixture on the PGA Tour since 1952, but has gone through five different sponsors and 11

South Course

Scorecard

different names, including an affiliation with entertainer Andy Williams for over 20 years. At one point, it had the longest title of any Tour event: The Shearson Lehman Brothers Andy Williams Open. However, today with Buick—the Tour's biggest sponsor—firmly in place, stability seems assured.

In its early years the tournament rotated through a half dozen different sites, but since 1968 Torrey Pines has been its constant home. The Tour eventually wants a TPC Course to host this event, but that remains in the future while Torrey Pines prospers in the present.

	North Course				South Course		
Hole	Yards	Par	PGA Tour Avg. Score	Hole	Yards	Par	PGA Tour Avg. Score
1	520	5	4.754	1	447	4	4.271
2	326	4	3.908	2	365	4	3.862
3	121	3	2.954	3	173	3	3.045
4	398	4	4.108	4	453	4	4.279
5	371	4	4.046	5	404	4	4.095
6	160	3	3.318	6	535	5	4.716
7	400	4	4.191	7	453	4	4.265
8	436	4	4.116	8	171	3	2.926
9	497	5	4.681	9	536	5	4.673
OUT	3229	36	36.076	OUT	3537	36	36.132
10	416	4	4.074	10	373	4	3.976
11	437	4	4.154	11	207	3	3.140
12	190	3	3.073	12	468	4	4.239
13	421	4	4.067	13	535	5	4.772
14	507	5	4.689	14	398	4	4.062
15	397	4	3.923	15	356	4	4.031
16	338	4	3.944	16	203	3	3.066
17	172	3	3.018	17	425	4	4.091
18	485	5	4.613	18	498	5	4.625
IN	3363	36	35.555	IN	3463	36	36.002
TOTAL	6592	72	71.631	TOTAL	7000	72	72.134

DORAL COUNTRY CLUB

9th hole

Doral—Ryder Open, Florida

"I t'll never work, Alfred. You're creating a monster." That's what everyone told Alfred Kaskel in 1960 when he decided to plunge his fortune into the construction of a golf resort smack in the center of a useless Florida swamp. His friends and business associates were unanimous in their disdain of the project they called "Kaskel's Folly."

Alfred called it Doral, a mellifluous meld of his own name and that of his wife, Doris. When he hired one of the era's preeminent golf architects, Dick Wilson, to create a course, then grabbed an open date on the 1962 pro circuit and started a tournament with a purse of $50,000 (twice that of any other Florida event), the skeptics assumed Alfred had lost his marbles as well as his shirt.

To no one's surprise, both the Doral Country Club and the Doral Open spewed red ink in their first year of operation. But in the three decades since, Doral has prospered, adding five more courses and a spectacular spa. In the eyes of avid golfers, it is one of the finest pure-golf resorts in America.

The original critics were accurate, however, in one prediction. Kaskel and Wilson created a monster of a golf course—the Blue Monster—on which the Doral-Ryder Open is annually staged. It was first designated simply the Blue Course, to distinguish it from the Red, White, Green, Gold, and Silver Courses which also snake through the Doral property. But this 6,939-yard demon is true blue, spread across almost as much water as grass.

The first difficult test comes at number four, a peninsular par three that preys on the mind as much as the muscles, playing 237 liquid yards to a green guarded on both sides by sand.

The eighth has been called one of the world's best par fives, its 528-yard fairway

Hitting a Draw
BY RAYMOND FLOYD

The right-to-left shot, or draw, has helped me on a couple of occasions at Doral. First was the high-drawing 6-iron I hit over palm trees to salvage a par on the 72nd hole in 1980. Then there's 1981, the year I beat David Graham in a playoff. I set up that victory with a long, low draw with a driver into the wind on the first playoff hole.

The key is to swing the club on a slightly flatter than normal plane, inside the target line. You can set up such a swing at address by taking a closed stance, with your feet, knees, hips, and shoulders aligned several feet to the right of the target. I don't change my grip for this shot, but it doesn't hurt to rotate your hands a quarter-turn clockwise on the club.

I trigger this swing by rotating my right shoulder, and concentrate on making a slow, strong turn. On the downswing the key is to make a good release of the club. Be sure that your right hand crosses over your left. This action closes the clubface as you move through the hitting area, imparting the counterclock-

wise spin that creates the right-to-left flight path. You can check yourself for the proper release: Make a couple of swings and stop as your arms reach a full extension in the follow-through (pointing to nine o'clock). If in this position your right wrist is on top of your left, you've made the correct release for a draw.

Raymond Floyd is a three-time winner (1980, 1981, 1992) of the Doral–Ryder Open.

18th hole

wiggling fiendishly between two lakes. Anyone hoping to hit the green in two will have to slug a lengthy second shot over the right-hand lake and hope it holds the sand-and-water-surrounded green. Scores of 6 and higher on this hole are not uncommon, even for the pros.

The back nine begins with a 563-yard par five that was the scene of one of Greg Norman's finest moments. In the final round of the 1990 Doral-Ryder Open, Norman charged home with a course-record 62 to come from seven strokes off the lead into a sudden-death playoff with Paul Azinger, Mark Calcavecchia, and Tim Simpson. The Great White Shark then struck two massive shots to the back fringe of the green, nearly hitting the stick with the second of them, before chipping in for a victorious eagle.

Another brute of a par three rears its head at number 13, at 246 yards one of the longest short holes in golf. Amateurs have trouble reaching it, and pros have trouble parring it. The green is broad but unusually shallow for a hole of this length, and it falls off quickly from front to back.

Seventeen is a classic dogleg par four of 406 yards, calling for a drive down the right center, just inside a trio of bunkers. From there it's a middle iron for the pros to a long, narrow green guarded by five sprawling traps.

The term "blue monster" is often used to refer solely to the 18th at Doral, a nerve-shattering journey of 425 yards along the edge of a big lake. The fairway is slim and serpentine, with the water looming large on the left and a row of

trees on the right. The second shot must be played to a green that is 175 feet long but only a few paces deep, with the lake to the left and bunkers to the right.

In 1988, Ben Crenshaw sank a lengthy birdie putt on 18 to win the tournament, but others have been less fortunate, most notably Paul Azinger. Needing a par to win in 1990, Azinger bogeyed the final

hole to fall into the playoff won by Norman. A year later, his elimination came much earlier. In the opening round, while addressing his second shot to 18, Azinger kicked away some rocks at the edge of the lake. A television viewer called in to report the violation, and the next day, after Azinger had shot a 65 to move into a tie for second place, he was disqualified. In 1968 Gardner Dickinson double-bogeyed this hole but still won the tournament, because Tom Weiskopf, needing a par to win and a bogey to tie, also took a 6.

"I've made 6's and 7's on it hundreds of times," says Raymond Floyd, who calls Doral's 18th the toughest par four in the world. That's high respect from a player who has won at Doral three times, back to back in 1980–81 and then again in an emotional week in 1992, just days after his home on nearby Indian Creek Island and all his possessions had been lost in a fire. Age 49 at the time, Floyd tied Sam Snead's record for most years between first and last victories (29), and claimed the devastating fire had actually had a

10th hole

4th hole

positive effect on his game, forcing him to focus on his golf the way his wife, Maria, had focused on restoring order to his home and family. He went on to have one of his best seasons on the Tour, then turned 50 in September and won in his second start on the Senior PGA Tour, becoming the first player ever to win on both Tours in the same season.

Also in 1992, Doral suffered a calamity of its own when Hurricane Andrew tore through southern Florida, wreaking several billion dollars worth of damage on the Miami area. Over 2,000 trees were ripped from the six golf courses. But within a short time Doral was back in operation, and even at age thirtysomething and minus a few teeth, its big course remains a Blue Monster.

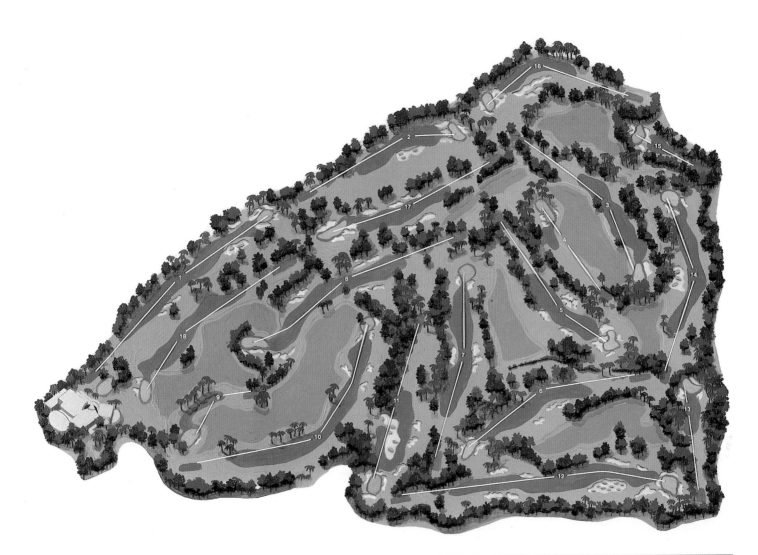

Scorecard

Hole	Yards	Par	PGA Tour Avg. Score
1	514	5	4.529
2	355	4	3.944
3	398	4	4.099
4	237	3	3.262
5	371	4	3.936
6	427	4	4.065
7	415	4	3.995
8	528	5	4.788
9	163	3	3.004
OUT	3408	36	35.622
10	563	5	4.904
11	348	4	3.935
12	591	5	4.909
13	246	3	3.314
14	418	4	4.038
15	174	3	2.949
16	360	4	3.888
17	406	4	4.029
18	425	4	4.277
IN	3531	36	36.243
TOTAL	6939	72	71.865

8th hole

WESTON HILLS COUNTRY CLUB

Weston Hills Country Club made its PGA Tour debut in 1992, and what a debut it was. On the par-five 72nd hole, Corey Pavin hit what *GOLF Magazine* called "the shot of the year," a 140-yard 8-iron shot that landed in the cup on the fly. The eagle 3 jumped Pavin into a first-place tie with Fred Couples, whom he beat on the second hole of sudden death.

Sudden death had also been the fate of the previous Honda Classic site, the TPC at Eagle Trace. The second of the Tour's Stadium Courses (after the TPC at Sawgrass), Eagle Trace was an Arthur Hills design that attempted to blend Scotland with Florida. It didn't work. The treeless, gently rolling terrain had a British feel, except for the presence of one element—water. A virtual canal system ran through 16 of the 18 holes, creating a crossbreed layout that was neither a target course nor a links. Since ponds guarded many of the greens, the traditional bump-and-run shots could only splash and sink, and in a stiff wind, the course could make even the world's best players look like Dorothy and Toto.

The course first hosted the Honda in 1984 and it never engendered much popularity. In 1987, the 36-hole cut was 151, a number that has not been equalled at any other Tour event in the ensuing years. The uneasy marriage reached its seven-year itch in 1991 when both weekend rounds were played in 40-mph winds. Over the two days, only three players broke 70 and ten players couldn't break 80, including former champion Curtis Strange, who finished with an 86.

"This place is a joke," said Greg Norman. "You won't see me back here next year. I don't need to be playing carnival golf." Dozens of his colleagues chorused in agreement, and the Tour administrators sensed it was time for a change.

Enter Weston Hills, the centerpiece of a 10,000-acre planned community near Ft. Lauderdale. At 7,069 yards, this par-72 layout is almost exactly the same length as Eagle Trace, but its holes are routed north-south, so that it plays either directly down or into the prevailing wind—good shots are rarely buffeted right or left. There is plenty of water here, and the hazards come into play on a dozen holes, but seldom is there a forced carry to a green.

The course begins with a 548-yard par five. Although it plays uphill, it is reachable to the Tour's longest hitters, as are two of the three other par fives at Weston Hills. In 1992, Dan Forsman took advantage of them, posting a record three eagles in his final round. (Forsman finished the year with 18 eagles, more than any other player on the Tour.)

Jones Jr.'s other Tour course, Poppy Hills, is known for its large and severely undulating greens. At Weston Hills, the slopes are far less fierce, except at the second hole, where the shortness of the 331-yard par four is balanced by a putting surface with a large slope at its center, the effect of which is to divide the green into three distinct sectors.

Each of the nines begins benignly and then builds to a crescendo, as the water hazards—not in play on the early holes—encroach more and more toward the finish. The most intimidating occurrence on the front nine is at the fifth hole, a 197-yard par three with water in front and to the left of the green.

Number six is a dead-straight par four with no sand but water down the entire left side and a series of mounds down the right. It's 436 yards into the prevailing wind, so this is a hole that requires length as well as accuracy.

As was the case at Eagle Trace, the ninth and 18th holes head back to a stately clubhouse. At Weston, however,

9th hole

Honda Classic, Florida

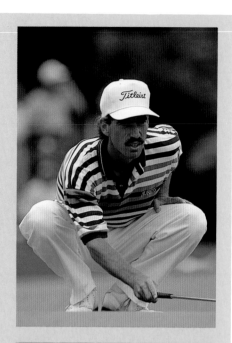

When my 8-iron shot fell into the cup on the last hole of the 1992 Honda Classic it was luck, but getting the ball close is a matter of accuracy.

Accuracy with the irons is comprised of two elements—direction and distance—and with the shorter irons, particularly the wedges, distance control becomes vital. So it's fundamentally important to know the exact yardages you hit each club. Then, be aware of the other factors that influence club selection. When you're playing uphill or to an elevated green, take at least one club more. Going downhill, take at least one less. From fluffy lies, beware the flyer—a backspinless shot that flies farther than a ball hit from the fairway—and take one club less. Obviously, use more club when hitting into a headwind, less club with a tailwind.

In the early-morning dew or when the grass is wet, you won't be able to put as much spin on the ball, so your shots will fly longer—use less club. Use more club also when playing left-to-right with a fade or slice, but less club when going right to left with a draw or hook. Finally, be aware of your emotions—when you're keyed up, allow for the extra adrenaline by taking one club less than you would under normal circumstances.

.

Corey Pavin won the 1992 Honda Classic in a playoff after holing-out an 8-iron on the final hole to tie Fred Couples.

Scorecard

Hole	Yards	Par	PGA Tour Avg. Score
1	548	5	4.701
2	331	4	3.955
3	149	3	2.983
4	385	4	4.071
5	197	3	3.156
6	436	4	4.109
7	535	5	4.759
8	419	4	3.986
9	435	4	4.164
OUT	3435	36	35.884
10	412	4	3.934
11	178	3	3.049
12	530	5	4.596
13	409	4	4.003
14	391	4	4.033
15	455	4	4.305
16	460	4	4.280
17	214	3	3.167
18	585	5	5.010
IN	3634	36	36.377
TOTAL	7069	72	72.261

18th hole

they merge at a mammoth double green. Number nine is the tougher par of the two, a 435-yarder that plays along the edge of a lake.

The sternest segment of the Weston Hills challenge is what the members call "The Final Four," a quartet of holes that stand up to any finish on the Tour. Fifteen doglegs 90 degrees around the edge of a wide lake, forcing players to decide how much water they want to carry in cutting the length of the approach. Into the wind, this 455-yard hole becomes a very stiff test.

Water haunts the 16th as well, as a lagoon stretches from tee to green along the right side of this 460-yard hole while a fairway bunker cautions against hitting the tee shot mindlessly left. The green is a peninsula that juts into the lagoon and is shored up by rocks. Players whose

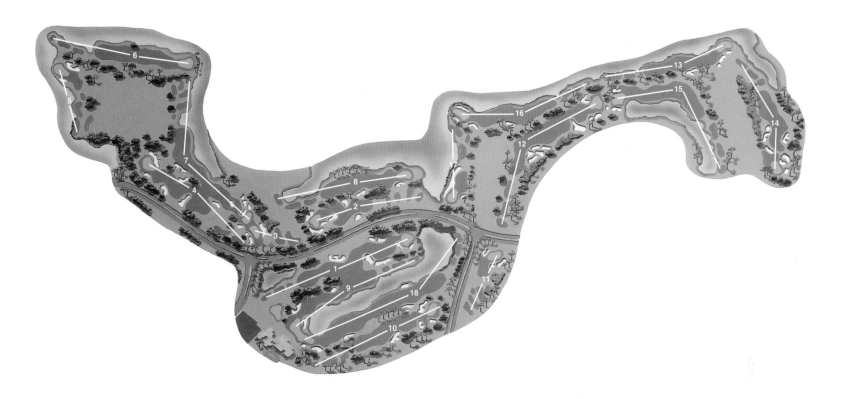

shots fall just short will see some strange caroms and some high numbers. Without question, this is the hardest hole on the course, particularly when it plays into the wind.

"Miss it left," is the credo at the 17th, Weston's longest par three. If you fade this 214-yard tee shot, your ball will splash into sand; if you slice, it will splash into water.

Number 18, the longest hole on the course, is a 585-yard par five that calls for two strong, straight shots to set up an approach over a lagoon to the shared green. Jones added some formidable undulations to this large green, so getting the ball to drop in the final hole can be a challenge, unless of course you can play an 8-iron with the accuracy of Corey Pavin.

17th hole

BAY HILL CLUB

1st hole

The Nestlé Invitational, Florida

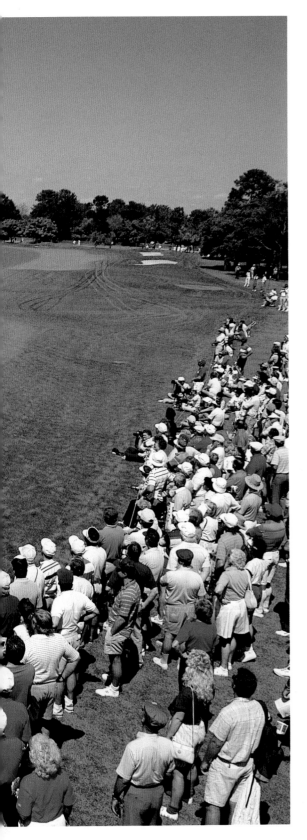

When 21-year-old Robert Gamez stepped to the tee of the final hole of the 1990 Nestlé Invitational, he knew he had little chance of victory. Not only was he a stroke behind co-leaders Greg Norman and Larry Mize, he was facing a hole then ranked as the toughest on the PGA Tour, a 441-yard par four with a blind tee shot and a long narrow green that curves along the shore of a lake. For Gamez, winning was a long shot.

But a long shot is exactly what he produced. After a perfect drive, the Tour rookie slashed a 7-iron 176 yards across the water, onto the green, and into the hole for a double-eagle 2 that vaulted him to the $162,000 first prize. No statistics are kept on such things, but it's safe to say that this was the longest winning shot in the history of professional golf.

The fantasyland finish was appropriate for this course, just a short drive from Walt Disney World. Appropriate, too, because this is the home of golf's most exciting player—the king of the closing charge—Arnold Palmer.

Palmer first laid eyes on the course in 1965 when he played an exhibition match with Jack Nicklaus. So struck was he by the quality of Dick Wilson's design and the surrounding terrain that he bought the place. Today, after much redesign work by Palmer and his partner Ed Seay, Bay Hill reflects Arnold's aggressive, virile spirit. It is long and tight, and most of the tough holes play into the face of a prevailing north wind, encouraging the hard, low, laserlike tee shot that remains Palmer's trademark even as a senior citizen. And when the holes at Bay Hill dogleg, they usually

17th hole

dogleg left, favoring the proprietor's preferred flight pattern, a draw.

Six water hazards and over 100 bunkers testify to Palmer's love of gambling, scrambling, heroic golf. In almost every round at Bay Hill there comes a moment when the player must hitch up his pants and go for broke.

One of the toughest tests comes right out of the box. Up until 1990, Bay Hill's opening hole was an easy par five. Now it's a par four of the same length as the finishing hole—441 yards—and almost as tough, doglegging left through trees to a sand-surrounded green. In its first year in play, it ranked as the hardest opening hole on the Tour.

Palmer and Seay made wholesale changes in 1990, and one of the most visible came at the third hole, a sickle-shaped par four that has cut many players to size. The hole winds sharply left along the edge of a lake, and now it culminates at a green buttressed on the lake side by a native rock wall. In 1993 Ben Crenshaw played one of the best shots of his life on this hole, a 3-iron from light rough that soared across, then bounded up on the green and curled to within six feet for an unanticipated birdie that helped him to victory.

Wrapping around the other side of that lake is number six, a 543-yard par five where John Daly could probably drive clear across the water and onto the green, but would never dare. Instead, he and the rest of the Tour try to play two—or three—solid shots that avoid the water. Anything's possible here, as Jim Colbert proved one year, making an eagle on Thursday and a 9 on Friday. Lee Trevino took an 11 here in 1979, then withdrew, muttering "I can make more money selling soda pop at the gate." And even the landlord has had his problems here. In 1983, Palmer took a 10 on this hole en route to an 85, his highest round as a professional.

3rd hole

18th hole

6th hole

Hitting Long Irons
BY ARNOLD PALMER

Bay Hill offers one of the most challenging finales in golf. The last five holes are long and demanding—two par threes, two par fours, and a gambler's par five. On almost every one of them the shot to the green must be played with a long iron.

The pros don't have much trouble with these clubs, but many amateurs do. They look down at these shallow-faced irons and wonder whether the loft is sufficient to get the ball airborne. As a result, they often hold back with their hands on the downswing, and throw the club at the ball in an attempt to scoop it into flight.

Rule one on the long irons is to trust them. The loft on even a 1-iron is sufficient to put the ball high into the air. All you need is a swing that applies the clubhead squarely to the ball—a level swing.

The more level the angle of attack—the longer the clubhead moves parallel to the ground—the better your chances of making solid impact. The best way to achieve this level clubhead path is to play the ball off your left instep and concentrate on making a smooth weight shift, to your right side on the backswing, then back to your left side on the downswing. One last point: Think of the ball simply as a point on your swing; don't hit at it, swing through it.

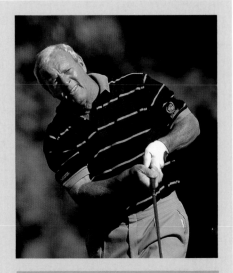

Arnold Palmer owns the Bay Hill Club and Lodge and is chairman of the Nestlé Invitational.

Scorecard

Hole	Yards	Par	PGA Tour Avg. Score
1	441	4	4.285
2	218	3	3.190
3	395	4	4.186
4	530	5	4.756
5	365	4	4.006
6	543	5	4.884
7	197	3	3.069
8	424	4	4.208
9	467	4	4.203
OUT	3580	36	36.787
10	400	4	4.035
11	428	4	4.194
12	570	5	4.916
13	364	4	3.908
14	206	3	3.111
15	425	4	4.042
16	481	5	4.491
17	219	3	3.215
18	441	4	4.409
IN	3534	36	36.321
TOTAL	7114	72	73.108

The back nine at Bay Hill features two of the longest and most difficult par threes on the Tour. The first of them, number 14, plays 206 yards slightly uphill to a sliver of green cinched by sand. Bob Gilder still winces over his experience here in 1983. He was in second place on Saturday when he pushed his tee shot high into a palm tree to the right of the green. When the ball didn't come down, Gilder tried to climb the tree to get at it, but abandoned his search when he drove a splinter into his left ring finger. Gilder eventually made a double-bogey and vanished from the leaderboard.

The other little devil is the 17th, a 219-yarder that plays almost entirely over a pond. It is a hole Don Pooley will never forget. Back in the final round of the 1987 tournament, Pooley struck a 4-iron into the hole here. It was his first ace ever, but more important, it earned a bonus of one million dollars— $500,000 for him and $500,000 donated to the Arnold Palmer Children's Hospital in Orlando. Pooley will receive after-tax payments of $2,083.33 every month until 2007.

Number 18 was a quiet little par five before Arnie got hold of it, lowering the elevated green so that it now cuddles at the edge of a rock-bound lake. Thick rough borders the fairway, making the approach so risky that many players simply lay up short of the green. Large bunkers cling to the amphitheater at the left and rear of the green so that anyone who hits into them will face a downhill explosion directly at the water and across the fastest green on the course. In the words of Ray Floyd, "The hole borders on the unfair."

But don't ever try to tell that to Robert Gamez.

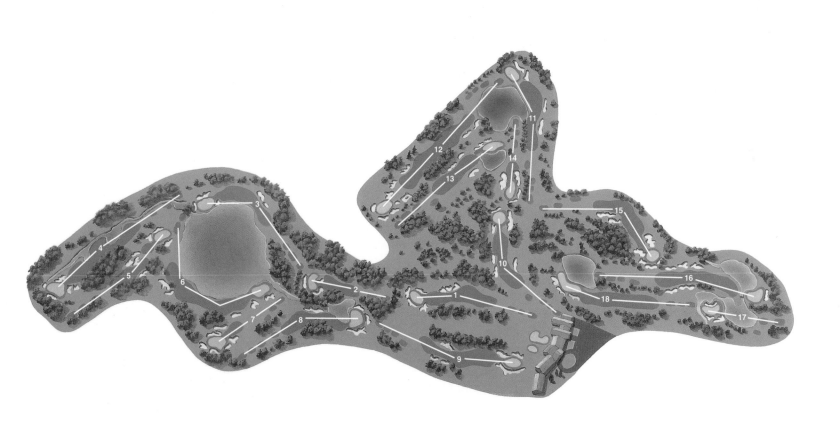

TPC AT SAWGRASS

It is the Ben Hogan of golf courses—the comeback kid. When the Tournament Players Club at Sawgrass opened in 1980, the initial reviews made then Commissioner Deane Beman's dream course seem like a nightmare. The design—by Pete Dye with consultation by Beman—was penal with a capital P, a malevolent collection of par-defying pranks: narrow fingers of fairway lined with long strips of sand and love grass; dozens of deep, diabolically placed pot bunkers; scores of rough-covered knolls and craters; tall trees everywhere; and, meanest of all, 18 hard, fast greens, each contoured like a clenched fist.

The loudest critics were the club's charter members, the Tour pros. When the first Players Championship came to the course in March of 1982, Jack Nicklaus was asked whether the layout suited his game. "No," he said, "I've never been very good at stopping a 5-iron on the hood of a car." Ben Crenshaw, normally the most diplomatic of players, pronounced the course "Star Wars Golf, designed by Darth Vader," and J.C. Snead, normally the most undiplomatic, called it "90 percent horse manure and 10 percent luck."

But the winner of that inaugural event, Jerry Pate, showed more perspective. "It's too early to rate this course," he said. "It's like trying to rate girls when they're born. They get better with age."

In the ensuing months, architect Dye joined with an advisory group of players to rework every one of the greens. Several bunkers also were altered, and

5th hole

11th hole

subtle but important changes were made to some of the fairways. Quickly, the bulges of baby fat became graceful, shapely curves, the sharp teeth softened into a comely smile. Today, the TPC is a charmer, and most of her suitors savor the challenge of conquering her.

"Now it's a darn good course," says Crenshaw. "There are no weak holes." His opinion is shared by the selectors in GOLF Magazine's international panel, which ranks the course 74th on its list of the 100 Greatest Courses in the World.

You can judge *this* book by its cover. The first tee at the TPC tells what's ahead in the next four hours. There is not so much a fairway as a landing strip. Miss it to the left, and you are standing amid tall pines. Miss it to the right, and you are in a bunker. The hole doglegs gently right to a narrow, contoured green that is protected by sand and grass bunkers. Most of the pros come to this hole with irons or fairway woods; all of them come to it with respect.

Stand on that first tee, look down the fairway, and you know you are at an interesting golf course. But stand there and look to your right, your left, or your back, and you know you are at the TPC. For encasing you on three sides is a 40-foot-high, bulkheaded grass amphitheater, tiered like a wedding cake, with seating capacity for 20,000.

The course is the fulfillment of Commissioner Beman's vision—a facility owned and operated by the PGA Tour and designed with the dual intent of challenging the pros and accommodating the spectators. Earlier layouts, notably Nicklaus's Muirfield Village, had incorporated features that enhance the visibility of tournament play, but this TPC was golf's first bona fide stadium, and it became the prototype for a network of 22 such facilities, spread across a dozen states and two foreign countries, with others on the way.

At Sawgrass, Beman's bulldozers literally moved mountains to improve the spectator views. Like most of Florida, this is flat terrain; at no point does it rise higher than five feet above sea level. But this did not stop Beman and Dye; 850,000 cubic feet of dirt were excavated and elevated to create the massive gallery mounds that line many of the holes. The course was also routed so that play returns to, or near, the clubhouse several times, allowing spectators to mill out to many holes without having to walk across the property. Finally, most of the underbrush was cleared so that when the going gets rough, it does not get too rough.

At least not for the spectators. For the pros it is another story. The toughest stretch of the course begins early—at the fourth hole, a 384-yard par four where Paul Azinger claims, "You can make double- or triple-bogey in a heartbeat." Although this is a hole short enough to be attacked with a 2-iron off the tee, the approach must be played to an angled green protected by water front and left, fiendish bunkers back and right.

Next comes the longest par four on the course. The 454-yard fifth hole sweeps right in a big banking turn. Mounds run along the left side of the fairway, and waste areas menace both the right and left sides of the landing area. The second shot is a long iron to a deep but slender green guarded by tall palms and bunkers, and, as if that were not enough, tall palms *within* bunkers.

Few greens present a more intimidating target than that of the 381-yard sixth hole. The small putting surface has severe breaks and is surrounded by a nest of deep bunkers and swales. If you fail to hit and hold this green on your second shot, you may not hit and hold it on your third.

Number seven, a 439-yarder with a huge strip bunker to carry on the approach, is a demanding par four under normal conditions; when played into a stiff breeze, it is a demanding bogey five.

Back-to-back at the eighth and ninth holes are the hardest par three and the hardest par five on the course. The "short" hole plays 215 yards slightly downhill to a green that is as difficult to putt as it is to reach. Although the island-green 17th gets most of the press, this par three taxes the pros for twice as many scores of bogey and worse.

17th hole

8th hole

Picturesque number nine is reachable in two, but few players try. Here is the smallest target on the course, perched above a large bunker on the left and a cluster of knolls and more bunkers on the right. In 1984, it was the toughest par five on the entire Tour. However, when Jacksonville native Mark McCumber won his emotional victory in 1988, he helped his cause by holing out a wedge shot here for an eagle 3.

Another of Commissioner Beman's aims was to give his course similar starts off the front and back nines. Since play during the first two rounds of The Players begins simultaneously on both sides, Beman felt that all competitors should have an equal opportunity to begin with a birdie—or a disaster.

The tenth fairway is only seven yards longer than its sibling rival on the front nine and in many ways is a mirror image. It doglegs slightly left in the same way that the first hole doglegs slightly right. The similar start continues with the par-five 11th hole as an analog to the second. Here is strategic golf architecture at its intriguing best. Two routes are available off the tee. A drive down the left side of the fairway allows a second shot to a landing area just short of the green, leaving a wedge pitch. A long drive down the right side leaves the better player an opportunity to go for the green in two. But that shot had better be a fine one. It must carry water and a strip bunker and then hold tight on an extremely narrow, rolling green surrounded by sand.

The second hardest hole on the course is number 14, a slim, straightaway par four of 438 yards. A huge spectator mound rises up on the right side of the right-to-left banked fairway, while the omnipresent strip bunker runs down the left.

Performing Under Pressure

BY STEVE ELKINGTON

The 3-iron shot I hit to the final hole in the 1991 Players Championship may have been my best shot ever under pressure. With water on the left, grassy mounds on the right, and the tournament on the line, it was all or nothing, and I'm proud that I was able to hit a solid shot straight at the flag.

Performing under pressure is something we all hope to be able to do. Of course, you don't know how good at it you are until the moment arrives, but there are certain things you can do to improve your chances.

First, it's important to have a swing you can trust. The swing doesn't have to be flawless, simply repeatable under the gun. You may have a high, floating fade—but if you can rely on that high floating fade, then you have a potent weapon. How do you get such a swing? Simple: Practice, play plenty of matches and tournaments, and then practice some more.

No matter what kind of swing you have, if I could make one recommendation, it would be to lighten your grip pressure when faced with a tense situation. The common tendency is to tighten the grip, which tightens your whole swing and leads to steering and veering.

Perhaps more important than the mechanics is your attitude—think positively. Remember your past successes, particularly the occasions when you've succeeded where the situation was similar to the one you're facing. Once over the ball, visualize that perfect shot—run a movie of the ball in flight and coming down next to the hole, as Jack Nicklaus

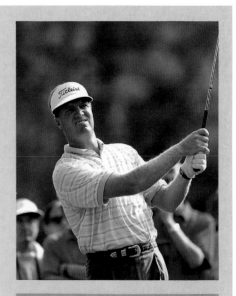

does. By focusing on the ideal outcome, you'll shut out negative thoughts and help insure a smooth, confident swing.

Steve Elkington won the 1991 Players Championship.

16th hole

The last three holes at the TPC are as mind-warping a finish as there is in golf. The 16th is a gambler's delight, a 497-yard par five that tempts the pros to go for it in two. The length of the second shot is no problem for most Tour players, but a lake on the right, trees and bunkers left, and a terrifyingly terraced green supply food for thought. In 1983, Hal Sutton came to this hole knowing he needed a birdie on one of the last three holes to win. After a 260-yard drive into position A, he slugged a 3-wood to the fringe of the green, chipped up, and made the birdie. He won by a stroke.

In only a few years, the 17th hole has become the most famous par three in golf. The hole is only 132 yards long, but there is no margin for error. Except for a tiny pot bunker to the front-right of the green, there is no place to land the ball but green—or water. In the blustery opening round of the 1984 TPC, 64 balls

plunked into the drink here, and the stroke average that day was 3.79, the highest ever recorded for a par three on the Tour. John Mahaffey called it "the easiest par five on the course." This is one hole that has seen almost no change since day one, and it has its detractors, including 1989 Champion Tom Kite. "We have 17 pretty good holes at the TPC and one bad one—17," says Kite. "It gives you no option."

Number 18 is one of the three or four closing par fours on the Tour that can be touted as the toughest finishing hole in golf. "It's a tremendous tournament hole because you can easily have a three-shot swing," says 1981 Players champion Ray Floyd. A large lake lurks along the entire left side of this doglegging 440-yard demon, adding a special penalty for any player who tries to cut off too much or allows an overly active right hand. The safe shot is to the right, but not too far

right because trees can block the lengthy approach. Near the green a cluster of thickly grown chocolate-drop mounds guards the right side, with grass bunkers in the back and sand and water to the left. If that's not enough pressure, consider the 40,000 pairs of eyes peering down from the huge natural grandstand to the right of the green.

Back in 1982, Jerry Pate handled it all nicely, with a perfect drive followed by a 5-iron 18 inches from the cup for a birdie to win by two. But it was after that tournament that the theatrics began. Pate, in his prime, was known for "celebratory aquatics," a predilection for capping his victories by diving into the nearest body of water. When that 5-iron came to rest, most of the gallery and television audience suspected what would come. Pate did not disappoint them. After signing his card, he did more than dunk himself, he grabbed course designer Dye and

18th hole

18th hole

Scorecard

Hole	Yards	Par	PGA Tour Avg. Score
1	388	4	4.035
2	526	5	4.738
3	162	3	3.061
4	384	4	3.931
5	454	4	4.129
6	381	4	4.045
7	439	4	4.099
8	215	3	3.161
9	582	5	4.877
OUT	3531	36	36.076
10	395	4	4.040
11	529	5	4.848
12	336	4	3.806
13	172	3	3.102
14	438	4	4.210
15	426	4	4.110
16	497	5	4.656
17	132	3	3.074
18	440	4	4.292
IN	3365	36	36.138
TOTAL	6896	72	72.214

Commissioner Beman and tossed them in as well.

With that baptism, The Players Championship officially settled into its permanent home. During its first three years (1974–76) the event had floated from course to course—first at the Atlanta Athletic Club, then Colonial in Ft. Worth, then Inverrary in Ft. Lauderdale, Florida. The Tour had intended it to be a prestigious event that would reward different Tour sites for past excellence in staging their events. But instead, it was viewed as an interloper. Thus, in 1977 the Tour moved the event to what they thought would be a permanent home at the Sawgrass resort course just outside Jacksonville, an Arnold Palmer/Ed Seay design. But the chem-

istry still wasn't right. Sawgrass is set less than a half mile from the ocean, and in March it can be one of the windiest places on earth. In the first two years there, no one broke par for 72 holes. This was not the showcase Beman had had in mind. So after searching far and wide for a new home, Beman found it in the marshland across the street.

Since The Players Club is two miles farther inland and well protected by trees, the winds rarely howl. And since the Tour has pushed the date of its event forward two weeks, to late March, softer conditions have prevailed.

Today, the TPC property also serves as the headquarters for the PGA Tour's offices, but the course itself is hardly the restricted province of the pros. In 1996,

the U.S. Amateur Championship will be held here, and in the meantime the Stadium Course is open to anyone who stays at the nearby Marriott resort, as part of a 99-hole golf complex that has earned a Gold Medal from *GOLF Magazine* as one of the finest golf resorts in the world.

So Deane Beman's dream has come to fulfillment—or almost. His ultimate wish was for The Players to reach the status of a major championship, equal in prominence to The Masters, U.S. Open, British Open, and PGA Championship. That's unlikely, since there is something nice and neat about four championships. But if the game can accommodate a fifth major, this tournament—played on this course—would seem to be it.

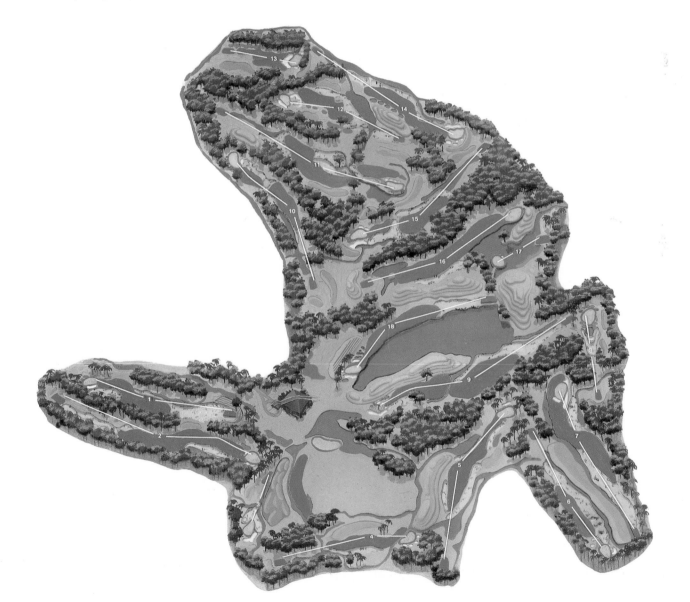

ENGLISH TURN GOLF AND COUNTRY CLUB

Back in 1699, the French and English were at war in bayou country. While sailing up the Mississippi near New Orleans, a British captain learned from some French rivermen that several well-armed French vessels were around the next bend in the river. Immediately, he turned his ship 180 degrees. But as it turned out, the Frenchmen were bluffing and the Brits sailed off on a wild goose chase. The spot in the river became known as English Turn.

Nearly three centuries later, the PGA Tour sailed into English Turn. This time it was a smart move.

Lakewood Country Club, which had been the tournament site since 1963, had outlived its usefulness. The practice facilities were inadequate, as was the parking. More important, the course had become too easy for today's professionals. In 1974, Lee Trevino won the tournament by playing four rounds without a single bogey. And in 1988, the last year at Lakewood, Chip Beck went him one better, winning the tournament with a record score of 262—26 under par, the worst battering of the year for a Tour course. It was time for a change.

The agent of change was Jack Nicklaus, whose course design company transformed a flat delta landscape into one of the more distinctive and challenging sites on the Tour. Facing immense drainage problems, Nicklaus's engineers excavated a waterway around the course, complete with five dams and a well. Then they used the 1.4 million cubic yards of dredged clay as fill to create mounds, tees, and greens, many of them with dramatic changes in elevation. They ensured good drainage by spreading 400,000 cubic yards of sand in a two-inch blanket across the 18 holes, then trucked in over 500 trees and planted them along the fairways for definition.

18th hole

4th hole

Nicklaus claims it was the most difficult piece of ground he had ever had to work with, and admits he's proud of the job he and his people did, particularly of their ability to "pace" the course by alternating tough, easy, and moderately difficult holes. "You can't have a difficult hole followed by another difficult hole," he says, "because that's discouraging for even the best of players." When English Turn was unveiled, it drew strong reviews from the Tour players.

No fewer than 21 water hazards dot the property and come into play on 13 holes. But those who give the water too wide a berth often risk an equally dire fate in sand—such as at the 349-yard fourth, where a shot that goes over the green will finish in a deep bunker, leaving a blast back across a two-tiered surface, with water beyond.

Nicklaus is generally known for the severe humps he puts in his greens—he calls them muffins—and initially English

Turn was fraught with English muffins. Between 1993 and 1994, however, the contours of several greens were softened and entrances leveled to allow more pin placements and enable run-on approaches, especially in downwind situations.

Ironically, the most challenging putting assignment may be at number nine, a par four where the contour of the green is deceptively subtle. Almost invariably on this surface, the ball breaks less than a player thinks it will.

Some of English Turn's other perils can be a bit more disquieting. In the first year the tournament was played here, a Rules official was called to the 12th green following a rain delay, and was forced to delay play further because he could not coax a water moccasin to slither off the green. And in 1992, a tournament marshall had to call in support to isolate an alligator that had taken up residence in the rough at 14, a 469-yard par four that is plenty difficult even without reptiles.

Scorecard

Hole	Yards	Par	PGA Tour Avg. Score
1	398	4	4.059
2	519	5	4.697
3	200	3	3.162
4	349	4	4.118
5	463	4	4.195
6	557	5	4.970
7	445	4	4.234
8	176	3	3.118
9	370	4	4.107
OUT	3477	36	36.660
10	420	4	4.174
11	550	5	4.757
12	158	3	3.071
13	380	4	4.000
14	469	4	4.187
15	542	5	4.950
16	442	4	4.151
17	207	3	3.189
18	471	4	4.493
IN	3639	36	36.972
TOTAL	7116	72	73.632

The signature hole at English Turn is number 15, a 542-yard par five that culminates at an island green. Nicklaus & Co. bulkheaded the green with pilings driven 60 feet into the ground. Depending on the length of the tee shot, this hole leaves a gambler's approach of between 190 and 230 yards. Otherwise, the second shot is a layup followed by a pitch to the island. It's the type of dramatic hole that Greg Norman loves, and he has a habit of eagling it in the heat of battle. In fact, although Norman has not won here, he finished second three of the first four years the tournament was played at English Turn, and in 1990, he looked to have won it until the last shot of the day.

It occurred at the final hole, a 471-yard par four that in that year ranked as the most difficult hole on the PGA Tour. The key shot here is the tee shot, which must be hit hard—to enable a reasonable chance of hitting and holding the sand-choked green—and straight, to avoid water and a massive waste bunker on the left and a series of deep pot bunkers to the right. Norman nailed a perfect drive and then stung a glorious 2-iron to within a foot of the flag to tie David Frost, playing just behind him.

Frost, needing a par to tie and a birdie to win, pulled his tee shot into the waste area. When his approach shot found the greenside bunker, most observers figured

14th hole

Frost had about a one-in-two chance of getting up and down for the sudden-death playoff. But three things were in David Frost's favor: 1) He had a good lie 2) He is one of the Tour's two or three finest sand players, and 3) He was up against Greg Norman, the same luckless Greg Norman who had been nipped by spectacular shots from Larry Mize (Masters), Bob Tway (PGA), and Robert Gamez (Nestlé Invitational).

It happened again. Frost nipped his ball beautifully from the sand and lofted it onto the green, where it took a bounce

and then rolled into the diametric center of the hole. Birdie three and victory. Norman, once again, could only shake his head.

It was a bitter defeat for the Great White Shark, as well as an eerie anniversary for this tournament whose history dates back over half a century. Twenty-five years earlier, another Australian, Bruce Devlin, had lost at New Orleans when on the 72nd hole Dick Mayer had birdied by sinking a pitch shot from 35 yards off the green.

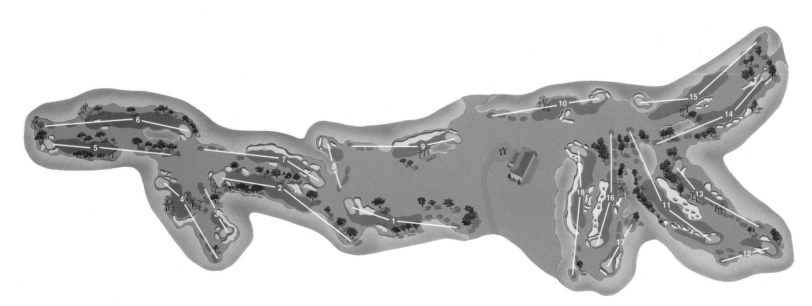

15th hole

The Tour doesn't get much farther south than New Orleans, and believe me we can get some hot, humid days during the Freeport-McMoRan Classic. But most Tour players know how to deal with heat. The fact is, as the temperature goes up, your scores can go down if you handle yourself properly.

First, don't overeat or overpractice before your play. Apply sunscreen to your exposed areas, dress in light clothing, and wear a hat. Keep your hands perspiration free by using a towel, and take off your glove between shots so that it doesn't become slippery. To protect yourself against dehydration and sunstroke, take a multiple vitamin before teeing off, and drink plenty of water along the way.

Be aware that in hot weather your muscles will be loose and elastic, the ball will be warm and resilient, and the fairways likely will be hard and dry. So you won't have to use your power swing to hit a long drive. And on those occasions when you're in between clubs for an approach shot, this may be one occasion when it's wise to go with the shorter club.

Chip Beck won the 1992 Freeport-McMoRan Classic.

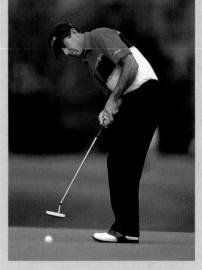

AUGUSTA NATIONAL GOLF CLUB

In 1930, shortly after he had completed the Grand Slam—winning the Amateur and Open Championships of America and Britain in the same year—Bobby Jones announced his retirement from competitive golf and declared his intention to design and build a golf course. After playing the world's best golf on the world's best courses for a decade and a half, he had developed some strong ideas about what a good golf course should and should not be. His course would incorporate those ideas. It would also be a place where he and his friends could enjoy golf in beautiful surroundings and with a degree of privacy.

Jones hoped to find a site within reasonable distance of his Atlanta home, and before long he did. Clifford Roberts, a tall, bespectacled Wall Street banker, had befriended Jones and knew of Jones's search. Roberts, who wintered in the antebellum resort of Augusta, home of Jones's wife, May, knew of a unique property there that was for sale.

It was called Fruitlands, the first nursery in the South. It had been owned for decades by a Belgian nobleman, Baron Prosper Jules Alphonse Berckmans. Throughout the 365 acres of pine forests, Berckmans had indulged his horticultural interest in a dazzling assortment of trees, shrubs, and flowers. Azaleas flourished

throughout the property, along with dogwood, redbud, daffodils, camellias, jasmine, woodbine, and a dozen types of plants and trees that existed nowhere else in the world—enough different varieties to name a hole after each one. Atop the highest hill on the property, a long driveway lined with magnolias led to the stately plantation home.

Alister Mackenzie, the famed Scottish architect, agreed to collaborate with Jones on the design of the course. Mackenzie had shown by his earlier work at Cypress Point that he knew how to take magnificent land and fashion an equally magnificent place to play golf.

From the start, the course reflected

6th hole

10th hole

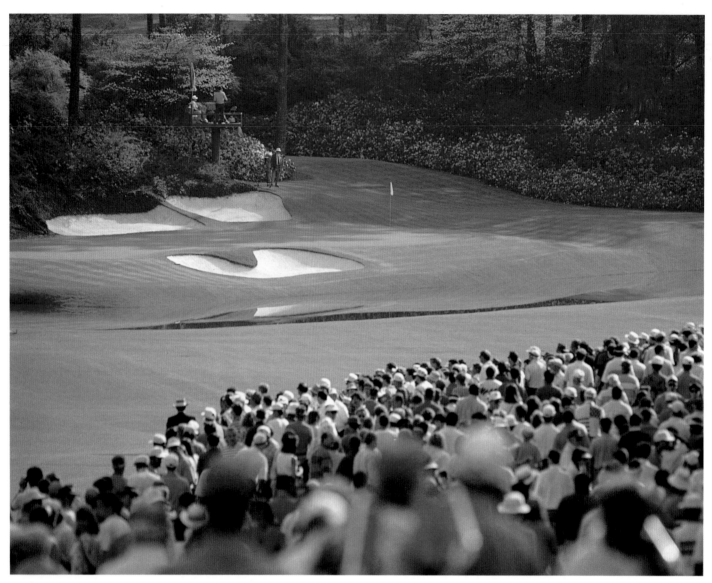

12th hole

two of Jones's fundamental desires: First, that it have a natural look, that it rise out of the terrain rather than be stamped onto it. In this way, Jones hoped to recall the softly rolling feel of the Scottish links he so loved. Second, the design would be strategic. Each hole would offer several lines of attack, permitting the player to choose among conservative, mildly aggressive, and audacious tactics, with the rewards in proportion to the difficulty of the attempted shot and the skill with which the shot was brought off.

Jones was particularly determined to apply this philosophy to his par fives. He disdained long, unreachable holes where "you don't start playing golf until your third shot." He therefore designed four

par fives, each of which could be reached in two by strong hitters. He also used menacing hazards, notably at the 13th and 15th holes, to punish the player who overestimated himself.

As Mackenzie drew the maps and oversaw the moving of earth, Jones played thousands of experimental shots from planned tees to planned greens. When the course was completed in 1933, Mackenzie, who would die a few months later, said, "Augusta National represented my best opportunity and, I believe, my finest achievement."

Despite numerous changes, Augusta National today remains the golf course Bobby Jones wanted it to be: a master-piece of strategic design and perhaps the

finest thinking man's course since St. Andrews.

With expansive fairways, virtually no rough, and only ten fairway bunkers, elbow room seems to abound on this course. And with enormous putting sur-faces and only 34 greenside bunkers (fewer than two per hole), the targets appear unmissable. But these greens are fiendishly fast and fearsomely swaled, and that combination of speed and undula-tion is more lethal than at any other course on the Tour.

Position play is therefore paramount. Approach shots must be directed to the sector of the green where putting will be least problematic. As Byron Nelson once observed, "At Augusta it's often better to

13th hole

be 20 feet to one side of the cup than six feet to the other."

But to find that ideal patch of green, one must attack from the most propitious angle, which means the tee shot must be played not simply to the fairway but to the proper sector of the fairway, a task that can require great discipline when the fairways are as wide as those at Augusta National.

As Jones put it, "There is not a hole out there that can't be birdied if you just think; and there is not a hole out there that can't be double-bogeyed if you stop thinking."

Soon after the course was completed, Jones decided to hold a tournament, an informal get-together for his amateur and professional friends. Roberts urged Jones to play in the event and suggested it be called The Masters. Jones, after much reluctance, agreed to the former on condition that he not accept prize money, but refused the latter, arguing that "Masters" was too presumptuous a name for his clambake.

Jones was never a threat in his tournament, either in the first year or in any of the 11 times he competed, his best finish being a tie for 13th (although in 1936 he did record a practice round of 64, a number that stood for more than a half century of Masters competition). In 1947 he withdrew after two rounds with what was diagnosed as bursitis. Years later it became apparent that his condition was more serious. Eventually, the ailment was identified as syringomyelia, a crippling spinal disease. Soon Jones was forced to walk with a cane, then he was confined to a wheelchair. The last Masters he attended was 1968, and he died in December of 1971.

But Bob Jones left behind a tournament that will live as long as golf is played. The first Augusta Invitational (1934) was won by young Horton Smith. This also was the last "Augusta Invitational." The press somehow got wind of the name "Masters," and by the end of the first week the newspaper reports carried the new name.

A year later the tournament had not only a new name but a storied tradition

13th hole

when Gene Sarazen surged to victory on the heels of "the shot heard round the world," an incredible 220-yard 4-wood that sailed across the water and into the hole at the par-five 15th in the final round. It enabled Sarazen to tie Craig Wood, whom he beat the next day in an 18-hole playoff.

Ever since that year, it seems, the Augusta National has had a gift for supplying the sensational, the unexpected. It is impossible to pick a hole on the course where something dramatic has not happened.

It was at the first hole in 1968 that Argentinian Robert DeVicenzo smashed an enormous drive and then holed out a 9-iron for eagle to take the lead in the final round, a lead he lost *after* the tournament when it was discovered that he had signed an incorrect scorecard.

The second hole, one of those reachable par fives, was reached in flamboyant style by Seve Ballesteros in 1983. In the

last round Ballesteros knocked a 4-wood 15 feet from the hole and sank the putt for an eagle. That day he scorched through the first four holes in birdie-eagle-par-birdie to jump over former champions Raymond Floyd, Craig Stadler, and Tom Watson for his second Masters victory. En route to victory in 1989, Nick Faldo sank a birdie putt that stretched from one side of this green to the other—over 100 feet—the longest putt in Masters history.

Number three is only 360 yards, an iron from the tee for most of the pros, but its green sits at the brink of a precipitous swale, and shots that miss short can spin back down the fairway 20 yards or more, leaving a ticklish pitch.

The longest par three on the course is the fourth, 205 yards downhill to a sweeping green that Mackenzie modeled after the green at number 11 of the Old Course at St. Andrews. For many years, this was the only hole on the course that

had never been eagled in The Masters. But Jeff Sluman did the deed, acing the hole with a 4-iron in 1992.

Mackenzie fashioned the 435-yard fifth hole after the famous and feared Road Hole (17) at St. Andrews. As at that hole, the nemesis is the large, treacherously sloped green. One year, Sam Snead stood at the front edge of the fifth, facing a 50-foot birdie putt up the steep bank to the second tier. He stroked it smoothly—too smoothly. The ball stopped on the upslope and then rolled all the way back to Snead's feet. From there, unbelievably, the Slammer holed it for par.

Conquering the Augusta greens became a bit easier as time progressed, as the original bermudagrass surfaces began to lose speed. They were still fast, to be sure, but not as fast as originally designed. So, in a daring gamble during 1980, the Masters people simply dug up all 18 surfaces and reseeded them with speedier bentgrass. Traditionally, bentgrass flourishes only in cooler climates, but at Augusta National, which closes from May to September each year, the changeover and the new greens were given the necessary tender loving care. The switch was a success.

A tough target greets mid-iron shots from the elevated tee of the par-three sixth. Amateur Billy Joe Patton solved this one in the last round of the 1954 Masters when he holed out his 5-iron shot for a 1. Patton led for most of that tournament, but in one of the saddest chapters in Masters history, the likable North Carolinian gave it back on the inward par fives, where on Sunday he took a calamitous 13 strokes. He finished one stroke out of the Snead-Hogan play-off, won by Sam.

Number seven is a tight, short, heavily bunkered par four that at first seems out of character with the expansive feel of the course, but it makes the same demands of its assailants—precision from the tee, care with the approach, and nerveless finesse on the green. Next comes the par-five eighth, 535 yards steeply uphill to a green tucked left in

back of a mound, making it difficult to reach except with a rolling draw on the second shot. In the final round of 1986, Tom Kite and Seve Ballesteros were paired together and among the leaders. Both eagled the hole, but then both collapsed as Jack Nicklaus charged to victory.

Nicklaus began his charge with a birdie at the ninth, a 435-yard par four dogleg left and uphill to a green that is banked so steeply from back to front, Ben Hogan is said to have purposely played short of it whenever the pin was up front. The inward nine of the Augusta National produces more cliffhanger finishes than an Alfred Hitchcock film festival.

It begins with a par four that tumbles 485 yards through a corridor in the pines, culminating at a huge green surrounded by azaleas and dogwood. It was in this cathedral-like setting in 1984 that Ben Crenshaw thrilled his fans with a 60-foot birdie putt that launched him to his only major championship victory.

The daunting 11th hole swoops 455 yards down to a green tucked between a

pond on the left and a deep swale to the right. In recent years it has been the center of drama, as four of the tournament's five sudden-death playoffs have been settled here. In 1979, Fuzzy Zoeller stung a brave 8-iron to 15 feet and sank the putt to beat Ed Sneed and Tom Watson. Five years later, Augusta native Larry Mize played one of golf's most electrifying shots, an 80-foot pitch from deep in the swale that rolled into the cup for a victory over the snakebit Greg Norman. And 11 has to be Nick Faldo's lucky number. In 1989, he sank a 20-foot birdie putt here to win his first Masters over Scott Hoch. Then, a year later, he joined Jack Nicklaus as the only back-to-back winners when, at 11 again, he won a playoff over Raymond Floyd.

It's a shame that no sudden-death play-off has reached the 12th hole, for there is no greater test of nerves and moxie than the tee shot on this little par three. A 155-yard shot over water to a green that is 105 feet wide but at its shallowest point only 28 feet deep, the Golden Bell has wrung every top player in the game. Three-time champion Gary Player calls it "the toughest par three in the world." Who knows what Tom Weiskopf calls it. In 1982 he took a 13 on it, the highest single-hole score in Masters history.

On Sunday afternoon, when the pin is at the right side of this green, close to the water, the time-honored strategy is to fire for the center of the green and hope for a safe par. In a playoff, with everything depending on one swing, it would be fun to see the tactics change.

The 11th, 12th, and 13th holes comprise Augusta's famed Amen Corner. It is at the 13th that players have an opportunity to redress—or amplify—their sins at 11 and 12. Surely, this picture-perfect, 465-yard dogleg has produced more triumphs and tragedies than any par five in golf.

It was here in 1937 that Byron Nelson sank a 50-foot eagle chip to surge toward his first Masters victory. And it was here, five years later, that he completed a three-birdie sweep of Amen Corner while beating Ben Hogan in a playoff. Much

15th hole

16th hole

later, Hogan did the same thing, birdieing 11, 12, and 13 at the age of 54 for a record 30 on the back nine, one of the most inspiring moments in golf history.

Thirteen is where the aforementioned Billy Joe Patton saw his title hopes go awry when his daring second shot fell into Rae's Creek. Three decades later, Curtis Strange suffered the same fate in the final round of the 1985 Masters,

dumping a 4-wood shot in the water.

The forgotten hole of the back nine is 14, sandwiched between two dramatic par fives. It's unassuming, an almost straight, slightly uphill, mid-length par four with not a grain of sand or a drop of water in sight, but the green is diabolically contoured and falls off to the front and right. More than on any hole on the course, careful placement of the approach shot is vital.

Fifteen, the water-guarded par five that was the site of Sarazen's heroics, has continued to provide thrilling moments through more than six decades of Masters competition. In 1986, Jack Nicklaus came to this tee at five under par, three strokes behind Seve Ballesteros, playing one group behind him. Moments later, after both players had finished the hole, they were even.

Nicklaus had made eagle 3, Ballesteros double-bogey 6.

The original design of the Augusta National has undergone many changes, but none more radical than that of the 16th hole, which in 1947 got a complete facelift from Robert Trent Jones, Sr. Alister Mackenzie's par three was 150 yards, with a small creek to the right of the green and two alternate tees, one to

the left of the 15th green and one to the right. Jones abolished the right-hand tee, lengthened the hole 20 yards, enlarged the creek into a pond, and repositioned the green to the right of that pond, banking the putting surface sharply from back-right to the water at the front left. The new green, he said, was far more receptive to the shots being played into it.

This was the site of the most famous putt in Masters history when in 1975 Jack Nicklaus rolled in an uphill-sidehill 40-footer for birdie in the final round. At the time he was in a wild three-way shootout with Johnny Miller and Tom Weiskopf, both playing directly behind him. Nicklaus's birdie gave him the lead, and when the other two missed birdie putts on 18, Jack won his fifth Masters, a record which stood until he himself broke it in 1986.

At 400 yards, number 17 is the shortest par four on the inward nine. The hole's landmark is the 80-foot oak that rises from the left-center of the fairway, called Ike's Tree because of the frequency with which Augusta National member President Eisenhower made contact with it. A deep front bunker catches its share of balata, and the green is full of subtle breaks. This is another hole that came to Nick Faldo's aid. Both Scott Hoch (1989) and Ray Floyd (1990) bogeyed it on the final day to allow Faldo to catch them.

Eleven holes on the course are doglegs, but only two—the first and the 18th—move from left to right. With trees lining the right side of 18 and two large bunkers on the outside corner, few players have the courage for an aggressive tee shot. Many in fact hit fairway woods or long irons to this fairway, which flows uphill to the green. The resulting mid-iron shot is played to a narrow target that slopes severely from back to front.

Virtually every top player of the last half century has won The Masters, and the very best have won it more than once: Nicklaus (6 times), Palmer (4), Jimmy Demaret, Player, and Snead (3), Ballesteros, Faldo, Hogan, Nelson, Watson, Bernhard Langer, and Horton Smith (2).

Masters tickets are not for sale, at least not for the four days of the tournament proper. Daily tickets may be purchased for the practice rounds and the traditional Par-3 Contest, but once the serious play begins, access to the course is limited to players and their immediate families, officials, press, and a few thousand lucky people called "patrons." These are the folks who years ago began coming to The Masters and have wisely renewed passes each year.

Any patron who does not renew the annual invitation is summarily debadged and a salivating member of the waiting list—cut off years ago and now estimated at just under 10,000—gets the nod. The patrons' badges may not be willed or transferred in any way.

18th hole

18th hole

Even more exclusive is the membership of the Augusta National Golf Club, a collection of titans of industry. As one reporter wrote, "The Augusta National is a golf club that looks as if it dropped out of heaven, and it's just as hard to get into." But the club was forced to revise its exclusionary ways in 1990 after the Shoal Creek controversy placed in jeopardy all tournament sites with discriminatory admission policies. A few weeks later, Augusta National accepted its first black member, Atlanta businessman Charles Townsend.

Tradition and privilege still pervade the old clubhouse, which includes a special grill room restricted to Masters champions and their guests, a "crow's nest" dormitory on the third floor, reserved each year for a handful of young amateurs who bunk there during the tournament, and a case on the main floor displaying one valued club from each of the past Masters champions.

Many enduring aspects of championship competition have originated at this, by far the youngest of the four major championships. The whole idea of stadium golf arguably had its roots here in the grassy knolls and terraces that shoulder Augusta's fairways and greens. The concept of multiple leaderboards also was born at The Masters, where an army of 200 scorekeepers relays up-to-the-minute results via underground telephone wires. It's no wonder that other events such as The Memorial, The Players, and The International have tried to imitate this one, in ambience as well as name.

Most of the gallery agree that the spectating is the easiest, the refreshments the tastiest (and most reasonably priced) of any tournament in golf. Most of the press agrees the facilities are the finest and most efficiently run. Most of the competitors agree that The Masters is the one golf tournament they would most like to win. That is a proper tribute to Bobby Jones.

Scorecard

Hole	Yards	Par	PGA Tour Avg. Score
1	400	4	4.069
2	555	5	4.732
3	360	4	4.068
4	205	3	3.212
5	435	4	4.174
6	180	3	3.142
7	360	4	4.031
8	535	5	4.748
9	435	4	4.063
OUT	3465	36	36.239
10	485	4	4.213
11	455	4	4.156
12	155	3	3.298
13	485	5	4.723
14	405	4	4.021
15	500	5	4.565
16	170	3	3.060
17	400	4	4.066
18	405	4	4.121
IN	3440	36	36.223
TOTAL	6905	72	72.462

High, Soft Irons

BY SEVE BALLESTEROS

The most important thing at Augusta is to hit your irons to the correct part of the green. Since the greens are usually hard, fast, and steeply sloped, it's particularly important to hit the ball high and soft with the long and middle irons.

I have three keys I practice each year before playing The Masters. First, I position the ball a bit more forward in my stance than I do on other courses. This helps ensure that I make impact on a slightly upward angle, helping to lift the ball upward. Second, I make a big turn, getting my arms well into the air on the backswing. Third, I stay back behind the ball on the downswing while letting my arms swing through the ball. You must not attack or hit at these shots. Perhaps more than in any other situation, you must make a smooth, flowing swing. In the follow-through, it's important to have the arms reach high into the air. Remember, to hit high, finish high.

Seve Ballesteros, a two-time Masters champion (1980, 1983), was also the youngest player (23) to win a green jacket.

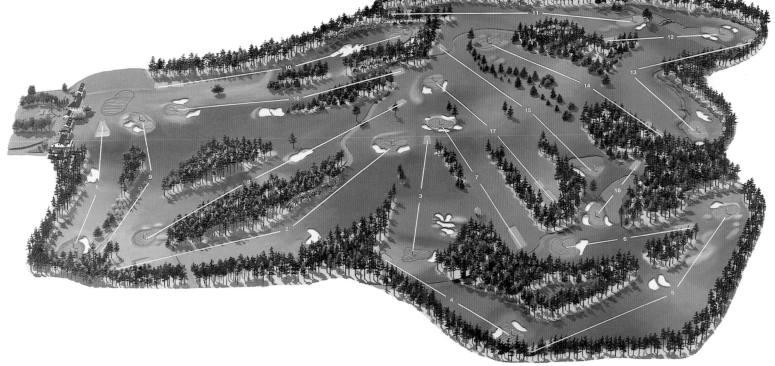

ANNANDALE COUNTRY CLUB

It happens every year—and nobody notices. For over a quarter century, the tournament now known as the Deposit Guaranty Golf Classic has been a fixture on the PGA Tour. And yet, except for the most ardent followers of professional golf, it has remained obscure. Why? Its traditional date has been the same week as The Masters.

The Deposit Guaranty Golf Classic has gone unnoticed, but rarely has it been unnoteworthy. Back in 1968, the inaugural year for the tournament (then known as the Magnolia Classic), B.R. "Mac" McLendon and Pete Fleming went nine holes of sudden death—a PGA Tour record—before McLendon prevailed with a 15-foot birdie putt.

McLendon needed 81 holes to gain his victory, but in 1980 Roger Maltbie took the first prize after only 18 holes of work. On Thursday, Maltbie posted a 65 to lead the field—then Mother Nature took over, with three straight days of pelting rain that left the course unplayable. On Sunday morning they called it off, declared Jolly Roger the winner, and everyone went home to watch Seve Ballesteros stride in victorious at Augusta. Since that fateful year, this tournament has had its share of April showers, being curtailed to 54 holes four times and to 36 holes once.

Since the game's royalty has always been at The Masters, the list of DGGC champions is hardly a Who's Who of Golf. Names like Blocker, Pace, Meyer, Walzel, and Silveira are the norm, and even the tournament's only two-time champion, Dwight Nevil, never finished higher than 59th on the Tour money list.

17th hole

Deposit Guarantee Golf Classic, Mississippi

9th hole

On the other hand, this has been a springboard for a few of today's household names. Craig Stadler (1978) and Payne Stewart (1982) won their first Tour events here, Paul Azinger finished runner-up in 1985 and 1986 before becoming Player of the Year in 1987, and a few weeks after finishing second in 1987, Nick Faldo won the first of his three British Opens.

For many years the tournament was played at the Hattiesburg Country Club, a cozy little course that was remarkable for its minimalism—6,490 yards laid out by Press Maxwell on barely 100 acres, with narrow tree-lined fairways, small greens, and an astonishing lack of sand—only 19 bunkers in its 18 holes. Even for the Tour's second-rank players,

Hattiesburg was a pushover. During the last few years the tournament was played there, the winning totals averaged nearly 15 under par.

So, in 1994, the show moved to a larger tent—the Annandale Country Club in Madison, Mississippi, a fast-expanding community six miles from Jackson. One of the first courses designed by Jack Nicklaus, Annandale reflects the Golden Bear's early predilection for bigness, measuring more than 7157 yards with a rating of 75.4. Its brawny holes call for powerful tee shots and lengthy approaches that soar high yet land softly, as if hit by the Golden Bear.

When it was completed in 1981, Annandale was the first course in Mississippi with bentgrass greens. Bent is

Swinging in the Rain
BY JIM
GALLAGHER, JR.

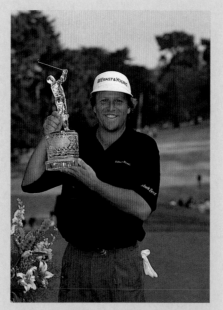

The year I won the Deposit Guaranty, there was so much rain the tournament went only 36 holes. Wet weather can make the going rough, whether you're playing the PGA Tour or a weekend nassau.

Get the most out of your umbrella—not just as a shelter but as a place to hang the single most useful item on a wet day—a dry towel. On a really wet day, you might want to take an extra towel—keep it in your bag and take it out when the first towel becomes sodden. You should also have a couple of extra gloves on hand.

Another great asset in rain is a handkerchief. Wrap it around the grip of your club, and you'll be amazed at how secure your hold will be. It's legal, too. And it should go without saying that rain gear—a hat, jacket, pants, and shoes—are vitally important.

The most significant key in playing shots is to accept the fact that you're going to lose distance. Slippery grips and wet fairways will insure this. So take

plenty of club on your approach shots, and swing within yourself. If you're a good enough player to make slight changes in your swing, use a flatter, more picking action, to minimize the digging that is inevitable with wet turf.

Finally, the ultimate edict: Don't *ever* play in an electrical storm. Get yourself off the course at the first sign of thunder or lightning.

Jim Gallagher, Jr. won the 1985 Deposit Guaranty Golf Classic.

The clubhouse

11th hole

generally the preferred surface among knowledgeable golfers, but it is a rarity in the deep South because it doesn't survive well in intense heat. But at Annandale the experiment has worked: The course has been ranked consistently among the top tests in the South, and in 1986 it earned the attention of the USGA, hosting the U.S. Mid-Amateur championship won by Bill Loeffler.

It doesn't wait long to assert itself. The second hole is a par three of 213 yards that plays over water to a slender green guarded by a tree and bunker to the left and two bunkers right. The green is 43 yards from front to back, so club selection can vary widely depending upon where the flag is positioned.

The easiest hole on the course is number five, a 522-yard par five that plays downhill. But with the second shot over water to the smallest green on the course, this hole provides plenty of excitement for both players and spectators.

One par five that few mortals can reach in two is number 11, a 579-yarder where the view from the tee is dominated by a huge bunker smack in the middle of the fairway. Most players, even pros, are forced to play short or left of it, accepting a three-shot route to the green, while the stronger hitters may try to hit over it—a carry of some 270 yards. But even if they clear the sand, there's a creek to be avoided off the tee, and in order to get home in two, the lengthy approach will have to find a green that is well bunkered and set at an angle to the fairway.

Like most good architects Nicklaus likes to give players alternative ways of playing his holes. Unlike most, however, he goes so far as to create multiple fairways, allowing—indeed forcing—a choice from the tee. Such is the case at Annandale's signature hole, number 17, where the choice is to play safely to the left side of a creek, leaving a middle-iron

approach to this 409-yard par four, or to gamble with a tee shot to an "island fairway," an expanse of land about 220–270 yards off the tee that is framed by creeks. If this bolder route is chosen, the reward is a wedge shot to the green.

More gambling comes into play at the final hole, another tempting par five. Anyone hoping to reach this green in two has to play a tee shot that avoids a lake to the left and a bunker right, then blast a second shot of 230 yards or more to a green with more water in front and more sand behind. It's a hole where a pro can make 3 or 6, a hole that can bring either victory or disaster.

Along with the new and improved site has come a new and improved slot on the PGA Tour schedule. At last, the tournament has crawled out from the shadow of The Masters. Now it is played during the third week of July—opposite the British Open!

Scorecard

Hole	Yards	Par
1	369	4
2	213	3
3	4061	4
4	465	4
5	522	5
6	398	4
7	556	5
8	209	3
9	450	4
OUT	3588	36
10	407	4
11	579	5
12	171	3
13	414	4
14	473	4
15	176	3
16	408	4
17	409	4
18	532	5
IN	3569	35
TOTAL	7157	72

HARBOUR TOWN GOLF LINKS

Surprise, and even shock, hit the golf fraternity when Pete Dye unveiled his design of the Harbour Town Golf Links. The year was 1969, the middle of an era when the trend was toward brutishly long courses, with fairways like airstrips, huge inkspot bunkers, and greens large enough to stage a football game.

Dye had already developed a reputation as the *enfant terrible* of golf architecture, but Harbour Town had been expected to be a traditional expansive course. For one thing, it was intended to be the site of a PGA Tour event. And for another, Dye's consultant on the project—making an historic debut in course architecture—was Jack Nicklaus, then the very embodiment of "brutishly long."

But the course they produced was unlike anything the Tour had ever seen. Said Dye, "It's different, but then, so was Garbo," and all agreed, this course was a rare and special star.

Spread among 300 acres of marshland on the inland coast of Hilton Head Island, South Carolina, Harbour Town has been variously called "Pebble Beach East," "Pine Valley South," and "St. Andrews with Spanish moss." The references are as different as California, New Jersey, and Scotland, but in each case the comparison to Harbour Town is valid.

Pebble Beach and Harbour Town each enjoy the most treasured asset a course can have: a spectacular natural setting. Sea Pines Plantation's founder Charles Fraser wisely reserved a large and attractive chunk of his Hilton Head property for the golf course. Dye took advantage of it by winding the fairways through forests of oak, pine, magnolia, and Spanish moss and placing the greens in menacing proximity to a dozen small lakes, ponds, and lagoons. He did not create long holes—his original par-71 design was barely 6800 yards from the back tees, and even today it is less than 7000 yards—but it was a course long on challenge.

Most of the holes are scenic, but the 17th and 18th are Monterey spectacular. The 192-yard 17th plays directly over water and is guarded by an 80-yard-long bunker that is bulkheaded with Dye's signature "railroad ties." The wind invariably is in the face of the late pairings at the MCI Heritage Classic, as is the setting sun, making club selection difficult.

Eighteen is similar in design to the famed finish at Pebble Beach, except that it is a par four instead of a par five. Recently lengthened, it now plays 478 yards from its back tee, and snakes along the edge of Calibogue Sound (pronounced Cali-bogey). The tee, the landing area, and the green sit on small promontories. Too far left and you're in the salt marshes; too far right and you're on someone's back porch, out-of-bounds. As for the second shot, depending on the wind direction, the green may be within reach of a soft 7-iron or unhittable with any club. A tall red-and-white-striped lighthouse stands to the rear, adding a touch of man-made beauty to one of the most scenically splendid holes in the world.

The analogy to Pine Valley is in the routing of the course. Pine Valley is carved from the wild Pine Barrens of southern New Jersey. It is one huge, magnificent bunker, dotted at perilous intervals with tees, fairways, and greens. In the same way, Harbour Town is cleverly cleaved from the swampland of coastal South Carolina.

Says codesigner Nicklaus, "I get angrier here than anywhere else. This place is designed for some shots I'm not supposed to be able to hit, and that's a challenge. Then, when I can't hit them, it just burns my rear end."

Indeed, it seems unlikely that any golfer can play all the shots Harbour

9th hole

116

Town demands: punches under the wind and cuts over mammoth trees, splashes from bunkers and thrashes from pampas grass, careful chips from clinging bahia-grass rough, and just plain old impossible straight shots.

Most of the landing areas are ample, but the groves of trees often encroach to give tee shots a claustrophobic feeling. On almost every long hole, the terrain and placement of hazards encourage the golfer to work the ball from left to right or right to left. Former PGA Champion and TV commentator Dave Marr, after playing a particularly frustrating round at an early Heritage Classic, captured the essence of Harbour Town in a wry comment to one of the tournament officials: "I never complain about pin positions," Marr said, "but you certainly have put the fairways in some strange places today."

The wise strategy is to find the fairway and hew to the best part of it, for the greens at Harbour Town are tiny, so tiny that this is the site of the PGA Tour record for fewest putts over 72 holes. In 1989, Kenny Knox got through the four rounds of the Heritage with only 93 rolls (breaking the old record of 94 by George Archer—also posted at Harbour Town). In one of those rounds, Knox used just 18 putts. His secret? He missed a lot of greens, then chipped close for short putts. Despite the hot blade that week, Knox finished tied for fifth, ten strokes behind Payne Stewart.

In recent years several of the greens have been enlarged, but they still average barely 4,000 square feet, far smaller than normal. And when you miss one, par can be as elusive as Garbo, especially if your ball finds a bunker. There are only 45 on this course, but they are not wasted. Sand completely encircles the par-three seventh, where the bunker also sprouts a huge tree. The ninth hole, one of the world's classic short par fours, was made more difficult in 1981 with the addition of a pot bunker behind the heart-shaped green.

The toughest stretch of the course comes at the turn with holes ten, 11, and 12. Each is a par four of over 400 yards, but each demands accuracy even more than distance. A lake to the left of the fairway haunts the tee shot at ten while chutes of trees must be threaded at 11 and 12.

The finest par four on the course is arguably number 13, just 378 yards, where the drive must be positioned to the right side of the fairway to set up the second shot, a field goal between two encroaching oaks. A large U-shaped bunker—banked with cypress planks—awaits the misplayed approach. Early during Heritage week, the pros can be seen practicing unusual sand shots—

18th hole

Chipping
BY DAVIS LOVE III

The smallest greens on the Tour are at Harbour Town. That means that even we pros miss several greens per round and find ourselves facing chip shots.

Chipping drives some weekend golfers crazy, but it shouldn't, because the chip is an uncomplicated shot. You begin by gripping down on the club about two inches. Address the ball with a slightly open stance, about 70 percent of your weight on your left side, and your feet positioned close together—so close that your heels are no more than a few inches apart. Position the ball back in your stance, about opposite your left heel.

The backswing for a chip shot is like a takeaway for a full swing, the club being drawn back just two or three feet. Your wrists should remain relatively firm, with just the slightest cocking motion, and your hands should be in front of the clubface. Try to feel as if your left hand controls the direction of the club while the right hand supplies the power.

Club selection for chipping is a matter of preference. Some players like to hit almost all of their chips with the same club, say a 9-iron or pitching wedge, while others prefer to rotate the assignment among several different irons, depending on the distance from the green and the distance from the fringe to the hole. The basic idea is to loft the ball over the fringe and get it rolling as soon as possible. The last piece of advice I'd give, however, may be the most important: Be aggressive on your chip shots—don't just try to get them close, try to sink them.

Davis Love III is a three-time winner of the MCI Heritage Classic.

8th hole

18th hole

bouncing the ball up the planks—in anticipation of an offbeat situation during the tournament.

One of the enlarged greens is at the par-three 14th, which plays 165 yards over water. But the new green contains more undulations than the original, and to its left side lurks the deepest pot bunker on the course.

Number 15 is a 575-yard par five that Lee Trevino once rated as his favorite on the Tour. "It's so long that it doesn't favor the long hitters," he said. "Even King Kong couldn't get on that green in two." Trevino made that statement back in the late 1970s, and in the meantime the green has been reached by several strong young players, a couple of them using irons. But the hole normally demands three carefully executed shots. Here, too, the green—at one time the smallest on the PGA Tour—has been enlarged, and the addition, to the back left, brings into

play a tall pine tree and a small lagoon just short and left of the green.

"Heritage" was not a capricious choice for the name of this tournament. A substantial body of evidence indicates that South Carolina's low country is the birthplace of American golf.

The English and Scottish settled in this region, and by the end of the eighteenth century they had civilized their society to the extent that their thoughts had turned to golf. In 1786, a group of Charleston men founded the South Carolina Golf Club, more than a century before the famous "Apple Tree Gang" established the first permanent club in Yonkers, New York. Sometime in the 1900s, the South Carolina Golf Club dissolved, but with the birth of the Heritage Classic the club was rechartered and given a home at Harbour Town, making that club arguably the St. Andrews of America.

Scorecard

Hole	Yards	Par	PGA Tour Avg. Score
1	414	4	4.115
2	505	5	4.616
3	411	4	4.073
4	198	3	3.208
5	535	5	4.739
6	419	4	4.038
7	180	3	3.088
8	462	4	4.250
9	337	4	3.960
OUT	3461	36	36.087
10	436	4	4.126
11	438	4	4.231
12	413	4	4.133
13	378	4	4.082
14	165	3	3.005
15	575	5	4.921
16	376	4	3.959
17	192	3	3.079
18	478	4	4.087
IN	3451	35	35.623
TOTAL	6912	71	71.710

Tradition is therefore an important part of this tournament. The festivities begin each year with the "playing-in" of the captain of the South Carolina Golf Club, a ceremony that starts with a parade of Scottish bagpipers and culminates with a tee shot by the defending Heritage champion, timed with the firing of a small cannon. It is similar to the ceremony staged at St. Andrews each fall to honor the incoming captain of The Royal & Ancient Golf Club.

Of course, any comparison to Scotland's venerable Home of Golf is inherently strained. But if venerability grows from a highly revered course, Harbour Town has a head start. And if additional prestige accrues from the list of champions who prevail on such a course, then Harbour Town already ranks ahead of nearly every Tour site. Virtually every player who has won here is also the winner of a major championship. Arnold Palmer won the inaugural Heritage Classic in 1969, and Jack Nicklaus, Nick Faldo, and Greg Norman have added their names to the trophy. Norman's win in 1988 was an emotional one dedicated to 17-year-old Jamie Hutton, a leukemia victim who had come to Hilton Head simply to meet Norman. Hale Irwin, Johnny Miller, Hubert Green, Tom Watson, Fuzzy Zoeller, and Payne Stewart each have won this tournament twice, and Davis Love III must be a big fan of long-distance MCI. Since the telecommunications company took over sponsorship of the Heritage in 1987, Love has marched home victorious a record three times, including back-to-back wins in 1991 and 1992.

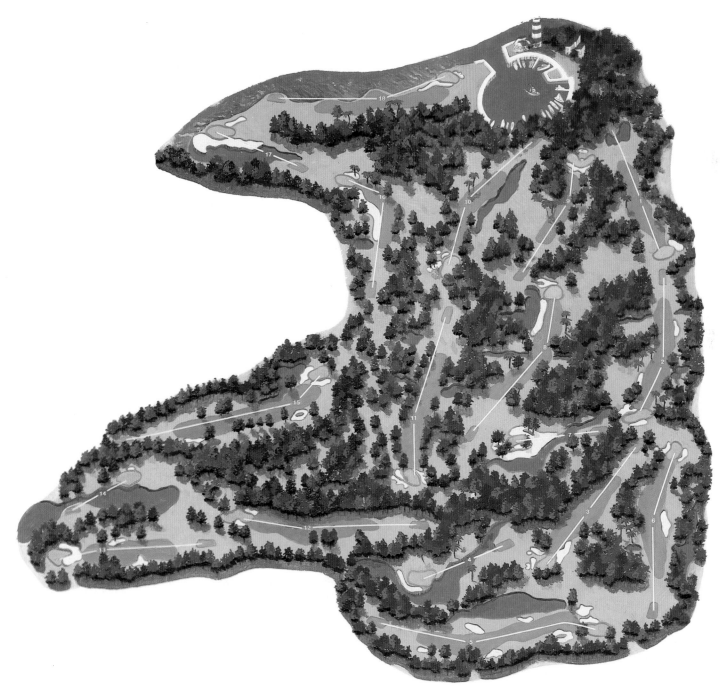

FOREST OAKS COUNTRY CLUB

3rd hole

Long before the era of recycling, Sam Snead is said to have stashed his prize winnings in tin cans and then buried the cans in his backyard. Surely, several vaults in that subterranean savings bank were reserved for the Greater Greensboro Open.

The first GGO was played in 1938, and Snead won it. He won it again in 1946, 1949, 1950, 1955, 1956, 1960, and 1965—a PGA Tour record total of eight victories in the same event. Seldom has anyone even approached that kind of dominance. In fact, there are only two other cases in which a player has compiled more than five victories in a single tournament. One is Jack Nicklaus's six Masters titles, and the other is the now-defunct Miami Open, won six times—by Sam Snead.

Snead took the first seven of his victories at Starmount Country Club. Indeed, he won both the first and last GGO's staged there. In 1961, the tournament moved to Sedgefield Country Club, where it stayed for 16 years. In 1977 it came to its present home.

Designed by Ellis Maples in 1964, the championship course at Forest Oaks is a par 72 of less than 7,000 yards, and yet bigness is the hallmark of this course. Large greens, large water hazards, large bunkers, and large trees make Forest Oaks play longer than its 6958 yards.

All these features come to bear at the third hole, a 409-yard par four that is the toughest challenge on the front nine. The tee shot must be played into a narrow fairway that has water running down its entire right side. The ball must be struck solidly, however, to afford a reasonable shot at the elevated three-tiered green, which is guarded by sand on both sides and to the rear.

The 13th is a gambler's par five—a 503-yard dogleg left with the second shot 250 yards downhill and over water. But the water appears at the early part of that 250, not near the green. The pros therefore enjoy this hole to the tune of about 4.8 strokes on average. The birdies here are needed, however, to balance the tough finish on this course.

In 1991, the already mammoth greens at holes 16 and 17 were expanded still further as major undulations were introduced. These targets are not tough to hit, but they can be hellish to putt. To

7th hole

The bunker at the 18th at Forest Oaks was about eight feet deep, and the pin was cut near the front lip, so I had to get the ball up quickly and make it stop just as quickly after it hit the green. To be honest, I was trying to keep it within ten feet of the flag, but to my good fortune it went into the hole to put me in a playoff that I eventually won.

The key to playing the explosion shot is to open the blade of the sand wedge as much as possible at address. The best way to do that is to turn the club to the open position in which you want to hold it, and then regrip it. The swing must be in the shape of a V, with a sharply ascending take-away, just as sharply a descending move into impact, and then another sharp ascent into the finish.

I try not to take too deep a divot of sand on this shot. I feel as if I'm bouncing the club off the bottom of the bunker at a point just beneath the ball. But the main key is to keep the wedge face open through impact. Do not let it close down by allowing your right hand to cross over your left the way it would in a normal release.

Larry Nelson won the 1981 Greater Greensboro Open in a playoff after sinking an 18th-hole bunker shot.

16th hole

get a feel for this assignment, imagine putting on a surface the size of a baseball diamond, with your ball at second base, the hole at home plate, and the pitcher's mound smack in your path.

The green at 18 also was reconfigured recently, with new bunkering, new pin positions, and a spectator mound added on the left. The net effect was to make this 426-yard par four a bit kinder, but it remains a difficult place to have to make a par. Just ask Larry Nelson. In 1981, he came to the home hole needing a 4 to reach a playoff, and he got it—by exploding from a greenside bunker into the hole. After that, winning the playoff was easy.

Forest Oaks is one of those courses that earns the Tour players' accolade "tough but fair." That toughness was accentuated during the years when the GGO was played one week before The Masters, the early-spring weather often bringing headaches. Tom Weiskopf claims that the best round of his career occurred here—a 64 amid 50 mph winds—and in 1987 it actually snowed during the tournament. But even today, with a slightly later date on the schedule, this remains a place where a score of even par means something, and where a

hot round on Sunday can bring victory.

In 1990, Steve Elkington shot 66 and came from six strokes back to win. A year later, Mark Brooks charged home with a 64 that took him from seven behind into a playoff which he won. But the ultimate final-day charge—and the round that *GOLF Magazine* called the best 18 holes of 1992—came from Davis Love III, who began the final day in a tie for ninth place and then unleashed a course-record 62 for a six-stroke victory. It was an unseasonably cold day, a day when no other player in the field could score better than 68. But Love came out of the box with birdies at one and two, holed a 117-yard wedge shot at the seventh for an eagle, and then birdied eight to reach the turn in 31. On the way in, he added birdies at 11 and 12, holed a 40-yard sand shot for an eagle at 15, and then struck his approach at 16 within gimme distance to finish off the record performance. It was the third victory in four weeks for Love, and the first prize brought his season winnings over the million-dollar mark before the end of April.

With that kind of money, Sam Snead would have needed a football field.

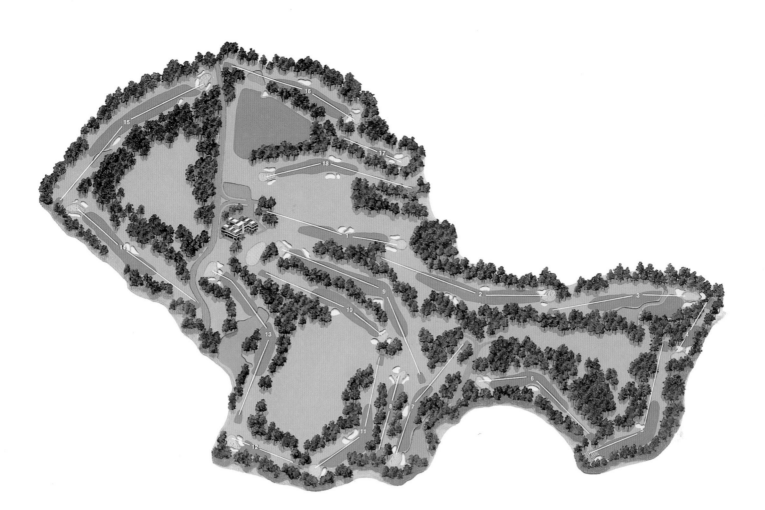

13th hole

Scorecard

Hole	Yards	Par	PGA Tour Avg. Score
1	407	4	4.047
2	511	5	4.618
3	409	4	4.251
4	190	3	3.218
5	415	4	4.014
6	386	4	4.020
7	372	4	4.007
8	215	3	3.117
9	574	5	4.878
OUT	3479	36	36.170
10	393	4	4.092
11	383	4	4.049
12	186	3	3.077
13	503	5	4.742
14	438	4	4.227
15	554	5	4.922
16	408	4	4.092
17	188	3	3.109
18	426	4	4.197
IN	3479	36	36.507
TOTAL	6958	72	72.677

TPC AT THE WOODLANDS

The USGA Handicap System doesn't allow most golfers to post a score of 9. Only players with handicaps of 30 and higher may return a number that big.

Except for pros. The guys on the PGA Tour don't get to pick up—they play out everything. That's why, if you look at the scorecard of David Graham on hole number one at The Woodlands in the third round of the 1983 Houston Open, you will see a 9. And a noteworthy 9 it is, for a couple of reasons. First, this is the easiest hole on the course—a 515-yard par five that the Tour dispatches with three times as many birdies as bogeys. Second, in a display of Australian grit, David Graham recovered from that 9 and won that Houston Open.

The course was designed by another Aussie, Bruce Devlin, along with his longtime associate, Bob Von Hagge. They carved it from a huge forest of oaks and pines as the centerpiece of a sprawling residential development, 27 miles north of Houston. The PGA Tour moved the Houston Open here in 1975, and in 1984 Commissioner Deane Beman announced that The Woodlands would be converted into a TPC Stadium Course.

Immediately the architects toughened it up. Ten bunkers were added, spectator mounds were sculpted on four holes, five tee boxes were relocated, one hole was overhauled, and another had its par changed. Today, this is a course where the average golfer might run up a 9 on any number of holes.

In fact, each of the other par fives is a likely candidate: the sixth, at 577 yards, the 13th, which culminates in an intimidating island green, and the 15th, which doglegs tensely through a corridor of trees with out-of-bounds haunting both sides of the fairway. It was at 15 that Jim McGovern struck back-to-back drivers

3rd hole

126

to within three feet of the cup on Sunday of the 1993 Houston Open. The eagle he scored enabled him to reach a sudden-death playoff with John Huston in which he prevailed for his first Tour victory.

There's a dash of Scottish feeling at the par-three 16th, where the back of the green tapers between two forgiving mounds. The middle-iron shot that is hit slightly astray may bounce off either of these hillocks and finish close to the hole.

One of the finest short fours on the Tour is the 17th, a sharp leftward dogleg of 383 yards with water in play most of the way. A large lake, one of nine hazards on the course, guards the left side of the fairway and pokes its nose directly in front of the green. Because the hole plays downhill, even a good tee shot will leave an awkward stance for the approach to this strip of a green guarded left, right, and front by water and in the rear by a bunker.

Flip 17 on its back, move the lake from the left to the right, add 60 yards, and you have an approximation of the heroic challenge at 18. A row of trees adds both definition and difficulty to the left side of this hole, while the lake laps menacingly at the front of the green. To the rear is a necklace of six bunkers. Even the pros play this approach with middle irons—and with caution.

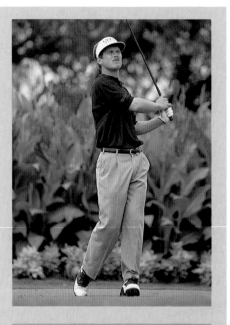

The Driver from the Fairway
BY JIM McGOVERN

The biggest shot of my Tour career was the driver I hit from the fairway of the 15th hole at Houston. It finished within three feet of the pin on that par five, and the ensuing eagle spurred me to a playoff victory over John Huston.

Many people think that hitting a driver off the fairway is a shot reserved for Tour professionals. That's no longer true. Today's metal woods, with their low centers of gravity, make this a shot that even middle-handicap players can pull off.

However, you do have to be careful about where you try to play. As a rule of thumb, don't haul out the driver unless your lie—in the fairway or light rough—has at least some part of the ball above the top of the driver's clubface.

Despite the distance you need to cover, the last thing you want to do on this shot is swing hard. Grip down a bit for control, and flex your knees to guard against the most common error—a top. The key to this swing is the takeaway, which should be long and low. This will enhance your chances of returning the clubface on that same shallow angle for the forward-driving impact that is necessary.

Don't make any other changes or adjustments. Just swing smoothly, trust your ability, and trust the club to get the ball into the air. When you nail this shot close to the hole, you'll really feel like a Tour pro. I sure did.

Jim McGovern's 1993 victory at Houston was his first win as a PGA Tour professional.

13th hole

1st hole

6th hole

It is the scene of one of Curtis Strange's proudest moments. In 1988, Strange nailed his approach shot to within four feet and then sank the putt for birdie to tie Greg Norman. Then, when the playoff returned to 18, he did it again, sinking from 25 feet. The victory made him the only three-time winner of this event, which dates back to 1946.

From 1988 through 1991, this tournament was sponsored by the Independent Insurance Agents of America. However, after the 1991 event they declined to renew coverage. It wasn't a case of cold feet so much as wet feet. In '91, the event was rained out. The storms that hit the Houston area that May were so unrelenting that the tournament got a mulligan and was restaged in the fall, when South Africa's Fulton Allem took home the prize.

A year later, however, the tournament was back, and with a new sponsor—a local business called Shell Oil—which promises to fuel the Houston Open for many years to come.

Scorecard

Hole	Yards	Par	PGA Tour Avg. Score
1	515	5	4.577
2	365	4	3.993
3	165	3	2.966
4	413	4	4.043
5	457	4	4.014
6	577	5	4.837
7	413	4	4.035
8	218	3	3.095
9	427	4	4.023
OUT	3550	36	35.583
10	428	4	3.984
11	421	4	3.923
12	388	4	3.915
13	525	5	4.806
14	195	3	3.136
15	530	5	4.628
16	177	3	2.954
17	383	4	4.044
18	445	4	4.090
IN	3492	36	35.480
TOTAL	7042	72	71.063

ATLANTA COUNTRY CLUB

9th hole

BellSouth Classic, Georgia

umber 18 at Pebble Beach gets most of the press, but the best finishing hole on the PGA Tour may be the one at Atlanta. The reason: This 499-yard par five, with a green guarded by water, is a place where anything can happen, from eagle to embarrassment.

To astonishment. Consider poor Johnny Miller, who in 1979 came to the tee of this hole needing a birdie to win the Atlanta Classic. He started his drawing tee shot just a shade too far to the right, and as the ball descended he noticed it was headed straight at a lone woman spectator perched on a metal seat just inside the gallery rope. The woman, sensing the same thing, hastily abandoned her post, and a split-second later Miller's ball pinged down onto the seat, bounced 100 feet into the air, and came to rest four inches out-of-bounds. Miller made a bogey and lost the tournament by a shot.

Still, he lost only the tournament, not his life. During the Civil War, all over Cobb County, the shots fired on this property were made with rifles. Particularly along the banks of Sope Creek, the armies of the North and South battled for the future of the Republic. The acreage that is now the Atlanta Country Club was the site of particularly furious action, in part because it housed a paper mill that was used to mint Confederate currency. In 1865, a brigade of Union soldiers finally torched the mill.

Today it is a battlefield of another sort, 18 testing holes designed by Willard Byrd in 1965. Thousands of pines and oaks line the fairways, and ten water hazards lurk within this test of accuracy, where no two holes run parallel. The gently contoured greens, grown with bentgrass (unusual this far south), are normally fast and always in splendid condition.

13th hole

7th hole

Even in its early years, Atlanta CC was recognized as a strong layout. It was chosen to host two different USGA Championships and was also the first site of the Tournament Players Championship, in 1974. Jack Nicklaus's company redesigned the course in 1979, and one of the first holes they changed was number three, a 196-yard par three. Although Nicklaus won the 1973 Atlanta Classic and six months later won that inaugural TPC, he never did like the third hole. On one occasion, after pushing his tee shot into the tangly kudzu grass to the right of the green, he struggled to a quintuple-bogey 8. Nicklaus's version of number three is shorter (188 yards) and does not invite disaster to the degree its progenitor did.

6th hole

Water is in play throughout the rest of the front nine, most demonically at the seventh, where Sope Creek must be crossed on both the tee shot and the approach to the narrow green. Georgia native and 1970 Champion Tommy Aaron once hit three balls into the drink here en route to a 9. The most difficult hole on the outward half is the closer, a 421-yard dogleg over water and through the trees, and it is followed by almost as tough a test. Number ten measures 457 yards, and the lengthy second must carry a stream just in front of the green.

The 13th hole is just 156 yards, but it is long on both beauty and history. Just to the right of the green are the remains of the Confederate mint. On the left side is something even more arresting—a waterfall. The entire left side of the green is set against a sheer rock face that drops off 15 feet to a small patch of grass, then drops off again to the waterfall. A

tee shot that lands on that patch must be played almost vertically upward to get back onto the dance floor.

The final round of the 1982 Atlanta Classic proved that the 452-yard 15th hole is the killer of the stretch run. A tantalizing par four, it invites a hard fade to the left-to-right bending fairway. But a creek down the right side penalizes the overly zealous drive. The creek winds back across the fairway about 35 yards short of the green to taunt the approach shot.

In that final round, the top four finishing players—Keith Fergus, Ray Floyd, Larry Nelson, and Wayne Levi—made scores of bogey 5, double-bogey 6, triple-bogey 7, and quadruple-bogey 8, respectively. Nelson, a former PGA and U.S. Open Champion (and twice a winner here), should have known better. His address is Country Club Lane, Marietta, Georgia. Larry lives on this course.

Scorecard

Hole	Yards	Par	PGA Tour Avg. Score
1	407	4	3.991
2	563	5	4.660
3	188	3	2.948
4	427	4	4.000
5	432	4	4.075
6	190	3	3.227
7	340	4	3.977
8	550	5	4.860
9	421	4	4.281
OUT	3518	36	36.019
10	457	4	4.176
11	548	5	4.667
12	426	4	4.039
13	156	3	2.978
14	335	4	3.996
15	452	4	4.296
16	206	3	3.155
17	421	4	4.184
18	499	5	4.877
IN	3500	36	36.368
TOTAL	7018	72	72.387

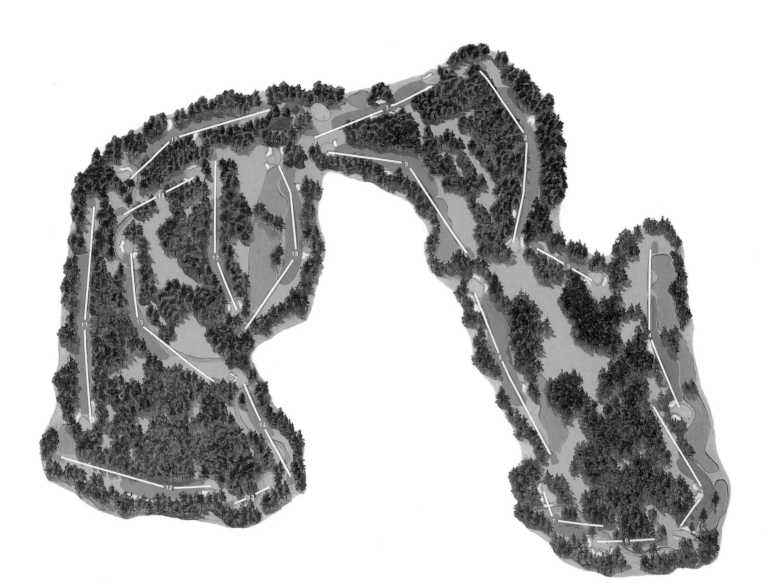

How to Play a Hole Backward

BY TOM KITE

Atlanta Country Club is not one of the longest par 72s we play, but it's demanding because it's tight and it makes you think. On a course like this one, there's no advantage to taking a driver and blasting it off the tee of every par four and five. This is one of those courses where it pays to play every hole backward in your mind before you play it forward from the tee. And that mental exercise is good discipline for anyone who wants to get the most out of his or her game.

If you haven't gone through this shot-planning on your home course, do so now. For each hole, ask yourself what spot in the fairway affords the ideal approach to the green. Take into consideration hazards as well as the slope of the greens, but also factor in the pattern of your shots. Position A for a person who hits a draw is probably on the left side of the fairway, while the player with a fade will usually prefer the right. On short par fours, the best position may be well short of the green, where you can make a full swing, rather than up close where you'd have to play a finesse shot of some kind.

Once you know where you want your tee shots to finish, ask yourself which clubs on your tee shots will give you the best opportunities to find those spots. Once you have that strategy, you've taken a big step toward good course management.

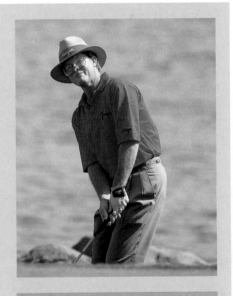

Tom Kite won the 1992 BellSouth Atlanta Classic a month before winning his first major championship, the U.S. Open at Pebble Beach.

TPC AT LAS COLINAS

The first big-time tournament ever played in Dallas—the Texas Victory Open—was won by a local boy named Byron Nelson, by a whopping 12 strokes. Nelson would never again win this event, which a year later became known as the Dallas Open, but his brief career (1932–46) was filled with other victories—65 in all—including a U.S. Open, two Masters, and two PGAs. So it was appropriate in 1968 when Dallas honored its finest player by renaming its tournament the Byron Nelson Golf Classic, the first professional event ever named after a player.

Today, a ten-foot-high bronze statue of Nelson stands near the first tee of the TPC at Las Colinas, the current site of the GTE Byron Nelson Classic.

When the Tour came to the Las Colinas resort in 1983, another Texan stepped into the winner's circle. Austin native Ben Crenshaw broke a lengthy victory drought and edged Hal Sutton by a stroke. One year after that—and exactly 40 years after Nelson's inaugural win—the Tour announced that Las Colinas would become the site of a Tournament Players Course. Golf course architect Jay Morrish would design a new 18-hole layout on the existing site, and he would be aided by two player consultants—Ben Crenshaw and Byron Nelson.

The original course at Las Colinas had been designed by Robert Trent Jones, Jr., son of the dean of American golf architects and a prolific, imaginative designer in his own right. Jones's course was as large and sprawling as Texas itself, with spacious fairways, expansive, heavily sloped greens, and mammoth flash bunkers. One green was shaped like the state of Texas, with Oklahoma as its back bunker. The course was big on everything but subtlety.

Enter understated Morrish and soft-spoken Crenshaw. Using the general route of Jones's back nine and blazing a new trail for the front, they created an entirely different golf course from the one that had been there.

Byron Nelson assumed a more passive, advisory role than did Crenshaw. Las Colinas was Crenshaw's first real involvement with course design (he has since pursued the profession with architect partner Bill Coore, their most notable design being the lavish Plantation Course which hosts the Lincoln Kapalua International in Hawaii), but he had been a student of golf architecture ever since his early amateur days, with a predilection for the old-style layouts, particularly the links courses of Great Britain.

One of Ben's strong beliefs is that a course should afford more than one route to most of its greens, accommodating not only the high-flying darts of the modern American pros but the low pinches and run-ups that are the bread-and-butter of British golf. At Las Colinas, where the wind is every bit as strong and persistent as in Britain, Crenshaw insisted on providing low-road access to most of the targets. The architects also provided plenty of interesting contours around the greens, so that the pitching and chipping game is more important here than at most Tour sites.

So strong are the Texas winds that during the 1984 Nelson, Dave Eichelberger cranked out the longest drive in the history of the Tour, a clout that traveled 397 yards. Also that week, Hal Sutton holed out a 3-wood shot on one of the par fives for the first double eagle on Tour in two years.

In his routing plan, Morrish strove for balance vis-à-vis the prevailing southerly wind, with some holes playing against it,

5th hole

GTE Byron Nelson Classic, Texas

11th hole

15th hole

The TPC at Las Colinas has honest, straightforward greens with relatively mild undulations. These are the kind I like, because they usually reward a solidly struck putt.

I think of the putting stroke as a miniature version of my golf swing. You should, too. For example, if you're a wristy player you should also use your wrists in your putting stroke.

I swing more with my arms than wrists. Thus, my stroke is slow and deliberate, my arms and shoulders swinging the putter back and through with my wrists firm.

I recommend a grip in which both thumbs are positioned on the top of the putter shaft. This grip helps give you a feel for the speed of a putt and is a must for holding the stroke on line.

Finally, get to know the various types of grass and grain and how they affect your putts. To save strokes on the green, know which putts must be lagged and which may be charged.

Ben Crenshaw was the design consultant on the TPC at Las Colinas, and is also the 1983 Byron Nelson champion.

17th hole

Scorecard

Hole	Yards	Par	PGA Tour Avg. Score
1	352	4	3.877
2	176	3	2.993
3	460	4	4.294
4	428	4	4.056
5	176	3	2.930
6	396	4	3.969
7	533	5	4.721
8	451	4	4.224
9	406	4	4.170
OUT	3378	35	35.234
10	447	4	4.139
11	341	4	3.973
12	426	4	4.124
13	183	3	3.018
14	390	4	4.204
15	412	4	4.119
16	554	5	4.716
17	196	3	3.111
18	415	4	4.010
IN	3364	35	35.414
TOTAL	6742	70	70.648

some with it, and some across it. He also gauged the yardages of several holes with the wind strongly in mind. A notable example is the third, a par four of 460 downwind yards. Tailwinds strengthen as well as lengthen shots, and that notion will be solace for slicers, because water lines the entire right side of this, the number-one handicap hole. The green is large, but so is one of the two bunkers guarding it, and the other bunker is a deep pot. God help those who catch this hole on a day when the prevailing wind is not prevailing. That's what happened during the 1990 Nelson, and even the PGA Tour struggled; with a scoring average of 4.587, this turned out to be the toughest hole on that year's Tour.

Morrish likes each of his designs to include at least one par four that is drivable, under ideal conditions, by the game's strongest players. At Las Colinas, the hole is the 341-yard 11th. Since it is

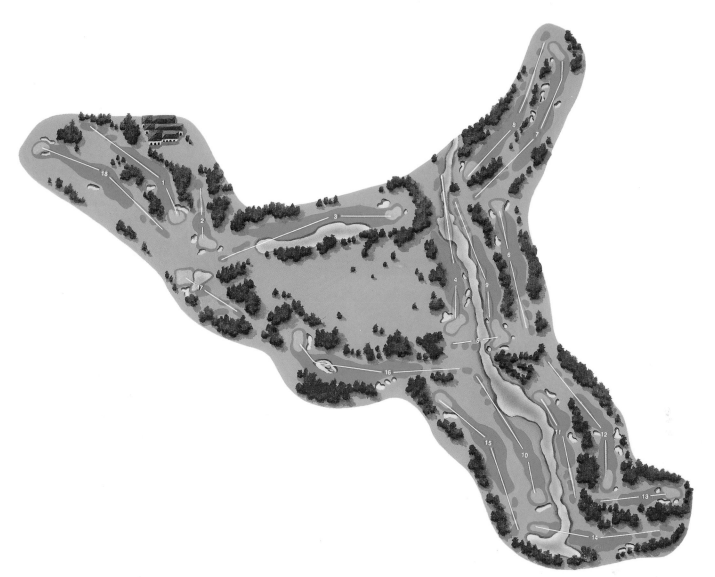

also a cuttable dogleg, the straight-line distance from tee to green is actually only 300 yards—but about 290 of those yards are over water. The 11th tee sits on the edge of a small river, and the fairway and green are on the other side. In 1991 Tom Kite was in contention on the final day when he pulled his tee shot into the water. Kite and his playing partner, Phil Blackmar, agreed that the ball had carried the far shore before falling back in, and that Kite was thus entitled to drop his ball on the other side of the river. But this was during the brief period when the PGA Tour used instant replay to settle Rules disputes, and the camera showed that Kite had never cleared the drink. Kite was forced to return to the tee, and he made a double bogey, eventually finishing in a tie for eighth place.

The most memorable hole on the course surely is the 14th, which plays from an elevated tee down to the edge of a river, leaving a short iron across the water to the green. Although only 390 yards, it plays into the prevailing wind, which adds terror as well as yardage to the river-crossing approach.

Crenshaw's Scottish proclivities arise at the 16th, a 554-yard uphill par five where the challenge is in the canny bunkering. The tee shot landing area is fronted by a trio of pot bunkers running diagonally from the left side. Then the second shot must deal with three cross bunkers coming diagonally from the right. At the green, roll-down bunkers guard the right while a grassy hollow catches shots that miss to the left.

The penultimate hole is a par three that plays 196 yards down a steep hill. In 1993, the hole was made considerably more challenging with the addition of a lake in front of the green. The course concludes with a sadly nondescript 415-yard par four that curls along the back-yard of the Four Seasons Hotel. The truth is that, while the middle of the course plays through wooded areas, the opening and closing stretches have a manufactured look despite recent attempts to add contour and definition around the greens. This is especially the case at holes 15 through 18, where stadium mounds predominate. During construction of the course, however, thousands of oaks, Mexican plums, and pine trees were added, many of them lowered by helicopter into waiting holes along the fairways. As these grow, so surely will the beauty and difficulty of the TPC at Las Colinas.

MUIRFIELD VILLAGE GOLF CLUB

*I*t's the course that Jack built. Back in 1974, in the 13th year of his reign as the greatest golfer of all time, Jack Nicklaus created a championship golf course near his hometown of Columbus, Ohio. He named it Muirfield Village, after the site of his first British Open victory, but he modeled it—and every aspect of the tournament staged on it—after another major championship. Nicklaus's Memorial Tournament is the Masters of the Midwest.

From the wide, rolling fairways, menacing hazards, and fiendishly fast, undulating greens to the tough ticket policy and invitational format, this carefully manicured event is rooted firmly in the soil of Augusta, Georgia.

It's also indisputable that Jack created this course in his own image. Muirfield Village favors a fade, and a fade is the shot with which Nicklaus won most of his championships. Muirfield Village favors a long, high approach shot that

can spin back on linoleum; Jack patented that shot. And Muirfield Village favors a player who can play from tee to green with canny caution, then putt without fear. That's Jack Nicklaus.

But a case could be made equally for the course fitting the piercing tee shots of Greg Norman, the deft touch of Paul Azinger, or the consistency of Tom Kite. The fact is, just as the Memorial Tournament honors fine players of the past, the Muirfield Village course rewards the best players of the present.

It is also a pleasure for spectators. This was one of the first courses designed with tournament galleries specifically in mind, predating all of the PGA Tour's Stadium Courses, and many of the tees and greens are situated within natural amphitheaters. Through the years, Nicklaus has tinkered constantly with the course, often shaving hills and adding mounds that improved visibility for spectators while also adding to the shot values of the course. The course

9th hole

17th hole

The Memorial Tournament, Ohio

3rd hole

currently ranks 24th on *GOLF Magazine's* list of the 100 Greatest Courses in the World, and in addition to hosting the Memorial, it has been the site of the 1987 Ryder Cup Matches (won by Europe, 15–13) and the 1992 U.S. Amateur Championship, won by Justin Leonard.

According to Nicklaus's longtime instructor, the late Jack Grout, "There are 18 bullies out there and you need to beat them up one at a time." One of the brawniest brutes puts up its dukes right at the opening bell. The 446-yard first plays from an elevated tee to a fairway that slopes from right to left while dog-legging from left to right. Bunkers guard the inside of the dogleg, woods and a creek run along the outside. The green is the largest on the course but is virtually surrounded by sand.

Number two is another monster—452 yards for the pros—and demanding of accuracy even more than length. The fairway slopes toward the right, where a creek runs along the entire length of the hole. Water seems omnipresent at Muirfield Village, and it almost is. Tom

Avoiding Three-Putts
BY HALE IRWIN

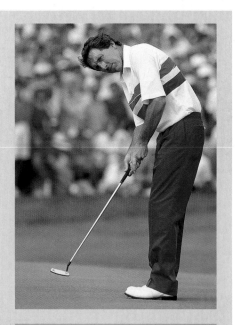

Muirfield Village has some of the most beautiful and well-conditioned greens in the world—and some of the toughest to putt. They were designed, after all, by one of the greatest putters in the history of the game. During the Memorial, the greens are very fast and full of subtle breaks; they demand nothing less than a Nicklaus touch.

One of the toughest aspects of putting fast bentgrass greens is adopting the correct attitude: neither too aggressive nor too cautious. I'm sure you've heard the expression, "Never up, never in." There can be no argument with its message. But this does not mean that charging the ball six feet past the hole is better than being one foot short. Ideally, you should hit every putt at a speed that will take it about one foot past the hole if you fail to hole it. Even on those rare occasions when you have hit a very bad putt and you can see it's going to miss the hole and finish well past—don't turn away in disgust. Watch the ball carefully. It could save you the embarrassment of missing the return. The amount of break the ball takes past the hole is exactly the amount of break you must allow for when trying to hole out.

Hale Irwin is a two-time winner (1983, 1985) of the Memorial Tournament.

9th hole

Weiskopf once observed incredulously, "Water comes into play on 18 shots here. That's *18 shots*."

As at the Augusta National, the first par three appears at hole number 4, and this one is not unlike the one at The Masters, a downhill shot of 204 yards to a well-bunkered, sloping green. Over the lifetime of the Memorial, this has proved to be the third-most-difficult hole on the course.

Nicklaus saved the best hole on the front for last, a taut 410-yard par four that calls for equal amounts of boldness and finesse. The drive must thread through a chute of trees and find not

simply the fairway but the best part of it to leave a good shot at the green, which is framed by a crossing creek, two bunkers, and a hillside.

Masters mimicry returns with the 12th hole, a par three over water that closely resembles the famous 12th at Augusta. The winds don't swirl as capriciously as they do through the Georgia pines, and this hole plays downhill instead of level, but its tiny, two-tiered green is far more difficult than that of its model; indeed, in one year this played as the hardest par three on the entire Tour. "I love this hole," Nicklaus said after he'd designed it, but in the first Memorial it

likely gave him warm feelings of another kind. In round three he dumped two tee shots into the water and had to make an eight-footer for a 7.

The greens at Muirfield Village are among the fastest on the Tour—up to 12 and more on the Stimpmeter, the device used for clocking green speed. Together with the fierce slopes, they could almost be unfair were it not for their consistently superb condition. As sportswriter Dan Jenkins once said, "You'd sooner put out a cigarette butt on your baby's tummy than on one of these greens."

It is rare to see a professional golfer play his third shot on a par four *purposely*

145

11th hole

12th hole

15th hole

18th hole

17th hole

into a greenside bunker, but at the 14th hole that happens frequently. Just 363 yards long, this hole has quickly earned a reputation as one of the most vexing holes in golf. Restraint is required from the tee, where most pros hit fairway woods and long irons to a valley just short of a creek that crosses the fairway. From there the target is a long, narrow strip of green, cut against a hill, with bunkers on the left and a steep bank down to the meandering creek on the right. A shot that strays left of the bunkers means that the next shot will not hold the green; that is why third shots are directed safely *into* the sand. In 1980, John Fought was tied for the lead in the final round when he took a quadruple-bogey 8 here. Three players have made 9.

All the par fives at Muirfield Village are reachable in two to the long hitters on the Tour, but the 15th hole is hittable

by everyone. Still, these 490 yards roll up and down hills and through a narrow valley Nicklaus created by cutting through the heart of a forest. And its small, sharply sloped green is elevated and fronted by a creek.

Some of the Memorial's most memorable moments have occurred on number 17, the 430-yard par four that winds past a 130-yard bunker through a valley of rough to a green flanked by a trio of the deepest bunkers on the course. It was here in the inaugural Memorial that Roger Maltbie "staked himself to victory" in a playoff over Hale Irwin. When Maltbie's approach soared well left of the green he looked to have blown any chance of victory. But the ball struck a gallery stake and bounded straight back onto the green. Roger then got down in two and then birdied 18 to win the tournament.

Eight years later, Jack Nicklaus chose

Scorecard

Hole	Yards	Par	PGA Tour Avg. Score
1	446	4	4.040
2	452	4	4.191
3	392	4	4.055
4	204	3	3.087
5	531	5	4.706
6	430	4	4.007
7	549	5	4.713
8	189	3	3.004
9	410	4	4.050
OUT	3603	36	35.853
10	441	4	4.031
11	538	5	4.857
12	156	3	3.045
13	442	4	4.129
14	363	4	4.125
15	490	5	4.562
16	204	3	3.084
17	430	4	4.093
18	437	4	4.255
IN	3501	36	36.181
TOTAL	7104	72	72.034

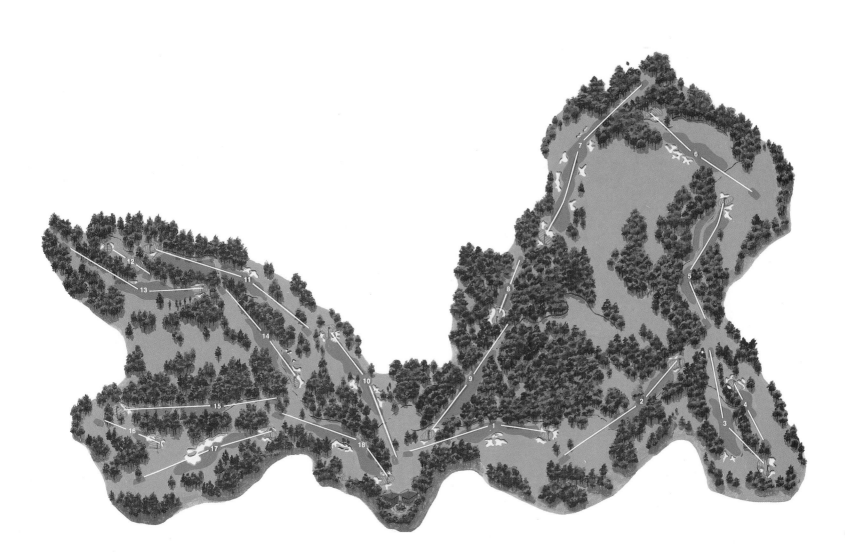

this hole to play perhaps his career worst tee shot under pressure. Tied with Andy Bean after 70 holes, Nicklaus slashed a rainbow slice so far and deep that it finished on the back porch of one of the Muirfield Village condos. But he rolled in a 25-foot putt for a bogey, then parred 18 as Bean missed a short putt. Nicklaus won the tournament in a playoff when Bean again missed a short one—on the 17th green.

If 18 has occasionally been anticlimactic, it is nonetheless the most difficult hole on the course, having played to a stroke average of 4.3 in the first 17 Memorials. A downhill-then-uphill dogleg right, it curls around a corner of trees and bunkers up to a heavily contoured green that is as hard to putt as it is to hit and hold. But in 1993, Paul Azinger avoided both of those assignments and still won the tournament.

One stroke behind his good friend

Payne Stewart as the two of them came to the 72nd hole, Azinger knocked his approach into the deep bunker that fronts the green. Stewart also missed the green but wedged his third shot to within eight feet of the hole. Advantage Stewart. But then Azinger hit the bunker shot of his life, a delicate explosion that barely cleared the lip and then trickled 15 feet down the sloping green and into the hole for a spectacular birdie. The stunned Stewart slid his par putt past the hole, and the 1993 Memorial became another chapter of an event whose history has included eight one-stroke victories and four playoffs in its first 18 years.

Greg Norman contends that Muirfield Village is the type of course that inspires great players to play their best golf. Certainly, the first two decades of Memorials have produced an impressive group of victors, including Norman, Hale Irwin, Tom Watson, David Graham,

Raymond Floyd, Curtis Strange, and the architect himself—twice.

However, each year the Memorial produces not only a champion but a special honoree as well. The Captains' Club, a group of graybeards led by Nicklaus, annually selects an individual who has "played golf with conspicuous honor," and dedicates the tournament to him or her. The first honoree was Nicklaus's idol Bobby Jones, and the role has by now gone to virtually every other great player in the game, from Old and Young Tom Morris to Arnold Palmer. But the perennial honoree is Nicklaus himself, who created this course and tournament in the same way Jones conceived Augusta National—as his own memorial.

COLONIAL COUNTRY CLUB

4th hole

Colonial National Invitation, Texas

They call it Hogan's Alley, but it is more than that. In one sense, Ft. Worth's Colonial Country Club *is* Ben Hogan. Linked together for nearly a half century, the course and the man developed a matchless affinity. Today, the terms that describe Hogan also describe the 18 holes he called home: proud, stern, brutally honest, and unremittingly tough; pursuant of precision, intolerant of mediocrity, and, when in top form, virtually unbeatable.

Founded in 1935 by Texas businessman Marvin Leonard, this big golf course on the banks of the Trinity River quickly became the favored practice ground of Hogan. When, in 1946, the first Colonial National Invitation Tournament was played, Hogan won by a stroke on a final round of 65, a score that would remain the course record. In the next seven years, The Hawk won three more Colonials, adding a record fifth in 1959 at the age of 46.

At his peak, Hogan hit balls with a swing whose power and repetitive consistency were likened to a machine stamping out bottle caps. So it is no wonder that he loved Colonial, a course that demands both accuracy and might, where one must be prepared either to hit the ball squarely or to hit it often. It is said that Hogan, having played so much of his formative golf at Colonial, found most other courses easy.

Most of the PGA Tour players agree that this design by Texas architect John Bredemus is one of the finest and most difficult tests they play. An extremely tight 7010 yards, it is, according to 1951 champion Cary Middlecoff, "the toughest par 70 in the world," and has retained its challenge. As its golden anniversary approaches, the Colonial tournament holds the title as the longest-running

13th hole

16th hole

PGA Tour event still played on its original site.

The cluster of holes three, four, and five is known as the Horrible Horseshoe. Number three is the longest par four on a course that is full of long par fours. A 476-yard dogleg left, it plays around a large tree and a trio of bunkers at the knee of the dogleg. When the U.S. Women's Open was played here in 1991, the USGA shortened this hole 16 yards

and then the world's best women golfers played it as a par five. The fourth hole is a Texas-size par three of 246 yards to a wide green with a shelf across the back. Hogan claimed it was "in between clubs; a 4-wood was too much and a 2-iron was not enough."

Number five is not simply the hardest hole at Colonial, it is consistently one of the toughest holes on the Tour. The 459-yard left-to-right dogleg is tightly

guarded by a tree-lined ditch on the left, trees to the shallow right, and the Trinity River to the deep right, all made more difficult by a prevailing left-to-right wind. The ideal tee shot is a power fade, which the long hitters play with a 3-wood, and with courage. This leaves a long-iron approach to the firm, well-bunkered green. All of which explains why the nickname of this hole is Death Valley.

18th hole

Middlecoff claimed he approaches the fifth this way: "First I pull out two brand-new Wilson balls and throw them into the Trinity River. Then I throw up. Then I go ahead and hit my tee shot into the river." In 1951 he played it a bit differently than that. In the final round, Middlecoff whistled his approach 60 feet over the green, next to a concession stand. From there he took a putter and rapped the ball under the trees, onto the green, and into the hole for a birdie. He went on to win by one.

When the U.S. Open came to Colonial in 1941, this hole brought Craig Wood to the brink of despair. After only four holes of play in the second round,

Wood was three over par. To make matters worse, his chronic back ailment was bothering him so much that he was playing in a corset. That was aggravated still further by the heavy rains during round two that had soaked both the course and the corset. And as a final touch of agony, the waterlogged Wood had hit his tee shot into the ditch at number five, only seconds before USGA officials had suspended play.

Wood did what most mortals would have done. He decided to quit and go home. But his playing partner, Tommy Armour, would not let him. "C'mon," said Armour, "everyone's struggling out here. Stick around."

Wood, the reigning Masters champion, decided that quitting was not such a good idea after all. When play resumed, he managed to get through number five with a bogey, then played even-par golf for the rest of the tournament. His 284 was good enough to win that Open by three strokes.

In 1968 the Army Corps of Engineers rerouted sections of the Trinity River as part of a major flood project. At Colonial that meant rebuilding nine holes and relocating the eighth and 13th greens, although the greens have since been restored. When Kel Nagle got the news about 13, he was upset. It was on this 178-yard par three in 1961 that

The Water Blast
BY IAN BAKER-FINCH

Although I won the Colonial in 1989, it's probable that I'm just as well remembered for the single shot I played on the 13th hole in 1993.

When my ball settled half-submerged at the edge of the greenside pond, I decided to blast it out. But first I took off my shoes, then my socks and then, yes, my slacks. There I stood in my undershorts and played the most daring shot of my life. Fortunately, I got the ball on the green, and immediately reclothed.

The fact is, whether you choose to remove any of your clothing or not, the blast from water often is a viable alternative to taking a penalty drop. If at least some part of the ball protrudes above the surface of the water, the shot is playable. You attack it exactly as you would a splash from a bunker, with the ball positioned toward the rear of your open stance. Hit down an inch or so behind the ball, and you'll create the same sort

of explosion and lifting effect as in a bunker. Swing with about the same force you'd use for a buried lie in sand. If you play the shot correctly, you'll be surprised at how high and softly the ball will fly.

Ian Baker-Finch won the 1989 Southwestern Bell Colonial.

Scorecard

Hole	Yards	Par	PGA Tour Avg. Score
1	565	5	4.719
2	400	4	3.892
3	476	4	4.162
4	246	3	3.104
5	459	4	4.256
6	393	4	3.919
7	420	4	3.978
8	192	3	3.019
9	391	4	4.053
OUT	3542	35	35.102
10	404	4	3.999
11	599	5	4.848
12	433	4	4.098
13	178	3	2.996
14	426	4	4.012
15	430	4	4.030
16	188	3	3.007
17	383	4	3.931
18	427	4	4.031
IN	3468	35	34.952
TOTAL	7010	70	70.054

Nagle scored the first hole-in-one in Colonial history. It is not the memory of that shot he savors, but the reaction of his playing companion.

The affable Australian had been paired with Hogan, and the Ice Mon, as usual, had wrapped himself in a cocoon of concentration and not spoken a word during the round. But after Nagle's flawless 2-iron found its mark, Hogan cracked. After waiting for the yells and whoops of the gallery to subside, he emerged from solitary confinement just long enough to mutter, "Nice shot."

Who knows what Hogan might have muttered if he had been accompanying Tom Purtzer on this hole in 1991. It was the final round of the Colonial and Purtzer was clinging to a one-stroke lead when he knocked his tee shot into the bunker behind the green. Facing a difficult downhill blast with water beyond, Purtzer opted not to blast at all—he

putted the ball. It hopped out of the sand and onto the green and then rolled into the hole for a birdie. What had looked like a bogey suddenly was a birdie. It spurred Purtzer to a round of 64 and a three-stroke victory.

One 64 is a great accomplishment on Colonial, but imagine two 64's in one day. That's what Keith Clearwater produced in 1987 after rain forced a 36-hole conclusion on Sunday. Clearwater won that event and also contributed some drama to the 1993 Colonial, when he posted a new course record of 61 which came courtesy of birdies on each of the last seven holes. After the 11th, Clearwater's scorecard showed no number higher than a 3, and his record total for the nine was 28. That was the year everyone tore up Colonial, particularly Fulton Allem, who beat Greg Norman by a stroke and won with a record score of 264, 16 under par.

Mention "Big Annie" to Jack Nicklaus, and he may give you a dirty look. Big Annie is a shady lady from Nicklaus's past. For years, she stood at the corner of the 17th hole, a 200-foot-high pecan tree waiting to snag second shots and turn pars into double-bogeys. In 1974, Nicklaus was leading the tournament when he tried to beat Big Annie by playing over the top of her. But his strategy backfired when his ball flew not only the tree but the green as well. A 6 went on his card, and Jack lost by a stroke. But in 1986, Nicklaus's revenge was wrought by Mother Nature, when a severe thunderstorm felled the tree. Almost immediately, several "Little Orphan Annies" were planted.

The 18th at Colonial is a 427-yard par four that doglegs softly left, culminating at a green tucked between an expanse of sand on the right and a large body of water on the left. A mound in the center of the fairway adds difficulty to the second shot by producing a side-hill lie with the ball above the feet, the kind of lie that encourages pull hooks that can find that water. On top of this, the fickle Texas wind can be a killer. One year, 280-pound George Bayer pumped his second shot high into the wind, and it sailed all the way to the roof of the clubhouse—at least that's where it is assumed to have finished.

In 1988, Lanny Wadkins rifled his approach three feet from the stick and sank the putt to win by a stroke, but that was only the second time in the history of the tournament that a player had birdied 18 to win. On the dark side of the coin is a man who must have nightmares about this hole—Bruce Crampton. Twice in his career Crampton came to this hole needing a par to win, a bogey to get into a playoff, and on both occasions he took double-bogey 6.

The Colonial Country Club has had its share of misfortune. In 1949 the Trinity River flooded so badly that the tournament was called off, and on three separate occasions the clubhouse has been destroyed by fire. But despite these disasters the Colonial Invitation has consistently ranked among the best run, most popular, most prestigious events on the Tour. The superb course always attracts a strong field of players, and that field invariably produces an exciting tournament with a dramatic finish.

The story of Clayton Heafner, the 1948 champion, says a lot about this event and the course on which it is played. As part of his victory euphoria, Heafner issued one of those breathless compliments to which winners are prone. "This is the way all golf tournaments should be run," he exclaimed. "Why, I'd rather finish last at the Colonial and get to take part than be up in the money at some other tournament."

In the very next Colonial, Heafner got his wish. His 72-hole total of 304 left him flat in the cellar.

TPC AT AVENEL

16th hole

The Kemper Open, Maryland

In Great Britain, a course such as Troon or Birkdale becomes known as Royal Troon or Royal Birkdale as the result of a grand gesture by a member of the royal family. Were there such a practice in America, The Kemper Open would now be played at Royal Avenel, for without question this course was christened by The King.

Arnold Palmer, that is. In 1986, just a few weeks after Avenel opened, an event known as The Chrysler Cup was played here. Sort of a Ryder Cup for seniors, it matched a team of America's best 50-and-over players against the best of the rest of the world. The captains of the two teams were Palmer and Gary Player.

A two-day pro-am preceded the event, and on the first day of that pro-am, when Palmer reached the then 187-yard third hole, he drew out a 5-iron and knocked the ball into the cup for a hole-in-one. A laudable feat, but nothing cataclysmic—it was, after all, the 13th ace for a man who has spent nearly a half century hitting the ball at the hole. No, the crowning glory came the next day, when Arnie came to the same hole, and took out the same 5-iron, and made the same score: 1.

The odds against a professional golfer—even Arnold Palmer—making a hole-in-one are roughly 3,000-to-one. The odds against his making two aces consecutively on the same hole are roughly 3,000-squared-to-one or 9,000,000-to-one. Needless to say, a plaque at Avenel's third tee commemorates the feat.

A few months later, when the PGA Tour came to Avenel for the 1987 Kemper Open, the players had a bit more trouble getting the ball into the hole. Although defending champion Greg Norman opened with a course-record 64, he closed with a barrage of bogeys and an even bigger barrage of complaints over the design and condition of the course. His feelings were shared by a significant number of his peers.

In fairness, Avenel had a tough act to follow. For the previous seven years the Kemper had been played at nearby Congressional Country Club, site of the 1964 U.S. Open and the 1976 PGA Championship, and slated to hold the Open again in 1997. Also, the first event at Avenel had been preceded by five straight days of rain, making conditions less than pleasant.

Tom Kite, who also opened the tournament with a 64, hung on to win, lend-

9th hole

11th hole

Playing from a Fairway Bunker

BY BILLY ANDRADE

The situation I fear more than any other is a ball in a fairway bunker. Since there's almost no room for error, you have to proceed with extreme caution.

Sure it's an intimidating spot, but if you use some common sense and control, you'll rarely get buried in fairway sand. The truth is, you should treat this shot like a shot from the fairway—but a bit more carefully.

To ensure clean contact, take one club more than you would for a shot of the same distance from the fairway. As with any lie in a bunker, grind your feet into the sand a bit for good footing and balance. Choke down on the grip an inch or so, to allow for your lowered platform and to further enhance control. Other than these adjustments, don't do anything except keep your leg action to a minimum. What you want is a compact, clean, picking swing—a lateral strike through the ball rather than a vertical chop down on it.

By the way, if you have a slice, there's good news and bad news. Your out-to-in swing will probably help you to raise the ball over the bunker's lip, but you'll probably produce a bigger banana ball than you would from the fairway or rough, so allow for the drift by aiming a bit to the left and taking two clubs more than you normally would.

Billy Andrade's first Tour victory came at the 1991 Kemper Open, where he set a tournament record of 263.

17th hole

18th hole

ing some legitimacy to the week, but over time the players' carping led to changes on virtually every hole on the course. Fairways were moved; bunkers were added in some places, eliminated in others, and reshaped everywhere; greens were reconfigured; and tees were added, lengthening the course nearly 150 yards.

Today, after almost a decade of maturing, Avenel is a diverse test of shot-making that gets kinder reviews from the players. It is set on a rolling tree-clad 200-acre tract in Potomac, Maryland, ten miles west of the White House. One of the Tour's TPC courses, it is distinguished by sizable spectator mounds on its finishing holes. The designer was Ed Ault, a D.C.-based architect famed for

his work at Baltimore's Five Farms as well as for the Las Vegas Country Club, one of the venues for the Las Vegas Invitational. Ault was assisted by Tom Clark; Ed Sneed acted as player consultant.

Although elements of their original design drew some harsh reviews, even the critics agreed that Avenel had a superb variety of holes and that it took good advantage of some dramatic terrain. Its great asset may be in its diversity of par fours, which range in length from just 301 yards to 472.

The two nines emanate from different sides of the clubhouse and run independent of each other, each ending in a slight loop. The front heads directly north for its first four holes before mak-

ing an about-face for the return to the clubhouse. The notable links in this chain are the second, a wide-open par five whose main challenge is its length —622 yards—and the sixth, another five but this one reachable even at a newly lengthened 520 yards. (In 1991 Mark Brooks did not simply reach it, he sank his second shot for a double-eagle en route to a tie for fourth.) But the toughest hole is the seventh, a 461-yard par four where the tee shot must be placed between a large bunker on the left and dense trees to the right.

One of the most controversial holes on the original course was the ninth, a downhill par three that left little room for error with its small, hard green just

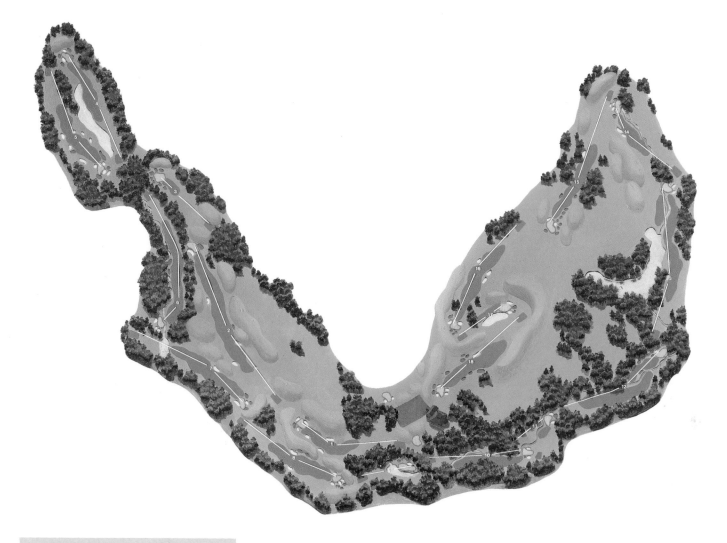

Scorecard

Hole	Yards	Par	PGA Tour Avg. Score
1	393	4	4.025
2	622	5	4.929
3	239	3	3.116
4	435	4	4.137
5	359	4	3.911
6	520	5	4.649
7	461	4	4.216
8	453	4	4.042
9	166	3	3.110
OUT	3648	36	36.135
10	374	4	3.997
11	165	3	2.989
12	472	4	4.319
13	524	5	4.779
14	301	4	3.845
15	467	4	4.194
16	415	4	4.086
17	195	3	3.118
18	444	4	4.186
IN	3357	35	35.513
TOTAL	7005	71	71.648

on the far side of a creek. Among the changes here were a new tee, a rebuilt green, reshaping of the water hazard, and expansion of the greenside bunkers. Today, it gets few complaints.

Number ten heads on an eastward path and begins a series of five heavily wooded holes where the creek comes constantly into play, most perilously at the 472-yard 12th, where water parallels the left side of the fairway and then crosses in front of the severely contoured green, making this the hardest hole on the course.

The course turns out of the woods at the 15th and heads homeward through a corridor of massive spectator mounds. The green at the par-three 17th is Colosseum-like; the mound not only wraps around the back of the green but extends more than halfway down the fairway. A 195-yard shot over water, this is the toughest of the four short holes and is often the deciding point of the tournament.

For Billy Andrade in 1991, however, it all came down to 18. The young pro from Rhode Island had never won a Tour event, and when he pushed his final tee shot into a bunker and then put his approach in more sand, it looked as if he might give away this one. But Andrade survived both bunkers and scrambled for his closing par to reach a playoff with Jeff Sluman, whom he beat on the first hole of sudden death. His winning score of 263—21 under par—is the tournament record at Avenel, and it spurred Andrade to his second career victory just one week later at the Buick Classic—back-to-back wins that surely were as exhilarating to Andrade as the pair of aces to Palmer.

WESTCHESTER COUNTRY CLUB

18th hole

The Buick Classic, New York

This is where country clubs are supposed to be found—in leafy, wealthy Westchester County—tucked among Tudor mansions and private tennis courts. And here, indeed, is the most imposing clubhouse on the Tour—hardly just a clubhouse, in fact, but a former grand hotel—overlooking a venerable layout that dates from the golden age of golf course design.

Westchester Country Club is one of the oldest courses on the PGA Tour, designed in 1922 by "The Old Man," Walter J. Travis. During the Roaring '20s, 4,000 courses were built in America—four times the number then in existence—and one of the plum projects was John Bowman's plan for his Westchester Biltmore Hotel, where he sought to establish a golf complex par excellence—not simply a course but a 400-room hotel, tennis courts, and polo field, all on a sprawling 500-acre tract perched on a hilltop near the town of Rye, 40 miles north of Manhattan.

Travis, a three-time U.S. Amateur champion in his younger years, was asked to find room for 36 holes over the property and managed to fit in 45—two regulation 18s plus a par-three course. The West Course, on which the Buick Classic is played, winds up and down rugged, rocky hills and loops through thick stands of pines, oaks, and maples. At 6,779 yards it is a short par 71, but it insists on accuracy, particularly from the tees. In 1992, five of the 20 toughest holes on the Tour were on this course.

During the tournament, the front and back nines are reversed, with the result that the first hole is a par three. It seems an unassuming 192-yarder, but its guile was sufficient for Arnold Palmer to rank it among his favorite 54 holes in golf.

The fourth hole has been ranked as one of the finest in the New York area. A

Putting Fast Greens

BY DAVID FROST

One of the reasons that the Buick Classic is regarded as great preparation for the U.S. Open is the speed of the greens at the Westchester Country Club. They're invariably as fast as those we see at Baltusrol or Medinah or Pebble Beach.

When you find yourself on surfaces such as these, remember a couple of things. First, watch carefully the putts of your playing companions—they're the best clue to a green's speed. Second, on putts of more than 15 feet, concentrate on distance rather than direction; if you hit the ball the proper length, you'll rarely be more than a foot or so from the hole. After you take your final look at the hole, keep a vivid mental picture of the distance to be covered—this will help you "feel the ball to the hole."

Of course, the most frightening putts on fast greens are the downhillers, and as such they require the most care. If you happen to have a pendulum stroke, using mostly the arms and shoulders, you're ahead of the game, since this is the "quietest" type of stroke, not susceptible to sudden acceleration from the wrists. But whatever type of stroke you use, do yourself a favor and hit fast downhill putts off the toe of the putter. By hitting the ball outside the sweetspot, you'll impart a softer strike so that it rolls a bit slower. Thus you'll get a gentler putt without having to change the pace or force of your putting stroke.

David Frost won the 1992 Buick Classic.

1st hole

14th hole

422-yard par four, it begins with a blind tee shot to a relatively small landing area, then calls for a middle iron uphill to a narrow, sloping green.

Water does not come into play until the eighth, a nearly right-angle par four that takes its hairpin left turn in front of a sizable pond. The pro must hit a draw off the tee or face a lengthy approach over water.

Number nine is a short par five of 505 yards, but the second half is steeply uphill. Still, lots of birdies are made here, and even more are made at the 314-yard 10th, which a few players drive each year. The traditional starting point for sudden-death playoffs, number ten is where Seve Ballesteros took the second of his two titles by getting up and down from the left greenside bunker for a birdie to beat David Frost, Ken Green, and Greg Norman.

Birdies at the turn are needed to balance the inevitable bogeys on holes 11 and 12. The par-four 11th is a winding downhill dogleg left with trouble on both sides all the way to the two-level green. It was here in 1993 that Vijay Singh became the first player from Fiji to win on the PGA Tour, when he covered the 444 yards with a drive and a 6-iron and sank a five-foot birdie putt to beat Mark Wiebe.

It's a tossup whether the hardest hole on the course is 11 or the hole that follows it. Normally a par five for the members and even for the Tour players until a few years ago, the 12th checks in at 476 yards. After a tight drive, the player faces a downhill/sidehill lie for a shot to the narrow green set at the top of a hill. Year in and year out, the pros use more strokes on this par four—about 4.4 on average—than they do on a dozen or so par *fives* on the circuit.

Such sternness is balanced by holes such as the 154-yard 14th. Although this hole recently was lengthened slightly, its green remains almost as inviting as in 1975, when Gene Littler made a hole-in-one here in the final round en route to a playoff victory over Julius Boros. He won the tournament on the first hole of sudden death.

That hole happened to be the very difficult 15th. At 477 yards it is the longest of the several long par fours on this course. It doglegs sharply to the right, but a towering tree forbids all but the strongest and most aggressive players from trying to cut the corner. Depending on where the tee shot finishes, the downhill second could be an 8-iron or a fairway wood. Littler won his playoff here with a one-putt par.

Westchester is blessed with a splendid finishing hole. It may not be as picturesque as the home hole at Pebble Beach or as intimidating as Doral's or as wind-blown as Harbour Town's, but the 18th at Westchester is as consistent at producing heartstopping finales as any closer on the Tour.

Two factors create the excitement. First is the hole's comparatively short length. At 535 yards it is reachable in

6th hole

8th hole

two by any player who catches his drive on the screws. Second is the bunker that guards the right side of the green. Large, steep-faced, and cunningly placed, it does what a great hazard should—control the play of a scratch golfer from the moment he puts his tee in the ground. Together, the green and the bunker tug at the Tour pro, coaxing and conning him into a bold approach.

It was on this hole in 1982 that Bob Gilder hit one of the most electrifying shots in golf, a 251-yard 3-wood that went into the hole for a double-eagle. It gave Gilder a three-day total of 192 (one stroke off the all-time Tour record), and spurred him to a record victory total of 261.

A year later, the tournament secured a new date on the Tour schedule, moving from mid-August to mid-June, with the result that the rough along the fairways became longer and thicker. That year, Seve Ballesteros's winning score was 15 strokes higher than Gilder's a year before, and only four strokes lower than the winning total in the U.S. Open that followed a week later at formidable Oakmont. In the decade since the change, most of the champions here have been players who also have at least one of the four major championships under their belts. Most notable was the 1990 champion, Hale Irwin. In that year, due to a shift in the schedule, the pros came

to Westchester the week after the Open instead of before. Irwin, who had won his third Open in an 18-hole playoff over Mike Donald at Medinah, kept right on going and took his second title of the week on Sunday.

Today, Walter Travis's compact little layout is a taut, nerve-wrenching test of shotmaking, loved by some, vilified by others, but respected by all who do battle with it. It retains its date a week before each year's Open, and most of the pros view the trip to New York as a valuable warm-up, reasoning, as the lyric goes, "If you can make it there, you'll make it anywhere."

TPC AT RIVER HIGHLANDS

*W*elcome to playoff city. Hartford—capital of Connecticut, bastion of the insurance industry, home of Mark Twain, Harriet Beecher Stowe, and the Whalers—is also the city most likely to produce overtime golf. Since the first Insurance City Open in 1952, 15 editions of this tournament—better than one out of every three—have ended regulation play in a deadlock. Arnold Palmer—who won this tournament twice—had to go extra innings both times.

Appropriately, the course on which the tension of Hartford now unfolds is itself a cliffhanger. As its name implies, the TPC at River Highlands sits atop a ridge overlooking the Connecticut River. It is a course of evolution, with 18 new holes stamped on the site of a 1928 design.

The original course, called Edgewood, was an old classic in the Donald Ross tradition—designed, in fact, by one of Ross's cousins, R. J. Ross, and built by Ross's construction engineer, Orrin Smith. But despite its bucolic New England location, the layout had a linkslike flavor—flat and barren.

Enter Pete Dye. In 1980, the Hartford Jaycees decided to move their PGA Tour event from the Wethersfield Country Club. (The tournament had been played on the cozy little layout since day one, and under the assault of today's long hitters, it had become more vulnerable than venerable.) Dye was hired to find a site and build a test for the big boys. After scouring the nearby countryside he settled on Edgewood, and did his best to transform the old design into a modern TPC course.

He got it about half right. When the course—then known as the TPC of Connecticut—was unveiled for the 1984 GHO, it met with decidedly mixed reviews from the pros. In truth, it was a decidedly mixed course. Dye had made few changes to the front of the old Edgewood layout; meanwhile, he had fashioned a target-golf Stadium Course on the inward nine. The two halves looked and played as if they were crafted by Jekyll and Hyde.

As complaints from the players mounted, the Tour initiated a redesign by Tour agronomist Bobby Weed. The day after Wayne Levi sank his final putt to win the 1990 tournament, the TPC of Connecticut was closed and work began on the TPC at River Highlands.

Weed took his assignment seriously and began by taking a reconnaissance

8th hole

Canon Greater Hartford Open, Connecticut

12th hole

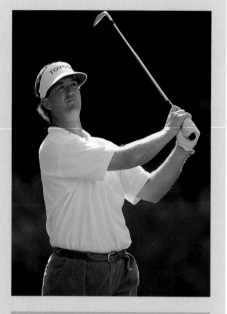
tour of classic Connecticut courses—C. B. Macdonald's jewel at Yale University, A.W. Tillinghast's Brooklawn in Bridgeport, and Willie Park's Woodway in Darien. "These are courses that blend in perfectly with the existing terrain. That was what I was trying to do with River Highlands."

He had some help. Fifty-two additional acres were purchased, including a dense forest, a majestic stretch along the river, and an abandoned salt and gravel quarry. The quarry had been an environmental eyesore, used mainly by dirt bike enthusiasts and by people junking unwanted cars and refrigerators—but it offered exciting possibilities as a site for golf holes.

The result: Seven new holes were created, including four beauties along the river. Each of the other 11 holes was changed in some way, including rebuilt

tees and greens. All the fairways were reworked as two lakes, 80 bunkers, and hundreds of trees were brought into play. The result of all this is that the course was lengthened 34 yards while the par lowered from 71 to 70.

The front nine now includes three par fours of 430 yards or more plus a par five that weighs in at 574 yards. The 15th hole from Dye's layout—one of the hardest on that course—is now the fourth hole at River Highlands, and this rightward-bending dogleg is tougher than ever, with bunkers added both in the drive zone and at the two-tiered green, and the tee pushed back 14 yards to make this a 460-yard struggle.

The eighth hole on the Dye course was a par three, as it is on River Highlands, but the similarity ends there. In place of the old mid-length hole is a 202-yarder straight over an elongated

18th hole

15th hole

16th hole

Scorecard

Hole	Yards	Par	PGA Tour Avg. Score
1	434	4	4.112
2	341	4	3.896
3	431	4	4.052
4	460	4	4.234
5	223	3	3.177
6	574	5	4.934
7	443	4	4.172
8	202	3	3.106
9	406	4	3.921
OUT	3514	35	35.604
10	462	4	4.205
11	158	3	2.894
12	411	4	4.141
13	523	5	5.023
14	421	4	4.138
15	296	4	3.923
16	171	3	3.156
17	420	4	4.249
18	444	4	4.209
IN	3306	35	35.938
TOTAL	6820	70	71.542

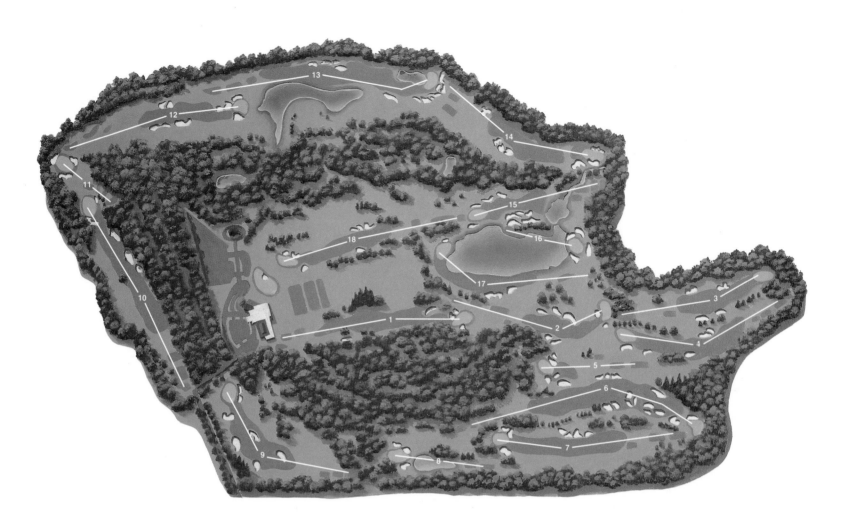

pond. Like many of the new greens, this one is slightly crowned, in the manner of Donald Ross's greens at Pinehurst Number 2. As a result, slightly errant shots will tend to drift off the green, leaving a tricky little shot back to the hole.

The hardest of the new holes may be number 10, a tree-lined 462-yard par four. Even after the required long, straight drive, the pros will be going at its slender green with a middle or long iron.

The elevated tee of the 158-yard 11th presents a postcard view of the Connecticut River, but players are advised to concentrate on the undulating green, where only an accurate tee shot will leave an uncomplicated route to the hole. Number 12 is a par four with out-of-bounds to the left, deep bunkers to the right, and a raised green guarded by three bunkers. In 1993, two players took 9's here. The 13th, like 12, plays along the ridge above the river. It's a reachable

par five, but man-made lakes menace both the tee shot and the approach.

A sizable lake comes into play on three of the four finishing holes, beginning with 15, a reconfigured version of Dye's 12th hole, where the lake runs along the entire left side of the hole. At 296 yards, this is a reachable par four for the Tour's longest hitters, and as the last few groups come down the stretch on Sunday, the pursuers invariably give it a go, hoping for a one-putt eagle.

On the former course, number 16 was a funky par three where the tee shot was played over the heads of players walking off the 17th hole. Now the hole plays back over the lake guarding 15, 171 yards to a green surrounded by a quartet of bunkers.

Holes 17 and 18, two of the strongest points of the Dye course, remain virtually unchanged today. Seventeen, a 420-yard par four, may present the most daunting view of any tee shot on the

Tour, with a mere sliver of a fairway squeezed between sand on the left and the ever-present lake to the right. Twenty-one yards longer than it used to be, the hole now calls for an even more nerve-wrenching second shot over the water to a green that formerly was bulk-headed but now is fronted by a grass slope that allows balls to slide back into the drink.

The final hole—a 444-yard par four played through shouldering ridges to a long, narrow amphitheater green—is the epitome of Commissioner Deane Beman's concept of stadium golf. Late on Sunday afternoon, this hole has been known to accommodate 40,000 spectators, each with a clear view of the action. When the last groups of players approach that green, they say the applause is deafening, the reception unlike any other in the game. It is an ideal place for a player to do something dramatic. Just ask Paul Azinger. In 1989, he chipped in from 45 feet for victory.

COG HILL GOLF & COUNTRY CLUB

4th hole

6th hole

Motorola Western Open, Illinois

Back in 1899, when a group of Chicago area golfers put up a $300 purse and started the Western Open, they didn't realize it, but they were also starting the PGA Tour. Up until then, there was only one professional golf tournament of consequence in America, the U.S. Open. Now, suddenly, the pros had a second major event at which to assemble and compete.

In a short time, other tournaments followed, all over the country. And as the pro circuit grew in venues, the Western Open grew in prestige, each year attracting a strong field at a top-notch course. Up until World War II, winning the Western was viewed as just a step below winning the National Open, and even as late as 1948, when Ben Hogan won the U.S. Open, PGA Championship, and Western Open in a

single year, his achievement was referred to as "golf's Triple Crown."

Today, nearly a century after its inception, the Western Open is no longer a major championship. Yet it remains one of the more prestigious victories on the Tour, a title that has been won by every prominent pro and multiple times by the very best: Hagen (5 victories), Sarazen, Hogan (2), Snead (2), Nelson, Demaret, Guldahl (3), Palmer (2), Nicklaus (2), Casper (4), and Watson (3).

"Western" is probably a misnomer for this tournament, which has been played mostly in and around the upper mid-section of America, while roaming as far west as California, as far south as Texas, and as far east as New York. For the last four decades, however, it has been rooted firmly in the soil of its birthplace, Chicago, including a lengthy run at fear-

somely difficult Butler National Golf Club from 1974 to 1990.

The current home is a place called Dubsdread, the featured layout at the Cog Hill Country Club, a four-course complex in Lemont, Illinois. A rarity among PGA Tour sites, this is a public course, owned and operated by Joe Jemsek, the impresario of daily-fee golf in Chicago. Born in 1913, Jemsek caddied at Cog Hill as a boy, earning 65 cents per loop. He turned pro at age 17 but eschewed the Tour in favor of a return to Cog Hill, where he learned the club management business. In 1939, he bought the nearby St. Andrews Golf Club for $100,000 with a goal of bringing country-club standards to public-course layouts. Jemsek's techniques succeeded, and in 1951 he bought Cog Hill. Today, he owns several facilities in the Chicago area and is revered nation-

13th hole

A major key to my success in the past few years has been my improved accuracy off the tee. Get the drive in play, especially on a course as stern as Cog Hill #4, and you'll make life a lot easier.

A straight drive begins with a square address position, the feet, knees, hips, and shoulders aligned parallel to an imaginary line that points from your ball to your target. I like to control the backswing mostly with my arms, leading the club straight back from the ball and then upward into a full turn of the hips and shoulders. If you keep a light grip and allow yourself to feel the pull of the clubhead on your hands at the top of the swing, then the club should swing on a natural path without any manipulation. And if you can resist the temptation to hit at the ball on the downswing, that same natural path will return the club to the ball with a square face and on a straight line through impact. It is that square face and straight line that produce accurate tee shots. Always maintain your balance, and be sure to finish with your weight on your left side.

Nick Price is the winner of the 1993 Motorola Western Open.

18th hole

wide as a champion of the public golfer. In 1988, when *GOLF Magazine* celebrated the centennial of American golf by selecting 100 of the game's heroes from the first century, Jemsek was one of those honored.

In 1964, when Jemsek added a fourth course at Cog Hill, his goal was to produce a layout playable by all but capable of testing the pros, even for a major championship. Architects Dick Wilson and Joe Lee gave him just that. From the front tees, Dubsdread is challenging but not oppressive, while from the tips it weighs in with a hefty course rating of 75.6. It's a course that could hold a major championship, and don't be surprised if the U.S. Open or PGA Championship is held here some day.

At 7073 yards, Dubsdread is not a long par-72, but it is spread across rolling, heavily wooded terrain and its holes weave among over 100 bunkers, most of them guarding fast bentgrass greens. This is a second-shot course, where the player who misses a lot of greens is an endangered species. In 1991, the first year Cog Hill was used for the tournament, three of its holes ranked among the 20 most difficult on the Tour.

The course is laid out in the shape of a V, with the two nines emanating from and returning to a central point in a pair of narrow, counterclockwise loops. The first difficult test of shotmaking comes at number four, a 416-yard dogleg right with a pair of bunkers at the corner and four more pinching the waist of the narrow hourglass green. Two holes later comes the toughest of the short holes. It plays downhill, but the distance is 213 yards, and a large bunker in front means that 213 is all carry. The expansive green is virtually surrounded by sand, so while slight misses are forgiven, anything more than slight is penalized.

Dubsdread's back nine is laid out across sidehills instead of from ridge to ridge in the manner of the front. As such, it is both more memorable and more difficult, particularly the stretch of holes from 12 to 14, known respectfully as Death Valley.

In 1991 it brought death to Greg Norman. In the final round the Great White Shark came to the 12th tee with a five-stroke lead. He then bogeyed four straight holes to lose the tournament by one to Russ Cochran. In fact, Norman finished second in each of the first three

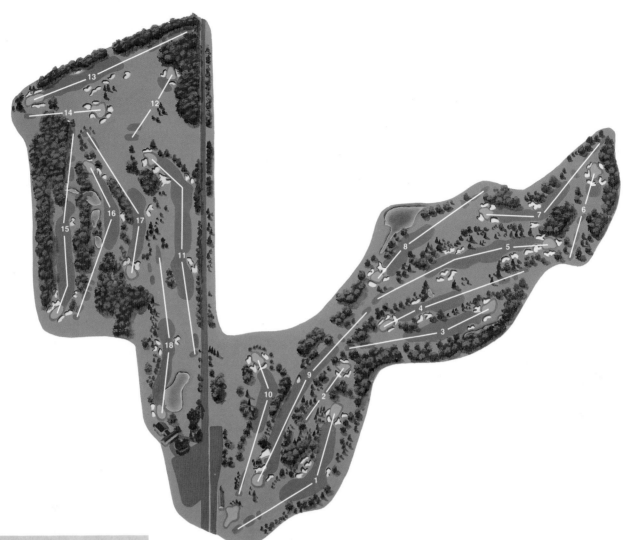

Scorecard

Hole	Yards	Par	PGA Tour Avg. Score
1	420	4	3.993
2	177	3	3.043
3	415	4	3.957
4	416	4	4.232
5	525	5	4.538
6	213	3	3.183
7	410	4	4.137
8	378	4	4.111
9	568	5	4.947
OUT	3522	36	36.141
10	372	4	3.912
11	564	5	4.793
12	209	3	3.134
13	446	4	4.333
14	192	3	3.079
15	519	5	4.750
16	409	4	4.041
17	388	4	4.084
18	452	4	4.360
IN	3551	36	36.486
TOTAL	7073	72	72.627

years the Western was played at Cog Hill.

The distinguishing feature at number 12, a lengthy, downhill par three, is the bunker at the elbow of the L-shaped green. It is the deepest and most difficult to escape on the course.

A straight drive is vital at 13, where a nest of bunkers haunts the left side of the fairway and trees and OB loom on the right. But care is equally important on the approach, since a deep gully crosses in front of the green and bunkers flank the extremely slender putting surface.

Another testing short hole presents itself at 14, where assignment number one is to avoid the six bunkers encircling the green, assignment number two is to find the correct level of this two-tiered target, and assignment number three is

to coax the ball across the slick slope to somewhere in the vicinity of the cup.

In its first year on the Tour, the 452-yard 18th at Dubsdread ranked as the fifth hardest on the Tour, thanks in large part to the sizable pond to the left of the green. More than one player has seen a good round end poorly here.

Proceeds from the Western Open go to a unique sort of charity, the Evans Caddie Scholarship Fund, founded in 1928 by Chick Evans, the first man to win the U.S. Amateur and Open in the same year (1916). Evans won the Western Open at age 20 and took a total of eight Western Amateurs. The first two caddies matriculated in 1930. Today, nearly 1,000 Evans Scholars are enrolled at colleges and universities across the country, with the financial aid totalling more than $5 million a year.

KINGSMILL GOLF CLUB

The Anheuser-Busch Golf Classic is only 25 years old, but the turf on which it is played has roots that go back several centuries.

When developers broke ground for Kingsmill-on-the-James, the brewer's residential resort community near Williamsburg, they uncovered some of Virginia's earliest settlements, including Burwell's Landing, Williamsburg's principal commercial wharf during Revolutionary times. Today, the Tour pros who play in this event pass near the sites of a prehistoric Indian settlement, a Colonial tavern, a Revolutionary breastworks, and the ruins of an eighteenth-century plantation.

But when Pete Dye turned his design talent toward Kingsmill, he built a few memorable features of his own. Ten of the greens are multitiered, and all of them have severe breaks reminiscent of the Scottish courses after which Kingsmill was patterned.

Two stretches of the course are particularly testing, the first of them starting at the eighth hole, a 413-yard par four with a narrow, banked landing area. Hit the tee shot too far right, and the ball will pitch toward out-of-bounds. Hit it too far left, and it will bound into thick rough if you are lucky, or water if you are not. With holes like this, the fate that befell Bill Kratzert in 1986 becomes a bit easier to believe. Kratzert was disqualified in the first round because ... he ran out of golf balls.

In 1981, architect Ed Ault made several changes on the course in response to comments from the Tour players. One of his biggest moves was to add a new tee at the ninth hole. The players now start at a point 125 yards behind the members' tee, making this a par four of 452 yards. Even so, this is a wide-open hole, so the drive is not a difficult one. It is the second shot that is vexing—normally a middle iron to a very shallow green that is guarded by sand and grass bunkers, with the latter variety the more difficult.

The rough on this course can be extremely penal during tournament time, as the mercurial Mac O'Grady will attest.

7th hole

5th hole

One year O'Grady hit a poor drive off the par-five seventh hole, then knocked his second from the left rough into worse trouble in the right rough, where a marshall marked the submerged ball with a small flag. Steaming mad when he arrived at the ball, O'Grady ripped away the flag. Then he marched forward a few yards to get a feel for his next shot. When he returned, he could not find the ball.

The second gauntlet is on the final three holes, a spectacular finish overlooking two miles of the James River. The 16th is thought by many to be the best hole on the course. A rightward dogleg of 427 yards, it normally plays into a headwind, increasing the need for both length and accuracy. The drive must be hit at least 240 yards to get past a long treeline on the right side and thereby leave a clear view of the green. Otherwise, the approach will have to be a slice or fade of nearly 200 yards. A half dozen bunkers and particularly deep rough surround the green.

Number 17 stretches 177 scenic yards along the bank of the James. (During the weekend of the tournament, the right

Bermuda Greens vs. Bentgrass Greens
BY CURTIS STRANGE

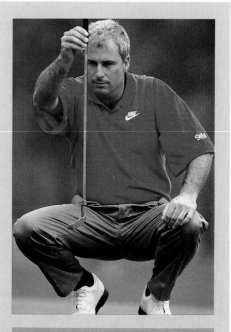

Kingsmill is fortunate to be far enough north to sustain bentgrass greens. Most of the courses north of here also have bent, but most of the courses farther south have bermuda greens. There's a big difference between the two.

Bermuda greens usually are slower and have a stronger grain than bent. Bentgrass is usually faster, smoother, and truer. A good putt on bent will usually go into the hole, a good putt on bermuda had better be perfect.

Bermuda's strong grain influences the break of a putt to the extent that, if it grows against the slope, it can negate up to three inches of break on a 10-foot putt. It also makes downgrain putts extremely fast and upgrain putts extremely slow.

I wouldn't recommend changing your stroke as you move from one type of grass to another unless you're making a permanent switch of residence. But it's worth observing that the players who have grown up on bermuda greens seem to have pop-type, rapping strokes, whereas the guys who have grown up on bentgrass have slower, silkier strokes.

Curtis Strange is the touring professional at the Kingsmill Golf Club.

Scorecard

Hole	Yards	Par	PGA Tour Avg. Score
1	360	4	3.928
2	204	3	3.101
3	538	5	4.695
4	437	4	4.165
5	183	3	3.103
6	365	4	3.842
7	516	5	4.742
8	413	4	4.169
9	452	4	4.109
OUT	3468	36	35.854
10	431	4	4.084
11	396	4	3.986
12	395	4	4.060
13	179	3	2.989
14	383	4	3.953
15	506	5	4.681
16	427	4	4.066
17	177	3	3.051
18	435	4	4.191
IN	3329	35	35.061
TOTAL	6797	71	70.915

17th hole

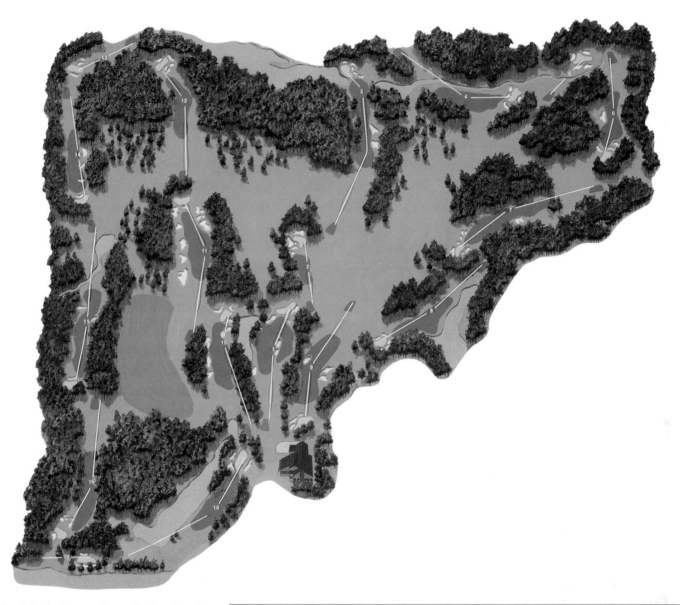

side of the hole is traditionally lined with dozens of nautical spectators as local boat owners moor within a few yards of the action.) The deepest green on the course allows for several pin positions, with all putts breaking softly toward the river. When the wind is up, par is a very welcome score here.

The finishing hole is a 435-yard punisher that was stiffened substantially in 1992 when its green was moved 60 yards left, converting the hole into a slight dogleg. The hole begins with a tee shot that must carry 200 yards over Moody's Pond. The pond also runs along the left side of the fairway, but a post-and-rail fence signals out-of-bounds on the right. A solid drive that avoids these perils will leave a middle iron to a tiered green with bunkers left and right.

18th hole

PLEASANT VALLEY COUNTRY CLUB

9th hole

New England Classic, Massachusetts

Sculpted from a huge apple orchard in the heart of Massachusetts, Pleasant Valley is the fruit of one man's dream. Cosmo E. "Cuz" Mingolla was a contractor who loved golf and believed that New England deserved and would support a major professional tournament. In 1961, he designed a golf course with the help of local pro Don Hoenig. Four years later, Pleasant Valley Country Club hosted the $200,000 Carling World Open, at that time the largest purse on the pro Tour.

The tournament attracted a spectacular field that included Ben Hogan, Arnold Palmer, Jack Nicklaus, and Gary Player among many others. After 70 holes, Palmer was tied with Tony Lema. Then both golfers played overly strong approaches to the 17th hole, but whereas Palmer's finished in a brook, Lema's struck a spectator and caromed to the edge of the green. Champagne Tony pulled ahead and went on to win the final tournament of his brief, brilliant career.

After a hiatus of two years, tournament golf returned to Pleasant Valley, this time as the Kemper Open. Palmer returned as well, charging in the final round from three strokes back to take a four-stroke victory over Bruce Crampton. The winner's check made him the first player to surpass a million dollars in career earnings.

Cuz Mingolla may not have had the big-business vision of PGA Tour Commissioner Deane Beman, but at Pleasant Valley he built the Tour's first true spectator course, two decades before Beman's TPC at Sawgrass. Eight of the 18 holes have their tees or greens within proximity of the clubhouse. In fact, spectators can watch play on the entire first hole without straying from home base, since this is the only course on the Tour designed to begin with a par three.

15th hole

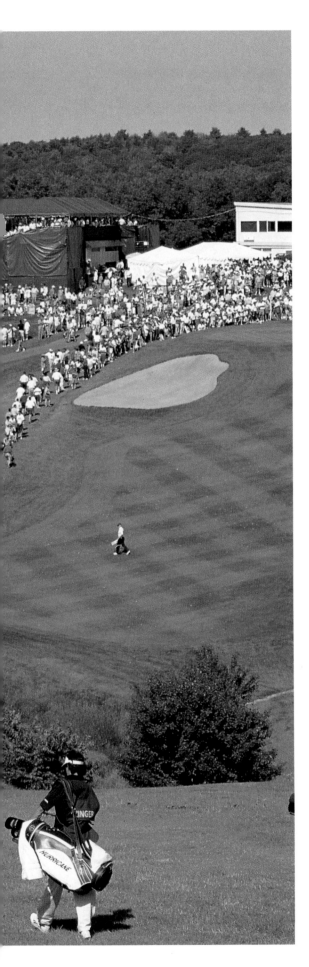

Long Putts

BY BRAD FAXON

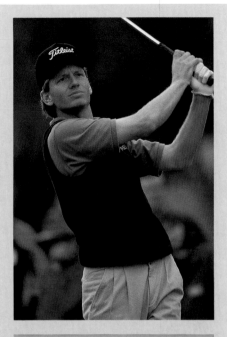

With some of the largest greens on the Tour, Pleasant Valley is a place that can serve up some very long putts. In a sense, these monsters are the most difficult shots in the game. They're small golf swings, requiring enormous care and finesse.

It should go without saying that the most important aspect of a long putt is the distance. If you can hit a 40-footer even with the hole, then you'll rarely have a second putt of longer than three feet. Misjudge the distance, however, and you might miss by five feet or more.

How do you regulate the distance? You'll have the best success if you use a wrist-free putting stroke, rolling the ball by rocking your arms and shoulders so that the putter swings with a pendulum motion. With such a stroke, you regulate the distance of the putt simply by increasing or decreasing the rocking of your shoulders.

This is far more reliable than trying to vary the amount of wrist break or the force of your wrist release into the ball. But there's one caveat: At a certain length of putt, it becomes difficult—if not impossible—to use the stiff-wristed style with fluidity and accuracy. So when the putt gets over, say, 50 feet or so, allow some natural hinging of the wrists

to occur. Watch Phil Mickelson or Ben Crenshaw—they've mastered the long, silky stroke, and Crenshaw claims that on the longest of putts he actually allows movement not only in his wrists but in his knees and head. There's also a softness in the legs—almost a weight shift.

No matter what method you use, the best way to conquer long putts is to develop a sense of touch, and the only way to do that is to give yourself lots of concentrated experience with putts of different lengths. In other words, practice!

Brad Faxon is the winner of the 1992 New England Classic.

17th hole

185

Occasionally, the Pleasant Valley clubhouse actually becomes part of the course, as in 1972, when Larry Ziegler found himself playing his third shot to the ninth green from the floor of the bag room.

The sadists in the gallery tend to cluster near the area overlooking the tenth tee and 11th green, for these two holes are the bruise brothers of the course. Ten plays 467 yards through a fairway bordered by trees, culminating at a green cinched by two large bunkers. Eleven runs back to the clubhouse, parallel to ten, and is even longer—at 480

yards one of the longer par fours in golf—and as if that's not enough, it is dotted with 11 bunkers.

But the star of the course is unquestionably number 17. It is the postcard hole and the killer. Picturesque and pugnacious, this downhill doglegging par four looms over the inward nine, ready to break the back of anyone who dares treat it lightly. The view from the tee is classic New England: densely wooded, rolling terrain, a quiet little pond, and even a weather-worn covered bridge. But this is no peaceful stroll. Ray Floyd calls it "a monster." In 1977, he won here *in spite*

of it. Leading the tournament by five strokes in the final round, Floyd pushed his tee shot into the right-hand woods and made a double-bogey 6 as his playing companion and closest pursuer, Jack Nicklaus birdied, cutting the lead to two. Then Nicklaus nearly chipped in for eagle at the 583-yard closing hole, his birdie leaving him one stroke short.

The thousands of spectators who were seated in the natural amphitheater surrounding the 18th green that day will swear that the Floyd/Nicklaus battle was the ultimate moment in Pleasant Valley history. But a few thousand others will

16th hole

argue that 1991 topped it. That was the year of the Cinderella story, when Bruce Fleisher outdueled Ian Baker-Finch through a seven-hole playoff, finally winning on a no-brainer 50-foot birdie putt at the 18th green. Fleisher, a former U.S. Amateur Champion who had never found success on the Tour, was the last alternate to make the field, and this was his first victory—at age 42.

In 27 years, the tournament has had 27 different winners—and almost as many different names: Carling World Open, Kemper Open, Avco International, Avco Golf Classic,

Massachusetts Classic, USI Classic, Pleasant Valley Classic, American Optical Classic, Pleasant Valley Jimmy Fund Classic, Bank of Boston Classic. Since 1991, however, it has been known as the New England Classic, one of the very few Tour events where there is no corporate sponsor and no plans to secure one. The tournament seems to be thriving under the support of a group of local sponsors, a dedicated force of volunteers headed by Cuz Mingolla's son Ted, and the loyal Massachusetts golf fans who make this consistently one of the largest, best-attended events on the Tour.

Scorecard

Hole	Yards	Par	PGA Tour Avg. Score
1	183	3	3.073
2	426	4	4.076
3	386	4	3.907
4	547	5	4.540
5	606	5	4.818
6	430	4	4.119
7	180	3	3.080
8	455	4	4.116
9	383	4	3.865
OUT	3596	36	35.594
10	467	4	4.218
11	480	4	4.104
12	377	4	3.908
13	394	4	4.066
14	230	3	3.079
15	371	4	4.002
16	200	3	3.129
17	412	4	4.159
18	583	5	4.725
IN	3514	35	35.390
TOTAL	7110	71	70.984

TPC AT SOUTHWIND

ohnny Miller said it best: "Every course should have one hole that makes your rear end pucker." At the TPC at Southwind, there's no question which hole it is—number 14. Two hundred and thirty-one yards—the last half of it across a lake—this demon is not only the hardest hole on the course, it ranks perennially as the most difficult par three on the PGA Tour, taxing the pros for an average of nearly three and a half shots. It is the type of hole—the type of all-or-nothing tee shot—that looms, that preys on a player's mind from the moment he arrives at the course.

Number 14 stands out all the more because this is not a brutish golf course. A par 71 of 7006 yards designed by Ron Pritchard, Southwind is a place where accuracy is more important than length. Eleven water hazards haunt the 18 holes, coming into play on 20 different shots, while only 24 of the 164 acres are main-

tained as fairway. The greens are small too—less than 4,500 square feet on average—making this a course where the wedge can be more powerful than the driver.

By keeping the ball in play, the pros have scored well here. The course record is 61, and in 1989, the first year Southwind hosted the Tour, Hubert Green, a player consultant on the design of the course, showed he knew his way around by posting a 30 on the front nine. Green got to ten under par for the day with two holes to go before bogeying his last two holes for a 63. Had he managed two birdies, he would have tied the all-time Tour record of 59, set by Al Geiberger in this tournament back in 1977, when it was played at the Colonial Country Club.

The course begins with a testing dog-leg par four of 426 yards with water on the left, a trio of bunkers on the right. The sloping green is set on an angle to

15th hole

4th hole

Federal Express St. Jude Classic, Tennessee

9th hole

14th hole

Scorecard

Hole	Yards	Par	PGA Tour Avg. Score
1	426	4	4.051
2	387	4	3.844
3	525	5	4.674
4	194	3	3.046
5	527	5	4.601
6	427	4	3.956
7	458	4	4.139
8	169	3	2.976
9	450	4	4.156
OUT	3563	36	35.443
10	447	4	4.080
11	146	3	3.022
12	375	4	4.079
13	430	4	3.997
14	231	3	3.365
15	385	4	3.934
16	528	5	4.588
17	464	4	4.126
18	437	4	4.170
IN	3443	3	35.361
TOTAL	7006	71	70.804

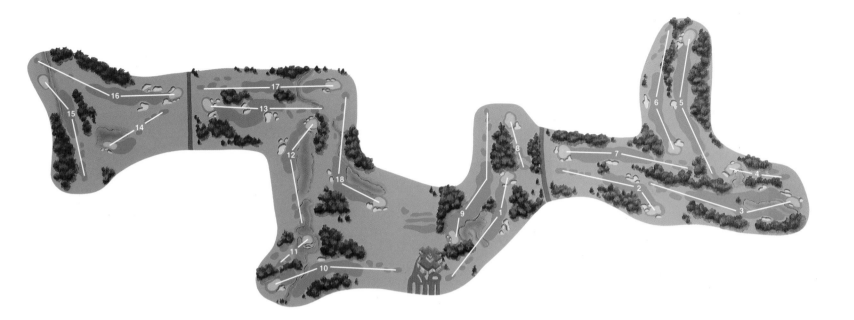

the approach of the fairway and three more bunkers make it difficult to find. Everyone welcomes an opening par here.

The eighth hole measures just 169 yards, but invariably plays longer since it heads into the teeth of the titular south wind. Only one bunker guards the green, but it is the deepest and most testing one on the course.

Water is unrelenting at the 12th, a 375-yard par four that plays longer because it wraps around the edge of a lake. The player who takes the aggressive route across the hazard on his tee shot may either shorten his approach shot or find himself with a stroke-and-distance penalty.

There is no such problem at 17, where the creek crosses the fairway about 40 yards beyond the driving area, but even the pros need middle and long irons to find the dance floor on this 464-yard par four. Back in 1990, Tom Kite fired a 3-iron to within a foot of the hole here in the final round. It gave him a birdie that enabled him to catch John Cook, whom he beat in sudden death. With the victory Kite became the first player in history to win over $6 million.

Putting with a Wedge
BY JAY HAAS

On a course like the TPC at Southwind, where the greens are relatively small, you're apt to encounter some unusual lies around the green. One of the most vexing is the situation where your ball comes to rest on the very edge of the green, its back to the fringe so that you can't swing your putter smoothly to the ball.

A couple of decades ago, Lee Trevino invented a shot for this situation. He took out his sand wedge and, using a putting stroke, he hit the ball with the leading edge of the club. The heavy-headed sand wedge can swing unimpeded through fringe or heavier grass with no catching or twisting.

As you can imagine, putting with a sand wedge feels a good deal different than putting with a putter, so give this shot some practice before you try it in play. Choke well down on the club, using your usual putting grip, and make your normal putting stroke as well. Your goal is to glide the club into the back of the ball, striking it at its equator. The thick flange at the bottom of the sand wedge will help you to do this—when you sole the club on its flange, the leading edge will be raised above the ground, at about the right height to strike the equator of the ball. So practice this a bit—get a feel for the distance you putt a ball with a sand wedge—and before long you'll develop good touch. Then, the next time you're up against the fringe, go ahead and impress your friends.

Jay Haas won the 1992 Federal Express St. Jude Classic.

WARWICK HILLS GOLF & COUNTRY CLUB

15th hole

Buick Open, Michigan

When the Buick Open came on the Tour in 1958, it offered the richest purse in golf— $52,000—and that was the total, not the winner's share. Billy Casper won the tournament on his 27th birthday, beating Arnold Palmer on the final hole. A year later, Art Wall added the Buick title to the Masters jacket he'd collected that spring. Long-hitting Mike Souchak took the 1960 title, and in 1961 another Masters champion, Jack Burke, Jr., was the victor. In those years, the money was good and so were the fields.

In 1963, the Buick drew an undesirable date, a week before the U.S. Open, and golf's big three—Palmer, Nicklaus, and Player—all skipped the tournament to get in some extra on-site practice at Boston's Brookline Country Club. But Julius Boros came, won, and then went on to win the Open, beating Palmer in an 18-hole play-off. A year later the Buick preceded the British Open. Again, many stars stayed away, but one exception was Tony Lema, who thrilled the fans by birdieing six holes in a row during the second round en route to victory. After toasting his victory with champagne, he flew to Scotland where, without a single practice round on the inscrutable Old Course at St. Andrews, he won the British Open.

Lema was in fact the darling of the early Buicks, winning again in 1965. But when Champagne Tony died in a plane crash in 1966, the tournament began to sag, and by 1970 it was off the Tour schedule. In 1972, however, locals resuscitated it as an event on the second tour, a sort of jayvee circuit equivalent to today's Nike Tour. Meanwhile, architect Joe Lee was brought in to soften what was the longest course on the Tour (7280 yards).

Lee took 260 yards off the back markers, replacing brute length with soft con-

8th hole

Breaking Putts
BY DAN FORSMAN

Sometimes I think Warwick Hills was named for the undulations in the greens. This is a course where you rarely see a perfectly level putt, and in every round you're sure to encounter at least one big breaker.

If you play on a course with sharply contoured greens, here are a couple of tricks. Number one, pay attention to the roll of your playing companions' putts. This will usually give you a key to the speed and roll of your own putt. Second, take a good look at the putt—try to view it from the back, from the hole to the ball, and from one side (just don't delay play). Once you have a read, trust it—more often than not, that initial read is the right one.

Next, visualize the ideal putt. Try to see your ball running along a path to the hole. Then pick out a spot on your intended line, and focus both your mind and your putterface on rolling the ball to that spot. Trust your read, trust your stroke, and you'll make your share of breaking putts.

Dan Forsman won the 1992 Buick Open.

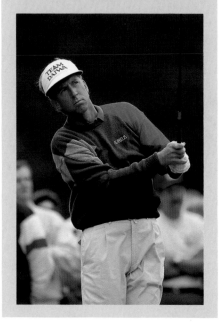

17th hole

18th hole

tours and curves on the fairways and undulations on the greens. And although he restored about half of that distance in the early 1990s, to keep pace with today's longer hitters, Warwick Hills remains a course where shotmaking and short-game skill are every bit as important as power.

After a good birdie opportunity at the first hole, the challenge begins at number two, a 431-yard par four that plays through two rows of trees plus out-of-bounds on the left. The fairway slopes slightly downward, and the second shot calls for a middle iron into a green guarded by a large bunker.

Long hitters will have to be careful off the tee of the fifth, where a slightly active right hand will produce a hook

out-of-bounds or into the lake on the left side of the landing area. Still, it is best to favor the left side of this mild dogleg right, where the right-hand greenside bunker, dotted with grassy mounds, is nearly as large as the green.

At the par-three eighth, Lee created a two-tiered green that is 43 yards from front to back, and with two bunkers to the left and one to the right, the 199-yard tee shot had best be struck with precision.

Lots of birdies are made at the start of the back nine, but few players do what Ken Green did in the final round of the 1985 Buick. At the 11th hole he chipped in for a birdie, then made three more at 12, 13, and 14, in the process passing leader Wayne Grady. Green's fast finish gave him a 67—268 (20 under par) and

the first Tour victory of his career.

Since that time, the 13th hole has been lengthened from 490 to 548 yards, giving the powerhitters a bit more pause as they contemplate their second shots over a pond to the right-front of the green.

In any case, the pros had best collect their birdies by the time they leave the 14th green, because the final four holes at Warwick constitute as strong a finish as there is on the Tour.

Number 15, a par four of 457 yards, is a hole that only an architect's mother could love. With trees lining both sides and out-of-bounds on the left, it de-mands a hard, straight drive and then a hard, straight long-iron shot into a green whose entrance is tightened by two vio-

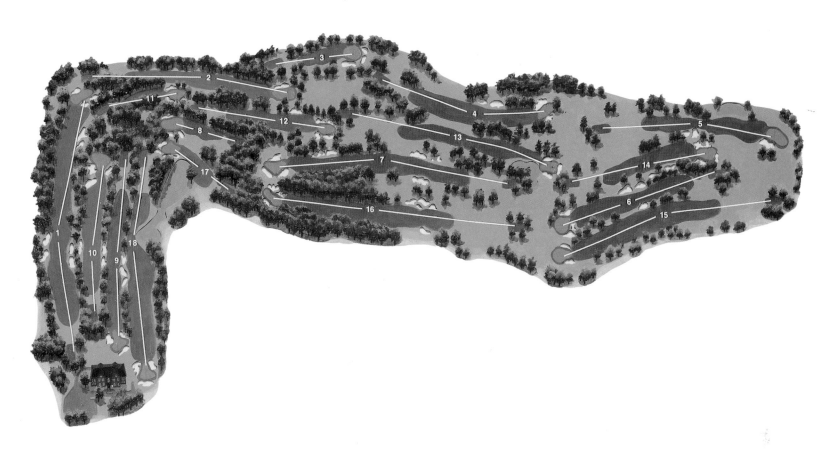

lin-shaped bunkers. Robert Wrenn bogeyed this hole in the final round in 1987. Had his score been a par, he would have finished the tournament at 27 under par, which would have tied the all-time PGA Tour record. A 63 in round two had spurred him to his seven-stroke victory, the largest margin in the history of the tournament.

Sixteen is a three-shot par five even for the pros. Again, accuracy is the number-one objective, with bunkers on both sides of the tee-shot landing area. The second must thread through a tight tunnel of trees to leave an unobstructed pitch to the angled, two-tiered green. In the Buick, pars and bogeys come with equal frequency on this hole.

In 1962, Jerry Barber scored the first televised hole-in-one on Warwick's 17th. Back then it played 222 yards; today it is only 197, but four bunkers gape at the approaching tee shots and the green is the most fiercely sloped on the course. Lee also reworked this green so that it sits in a natural amphitheater, one of the first examples of stadium golf.

When Jack Nicklaus played in his first Buick Open as an amateur, he looked at

the 18th and said, "Now this is a good finishing hole. It would be so easy to tighten up and sail one out-of-bounds on the left. I must remember to keep the tee shot way right." A few years later, Jack came to that hole needing a birdie to have a chance of tying Tony Lema and forcing a playoff. In one of the rare instances in which he did not rise to the occasion, Nicklaus unloaded a hook so wide and deep that it was still rising as it passed over the OB fence.

The hole psyched out Nicklaus, and it has conquered scores of lesser players in the past four decades. A par four of 435 yards, it plays into the teeth of the prevailing wind to the shallowest target on the course. Indeed, anyone who can birdie this monster deserves to win something.

And yet this hole, and the golf course in general, have won the praise of the pros. Players such as Ben Crenshaw, Tom Kite, and Lanny Wadkins count Warwick among their favorite courses on the Tour and have proved their loyalty with consistent attendance at the Buick Open.

Scorecard

Hole	Yards	Par	PGA Tour Avg. Score
1	567	5	4.866
2	431	4	4.118
3	187	3	3.039
4	401	4	4.028
5	437	4	4.073
6	421	4	4.019
7	584	5	4.816
8	199	3	3.060
9	413	4	4.058
OUT	3640	36	36.077
10	401	4	3.998
11	190	3	3.033
12	335	4	3.806
13	548	5	4.794
14	322	4	3.769
15	457	4	4.246
16	580	5	4.784
17	197	3	3.022
18	435	4	4.204
IN	3465	36	35.656
TOTAL	7105	72	71.733

CASTLE PINES GOLF CLUB

t's the only tournament on the Tour where the average winning score is Plus 13. It's the only tournament where playoffs occur on Friday and Saturday. It's the only tournament where the course weighs in at over 7,500 yards and one hole measures 644 yards. And it's the only tournament where birdies don't cancel bogeys and eagles are like gold. Since its inception, The International has been something different.

It was the brainchild of businessman Jack Vickers, whose long-held dream was to create his own golf course for a major tournament. In the late 1970s Vickers acquired a 5,000-acre tract near Castle Rock, Colorado, about half an hour and 1,000 feet above Denver. Immediately, Vickers called in Jack Nicklaus as his architect. Together they walked the land several times, then buzzed it several times more in a helicopter. In 1979 Nicklaus and his crew began construction, and in 1981 Castle Pines opened to strongly favorable reviews.

With the course in place, Vickers turned his attention to the matter of the golf tournament. With 40 events already cramming the calendar, the PGA Tour was not looking for another tournament. But Vickers had that problem solved—his would not be just another tournament. First, The International would be an invitational that would live up to its name, with a field of pros from all over the world. Second—and the true "hook" for this event—was Vickers's proposed format, a 72-hole stroke-play event based upon a variation of the Stableford System, with points awarded in relation to par: Double bogey or worse is –3 points, bogey is –1, par 0, birdie 2, eagle 5, and double-eagle 8.

For the first eight years of the tournament, each new round was a tournament in itself—the previous day's points were not carried over and everyone began again from scratch. In 1993, however, the format was changed, and now points are accumulated throughout the four days. After round two the 144-man field is cut in half, and

after the third round a second cut pares the field to 24 players who go at it on Sunday. The player with the most Stableford points at the end of the week wins.

The Stableford has long been a popular format for club golf events, but until Vickers, no one had suggested it for the PGA Tour. A gimmick? Perhaps, but it came at a time when the Tour was looking for new and different formats to help sustain interest in the professional side of the game. With events such as the Skins Game and the Legends of Golf attracting attention, Vickers's proposal seemed cogent. Commissioner Beman decided it was good for golf—especially since Vickers guaranteed TV sponsorship and offered the players a $1-million-dollar purse. So the Tour found a spot for The International.

Nicklaus predicted the new format would breed aggressive golf. "In playing for points rather than protecting a total score, a player is forced to attack the course more than usual," he said, and invariably the action at Castle Pines bears that out.

At 7559 yards this is by far the biggest battlefield on the Tour, and it begins with the Tour's longest hole, a 644-yard par five. If that sounds like an unlikely place to expect a birdie, keep in mind that the hole plays downhill all the way and that the thin Colorado air means a 10 to 15 percent increase in hitting distance. A player such as John Daly, Fred Couples, or Greg Norman can reach this green with an iron.

Wind is a factor at the linkslike third and fourth holes, the only part of the course that is not lined with trees. Into a stiff wind, the teé shot at the 205-yard fourth is one of the most difficult assignments of the day, and there is no letup at the fifth, a 477-yard par four that plays uphill with bunkers in both the drive area and the approach.

9th hole

The International, Colorado

5th hole

12th hole

Downhill Lies

BY JACK NICKLAUS

If I could design my ideal golf course, all of the holes would play downhill, so that on each tee the golfer could see everything that he was about to face. At Castle Pines, each nine begins with a steeply downhill hole, and the second shots on those holes can be demanding ones.

When playing downhill from the fairway, the first key is to tilt yourself so that you're perpendicular to the slope. In effect, give yourself a flat lie. To prevent falling forward, put most of your weight on your back foot at address and keep it there throughout the swing. To help maintain balance, you should make this an arm-and-wrist swing and minimize your body turn. On the downswing, try to make your clubhead "chase" out after the ball through impact.

Off a downhill lie, the ball will tend to fly lower and thus travel farther than normal, so club appropriately. And if the slope is so severe that you are bound to lose balance, allow for a pushed shot by aiming a few yards left of your target.

Jack Nicklaus is the designer of the Castle Pines course.

One of Nicklaus's architectural preferences is for downhill holes, and the tenth at Castle Pines may be his best example. This par four of 485 yards seems to play almost as many yards downhill. A lush, tumbling carpet of fairway through thick stands of pine and oak, it is reminiscent of and every bit as beautiful as the tenth hole at Augusta National. The major difference is that this hole is even more difficult. Although the fairway is amply wide, the second shot of 200 yards or more must be played

from a downhill and/or sidehill lie to an angled green that is guarded by a large pond. Four is an excellent score here.

Four is also a good score at the 12th, a tight 440-yarder where the approach is to a narrow green with a bunker on the right and a rocky stream on the left.

If Nicklaus had a weak moment in designing this course, it was at the par-three 16th, where he plotted a "gathering bunker" at the left-front of the green. Gathering bunkers are throwbacks to the old pot bunkers of Scotland. They gobble

up anything that bounces or rolls near their lips. The three such bunkers at Castle Pines have no sand but do have steep-faced banks. When the pin on this lengthy par three is at the brink of such a bank, at the top of the gathering bunker, there is virtually no way to get a ball close to the hole. Even some of Castle Pines's most loyal members concede that this gambit is a bit strained.

But if a four is wrought at 16, another four may be gotten easily at the 17th, at 492 yards the shortest par five on the

18th hole

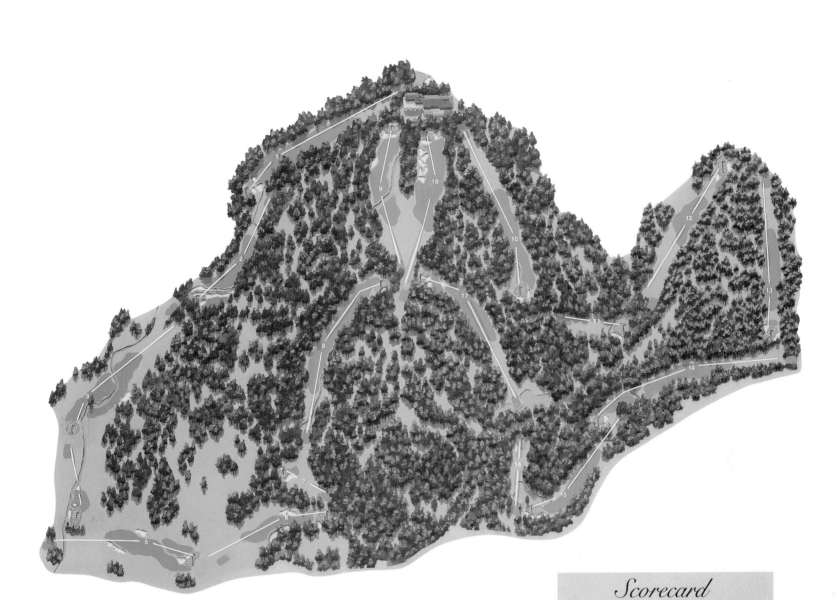

course. It is here that the potential of The International's scoring system becomes most dramatic. John Cook clinched his victory in 1987 when on Sunday he hit a 4-iron to 12 feet and sank the putt for an eagle and five points, and Jim Gallagher has the distinction of scoring 8 points on this hole with the double-eagle he recorded in 1990.

Number 18 is marked by another Nicklaus signature, the double fairway. Long hitters usually will take the high road to the right, a tee shot over a bunker-filled hill which, once carried, produces a long, bounding draw to within short-iron distance of the hole. Shorter hitters may opt for the lower fairway, actually a more direct route, where an accurate drive leaves a level lie and an approach over bunkers to the amphitheater green.

Castle Pines is an extremely private club and as such it gets less play than any other venue on the Tour—roughly 14,000 rounds a year, or about 40 players per day. Consequently, the course is usually in pristine condition, with the greens rolling at a smooth, fast 10 on the Stimpmeter even for member play.

As at the Augusta National Golf Club, home of The Masters, membership is by invitation only, and it has been so from the beginning. Founder Vickers invited 12 of his friends to join as partners in his venture—at a cost of $500,000 each. Then each of those 12 disciples, as they are known, was asked to invite a few friends of his own. And so on until the membership of grand old men reached the planned number of 350.

Scorecard

Hole	Yards	Par
1	644	5
2	408	4
3	462	4
4	205	3
5	477	4
6	417	4
7	185	3
8	535	5
9	458	4
OUT	3791	36
10	485	4
11	197	3
12	440	4
13	439	4
14	623	5
15	403	4
16	209	3
17	492	5
18	480	4
IN	3768	36
TOTAL	7559	72

FIRESTONE COUNTRY CLUB

When Akron's Harvey S. Firestone opened his course in 1929, professional golf was the furthest thing from his mind. He had built the course purely as a recreational facility for the employees of his Firestone Tire and Rubber Company. Still, in 1954 it was strong enough to host the first Rubber City Open, in which Tommy Bolt shot a torrid 265—23 under par—and took home the first prize of $2,400.

The course lasted five more years, but when Firestone was nominated to host the 1960 PGA Championship, Robert Trent Jones, Sr., was called in to stiffen the challenge. The result was major surgery; he built 50 new bunkers, added two ponds, enlarged the greens to twice their original size, and stretched the rubber man's course to a backbreaking 7,173 yards—while reducing the par from 72 to 70.

That PGA was won by Jay Hebert on a score of 281—one over par—and 14 strokes higher than Tom Neiporte's victory on the "same" course a year earlier. The success of that tournament spurred the birth of the American Golf Classic, which replaced the Rubber City at Firestone and ran for a decade and a half.

Two years later, a Chicago entrepreneur named Walter Schwimmer hatched the idea of bringing together the winners of the four major championships—The Masters, U.S. Open, British Open, and PGA—in a late-season mini-event over 36 holes. In 1962, the World Series of Golf was born, with a field of just three players—Arnold Palmer (who had won both The Masters and British Open), Jack Nicklaus, and Gary Player. With golf's Big Three in its first staging, the World Series got off to a flying start.

Nicklaus won the $50,000 first prize, and the tournament became a fixture on the PGA Tour. It has since expanded to include a large field of both American and international players—anyone who has won a qualifying tournament during the previous 12 months.

During the '60s and '70s, Firestone hosted 14 American Golf Classics, three PGA Championships, eight CBS Golf Classics, and the World Series every year.

10th hole

3rd hole

11th hole

Since most of those events were televised, Firestone quickly became the most recognizable golf course in America.

Critics say the course is charmless, monotonous. Virtually all of its fairways run straight and parallel to one another, and few of the par threes and fours call for an approach with anything shorter than a long iron. Subtlety is not the long suit at Firestone. However, the course has the near-unanimous admiration of the Tour players, who see it as a supremely honest, straightforward examination of their skills.

"It's a great test of golf. Every shot is demanding," says Nicklaus, whose record on the course is incredible even by his herculean standards. Jack has won seven tournaments at Firestone—five World Series, one American Golf Classic, and the 1975 PGA. It's no wonder that, when the club decided to fine-tune the course in 1986, the architect they brought in was Jack, who reworked several of the greens, added a few bunkers, and introduced a couple of greenside mounds for improved spectator viewing.

The front nine features a string of holes that perhaps only Nicklaus could love. After a comparatively benign (399-yard) opening hole and a bona fide birdie opportunity at the second (a par five of only 497 yards), Firestone bares its teeth with a stretch that includes five par fours averaging 455 yards and two "short holes" of 210 and 219 yards. The biggest bruiser of this stretch comes at the end—number nine is a par four that winds 470 yards back toward the clubhouse, culminating at a green ringed by bunkers. The length of this par-35 front nine is 3614 yards, a fact that adds wonder to the accomplishment of José Maria Olazabal. The young Spaniard opened the 1990 tournament with five straight 3's—birdie, eagle, birdie, birdie, par—and went on to shoot a course-record 61. After that, he strung together three straight 67's, setting tournament records at the 36- and 54-hole points and winning the tournament by a phenomenal 12 strokes with a score of 262—18 under par and five strokes lower than the previous best. No one had ever humbled the post-Jonesian Firestone to such an extent.

The inward nine starts similarly to the front, with two relatively manageable holes. Ten is the tougher of the two, calling for a pin-straight drive through a chute of trees. The greens at both ten and 11 are closely bunkered and nightmarishly difficult to hold. Such is also the case at the par-three 12th, where an elevated green is guarded in front, left, and right by sand. Accuracy is doubly important here because the hole normally plays into the face of the wind.

Number 13 is thought by many to be the finest hole on the course, a 457-yard dogleg to the right. The tee shot landing area is guarded by a bunker on the left and a large, encroaching tree on the right, encouraging the golfer to play a fade between the two and lengthening a long hole still further. Four bunkers ring the green, which slopes hard from back to front. A shot that strays into the heavy rough beyond the green virtually guarantees bogey or worse.

Par is a good score at the 221-yard 15th, where the narrow green is bunkered closely on both sides. The pros play anything from a 4-iron to a 3-wood. Gary Player would have been pleased to take par here on Monday morning in 1974, for it was on this hole that Lee Trevino sank a three-foot putt for par to beat Player in the longest playoff in the history of the Series. The two had tied with one-under-par 139's that year, then had gone back to the 14th for sudden death. But they then had tied five holes in a row. With darkness closing in, tournament director Jack Tuthill called an overnight moratorium. The next morning both teed off again on 14 and both made birdies. Then Trevino's 1-iron found the green at 15 while Player's 2-iron hit sand. Gary two-putted for bogey, and Lee sank a three-footer to win.

The 625-yard 16th hole is one of the most famous and feared in golf. For decades it has elicited the best and worst play. It was here in 1960 that Arnold Palmer saw the end of his bid to become the first player to win the American Slam. Palmer had won The Masters and the U.S. Open, and had finished second in the British Open. In the PGA at Firestone, he was in strong contention when he came to the 16th tee in the third round. But he hit a succession of less than desirable shots and finally wrote an 8 on his card. Later, he dubbed the hole "The Monster" and included it in a book listing his all-time favorite 18 holes in golf. "It has everything mean and nasty," Palmer wrote. "Bunkers, ditches, trees, water—you name it— everything that's troublesome, plus a green that is so hard the ball winces when it lands."

The hole plays downwind and sharply downhill, with the fairway banked hard from right to left. A well-hit, drawing drive can run a long way. Still, 625 yards is 625 yards; this is not a green that is

The Lob Shot
BY CRAIG STADLER

On a course as long as Firestone, even we Tour players miss a lot of greens. As a result, we often find ourselves wedging the ball from the rough to a tight pin placement. For such a situation, there is only one shot: the lob.

In one sense, this is the easiest shot in the game, because it calls for the slowest, easiest swing. The idea is to slip the face of your wedge underneath the ball to pop it lazily upward so that it drops softly on the green with virtually no roll.

The proper technique is not unlike that for a bunker shot. You begin with an open stance and an open-faced sand wedge, or even better, a lofted (60-degree) wedge. The ball should be positioned just in back of your left heel—a bit farther forward than where you'd position it for a bunker shot—because you don't want to hit down too vertically on this ball.

But the main key remains a slowly paced swing, particularly if you have a shot of less than 20 feet or so. You should almost feel as if the clubface is dropping down to the ball from the force of gravity. Don't quit on the shot—be sure you finish your swing—but be sure that swing is the softest one you can make.

Craig Stadler is a two-time winner (1982, 1992) of the NEC World Series of Golf.

12th hole

16th hole

18th hole

Scorecard

Hole	Yards	Par	PGA Tour Avg. Score
1	399	4	4.086
2	497	5	4.572
3	442	4	4.145
4	458	4	4.387
5	210	3	3.125
6	469	4	4.241
7	219	3	3.106
8	450	4	4.068
9	470	4	4.278
OUT	3614	35	36.008
10	410	4	4.109
11	370	4	3.952
12	178	3	3.047
13	457	4	4.209
14	418	4	4.135
15	221	3	3.141
16	625	5	5.040
17	392	4	4.091
18	464	4	4.201
IN	3535	35	35.925
TOTAL	7149	70	71.933

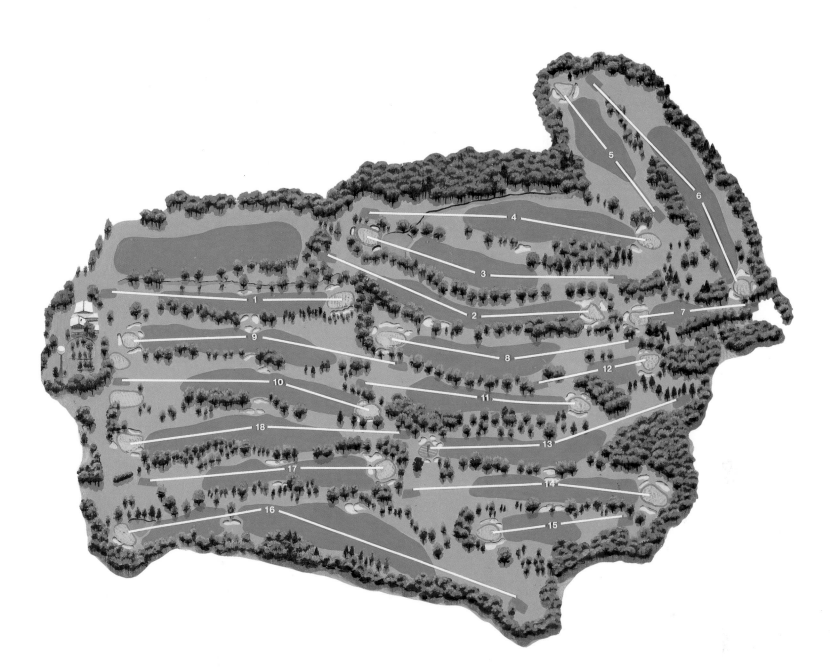

reachable in two, at least not by mere mortals. Palmer and a few others have done it, but with a 50-yard pond smack in front of the green, a gambling 3-wood shot of 250 yards is generally not advised. Most players will cozy long irons to a position about 100 yards or so short of the green, then hit a fast-spinning wedge shot at the pin.

In the 1975 PGA Championship Jack Nicklaus hit his tee shot at 16 into trees on the left, took a penalty drop, and then hit his third shot into trees on the right; from there he played a gargantuan 8-iron over the tops of the trees and over the water to 20 feet from the pin. He sank the putt for a par and went on to win.

Somewhat less heroic—but no less inventive—was the par made by Lon Hinkle in the final round of the 1979 World Series. After pushing his third shot into trees on the right, Hinkle was stymied. The trees blocked a high shot, the water prevented a low shot—at least that was the way it looked. But Hinkle closed the face of his iron, took the club back low, and punched the ball straight at the water. It skipped once, twice, three times, and bumped up the bank and onto the green. He made his par and went on to win the tournament.

The 17th hole is short by Firestone standards—392 yards—but the driving area is pinched tight by four bunkers, so most players lead with an iron, then play

a blind second shot over a pot bunker to the elevated green. A large hogback runs across this green, making it the site of frequent three-putts.

Eighteen is a superb finishing hole—464 tree-lined yards, slightly downhill, and turned softly from right to left. The better side of the fairway for the approach is the right, but two bunkers there caution against too-aggressive a drive. The once-enormous green was made smaller by Nicklaus and is surrounded by bunkers and nestled in a natural amphitheater. Hundred-foot putts are not uncommon here, and neither are three-putt bogeys. Like the course itself, 18 is long, tough, and—like the rest of Firestone—pure golf from start to finish.

BROWN DEER PARK CLUB

The newest tournament site on the PGA Tour is a place with the unlikely name Brown Deer Park. In 1994 the Milwaukee Open moved here after a 21-year run at Tuckaway Country Club. But this is hardly a new layout. Designed in 1926 by George Hansen, a Milwaukee greenkeeper and low-handicap golfer, it is a golf course with a past.

For half a century, Brown Deer ranked consistently among the best public courses in America, and in 1951 it earned the ultimate accolade for a daily-fee layout when it hosted the U.S. Amateur Public Links Championship. Then two years of horrendous weather, combined with lackadaisical maintenance by the County of Milwaukee, put the course in such poor condition it was closed for two years. But in the early

'90s, spurred by local sportscaster and golf fanatic Lloyd Pettit, the County changed its attitude and began to invest in Brown Deer, installing a new drainage system and commissioning a redesign under the supervision of local boy Andy North.

North, a native of Madison, has been the unofficial ambassador for the Greater Milwaukee Open, and it was partly through his involvement that the Tour became interested in Brown Deer.

The most distinguishing characteristic of this course is its rough—high, dense, gnarly grass usually reserved for the U.S. Open (it may be more than a coincidence that North is a two-time Open champion). And those who find that rough likely will also find tree trouble. The course is lined with hundreds of mature oaks, maples, and black wal-

nuts—ideal habitat for brown deer but somewhat less welcoming to errant golfers.

The pros do not have to contend with terrain as hilly as they faced at Tuckaway, but Brown Deer does serve up its share of uneven lies, and these can combine with a brisk wind off nearby Lake Michigan to make approach shots a challenge. The greens, many of which were redesigned for the Tour, feature subtle drifts rather than severe breaks, and as such can be difficult to decipher. It's not uncommon to face an eight-foot putt, knowing it breaks two or three inches, but not sure which way.

Doglegs—long, severe doglegs—are the central challenge at Brown Deer, and the first of them comes at hole number four, a 486-yard par four that the members play as a par five. The key to this

4th hole

Greater Milwaukee Open, Wisconsin

11th hole

13th hole

Rough Going

BY MARK BROOKS

Thick rough is the most penal feature of Brown Deer Park, and those who stray off these fairways can sometimes feel as if they're playing in the U.S. Open.

When your ball settles into lush, dense rough your first concern should be damage control. Don't be a hero—select the club that you know will get you back into play, even if that club is a sand wedge.

Whatever club you choose, play the ball back in your stance, and stand a bit closer to the ball than you would for a shot from the fairway. These two adjustments will set you up for the downward attack on the ball that will help you extricate it.

In the thickest of rough, go ahead and give it your hardest swing. Just make two further adjustments at address: aim a bit to the right of your target and take a firm hold on the club, particularly in your left hand. Why? Because thick grass tends to turn the club in your hand, and when that happens you'll pull the ball to the left.

Mark Brooks won the 1991 Greater Milwaukee Open.

hole is a huge oak tree that looms in the right rough of the left-to-right hole, about 120 yards short of the green, effectively blocking anything but a very large drive or one directed well left, to give the tree a sufficiently wide berth (while lengthening an already long second shot).

Four holes later another big tree-lined dogleg growls, this one bending counter-clockwise for 426 yards. Once again a drive of at least 250 yards is needed to leave a clear view of the well-bunkered green. And at number ten the assignment is much the same. The entire right side of this hole is blocked by 80-foot-high trees, with the result that the tee shot must travel nearly 280 yards or the second shot must be a massive power fade.

The stretch run is marked by two par fives which must be played shot by shot and not simply brutalized with power. At

Scorecard

Hole	Yards	Par
1	443	4
2	421	4
3	170	3
4	486	4
5	170	3
6	550	5
7	215	3
8	426	4
9	355	4
OUT	3236	34
10	455	4
11	198	3
12	371	4
13	413	4
14	195	3
15	527	5
16	371	4
17	370	4
18	565	5
IN	3465	36
TOTAL	6701	70

15th hole

number 15, a creek crosses at about the 280-yard mark, leaving even a second shot of nearly 250 yards, and at the closing hole the creek crosses at about 240 yards off the tee, calling for a decision from the Tour players. If they try to clear the water, they'll have a chance of reaching the green. If they lay up, then the green will be 350 yards away. Now, a 240-yard carry is within the ability of 90 percent of the Tour, but what complicates this finishing tee shot is the prevailing westerly wind. In the late afternoon, when a gust whips up off Lake Michigan, it blows smack into the face of the players on this hole. So on Sunday, with the tournament on the line, the last few groups must summon either strength or restraint.

18th hole

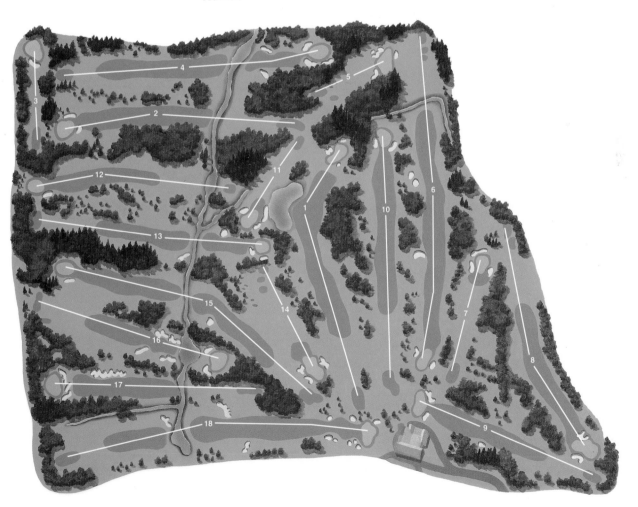

GLEN ABBEY GOLF CLUB

It is the first major course designed completely by Jack Nicklaus, and site of the only major event he has never won. Glen Abbey is a bear of a place to play.

Home of the Canadian Open continuously since 1981, and headquarters of the Royal Canadian Golf Association, this big, exhilarating course set on a lush estate in Oakville, Ontario, has been called Nicklaus's finest, and even the Golden Bear admits that at Glen Abbey he corrected several of the mistakes he made (in collaboration with architect Desmond Muirhead) at his pride and joy, Muirfield Village.

What's more, this is a course that is getting better with age. Although the Canadian is the world's fourth-oldest tournament, Glen Abbey is barely two decades old, and its challenge has increased in recent years as thousands of small trees planted in 1975 have matured and thickened.

Nowhere is this more true than at the fourth hole, a par four of 417 yards that literally grows tougher each year. Trees down the right of this slight dogleg encourage a drive to the left side of the fairway where three bunkers await. The second shot here had better be just as sharp. Miss the terraced putting green, backed by mounds, and the comeback chip will require the imagination of Steven Spielberg.

Number seven is a par three that reads 197 yards on the card but can be stretched or compressed markedly by adjusting the tee blocks. Wind conditions also have a big effect on the playing distance of this hole. The last 30 yards play over water, and the light-bulb-shaped green is surrounded by four big bunkers. It was here that Craig Stadler had one of his most embarrassing moments. In the middle of a less than stellar round, Stadler knocked his ball into the edge of the water hazard. Without much preparation he waded in and whacked it, losing his balance just after impact. The ball came out, but the Walrus went in, hitting the lake with a sizable splash.

Nicklaus says the eighth hole may be his favorite on the course, a par four of 433 yards that doglegs slightly right to a green that is raised in the center. Two bunkers down the right side of the land-

9th hole

11th hole

Canadian Open, Ontario

3rd hole

12th hole

ing area discourage boldness on the drive, and a grass bunker leads to a cluster of sand bunkers near the green.

The ninth through 12th holes represent one of the toughest stretches in competitive golf. More than once, all four of them have ranked among the 100 toughest holes on the Tour. Nine, ten, and 11 are par fours averaging 451 yards in length, the longest being number nine, a 458-yarder that can seem like 548 yards when it plays into an Alberta clipper.

From day one of his career as an architect, Jack Nicklaus has believed that the best golf hole is one that plays downhill, where the golfer can see clearly from the tee everything that confronts him. Eleven is just such a hole, although the view may be a mixed blessing. The tee sits 120 feet above the fairway. Two-thirds down the fairway a pair of bunkers wait, and a bit beyond them Sixteen Mile Creek crosses in front of the green, which is surrounded by pot bunkers. Not a particularly encouraging sight.

The 11th hole is also the start of a five-hole stretch known as The Hole, an area of the course that rambles through a 100-foot deep gorge where water comes constantly into play.

At the par-three 12th, swirling winds make club selection a constant challenge. The shot must carry water and avert sand in both the front and back.

Par for the incoming nine at Glen Abbey is 37, owing to the fact that three of the last six holes are par fives—reachable par fives. The 13th is the longest of them at 529 yards, and the second shot must carry the creek as well as a front bunker, then grab tight on the fast, narrow green before rolling down into a deep, grassy swale toward the back left. Birdies here are frequent, but so are double-bogeys.

Birdies are infrequent at the par-four 14th, traditionally the hardest hole on the back nine. It is a moderate dogleg right that invites gambling players to take a big bite off its water-guarded corner. A large hollow cuts across the right-middle of the green, making every pin position a tough one. For the pros, par on 14 is about 4.3.

Driving for Power
BY GREG NORMAN

One of the reasons I love the Glen Abbey course is that it suits my game. I'm a long hitter, and on a good day I can save a few strokes by hitting the par fives in two.

To me, the essence of power lies in the basics of grip, stance, and posture. In my grip the palms are parallel and face the target. I stand tall to the ball with my chin up, my back straight, and my knees slightly flexed.

A powerful swing begins with a take-away in which everything moves together—hands, arms, and shoulders start back from the ball in one piece. Next is the turn—a full body turn—where the hips and shoulders rotate around a firmly planted right leg. The resistance built up in that leg triggers an uncoiling into the forwardswing.

Just before my hands and club reach the top of the swing I drive my right knee toward the left. This shifts my lower body laterally and allows my hips to clear the way so that my arms and hands can whip through the ball.

There's nothing fancy to this swing, just sound fundamentals. But if you practice and learn to apply these fundamentals, you'll always hit the ball squarely and with good clubhead speed, and that's the only way to create power.

Greg Norman is a two-time Canadian Open champion (1984 and 1992).

The 15th, a par three of 141 yards, is the site of an expensive blunder by Andy Bean. In the third round of the 1983 Canadian Open, after narrowly missing his approach putt, Bean playfully tapped in his ball billiard-style with the grip end of his putter. This was a miscue of Rule 14-1 of the Rules of Golf, which states: "The ball shall be fairly struck at with the head of the club and must not be pushed, scraped, or spooned." At the time, of course, Bean did not realize his error; neither did any of his playing companions nor any of the officials or observers on the scene. But Clyde Mangum, then Deputy Commissioner of the PGA Tour, happened to be watching the event on television and immediately recognized the infraction. He called the tournament headquarters and reported what he'd seen, and in minutes Bean was assessed a two-stroke penalty for his violation.

Bean, who had been in the thick of contention, slipped quickly to a 77 and dropped well back in the pack. "If I lose by one or two strokes, I'll really have paid for it," he said. He paid dearly. The next day, big Andy birdied eight of the first 11, made the turn in 29, and came

13th hole

16th hole

15th hole

18th hole

Scorecard

Hole	Yards	Par	PGA Tour Avg. Score
1	435	4	4.224
2	414	4	4.138
3	156	3	3.055
4	417	4	3.989
5	527	5	4.739
6	437	4	4.076
7	197	3	3.135
8	433	4	4.168
9	458	4	4.247
OUT	3474	35	35.771
10	443	4	4.226
11	452	4	4.260
12	187	3	3.218
13	529	5	4.918
14	426	4	4.294
15	141	3	3.034
16	516	5	4.670
17	436	4	4.226
18	508	5	4.788
IN	3638	37	37.634
TOTAL	7112	72	73.405

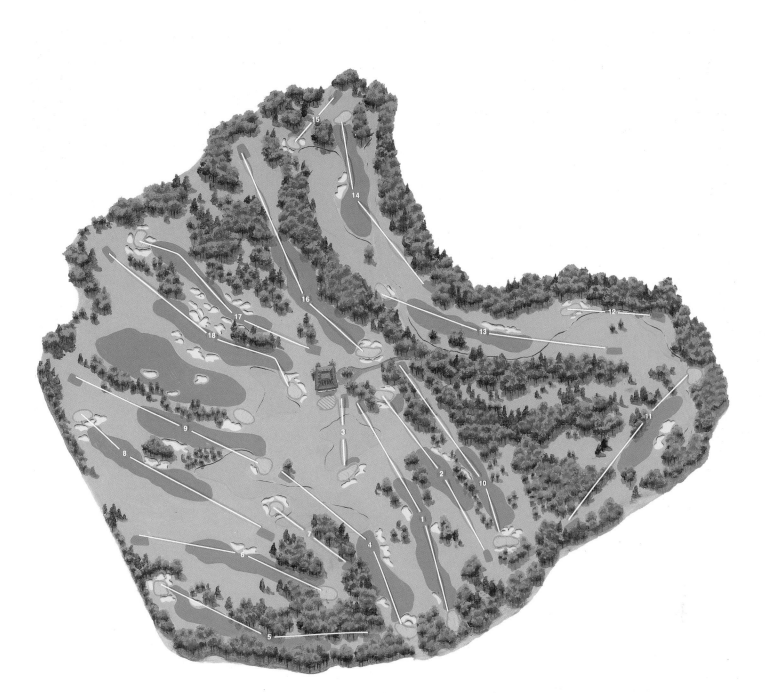

back in 33 for a course-record 62 to finish the tournament at 279, two strokes out of a playoff.

The 16th hole was originally a par four, but in 1983 it was lengthened and is now a vulnerable five. With no water in front of the green, most of the field will go for this one, especially when it is downwind. In 1985, Nicklaus was two strokes in back of Curtis Strange when he hit this green in two. Curtis was still in the fringe after three shots, and as Jack addressed his 30-foot eagle putt, it

seemed as if this might be his year. But he left it two feet short, then missed that one. Strange equalled the Golden Bear's par, and two holes later Jack had his seventh bridesmaid finish. It was the 17th that cost Nicklaus the 1981 tournament when he bogeyed the hole and then lost by one stroke to Peter Oosterhuis. Fourteen bunkers, including ten in the tee-shot landing area, make this a very tough four.

Downwind, the 18th at Glen Abbey may be the shortest par five on the Tour.

Only 508 yards long, it can play like 400. In 1985 defending champion Greg Norman reached it one day with his driver and an 8-iron. Nicklaus had grumbled that, with the 16th now a par five, the RCGA people should make this one a long par four, but so far there has been no change. Evidently, the officials like the notion of a player being able to eagle the final hole for a dramatic victory, and even Jack would be hard-pressed to fault that reasoning.

OAKWOOD COUNTRY CLUB

11th hole

*V*irtually every golfer has made a birdie. Many have made two back-to-back. The better players—and luckier ones—have scored three in a row. And among the PGA Tour pros, four straight birdies is not uncommon. Beyond that, however, we're in the realm of rarities and records.

After all, even the world's most skilled players tend to tense up a bit as the birdie streak lengthens. The brain sends strange messages to the muscles, messages that translate into a fear of failure, or at least a desire to return to the comfort zone of par. But a few players seem immune to such messages, and one such player is Fuzzy Zoeller.

In 1976, his rookie year, Zoeller came to the Quad Cities Open and set the scoreboard on fire. After playing his first nine holes in even par and then adding another par at number ten (the easiest hole on the inward nine), Zoeller unleashed a string of birdies—at 11, 12,

12th hole

13th hole

Wedging It Close
BY SCOTT HOCH

A short course and a particularly tight one, Oakwood Country Club always yields low scores. With a bunch of short par fours, the secret is to be able to hit wedge shots close to the hole.

One of the keys to good wedge play is often forgotten and has to do with the shot you play *before* the wedge. On a short par four, a strong player should hit his tee shot with the club that he knows will leave him at precisely the distance he hits a full wedge. Almost everyone has an easier time hitting full wedge shots than trying to throttle down for a half or three-quarter shot. So if you're playing a 320-yard par four and you normally hit a full wedge 100 yards, select the club that will enable you to hit a tee shot of 220 yards.

Second, don't construe "full wedge" to mean hard wedge. The key to this shot is to maintain smoothness and control throughout the swing. On a wedge, you should use less leg action, a shorter backswing turn, and quieter hand action than on any other full shot.

Finally, since most wedge shots have enough backspin to stop quickly, be sure you get the ball to the hole. One good trick is to play your shot for the top of the flag, not the cup. With wedges as with short putts, never up, never in.

Scott Hoch is a two-time winner of the Hardee's Golf Classic (1980, 1984).

13, 14, 15, 16, and 17. Then, at the final hole, he knocked his approach shot 25 feet from the pin, an opportunity for another birdie and a final-nine score of 28.

"As I stood over that putt, my caddie reminded me that I'd already birdied seven straight," says Zoeller. "By that time the hole looked like a barrel." Fuzzy put his characteristic smooth stroke on the ball, and in it went for a PGA Tour record, the only time in Tour history a player has finished with eight straight birdies. Zoeller went on to finish second in the tournament, two strokes behind John Lister.

The site of Zoeller's feat, Oakwood Country Club, is the improbable answer to the golf trivia question: "What was the first PGA Tour site designed by Pete Dye?" Completed in 1964, Oakwood lacks the fiendish features usually associated with Dye—no railroad ties, no pot bunkers, no bulkheaded water hazards, no small, gnarly greens. Dye began incorporating those ploys after his first visit to Scotland in 1963. By that time, Oakwood had been laid out and seeded.

Despite Zoeller's exploits, it is the front nine at Oakwood that is more vulnerable. Indeed, for several years more birdies were made here than on any nine holes on the Tour. In recent years, however, the course has been lengthened over 200 yards, and 150 of those yards have been added to the front nine.

Holes one and two, a pair of par fours which once averaged a mere 370 yards, now weigh in at 413 and 400—and they're still among the easier holes. At the 435-yard third, out-of-bounds and a pond rise up on the left, and the approach shot to the narrow green is complicated by the looming presence of a rear bunker.

Number four, a whopping 495 yards, is probably the hardest hole on the outward half. A pond and a fairway bunker

3rd hole

4th hole

Scorecard

Hole	Yards	Par	PGA Tour Avg. Score
1	413	4	4.080
2	400	4	3.945
3	435	4	4.114
4	495	4	4.350
5	169	3	2.970
6	515	5	4.468
7	350	4	3.875
8	183	3	3.045
9	436	4	4.042
OUT	3396	35	34.889
10	515	5	4.602
11	386	4	3.935
12	174	3	3.049
13	435	4	4.138
14	446	4	4.119
15	409	4	4.007
16	389	4	3.987
17	214	3	3.081
18	391	4	4.079
IN	3359	35	34.997
TOTAL	6755	70	69.886

18th hole

are on the left side and heavy rough is to the right, so accuracy is as important as distance off this tee. From position A, a long iron will be needed for the approach to the huge, sloping green.

The 12th hole, a par three of 174 yards, looks harmless enough, but should the tee shot fall short, it will plunk into sand or water. Correct club selection is a must. On Sunday in 1983, Curt Byrum came to this hole at 12 under par for the tournament; he made a double-bogey here, then a bogey at 15, another double-bogey at 16, and a bogey at 17. Byrum, who had opened the tournament with a 63, finished tied for 19th. (To his credit, he came back and won here in 1989.)

A deep gully runs along the left side of the 13th fairway, a 435-yard par four

where the green plays tricks with the mind of anyone hitting into it. It slopes so steeply from front to back that when the pin is in the front portion of the green, a ball must pitch short of the putting surface to leave a makeable birdie putt. But a bunker guarding the front-right of the green adds risk to such a shot.

The longest par four on the inward nine is the 446-yard 14th. Out-of-bounds on the left and heavy rough on the right narrow the fairway. The subtly sloped green is deep but slender, and shots missed to the left invite disaster.

The back and front nines of Oak-wood as the members play them flip-flop for the Hardee's Classic, and one result is that the 18th (ninth for the members) is

one of the less formidable finishing holes on the Tour. It's only 391 yards, but is tight. To the left is a deep ravine, to the right, out-of-bounds.

This tournament began as a satellite event in 1971 and was won by Deane Beman, then a Tour player. The next year it was elevated to full Tour-event status, and Beman won again, this time finishing just ahead of an unknown young pro named Tom Watson. In those days, the tournament was played at the Crow Valley Golf Club in Bettendorf, Iowa. But in 1975 it moved across the state line for good.

EN-JOIE GOLF CLUB

The name of the club is "En-Joie," and that is more than a cute attempt at Gallicism. "En" is short for "Endicott," the quiet town in upstate New York where the club is situated. "Joie" stands for "Johnson," more specifically George F. Johnson, the man who built the course. Together they are Endicott-Johnson, one of America's largest shoe manufacturers, a company that was, not coincidentally, based in Endicott and owned by George Johnson.

Johnson had always wanted to build a golf course exclusively for the Endicott-Johnson employees. In 1927, he commissioned Ed Moran, who operated a steam shovel at a granite pit near the company plant, to take a crew of men and begin developing the course. Two years later Endicott-Johnson opened the doors to the first corporate golf course in America. Each hole was named after a different department in the company, and the 15th green was actually designed in the shape of a shoe. Golf clubs were sold to the workers for a dollar each, and group lessons were made available for 50 cents. The local paper hailed the project as the "first attempt by an industry to inject democracy into the white-collar men's game of golf."

The democratic spirit fostered by George Johnson has spread throughout much of New York's rural southern tier, where today hundreds of volunteers work to make the B.C. Open a big-time event with small-town charm. At perhaps no other tournament on the PGA Tour is there the same feeling of warmth, almost a familial bond between the players and the event. As Lee Trevino, one of the first supporters of the B.C., put it, "Most tournaments on the Tour cater to three or four big guns. At the B.C., a rookie gets the same treatment as a star."

Today, the tournament is named in honor of Johnny Hart, the Endicott resident and golf fanatic whose comic strip,

1st hole

2nd hole

B.C. Open, New York

"B.C.," is syndicated all over the world. But in 1971, the event was known as the Broome County Open. At that time it was a one-day pro-am with a total purse of $10,000. A year later it expanded to 36 holes, with double the prize money. Then, in 1973, the first full-scale Tour event took place as a satellite tournament opposite the Cleveland Open. Since then, the Cleveland tournament has vanished, while the B.C. has grown into one of the liveliest stops on the circuit.

But that growth has not come without some pain. In 1974, fire demolished the clubhouse just five weeks before the tournament. A distress call was placed to PGA Tour Commissioner Deane Beman.

"Was there any damage to the course?" Beman asked.

"None" was the reply.

"Then we'll be there as scheduled," said the Commissioner. "We haven't played a clubhouse yet."

A year later, a raging storm hit Endicott on Tuesday night of tournament week, uprooting several trees and leaving some of the fairways under five feet of water. But the next morning more than 500 volunteers pitched in and raked, pumped, shoveled, and squeegeed the course into playable condition in time for the pro-am.

That same year, Andy North opened the tournament with an incredible back-nine score of 27, an all-time PGA Tour record which apparently caught the eye of the Commissioner. Not long thereafter Beman began to question the quality of the En-Joie course and the viability of the rural New York market as a tournament venue.

When tournament officials got wind of Beman's feelings, they invited the Commissioner to Endicott to see for himself.

7th hole

Beman came and rapidly changed his mind. Today, the B.C. tournament is secure and the En-Joie course, which has had a redesign, remains the permanent site.

The most drastic change came on the first hole, a par four that had been the easiest hole on the course. At the suggestion of 1979 champion Howard Twitty, a lake was added near the green. In 1984, the year following the change, the pros played this hole in an average of 4.35 strokes. It was not only the most difficult hole on the course, it was one of the hardest par fours on the entire Tour. Lake Twitty took its toll.

The other tough tests on the front nine are the par-three holes, four and seven, which measure 221 and 200 yards respectively. In fact, all five par threes at En-Joie are brutes, with an average distance in excess of 200 yards. No wonder John Daly won here—he was probably the only guy in the field who could play the "short" holes with short irons.

An unusual aspect of the En-Joie course is the fact that its par 71 is divided into nines of 37 and 34. The front nine measures 3702 yards and includes three par fives against two threes, while the

back features three threes and only one five and measures just 3264.

As part of the redesign, the relatively easy par-five 15th was changed in yardage and par to a 476-yard par four. Set as it is among par threes at the 14th, 16th, and 17th, this hole stands out like King Kong in a kindergarten. It is by far the longest par four on the back nine.

But it is not the sternest test—number 13 is. An extremely tight 441-yarder, played to an elevated green, this is the hole that beckons the best from the pros. At least it did from Calvin Peete, who in 1982 laced a 2-iron into the cup for an eagle 2, spurring him to a three-stroke victory.

The final tee shot on most courses is a psychologically demanding one, but at En-Joie it is made doubly difficult by out-of-bounds to the right and two large ponds to the left. Adding to the intimidating beauty of the ponds is a waterfall that connects them, with the cascading waters very much in play.

The waterfall, unquestionably the most distinctive feature on the En-Joie layout, was, appropriately, the idea of a fellow named Alex Alexander. Since the inception of the B.C., Alexander has

Short Putts
BY JOHN DALY

My first years as a PGA Tour player have taught me to respect that old adage: You drive for show but putt for dough. I may win over the fans with my long tee shots, but to win money and tournaments, you have to sink your short putts.

If these putts make you tense, I recommend that you grip the putter lightly and don't sole it at address—keep it an inch or so off the ground. These adjustments will help you reduce the tension and make a free, unhurried stroke.

I'm also a firm believer in playing without delay, particularly on the green, where GOLF Magazine found me to be the fastest putter on the Tour. Do your prestroke reading carefully and deliberately while others putt. Also, take some care in setting the blade of the putter precisely on your intended line. But after that, pull the trigger promptly. Too many players spend too much time agonizing over putts, especially short putts, to the point that they have difficulty pulling the putter back. So do as I do—take a short time on those short putts.

John Daly won the 1992 B.C. Open.

10th hole

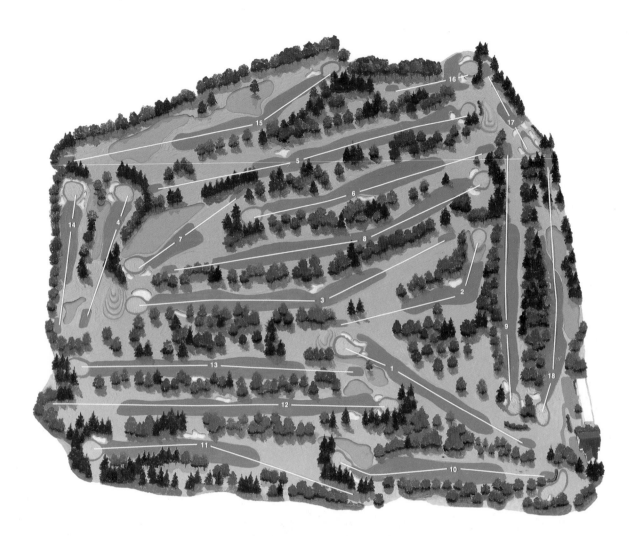

Scorecard

Hole	Yards	Par	PGA Tour Avg. Score
1	388	4	4.152
2	363	4	4.013
3	554	5	4.794
4	221	3	3.098
5	565	5	4.816
6	433	4	4.103
7	200	3	3.093
8	553	5	4.875
9	425	4	4.049
OUT	3702	37	36.993
10	360	4	3.990
11	433	4	4.180
12	556	5	4.759
13	441	4	4.162
14	212	3	3.147
15	476	4	4.373
16	182	3	3.082
17	198	3	3.034
18	406	4	4.082
IN	3264	34	34.809
TOTAL	6966	71	71.802

13th hole

been a combination tournament director, traffic cop, social secretary, messiah, and den mother. He has guided the tournament from its modest beginning, nursing and nurturing it every step of the way. It was he who made the frantic call after the clubhouse fire, he who marshaled the cleanup effort after the storm, he who stood up to the doubting Commissioner. Alexander also founded an annual golf championship for the caddies.

It is all part of that spirit of democracy, of favoritism to no man, commitment to every man. At no time was that spirit more clearly reflected than in 1974, a year when the B.C. produced one of the more surprising victors in modern golf.

Richie Karl, a struggling 29-year-old pro, had earned only $256 when the Tour arrived in Endicott. But Richie had

reason for hope. Endicott was his home, and he had played at the En-Joie course since the age of six. When he turned professional, he went to work at En-Joie as the assistant to head pro Bill Dennis. Outside Endicott, no one knew Richie, but Richie knew Endicott inside-out.

He opened the tournament with a 70, then followed with rounds of 67 and 68. On Sunday, Karl blitzed through the front nine in 31. With nine holes to go, he had a six-stroke lead and a gallery of 30,000 friends and neighbors.

At the tenth tee, however, Karl made a mistake; he looked at the leaderboard. Seeing his huge lead, he began to play defensively. He bogeyed ten and 13 while one of his pursuers, Bruce Crampton, birdied 12 and 13. Karl three-putted the 16th, and with a 37 on the back nine, he

had blown six strokes in nine holes. The law of momentum said Crampton would win the sudden-death playoff.

But the spirit of the B.C. said otherwise. Crampton failed to reach the green of the first playoff hole and chipped to within a foot of the hole for a sure par. Karl, however, hit the green and stroked his uphill putt directly into the hole for a victorious birdie. The crowd erupted into one of the wildest whoops Broome County had ever heard.

"The first thing I saw was my caddie running up to me. He was crying," said a joyous Karl. "Then something dressed in white [Natalie, his wife] was in my arms and she was sobbing, and I guess, well, I was sobbing a little, too." Sobbing for joy.

18th hole

CALLAWAY GARDENS RESORT

From the family that brought you Big Bertha comes the new site of the Buick Southern Open. In 1952, Cason and Virginia Callaway, cousins of golf club manufacturer Ely Callaway, opened a 14,000-acre fishing retreat near Pine Mountain, Georgia, about 70 miles from Atlanta. Today, Callaway Gardens is one of the premier golf resorts in the southeast, winner of the prestigious Silver Medal from *GOLF Magazine*, with an expansive hotel and four courses that attract more than 750,000 guests annually. In 1991, after 21 years at the Green Island Country Club in nearby Colum-

bus, the Southern moved to Callaway's Mountain View Course.

The shift was prompted by a need for easier access and better parking facilities, but in the bargain the tournament got an excellent golf course. The Mountain View course was designed by Joe Lee and Dick Wilson in the mid-1960s, at about the same time that Wilson was completing two other PGA Tour venues, the Blue Course at Doral (site of the Doral-Ryder Open) and the Dubsdread Course at Cog Hill (site of the Western Open). Prior to the Tour's arrival, a half million dollars of improvements had been made, including new Tifdwarf bermuda greens,

new tees on several holes, and rebuilding of all 65 bunkers on the course.

It was love at first site for the Tour pros. In a survey they rated Mountain View the second-best-conditioned course on the Tour, at the same time that *USA Today* ranked this par 72 of 7057 yards (with a rating of 73) as the fifth most difficult course on the circuit. When David Peoples won the inaugural Buick Southern Open here, his 72-hole total was 276, 11 strokes higher than that of the 1990 winner at Green Island, Kenny Knox.

The Mountain View Course is aptly named, as several holes meander up and

9th hole

Buick Southern Open, Georgia

15th hole

down hills. The narrow fairways are lined with thick rough shaded by stands of pine trees, so a straight ball is important, particularly because of the deep green-side bunkers that call for an all-carry approach at most greens.

The front and back nines of the course are flip-flopped for the tournament, partly because most of the testing holes are on the inward half, beginning with the par-three 12th. One of only two holes where water is in play, it calls for a carry of 202 yards. The four par threes

here are arguably the key to the course, averaging 200 yards in length, with the longest of them the 218-yard 16th. This was the pivotal hole of the 1992 Buick Southern Open, as Gary Hallberg, holding a one-stroke lead, struck his tee shot ten feet from the cup while his nearest pursuer, Jim Gallagher, hit his ball to six feet. Had a miss by Hallberg combined with a sink by Gallagher, the tournament would have been tied. Instead, it went the other way, and Hallberg held on for a one-stroke victory.

In contrast to the par threes, the par fives are relatively short, an average of barely 534 yards with none longer than 546. The pivotal hole on the second nine may be number 15, a three-shotter of 539 that is reachable in two shots, but they had better be excellent ones. A 17-acre lake lurks on the right side and pokes in front of the green, and the fairway banks toward the water. Despite its lack of length, it is one of the more difficult par fives on the Tour.

18th hole

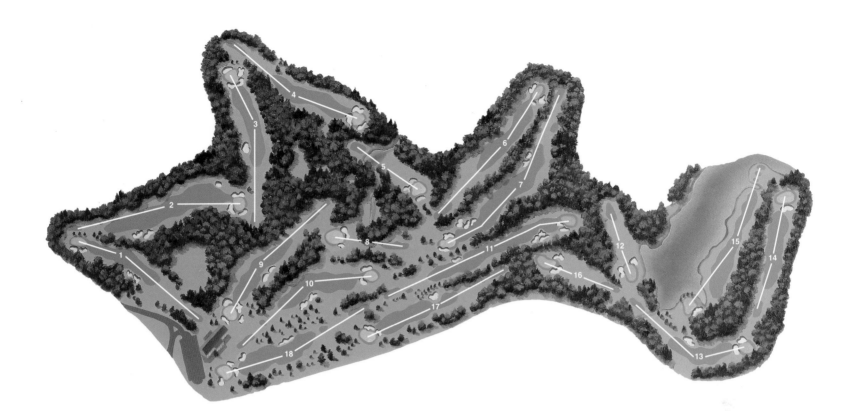

Scorecard

Hole	Yards	Par	PGA Tour Avg. Score
1	412	4	4.116
2	508	5	4.637
3	400	4	4.195
4	397	4	4.132
5	212	3	3.159
6	432	4	4.147
7	543	5	4.728
8	178	3	3.071
9	427	4	4.242
OUT	3509	36	36.427
10	431	4	4.096
11	546	5	4.733
12	186	3	3.090
13	367	4	3.948
14	421	4	4.228
15	539	5	4.970
16	218	3	3.174
17	408	4	4.111
18	432	4	4.199
IN	3548	36	36.549
TOTAL	7057	72	72.976

Sidehill Lies

BY GARY HALLBERG

The Mountain View Course, as its name implies, is full of hilly lies. The most vexing are those where the ball is either well above or well below your feet.

With a sidehill lie where the ball is above your feet, your tendency will be to pull the ball to the left. You should allow for this by aiming a bit farther right than normal. (In the case of a severe slope, open the face of your club a bit to counteract the pulling effect.) The ball also will be closer to your hands than with a level fairway lie, so you should adjust by gripping down a bit on the club—this may also mean that you'll have to take one club more than for a level shot.

For the lie where the ball is below your feet, everything is just the opposite. Expect a push to the right and compensate by aiming a bit left. (On a severe lie, address the ball with a slightly closed clubface.) Be aware that the ball is farther from your hands than usual, and adjust by putting some extra flex into your knees to lower your hands.

No matter which type of lie you have, keep your swing "quiet" and compact. With an awkward stance, you must stay centered over the ball to ensure solid contact.

Gary Hallberg won the 1992 Buick Southern Open.

MAGNOLIA, PALM, LAKE BUENA VISTA GOLF COURSES

Four brats, that band of kids whose fathers play professional golf for a living, couldn't care less whether Dad makes it to The Masters or U.S. Open. The main event of the year, after all, is the Walt Disney World/Oldsmobile Classic, that golden week in the fall when they get to eat lunch with sea lions, shake hands with Goofy and Pluto, and hurtle themselves repeatedly down Space Mountain.

Meanwhile, their fathers go to work at the Magic Linkdom, a network of three testing courses produced by Joe Lee, the protégé and eventual partner of Dick Wilson. Lee designed dozens of resort and real estate community courses in the Sun Belt, collaborated with Ben Hogan on the Trophy Club in Ft. Worth (Hogan's only serious foray into architecture), and also reworked the layout of Warwick Hills, site of the Buick Open.

Although the three courses sit within a few thousand yards of each other and

Magnolia, 12th hole

all three are par 72s, they have separate personalities. The Magnolia is the long-ball course at 7,190 yards. When the wind is blowing it is much longer, especially when playing across and around its 97 bunkers and ten water hazards. This is the course played twice during the Disney and always used for the final round.

The Palm, which emanates from the same clubhouse as its big sister, is 223 yards shorter, but it sometimes seems as if those yards were pared from the width of the fairways. With encroaching trees and water in play on ten holes, the average player has two options: Keep in play or bring lots of balls.

Lake Buena Vista is shorter yet at 6829 yards, but may be the tightest of the three. In 1991 the course was lengthened 123 yards and the back and front nines were reversed for tournament play. Half of the additional yardage went into the old ninth hole, which has become a 448-yard finisher, the most formidable assignment on the course.

The Palm and Magnolia were opened in 1970 and hosted the Disney Classic from 1971 through 1973. In each of those years it was won by Jack Nicklaus. Perhaps the Bear's stranglehold reminded the promoters of a brutally one-sided boxing match for after 12 rounds they converted the tournament to a pro-pro

team format, where twosomes pooled their efforts, using the lower score on each hole. That lasted through 1981, when the event returned to the standard format, adding play on the Lake Buena Vista course.

Two holes at the Palm and two at the Magnolia course deserve special mention. The toughest test at the former is number six, a 412-yard bowling alley with water in the left gutter, trees and swamp in the right. Water also cuts directly in front of the green. The hole was immortalized when Arnold Palmer took an 11 on it.

The longest par four on the course is the 454-yard 18th, where the last third of the hole is an island. The right edge of the green is hard by the water, while the left is guarded by four bunkers. The pros will tell you they're glad they have to face this hole only once a year.

The fourth hole at the Magnolia is a place only Lawrence of Arabia could love. From tee to green are scattered 14

Palm, 6th hole

bunkers—more than two acres of sand. Half of them are at the green, which they encircle like a malevolent gallery, in some spots hovering two deep. Still, if you can keep yourself out of buried lies, this 552-yard par five is one of the easier holes on the course. One year it yielded ten eagles, 115 birdies, and only two bogeys in two days' play as the pros ravaged it in 4.3 strokes.

The finishing hole at the Magnolia, as at the two other courses, is the longest par four on the course. Anyone who can come down the stretch in the last group on Sunday and finish with a birdie here will have earned his victory, as Larry Nelson did in 1987. In fact, Nelson made five birdies and an eagle in his last ten holes for a then course-record 63. With his final birdie at 18, he overcame a six-stroke deficit and beat Mark O'Meara by a shot.

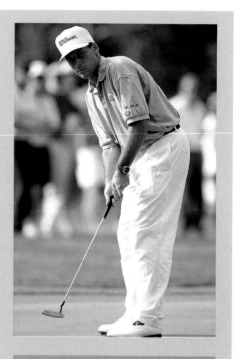

In-Between Shots

BY JOHN HUSTON

Courses such as those at the Walt Disney World/Oldsmobile Classic call for accurate iron play, not only with regard to direction but also distance. One of the most demanding aspects of getting the ball close is dealing with the situation where you're in between clubs.

Obviously, you have two alternatives—take the shorter club and hit it hard or take the longer club and smooth it. Let your psychological makeup determine your decision. If you're an aggressive person, you want to make a full-blooded swing at the shorter club. If you're more passive, put your smooth swing on the longer club.

But there's a third option as well. Take the longer club and grip down on it an inch or so. This effectively shortens the club and lessens the distance you'll get with it, allowing you to make your normal swing and hit that in-between shot.

John Huston won the 1992 Walt Disney World/Oldsmobile Classic.

Palm, 16th hole

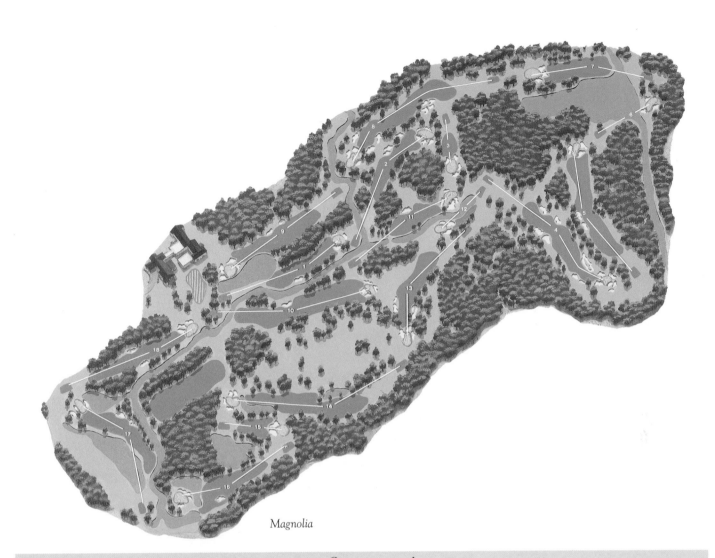

Magnolia

Scorecard

Magnolia			
Hole	Yards	Par	PGA Tour Avg. Score
1	428	4	3.992
2	417	4	3.980
3	160	3	2.845
4	552	5	4.613
5	448	4	4.045
6	195	3	2.953
7	410	4	3.862
8	614	5	4.816
9	431	4	3.993
OUT	3655	36	35.099
10	526	5	4.532
11	385	4	3.816
12	169	3	2.928
13	375	4	3.784
14	595	5	4.819
15	203	3	3.065
16	400	4	3.847
17	427	4	4.109
18	455	4	4.106
IN	3535	36	35.006
TOTAL	7190	72	70.105

Palm			
Hole	Yards	Par	PGA Tour Avg. Score
1	495	5	4.386
2	389	4	3.938
3	175	3	2.875
4	422	4	4.086
5	403	4	3.908
6	412	4	4.165
7	532	5	4.549
8	205	3	2.995
9	373	4	3.977
OUT	3406	36	34.879
10	450	4	4.157
11	552	5	4.666
12	199	3	3.005
13	364	4	3.771
14	547	5	4.804
15	426	4	3.939
16	172	3	2.895
17	397	4	3.921
18	454	4	4.170
IN	3561	36	35.328
TOTAL	6967	72	70.207

Lake Buena Vista			
Hole	Yards	Par	PGA Tour Avg. Score
1	385	4	3.889
2	442	4	4.080
3	197	3	3.095
4	397	4	3.874
5	506	5	4.475
6	384	4	3.938
7	200	3	2.965
8	526	5	4.739
9	438	4	4.192
OUT	3475	36	35.247
10	514	5	4.574
11	176	3	2.912
12	409	4	3.889
13	382	4	3.845
14	390	4	3.884
15	354	4	3.932
16	157	3	2.851
17	524	5	4.656
18	448	4	3.853
IN	3354	36	34.396
TOTAL	6829	72	69.643

OAK HILLS COUNTRY CLUB

6th hole

Texas Open

Albert W. Tillinghast was not a particularly prolific golf course architect, nor did he ever get a chance to design on scenically spectacular land, but his designs had integrity, artfulness, and an ability to test players of all levels. Today, "Tillie the Terror" continues to challenge all who are fortunate enough to play at the Baltusrol, Winged Foot, Somerset Hills, Baltimore, Bethpage, Brook Hollow, and San Francisco Golf Clubs.

The PGA Tour gets just one chance per year to tangle with Tillinghast—at Oak Hills. Although Jay Morrish reworked this course a bit in 1984, the fundamental Tillinghast virtues remain intact.

"It has such great balance," says Ben Crenshaw, a Texan who has won here twice, in 1973 and 1986, the first victory coming in his debut as a Tour pro. But Crenshaw's fond memories of Oak Hills go back even further than that.

"I'll never forget the day I went to San Antonio with my Dad, at age 11, and watched Arnold Palmer play," he recalls. "I particularly remember the third hole, one of the longest, toughest par fours on the course. It doglegs right, and the land also slopes to the right, toward a series of mesquite trees. On that day, it was also playing straight into the face of the wind. I can recall standing in the gallery and watching my hero smack a long, low drive up the center of that fairway and then a tremendous 1-iron up to the green.

"Oak Hills is not an overpowering course," says Crenshaw, "but neither is it the kind of course that can be overpowered. Its strength, I believe, is its short par fours, some of the best I've ever seen."

Holes such as the first, sixth, eighth, 14th, and 17th average less than 350 yards yet provide some of the most test-

4th hole

Getting Unburied
BY LEE TREVINO

There is not a green at Oak Hills that isn't closely guarded by bunkers, and if the Texas wind gets up, you can find yourself with some balls that drop straight down into the sand, leaving a buried lie.

Most golfers play this shot by cutting into the sand with the clubhead square or closed, to insure that the leading edge will dig down and under the buried ball. Personally, I don't care for that technique because the ball comes out too low and too hot. I want a softer shot with more backspin that will settle quickly on even a small area of green.

So I play the ball back about in the center of my stance with most of my weight on my left foot. I swing the club practically straight up and down and give the ball a judo chop with the clubface, just stick the clubhead into the sand with no follow-through. The ball rides up the clubface, taking on tremendous backspin, then flies up nice and high and floats onto the green like a feather dropping on a pond. I suggest, however, that you practice this shot a few times to see if you're precise enough to catch the ball instead of the sand behind it.

Lee Trevino won the 1980 Texas Open.

9th hole

ing golf on the course. All demand tee shots into the ideal part of the fairway to ensure a good chance at birdie.

Miss a green, such as the one at number four, even by a little bit, and the ensuing assignment is a stern one. Like many a Tillinghast target, this green sits toward the player. Thus, an approach that goes into the swale beyond it will leave a difficult pitch to a severely canted surface.

At the seventh hole, a par four that doglegs right, Morrish created a double-tiered target. When the pin is on the back half, the approach had better find its way back there as well. If not, a three-putt is almost assured.

As at many Texas courses, two formidable opponents at Oak Hills are the wind and the mesquite tree. A southeaster blows almost constantly at 15 miles per hour or so, guiding even slightly wayward shots toward the pesky mesquites. These are thorny, low-lying tree-bushes, rarely reaching more than 20 feet in height. They are easy enough to play over but nearly impossible to play under, through, or out of. As such, mesquites are perhaps the most vexing of golf's arboreal perils.

There's more tree trouble off the tee of the par-five 15th. Although a 1987 tornado ripped dozens of centuries-old oaks from the course, this hole remains lined with timber. Crenshaw favors a "holding shot," a hard-hit fade down the left side of this slightly left-to-right fairway.

Should that fade grow into a slice, the ball will go out-of-bounds.

Oak Hill is unique among the Tour courses, and rare among the world's courses, in that both its front and back nines conclude with par threes. Both the ninth and the 18th play over lakes and toward the clubhouse. The 18th is the more difficult of the two, a 6- or 7-iron to a broad, shallow green that has provided plenty of drama. In 1986, when Payne Stewart bogeyed this hole in the third round, he thought he'd merely lost a share of the lead, but when heavy rain then soaked the course and the final round was canceled, it meant a one-stroke victory for Crenshaw. But Crenshaw has also suffered here—in

15th hole

18th hole

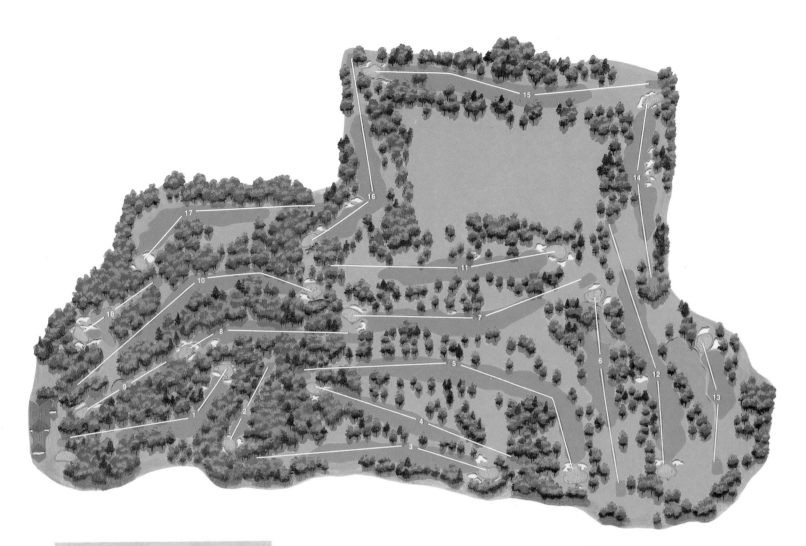

Scorecard

Hole	Yards	Par	PGA Tour Avg. Score
1	349	4	3.967
2	175	3	2.905
3	456	4	4.083
4	389	4	4.079
5	604	5	4.763
6	352	4	4.015
7	460	4	4.188
8	309	4	3.795
9	155	3	2.918
OUT	3249	35	34.713
10	506	5	4.549
11	426	4	3.998
12	444	4	4.082
13	220	3	3.232
14	328	4	3.903
15	527	5	4.581
16	385	4	4.027
17	367	4	3.882
18	198	3	3.037
IN	3401	36	35.291
TOTAL	6650	71	70.004

1981, his fellow Texan Bill Rogers birdied 18 to force a playoff which Rogers won.

It's not a particularly vexing green to putt, but don't tell that to Gary Hallberg. In 1990 he three-putted the 72nd hole to give Mark O'Meara the win. Then, a year later, and from virtually the same position, he shakily two-putted to tie Blaine McCallister, who won on the second hole of sudden death.

In 1987, Tom Watson birdied the hole to win a tournament that, in addition to being the Texas Open, was a limited field event that turned out to be the progenitor of the Tour Championship. But as Texas Open champ, Watson added his name to a long list of illustrious winners, including Walter Hagen,

Sam Snead, Byron Nelson, Ben Hogan, and Arnold Palmer. This is a tournament that dates back to 1922, when a Scotsman named Bob MacDonald sank a putt on the final hole to beat Cyril Walker by a stroke with a score of 281, then an American competitive record for 72 holes.

In those days, the Texas Open was held at Brackenridge Park, then regarded as one of the top three public courses in the country. The pros loved to play Brackenridge, and they played it well. In fact, the all-time PGA Tour record for 72 holes was made in the Texas Open in 1955 when Mike Souchak completed four rounds in 257 strokes—27 under par.

DESERT INN COUNTRY CLUB
LAS VEGAS COUNTRY CLUB
TPC AT SUMMERLIN

One of the youngest events on the Tour, the Las Vegas Invitational is also one of the most lucrative, having started in 1983 with a purse of more than $1 million, at that time the highest on the Tour. The extra pay was for extra play—90 holes instead of the standard 72—and for hazardous duty. Each pro plays with three amateurs in each of the first three days of the tournament. It's similar to the Bob Hope format, except that the amateurs play in teams at the Hope. Here, it's every man for himself. After round three a cut is made and the low 30 amateurs are paired with pros for a shootout on Saturday. On Sunday, it's pros only.

During the first three days, play is spread among the courses at the Desert Inn Country Club, the Las Vegas Country Club, and the Tournament Players Club at Summerlin. On Saturday and Sunday, all play is at Summerlin.

The oldest of the three venues is the Desert Inn course, which brought golf to Vegas in 1950 and three years later brought big-time golf by hosting the first 14 editions of the Tournament of Champions. Since then it has played host to events on the LPGA and Senior Tours as well as the PGA Tour.

This is a flat but long course with several tough holes, notably the stretch from holes seven to nine. The sternest hole on the course is probably the seventh, a 205-yard par three surrounded by both sand and water. In the first year of the tournament, it ranked as the second toughest one-shotter on the Tour. That year, the only par three that played harder was the famed 16th at Cypress Point, now no longer a Tour site.

Las Vegas, 17th hole

Las Vegas Invitational, Nevada

Las Vegas, 18th hole

The Las Vegas Country Club course was designed by Ed Ault in 1967 and updated by Ron Garl in 1979, with an additional update in 1993. Each of the nines ends with a Las Vegas par five, calling for a gambling second shot over water. Number nine is by far the easier of the two, its deep green coming at the end of 474 yards. But 18 is a 525-yarder where anyone gunning for the green in two (or for that matter, three) must carry a moatlike pond in front of the green. Should your drive reach the crest of the

hill at the corner of this dogleg right, you'll feel as if you've just been dealt 16 at blackjack. You can stay pat and lay up shy of the pond, taking your chances with the short, tricky pitch; or you can take a hit with a wood shot that will have to carry not only the water but a stone wall (courtesy of architect Garl) at its far edge.

Bunkers line the back of the green, and shooting out of them means exploding to a fast green that slopes down to the water. Many a hapless powerhitter

has boomed his second shot over the pond but over the green as well, then watched in agony as his mediocre blast rolled back across the green and into the drink. Still, this is a great place to settle a nassau, and rumor has it that in one foursome of high rollers the payoff was $1.8 million. The hole also was decisive in several of the early Las Vegas Invitationals, most notably 1987 when Paul Azinger reached the green in two and then sank his eagle putt to break a three-way tie and earn the victory.

While the Desert Inn and Las Vegas Country Club courses have been consistent venues for this event, the third venue has varied. Originally the courses at the Dunes, Showboat, and Tropicana Hotels were used, then the Spanish Trail Golf & Country Club took a few turns, and in 1991, Sunrise Golf Club became the site. Although it was used only one year, Sunrise will always be remembered because it was there that Chip Beck became the second player in PGA Tour history to break 60. Beck's 59 tied the record set by Al Geiberger in the 1977 Memphis Classic.

In 1992, the tournament acquired not only a new venue but a new home at the TPC at Summerlin. Twenty minutes from the Las Vegas strip, Summerlin is more than a golf course— it is the largest master-planned community in America, a 22,000-acre project that eventually will be the home of 150,000 people. It was developed by the Summa Corporation, heirs of billionaire Howard Hughes's empire; Summerlin was the name of Hughes's mother.

Designed by Bobby Weed with player consultant (and 1983 LVI champion) Fuzzy Zoeller, the TPC received strongly favorable reviews from both the pros and amateurs. Zoeller, who likes to build courses that are fun, said his goals at Summerlin were simple: to give players clear targets from the tees, to allow them a chance to roll their approach shots onto the greens, and to keep the green undulations subtle.

But in sharp contrast to the Desert Inn and Las Vegas Country Clubs, two established, old-style, in-town tracks, the TPC is a desert course, its lush green fairways sprawled across a no-man's-land.

The desert wash is a constant factor, beginning at number three, where the second shot to the reachable par five must cross the expanse of sand and scrub or the player will pay a penalty of at least one stroke, probably more. The toughest tee shot of the day occurs at the sixth hole, where a narrow path of fairway snakes between desert on both sides.

Fuzzy's fun comes at number 15, a 341-yard par four that dares the pros to

Summerlin, 11th hole

Desert Inn, 16th hole

TPC at Summerlin			
Hole	Yards	Par	PGA Tour Avg. Score
1	408	4	3.865
2	469	4	4.047
3	492	5	4.377
4	450	4	4.025
5	197	3	3.058
6	430	4	4.020
7	382	4	3.863
8	239	3	3.253
9	563	5	4.625
OUT	3630	36	35.133
10	420	4	3.973
11	448	4	4.057
12	442	4	4.059
13	606	5	4.828
14	156	3	2.858
15	341	4	3.902
16	560	5	4.581
17	196	3	3.170
18	444	4	4.098
IN	3613	36	35.526
TOTAL	7243	72	70.659

Desert Inn			
Hole	Yards	Par	PGA Tour Avg. Score
1	515	5	4.566
2	433	4	4.085
3	414	4	4.139
4	191	3	2.953
5	578	5	4.922
6	424	4	4.002
7	205	3	3.179
8	442	4	4.163
9	432	4	4.082
OUT	3634	36	36.091
10	518	5	4.569
11	209	3	3.091
12	420	4	4.028
13	407	4	4.077
14	411	4	4.063
15	512	5	4.613
16	173	3	3.016
17	395	4	3.937
18	432	4	4.026
IN	3477	36	35.420
TOTAL	7111	72	71.511

Las Vegas			
Hole	Yards	Par	PGA Tour Avg. Score
1	435	4	3.979
2	405	4	3.937
3	199	3	3.007
4	365	4	3.769
5	468	4	4.147
6	546	5	4.573
7	179	3	2.986
8	440	4	3.937
9	474	5	4.343
OUT	3511	36	34.678
10	552	5	4.622
11	447	4	3.993
12	401	4	3.846
13	449	4	4.077
14	192	3	2.958
15	430	4	3.972
16	447	4	3.951
17	210	3	3.000
18	525	5	4.629
IN	3653	36	35.048
TOTAL	7164	72	69.726

Summerlin, 17th hole

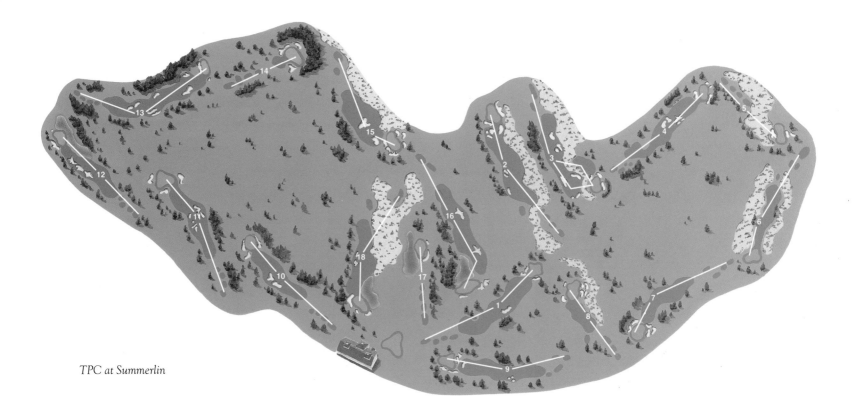

TPC at Summerlin

drive its green. The longer hitters like to give it a go, but with desert on the left and bunkers surrounding the green, the majority of the field lays back with an iron from the tee.

Sixteen is another gambler's par five, very reachable at 560 yards but with a second shot over water. Then it's long irons to the greens of the last two holes, a 196-yard par three at 17 followed by the 444-yard 18th, a classic dogleg finisher in the tradition of the TPC at Sawgrass, with water running down its entire left side.

Despite its 7243 yards, Summerlin was roundly conquered in its first year. Every player in the top 25 finishers played it in par or better on Saturday and Sunday, most posted at least one round in the mid-60s, and the champion, John Cook, posted a record 62 on his first competitive trip through. Of course, Cook had a bit of local knowledge on his side. His father, Jim Cook, is the longtime tournament director of the Las Vegas Invitational. Still, the victory at Vegas capped the best season in Cook's 13-year career as a pro—three Tour wins plus runner-up finishes in both the British Open and the PGA Championship.

Tackling Crosswinds
BY FUZZY ZOELLER

Windy courses, such as those in Vegas, play differently every day, and anyone who wants to play them consistently had better have a good strategy for handling crosswinds.

The better player you are, the fancier you can get with the wind. If you're a player of average or less-than-average ability, you probably shouldn't try to "doctor" shots to suit the winds. Go with your normal pattern, whether that is a low hook, a high fade, or whatever. Sometimes the wind will help you, sometimes it will hurt you, but the key is to take the breaks as they come. In windy conditions, you don't want to start trying low-percentage shots: Let your opponent make that mistake.

If you have the ability to play both right-to-left and left-to-right shots with some degree of confidence, follow this general rule: When you want accuracy, fight the crosswind; when you want distance, ride it. On a tight tee shot or approach in a right-to-left wind, play a fade that will work against the wind and give you a straight shot. But on a wide-open shot or in a situation in which you need maximum distance, take advantage of that right-to-left wind by playing a high draw or hook. Just allow plenty of room for the ball to work from right to left.

Fuzzy Zoeller won the inaugural (1983) Las Vegas Invitational (playing in 30 mph winds) and was the player consultant on the design of the TPC at Summerlin.

THE TOUR CHAMPIONSHIP

Donald Regan, the Wall Street financier who won a measure of fame first as Ronald Reagan's Treasury Secretary and later as the strong-willed White House Chief of Staff, surely gained experience for those posts when he served on the PGA Tour's Policy Board during the late 1970s.

In the politics of professional golf Don Regan seldom failed to make his point, and one of his strongest beliefs related to the Tour schedule. Commissioner Deane Beman's notes from a 1979 board meeting include an adamant assertion from Regan: "Must end with something!"

Regan was the board's most fervent proponent of a season-ending championship, a Super Bowl of golf. But he left the board and served his first term with Reagan before anything happened, and what did take place was a mistake of near-Watergate proportions: the Seiko-Tucson Match Play Championship.

"At the time, I was convinced that the world's players, the media, and the fans wanted a match-play event," says Beman, "but that just shows you can't be right all the time." With a restricted field seeded with marquee players, Beman hoped to ensure high interest and television ratings—instead he merely offended the rank-and-file Tour players, and two years after it began, the tournament was abandoned.

In its place came something called the Vantage Championship, a Nabisco-sponsored event played at Oak Hills Country Club (site of the current Texas Open) and won by Ben Crenshaw. The tournament had a standard field of 144 players and a purse of $1 million. A year later, however, two big changes took place—the field was limited to the season's top 30 money winners and the purse was doubled to $2 million (the Tour's largest), with the winner taking home $360,000. Appropriately, that first-place check went to the man who had dominated the PGA Tour for the previous decade, Tom Watson, who sank a six-foot birdie putt at the 72nd hole. It turned out to be the last of Watson's 32 Tour victories, but the start of something big for the Tour.

The elite field and the huge purse have helped, but the true key to the success of this tournament may have been the Tour's decision to rotate it among the nation's top golf courses—Pebble Beach in 1988, then Harbour Town, then Champions, followed by two years at Pinehurst Number 2 and two more at Olympic. Those great courses have inspired great finishes by great players.

At Pebble, Curtis Strange and Tom Kite dueled to a dead heat before Strange settled matters on the first hole of sudden death when he nearly scored a hole in one at the 17th hole. A year

later, it was a playoff again, a par-three 17th again, but this time at Harbour Town, and Tom Kite again, but this time he became the victor when Payne Stewart missed a four-foot putt to tie.

The next year may have produced the most stirring victory of all, as Jodie Mudd sank lengthy birdie putts at the 17th and 18th holes at Houston's Champions Golf Club to tie Billy Mayfair, then ran home a 15-footer for another birdie at the first playoff hole to earn the biggest paycheck of his life. At Pinehurst Number 2, Craig Stadler and Russ Cochran tied in regulation, and again it was a par-three 17th hole that proved pivotal when Stadler struck his tee shot to eight feet and made the deciding birdie. A year later, Paul Azinger clinched victory at Pinehurst's par-five 16th, striking two long, straight shots to the edge of the green and then using a strange-looking putter he called "The Thing" to sink a mammoth putt for eagle.

Qualifying for each of the first half-dozen Tour Championships, Azinger finished first, second, and fourth. From this tournament alone, he has banked nearly a million dollars. But the biggest winner has been the Tour itself, for with the Tour Championship, the season's grand finale is firmly in place.

Pressure Putting
BY PAUL AZINGER

Bobby Jones once observed that there is golf and there is tournament golf, and the two are not remotely alike. Anyone who has ever played in even a club tournament knows that Jones was right. And his words surely ring truest on the putting green.

The best advice I can give you when you're putting under pressure is to trust your stroke. If you don't have a stroke you can trust, do yourself a favor and on the day of your big round: Arrive early

and work on your stroke until you find a key—any key—that helps you. Then focus on that key during the round. Even if it's only a "w.o.o.d." key—works only one day—that may be enough.

The other important point is mental. Work hard on getting the line of your putt, and then work hard on visualizing your ball rolling along that line. When you do this, you focus your thoughts on something positive rather than worrying about missing the putt.

Paul Azinger won the 1992 Tour Championship at Pinehurst Number 2.

Southern Hills, 4th hole

UNOFFICIAL EVENTS

*I*n addition to the tournaments on its regular schedule, the PGA Tour co-stages five "unofficial" events at the end of each year. Prize winnings from these events are not applied to the official money list for the year, nor does a victory in any of these entitle the winner to any of the exemptions that accrue to victors in the core events. In most other ways, however, these five tournaments—each with a unique personality—enjoy the full sanction and support of the Tour.

LINCOLN-MERCURY KAPALUA INTERNATIONAL

Back in 1983, the spectacular Kapalua Bay resort in Maui, Hawaii, initiated this limited field event with competitors from around the world. Since then its list of champions has included Greg Norman, Sandy Lyle, Mark O'Meara, Davis Love, and Fred Couples.

This tournament has a major advantage over virtually every other event in golf. With a six-hour time difference between Maui and New York, its afternoon finish can be televised live during prime-time hours on the East Coast.

For its first decade, the tournament was played exclusively on the Bay Course at Kapalua. But in 1991, when Ben Crenshaw and Bill Coore unveiled their Plantation Course at the resort, the event switched to a two-course format with the final two rounds over the Plantation, an expansive layout with broad, tumbling fairways and enormous, undulating greens, a par of 73, and a final hole of 663 yards.

Although this is a comparatively young event, it is a week in Paradise that has quickly engendered great loyalty among the world's top players. One of them is Davis Love, and in 1992 he proved the extent of that loyalty. After sinking a 25-foot putt to win the individ-

ual title in the World Cup in Madrid, Spain, Love jumped on a plane and flew nearly 10,000 miles to Kapalua, where at the end of the week he sank another putt—this time 50 feet and this time for an eagle—to win for the second time in two weeks.

THE SKINS GAME

Most weekend golfers have played "skins" golf at least once, "the two tie, all tie" format for three or more players. Each player competes against all others on a hole-by-hole basis, and the only way to win the hole (or skin) is to score lower than all other players. If Player A makes a par and Players B, C, and D make bogeys, Player A wins the skin. If, however, A is tied by B, then no matter what the others players score, all four players tie the hole and the "skin" carries over to the next hole. If the group is playing for a one-dollar skin, then the next hole is worth two dollars. Theoretically, the group could tie the first 17 holes and then one player could win it all—18 dol-

lars from each of his or her opponents—with an outright victory at the final hole.

It is a format played all over the world, but never had the skins found its way to the pro ranks until 1983, when Arnold Palmer, Jack Nicklaus, Tom Watson, and Gary Player teed up at Nicklaus's Desert Highlands course in Arizona. In their case, however, the skins were not a dollar a hole, they started at $10,000 per hole for the first six, doubled to $20,000 for holes seven through 12, then upped to $30,000 for the final six holes. The total purse was $360,000, and with lots of ties along the way, large chunks of that total often hinged on single holes. Of course, in this case the players themselves did not ante up the cash, tournament sponsors did. But a percentage of each player's winnings went to charity. Gary Player was the winner with $170,000 for his efforts.

After two years at Desert Highlands, the event moved to another Nicklaus course, Bear Creek in Murietta, California, then settled in for a six-year run at

Kapalua Bay, Plantation Course, 17th hole

Riding a Tailwind

BY SANDY LYLE

The wind blows constantly in Hawaii, but on certain holes at Kapalua, you have it at your back. That's the time to be aggressive on the tee shot.

You want to get your ball up high so that you can ride that wind. Some teachers recommend teeing the drive a bit higher than normal. I disagree. I think an abnormally high tee forces most golfers to make compensations in their swings. Very often, they end up hitting under the ball and popping it straight up. I prefer teeing the ball at its usual height but positioning it farther forward in my stance, up near my left instep where I'll be sure to hit it on the upswing.

Other than that, I concentrate on keeping my right shoulder below my left throughout most of the swing. This helps me to stay behind and under the shot to ensure a high flight. You don't want to overswing on this shot and completely mishit it, but it's nice to know that on downwind shots you can afford to make a hard swing because the tailwind will straighten out a hook or slice.

On downwind approach shots, bear in mind that your ball will not only fly farther than usual, it will tend to bounce and roll farther as well because the wind strips it of normal backspin. Thus, depending on the strength of the helping breeze, take one, two, three, or even four clubs less than normal for the distance in question.

Sandy Lyle is the 1984 Lincoln-Mercury Kapalua International Champion.

Scorecard

Kapalua Bay, Plantation Course		
Hole	Yards	Par
1	473	4
2	218	3
3	380	4
4	382	4
5	532	5
6	398	4
7	484	4
8	203	3
9	521	5
OUT	3591	36
10	354	4
11	164	3
12	373	4
13	407	4
14	305	4
15	555	5
16	365	4
17	486	4
18	663	5
IN	3672	37
TOTAL	7263	73

Pete Dye's Stadium Course in La Quinta before moving to its current site, Bighorn, an Arthur Hills design carved into the foothills of the Santa Rosa Mountains.

The 18 holes are played over two days to stretch the live television coverage of this event, which is annually one of the highest rated telecasts. The foursome of players is composed of the defending champion, one player chosen by the sponsors, and two players chosen by a blue-ribbon panel of golf officials and journalists. The purse split among the four players now tops a half million dollars.

FRANKLIN FUNDS SHARK SHOOTOUT

In 1989 Greg Norman brought together about two dozen of his best Tour pro friends and staged a made-for-television competition among two-man teams. Norman had been inspired by a victory three years earlier (not one of his better-known triumphs) in the Bay Hill Golf Club member-guest, where he had teamed with golf photographer Lawrence Levy, playing under the same format, which calls for a different mode of competition each of the three days—alternate shot, best ball, and scramble.

Norman and his partner in the first Shootout, Jack Nicklaus, could muster only a 74 in the opening round but roared back with a 14-under-par 58 on Sunday over the Nicklaus-designed course at the Sherwood Country Club, a lavish enclave near Thousand Oaks, California. That year the tournament was won by Curtis Strange and Mark O'Meara with a score of 190, and the following year the team of Ray Floyd and

Fred Couples steamrolled the field with a 182, an average of less than 61 per round.

It is a small field but an elite and charismatic one, the mood is usually lighthearted, the birdies prevalent, and the TV ratings for this end-of-the-year event are usually good.

JC PENNEY MIXED TEAM CHAMPIONSHIP

The Innisbrook Resort in Tarpon Springs, Florida, is the annual site of the only major tournament that teams PGA Tour pros with their counterparts from the Ladies Professional Golf Association.

The event got its start in 1960, when it was known as the Haig & Haig Scotch Foursome. It ran for seven years, stopped for a decade, and returned in 1976. Virtually every top LPGA player has shared in a victory, including Mickey Wright, Kathy Whitworth, and Ruth Jessen in the original version and Pat Bradley, Nancy Lopez, JoAnne Carner, and Beth Daniel in recent years.

Play proceeds according to the Pinehurst format, in which each member of the team plays a drive, then the partners

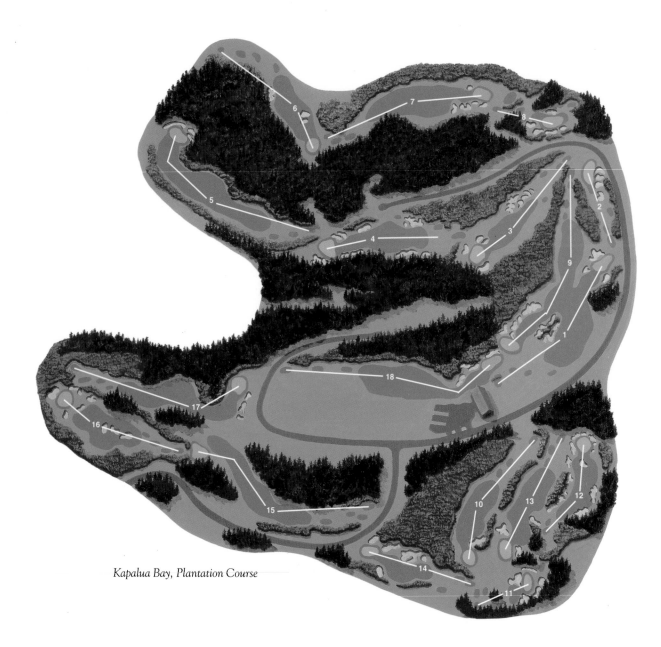

Kapalua Bay, Plantation Course

hit second shots from each other's drives, then decide which of the two second shots offers the better potential for success. Once that choice is made, they take the other ball out of play and finish the hole with the selected ball, alternating shots until the ball is holed.

Strategy in this event is both more complicated and more important than in a standard tournament. On a 520-yard par five, for example, a male pro may hit a 260-yard drive, then his female partner will add a 210-yard fairway wood straight down the middle. They must weight the promise of that position against that of their other ball, driven 240 yards by the female pro and boosted another 260 off

the fairway wood of the male pro, but into a greenside bunker. Should the man play a 50-yard pitch shot or the woman play a 60-foot explosion? Such decision-making is the key to the excitement of this format for both players and spectators.

DINERS CLUB MATCHES

Match play—the hole-by-hole game played by most weekend golfers— has only one slot in pro golf, the Diners Club Matches. The event, which began in 1994, was spurred by the revived interest in the Ryder Cup Matches, in which a team of players from America competes at match play against a team from Europe.

The Diners Club format is a single-elimination competition for two-player teams, with separate divisions for the PGA Tour, Senior Tour, and LPGA Tour. Sixteen teams compete in the regular Tour division with eight teams each in the women's and seniors' brackets. Seeded players earn their way into the field through victories in specific events or their finishes on the money list during the season. Each seeded player then chooses a partner from those not already qualified. The idea for the tournament came from LPGA Commissioner Charles Mechem along with Jack Nicklaus, whose TV production company brought the project to fruition.

All-Time Tournament Records

MERCEDES CHAMPIONSHIPS
(formerly Tournament of Champions)

Record	Player(s)	Score	Year
Low 18	Jack Nicklaus	64	1963
	Arnold Palmer		1967
	Frank Beard		1970
	Craig Stadler		1982
	David Graham		1984
	Tom Kite		1985, 1993
	Calvin Peete		1986
Low first 36	Tom Watson	131 (65-66)	1980
Low 36	Tom Watson	131 (65-66)	1980
Low first 54	Calvin Peete	199 (68-67-64)	1986
Low 54	Calvin Peete	199 (68-67-64)	1986
Low 72	Calvin Peete	267 (68-67-64-68)	1986
Highest winning score	Gene Littler	285	1957
Largest winning margin	Gene Littler	13 strokes (280)	1955
Largest 18-hole lead	Tom Kite	4 strokes (64)	1985
Largest 36-hole lead	Bobby Mitchell	4 strokes (136)	1972
	Bud Allin	(135)	1974
Largest 54-hole lead	Jack Nicklaus	5 strokes (209)	1971
	Don January	(208)	1976
	Tom Watson	(203)	1980
Lowest start by winner	Tom Kite	64	1985
Highest start by winner	Johnny Miller	75	1974
Lowest finish by winner	Gary Player	67	1978
	Tom Watson		1984
Highest finish by winner	Al Geiberger	73	1975
	Tom Watson		1980
	Lanny Wadkins		1982
Best final-round comeback	Gary Player	7 back	1978
Lowest 36-hole Cut score	No cut		

UNITED AIRLINES HAWAIIAN OPEN

Record	Player(s)	Score	Year
Low 18	Davis Love III	60	1994
Low first 36	Davis Love III	128 (68–60)	1994

Low 36	Hale Irwin	128 (66-62)	1981 (rounds 2-3)
	Davis Love III	128 (60-68)	1994
Low first 54	Hale Irwin	196 (68-66-62)	1981
Low 54	Andy Bean	195 (63-66-66)	1980 (rounds 2-3-4)
Low 72	Hale Irwin	265 (68-66-62-69)	1981
	John Cook	265 (67-68-65-65)	1992
Highest winning score	Dudley Wysong	284 (72-69-70-73)	1967
Largest winning margin	Hale Irwin (265)	6 strokes	1981
Largest 18-hole lead	Jack Nicklaus (63)	4 strokes	1969
Largest 36-hole lead	Jack Nicklaus (134)	4 strokes	1969
	Tom Watson (133)		1973
	Jack Nicklaus (132)		1974
	Davis Love III (128)		1994
Largest 54-hole lead	Jack Nicklaus (201)	6 strokes	1974
Lowest start by winner	Howard Twitty	63	1993
Highest start by winner	Gay Brewer	74	1965
Lowest finish by winner	Grier Jones	64	1972
	Corey Pavin		1987
Highest finish by winner	Dudley Wysong	73	1967
Best final-round comeback	Corey Pavin	6 back	1987
	Lanny Wadkins		1991
Lowest 36-hole cut score		141	1989, 1991, 1994
Highest 36-hole cut score		152	1965

NORTHERN TELECOM OPEN (TUCSON)

Record	Player(s)	Score	Year
Low 18	David Frost	60	1990
Low first 36	Joe Campbell	129 (65-64)	1959
	Julius Boros	(65-64)	1959
	Bruce Lietzke	(63-66)	1979
	Craig Stadler	(65-64)	1982
Low 36	Johnny Palmer	126 (62-64)	1948 (rounds 3-4)
	Mark Wiebe	126 (65-61)	1988 (rounds 2-3)
Low first 54	Joe Campbell	194 (65-64-65)	1959
Low 54	Joe Campbell	194 (65-64-65)	1959
Low 72	Lloyd Mangrum	263	1949
	Phil Rodgers		1962
	Johnny Miller		1975

Highest winning score	Joe Campbell	278	1966
Largest winning margin	Don January (266)	11 strokes	1963
Lowest start by winner	Johnny Miller	62	1974
Highest start by winner	Lee Janzen	71	1992
Lowest finish by winner	Johnny Miller	61	1975
Highest finish by winner	Arnold Palmer	73	1967
	Miller Barber		1972
	Tom Watson		1978
Lowest 36-hole cut score		139	1959
Highest 36-hole cut score		148	1964

PHOENIX OPEN

Record	Player(s)	Score	Year
Low 18	Johnny Miller	61	1970, 1975
	Homero Blancas		1972
	Ben Crenshaw		1979
	Don Pooley		1986
Low first 36	Johnny Miller	128 (67-61)	1975
	Ben Crenshaw	128 (67-61)	1979
	Hal Sutton	128 (64-64)	1986
Low 36	Johnny Miller	128 (67-61)	1975
	Ben Crenshaw	128 (67-61)	1979
	Lanny Wadkins	128 (63-65)	1982 (rounds 3-4)
	Hal Sutton	128 (64-64)	1986
	Don Pooley	128 (61-67)	1986 (rounds 2-3)
Low first 54	Johnny Miller	196 (67-61-68)	1975
	Hal Sutton	196 (64-64-68)	1986
Low 54	Johnny Miller	193 (61-68-64)	1975 (rounds 2-3-4)
Low 72	Johnny Miller	260 (67-61-68-64)	1975
Highest winning score	Ky Laffoon	281	1935
Largest winning margin	Johnny Miller (260)	14 strokes	1975
Largest 18-hole lead	Arnold Palmer (64)	3 strokes	1962
	Davis Love III (63)		1988
Largest 36-hole lead	Byron Nelson (133)	6 strokes	1939
	Johnny Miller (128)		1975
Largest 54-hole lead	Byron Nelson (198)	12 strokes	1939
Lowest start by winner	Jimmy Demaret	64	1950
	Arnold Palmer		1962
	Hal Sutton		1986
Highest start by winner	Dudley Wysong	73	1966
Lowest finish by winner	Mark Calcavecchia	63	1992

Highest finish by winner	Jimmy Demaret	73	1949
	Jerry Pate		1977
Best final-round comeback	Sandy Lyle	7 back	1988
Lowest 36-hole cut score		140	1991
Highest 36-hole cut score		153	1953

AT&T PEBBLE BEACH NATIONAL PRO-AM

Record	Player(s)	Score	Year
Low 18	Tom Kite	62	1983
Low first 36	Bob Rosburg	132 (65-67)	1958
Low 36	Bob Rosburg	132 (65-67)	1958
	Mike Morley	(65-67)	1982 (rounds 3-4)
	Paul Azinger	(64-68)	1992 (rounds 3-4)
Low first 54	Cary Middlecoff	202 (66-68-68)	1956*
	Tom Watson	(66-69-67)	1977
Low 54	Cary Middlecoff	202 (66-68-68)	1956*
	Tom Watson	(66-69-67)	1977
	Paul Azinger	(70-64-68)	1992 (rounds 2-3-4)
Low 72	Tom Watson	273 (66-69-67-71)	1977
Highest winning score	Ken Venturi	286 (70-71-68-77)	1960
Largest winning margin	Lloyd Mangrum (205)	5 strokes	1948*
	Cary Middlecoff (202)		1956*
	Jack Nicklaus (284)		1967
	Fuzzy Zoeller (205)		1986*
Largest 18-hole lead	Jack Nicklaus (66)	3 strokes	1972
	Billy Casper (66)		1973
	Tom Watson (66)		1978
Largest 36-hole lead	Bob Rosburg (132)	5 strokes	1958
Largest 54-hole lead	Ted Kroll (203)	5 strokes	1961
	Lon Hinkle (207)		1979
	Fuzzy Zoeller (205)		1986
Lowest start by winner	John Dawson**	66	1942t
	Cary Middlecoff		1956*
	Jack Nicklaus		1972
	Tom Watson		1977, 1978
	John Cook		1981*
	Mark O'Meara		1989
Highest start by winner	Jack Burke	75	1950*
	Bruce Crampton		1965
	Ben Crenshaw		1976
Lowest finish by winner	Jim Simons	66	1982
	Johnny Miller		1987
Highest finish by winner	Ken Venturi	77	1960
	Lon Hinkle		1979
Best final-round comeback	Bob Rosburg	7 back	1961

Lowest 54-hole cut score		215	1992
Highest 54-hole cut score		227	1967

* 54-hole tournament
** amateur
t 36-hole tournament

NISSAN LOS ANGELES OPEN

Record	Player(s)	Score	Year
Low 18	George Archer	61	1983
Low first 36	Davis Love III	130 (67-63)	1992
Low 36	Arnold Palmer	128 (66-62)	1966 (rounds 2-3)
Low first 54	Fred Couples	197 (68-67-62)	1990
Low 54	Fred Couples	197 (68-67-62)	1990
Low 72	Lanny Wadkins	264 (63-70-67-64)	1985
Highest winning score	Denny Shute	296	1930
Largest winning margin	Phil Rodgers (268)	9 strokes	1962
Largest 18-hole lead	Terry Mauney	4 strokes	1982
Largest 36-hole lead	Henry Ransom	4 strokes	1951
	Davis Love III		1992
Largest 54-hole lead	Pat Fitzsimons	6 strokes	1975
Lowest start by winner	Charles Sifford	63	1969
	Lanny Wadkins		1985
Highest start by winner	Jimmy Thomson	75	1938
Lowest finish by winner	Phil Rodgers	62	1962
Highest finish by winner	Fred Wampler	75	1954
Best final-round comeback	Ken Venturi	7 back	1959
Lowest 36-hole cut score		140	1991
Highest 36-hole cut score		156	1952

BOB HOPE CHRYSLER CLASSIC

Record	Player(s)	Score	Year
Low 18	Bert Yancey	61	1974
	David Edwards		1987
Low first 36	Lennie Clemente	128 (66-62)	1994
	Scott Hoch		1994
Low 36	John Cook	127 (63-64)	1991 (rounds 4-5)
	Tom Kite		1993
		(65-62)	(rounds 4-5)
Low first 54	Bruce Lietzke	196 (65-66-65)	1981
Low 54	Tom Kite	191 (64-65-62)	1993 (rounds 3-4-5)
Low first 72	Tom Kite	263 (67-67-64-65)	1993
Low 72	Tom Kite	258 (67-64-65-62)	1993 (rounds 2-3-4-5)
Low 90	Tom Kite	325 (67-67-64-65-62)	1993

Highest winning score	Doug Sanders	349	1966
	Tom Nieporte		1967
Largest winning margin	Rik Massengale (337)	6 strokes	1977
	Tom Kite (325)		1993
Largest 18-hole lead	Rik Massengale (64)	3 strokes	1977
	Craig Stadler (63)		1983
Largest 36-hole lead	Craig Stadler (129)	6 strokes	1983
Largest 54-hole lead	Jack Nicklaus (207)	5 strokes	1963
	Bruce Lietzke (196)		1981
Largest 72-hole lead	Rik Massengale (270)	6 strokes	1977
Lowest start by winner	Jay Haas	63	1988
Highest start by winner	Tom Nieporte	76	1967
	Steve Jones		1989
Lowest finish by winner	Tom Kite	62	1993
Highest finish by winner	Jack Nicklaus	72	1963
	Billy Casper		1965
Best final-round comeback	Tommy Jacobs	4 back	1964
	Doug Sanders		1966
	John Mahaffey		1984
Lowest 72-hole cut score		278	1993
Highest 72-hole cut score		295	1976

BUICK INVITATIONAL OF CALIFORNIA

Record	Player(s)	Score	Year
Low 18	Gene Littler	62	1965
	Craig Stadler		1987
	Andy Bean		1987
	Gil Morgan		1988
Low first 36	Gary Player	130	1963
	Bob Eastwood		1990
	David Toms		1994
Low 36	Billy Casper	127 (63-64)	1965 (rounds 3-4)
Low first 54	Woody Blackburn	198 (66-66-66)	1985
Low 54	Gil Morgan	197 (62-67-68)	1988 (rounds 2-3-4)
Low 72	George Burns	266 (63-68-70-65)	1987
Highest winning score	Jack Nicklaus	284 (68-72-71-73)	1969
Largest winning margin	Tom Watson (269)	5 strokes	1977
	Fuzzy Zoeller (282)		1979
Largest 18-hole lead	Jimmy Powell (64)	2 strokes	1968
	Gene Littler (66)		1972
	Tommy Aaron (69)		1979
	Jay Haas (70)		1993
Largest 36-hole lead	Jay Haas (136)	3 strokes	1978
	Johnny Miller (132)		1982
	Tom Kite (133)		1983

Record	Player(s)	Score	Year
	Payne Stewart (138)		1993
	David Toms (130)		1994
Largest 54-hole lead	J.C. Snead (200)	5 strokes	1976
Lowest start by winner	George Burns	63	1987
Highest start by winner	Pete Brown	76	1970
	Fuzzy Zoeller		1979
Lowest finish by winner	Billy Casper	64	1966
Highest finish by winner	Jack Nicklaus	73	1969
Best final-round comeback	Pete Brown	7 back	1970
Lowest 36-hole cut score		139	1985
Highest 36-hole cut score		151	1993

DORAL-RYDER OPEN

Record	Player(s)	Score	Year
Low 18	Greg Norman	62	1990, 1993
Low first 36	Tom Weiskopf	133 (67-66)	1968
	Jerry Heard	(65-68)	1974
	Kenny Perry	(69-64)	1991
	Greg Norman	(65-68)	1993
	Paul Azinger	(67-66)	1993
Low 36	Greg Norman	130 (68-62)	1993 (rounds 2-3)
Low first 54	Greg Norman	195 (65-68-62)	1993
Low 54	Greg Norman	195 (65-68-62)	1993
Low 72	Greg Norman	265 (65-68-62-70)	1993
Highest winning score	Mark McCumber	284 (70-71-72-71)	1985
Largest winning margin	Hubert Green (270)	6 strokes	1976
Largest 18-hole lead	Lee Trevino (64)	4 strokes	1973
Largest 36-hole lead	Lee Trevino (134)	4 strokes	1973
Largest 54-hole lead	Greg Norman (195)	6 strokes	1993
Lowest start by winner	Lee Trevino	64	1973
Highest start by winner	Dan Sikes	76	1963
Lowest finish by winner	Greg Norman	62	1990
Highest finish by winner	Gardner Dickinson	72	1968
	Andy Bean		1977
	Mark McCumber		1979
	Bill Glasson		1989
	Rocco Mediate		1991
Best final-round comeback	Greg Norman	7 back	1990
Lowest 36-hole cut score		143	1986, 1991, 1993
Highest 36-hole cut score		153	1962

HONDA CLASSIC

Record	Player(s)	Score	Year
Low 18	Dan Pohl	62	1989
Low first 36	Dan Pohl	128 (66-62)	1989
Low 36	Dan Pohl	128 (66-62)	1989
Low first 54	George Burns	200 (66-67-67)	1982
Low 54	Blaine McCallister	196 (67-65-64)	1989 (rounds 2-3-4)
Low 72	Blaine McCallister	266 (70-67-65-64)	1989
Highest winning score	Kenny Knox	287 (66-71-80-70)	1986
Largest winning margin	Jack Nicklaus (275)	5 strokes	1977
Largest 18-hole lead	Mike Sullivan (65)	4 strokes	1987
Largest 36-hole lead	Jack Nicklaus (136)	4 strokes	1977
Largest 54-hole lead	Steve Pate (204)	5 strokes	1991
Lowest start by winner	Fred Couples	64	1993
Highest start by winner	Bruce Lietzke	72	1984
Lowest finish by winner	Blaine McCallister	64	1989
Highest finish by winner	Steve Pate	75	1991
Best final-round comeback	Bruce Lietzke	4 back	1984
Lowest 36-hole cut score		140	1989
Highest 36-hole cut score		151	1987, 1990

NESTLÉ INVITATIONAL

Record	Player(s)	Score	Year
Low 18	Andy Bean	62	1981
	Greg Norman		1984
Low first 36	Andy Bean	130 (68-62)	1981
	Tom Watson	(64-66)	1981
Low 36	Payne Stewart	128 (63-65)	1987 (rounds 3-4)
Low first 54	Andy Bean	197 (68-62-67)	1981
Low 54	Payne Stewart	195 (67-63-65)	1987
Low 72	Payne Stewart	264 (69-67-63-65)	1987
Highest winning score	Mike Nicolette	283 (66-72-71-74)	1983
Largest winning margin	Fred Couples (269)	9 strokes	1992
Largest 18-hole lead	Tom Byrum (64)	3 strokes	1990
Largest 36-hole lead	Paul Azinger (132)	4 strokes	1988
Largest 54-hole lead	Mike Nicolette (209)	6 strokes	1983
	Fred Couples (199)		1992
Lowest start by winner	Mike Nicolette	66	1983
	Paul Azinger		1988

Highest start by winner	Robert Gamez Ben Crenshaw	71	1990 1993
Lowest finish by winner	Gary Koch	63	1984
Highest finish by winner	Dave Eichelberger	74	1980
Best final-round comeback	Tom Kite Gary Koch	6 back	1982 1984
Lowest 36-hole cut score		143	1982
Highest 36-hole cut score		152	1983

THE PLAYERS CHAMPIONSHIP

Record	Player(s)	Score	Year
Low 18	Fred Couples Greg Norman	63	1992 1994
Low first 36	Greg Norman	130 (63-67)	1994
Low 36	Greg Norman	130 (63-67)	1994
Low first 54	Greg Norman	197 (63-67-67)	1994
Low 54	Greg Norman	197 ((63-67-67)	1994
Low 72	Greg Norman	264 ((63-67-67-67)	1994
Highest winning score	Mark Hayes	289 (72-74-71-72)	1977
	Jack Nicklaus	289 (70-71-73-75)	1978
Largest winning margin	Lanny Wadkins (283)	5 strokes	1979
	Nick Price (270)		1993
Largest 18-hole lead	Billy Ray Brown (64)	3 strokes	1992
Largest 36-hole lead	Lanny Wadkins (135)	3 strokes	1979
	Greg Norman (130)		1994
Largest 54-hole lead	Larry Mize (200)	4 strokes	1986
Lowest start by winner	Greg Norman	63	1994
Highest start by winner	Hal Sutton	73	1983
Lowest finish by winner	Jack Nicklaus	65	1976
Highest finish by winner	Jack Nicklaus	75	1978
Best final-round comeback	Raymond Floyd	6 strokes	1981
Lowest 36-hole cut score		142	1993
Highest 36-hole cut score		155	1977

FREEPORT-McMoRan CLASSIC

Record	Player(s)	Score	Year
Low 18	Bob Gilder Dennis Paulson	62	1979 1994
Low first 36	Dick Mast	132 (64-68)	1987
	Lanny Wadkins	(67-65)	1988
	Chip Beck	(67-65)	1992

Low 36	Chip Beck	129 (64-65) (65-64)	1988 (rounds 2-3) (rounds 3-4)
Low first 54	Chip Beck	198 (69-64-65)	1988
Low 54	Chip Beck	193 (64-65-64)	1988 (rounds 2-3-4)
Low 72	Chip Beck	262 (69-64-65-64)	1988
Highest winning score	Jimmy Demaret	286	1940
Largest winning margin	Lee Trevino (267)	8 strokes	1974
Largest 18-hole lead	José Maria Olazabal (63)	4 strokes	1994
	Mike Reasor (65)		1976
	Skip Dunaway (64)		1981
	John Mahaffey (63)		1985
	Dan Forsman (66)		1989
Largest 36-hole lead	Chip Beck (132)	4 strokes	1992
Largest 54-hole lead	Billy Casper (201)	5 strokes	1975
	Calvin Peete (201)		1986
Lowest start by winner	Tom Watson Bob Eastwood Ben Crenshaw	66	1980 1984 1987
Highest start by winner	Lon Hinkle	74	1978
Lowest finish by winner	Chip Beck	64	1988
Highest finish by winner	Mason Rudolph	75	1964
Best final-round comeback	Larry Hinson	5 back	1969
Lowest 36-hole cut score		141	1988
Highest 36-hole cut score		152	1993

THE MASTERS

Record	Player(s)	Score	Year
Low 18	Nick Price	63	1986
Low first 36	Raymond Floyd	131 (65-66)	1976
Low 36	Johnny Miller	131 (65-66)	1975 (rounds 3-4)
	Raymond Floyd	(65-66)	1976
Low first 54	Raymond Floyd	201 (65-66-70)	1976
Low 54	Raymond Floyd	201 (65-66-70)	1976
Low 72	Jack Nicklaus	271 (67-71-64-69)	1965
	Raymond Floyd	271 (65-66-70-70)	1976
Highest winning score	Sam Snead	289 (74-73-70-72)	1954
	Jack Burke Jr.	(72-71-75-71)	1956
Largest winning margin	Jack Nicklaus	9 strokes	1965
Largest 18-hole lead	Craig Wood (66)	5 strokes	1941
Largest 36-hole lead	Herman Keiser (137)	5 strokes	1946

Record	Player(s)	Score	Year
	Jack Nicklaus (135)		1975
	Raymond Floyd (131)		1976
Largest 54-hole lead	Raymond Floyd (201)	8 strokes	1976
Lowest start by winner	Raymond Floyd	65	1976
Highest start by winner	Craig Stadler	75	1982
Lowest finish by winner	Gary Player	64	1978
Highest finish by winner	Arnold Palmer	75	1962
Best final-round comeback	Jack Burke Jr.	8 back	1956
Lowest 36-hole cut score		145	1979, 1992
Highest 36-hole cut score		154	1982

DEPOSIT GUARANTY GOLF CLASSIC

Record	Player(s)	Score	Year
Low 18	Ernie Gonzalez	62	1986
	Mike West		1987
	Robert Wrenn		1987
	Emlyn Aubrey		1991
	Mike Donald		1992
Low first 36	Allan Strange	129 (66-63)	1981
Low 36	Mike Nicolette	128 (64-64)	1992
Low first 54	Dan Halldorson	197 (64-67-66)	1986
	Mike Donald	(68-62-67)	1992
Low 54	Dan Halldorson	197 (64-67-66)	1986
	Brandel Chamblee	(67-64-66)	1991 (rounds 2-3-4)
	Russ Cochran	(65-69-63)	1991 (rounds 2-3-4)
	Ed Fiori	(65-67-65)	1991 (rounds 2-3-4)
	Mike Donald	(68-62-67)	1992
	Mike Nicolette	(64-64-69)	1992 (rounds 2-3-4)
	Grant Waite	(65-69-63)	1993 (rounds 2-3-4)
Low 72	Dan Halldorson	263 (64-67-66-66)	1986
Highest winning score	Larry Mowry	272 (71-67-66-68)	1969
	Bobby Walzel	(72-68-67-65)	1979
Largest winning margin	Frank Conner (267)	5 strokes	1988
Largest 18-hole lead	Several players	2 strokes	
Largest 36-hole lead	Dwight Nevil (131)	4 strokes	1973
	Allan Strange (129)		1981
Largest 54-hole lead	Mike Morley (200)	4 strokes	1972
Lowest start by winner	Dwight Nevil	64	1973
	Dan Halldorson		1986
	Jim Booros		1989
Highest start by winner	Bobby Walzel	72	1979
Lowest finish by winner	Craig Stadler	63	1978
	Russ Cochran		1983
	Frank Conner		1988

Record	Player(s)	Score	Year
	Larry Silveira		1991
Highest finish by winner	Bob Wynn	71	1975
Best final-round comeback	Russ Cochran	7 back	1983
Lowest 36-hole cut score		140	1981, 1991, 1992
Highest 36-hole cut score		145	1973, 1975, 1983, 1989

MCI HERITAGE CLASSIC

Record	Player(s)	Score	Year
Low 18	David Frost	61	1994
Low first 36	Jack Nicklaus	129 (66-63)	1992 1975
Low 36	Jack Nicklaus	129 (66-63)	1975
	David Edwards	129 (65-64)	1994 (rounds 3-4)
	Ian Baker-Finch	(64-65)	1991 (rounds 2-3)
Low first 54	Hale Irwin	198 (68-65-65)	1994
	Payne Stewart	199 (65-67-67)	1989
Low 54	Ian Baker-Finch	198 (64-65-69)	1991 (rounds 2-3-4)
	Hale Irwin	198 (68-65-65)	1994
Low 72	Hale Irwin	266 (68-65-65-68)	1994
Highest winning score	Arnold Palmer	283 (68-71-70-74)	1969
Largest winning margin	Hale Irwin (272)	5 strokes	1973
	Hubert Green (274)		1976
	Tom Watson (270)		1979
	Payne Stewart (268)		1989
Largest 18-hole lead	Jack Nicklaus (66)	3 strokes	1975
Largest 36-hole lead	Johnny Miller (134)	6 strokes	1974
	Jack Nicklaus (129)		1975
Largest 54-hole lead	Tom Watson (199)	8 strokes	1979
Lowest start by winner	Graham Marsh	65	1977
	Tom Watson		1979
	Greg Norman		1988
	Payne Stewart		1989
	Davis Love III		1991
Highest start by winner	Bob Goalby	74	1970
Lowest finish by winner	Bob Goalby	66	1970
	Greg Norman		1988
Best final-round comeback	Hubert Green	5 back	1978
Lowest 36-hole cut score		143	1993, 1994
Highest 36-hole cut score		152	1971

Kmart Greater Greensboro Open

Record	Player(s)	Score	Year
Low 18	Davis Love III	62	1992
Low first 36	Jeff Sluman	129 (64-65)	1988
Low 36	Jeff Sluman	129 (64-65)	1988
Low first 54	George Archer	199 (67-64-68)	1967
	Dave Stockton	(67-67-65)	1967
	Billy Casper	(67-64-68)	1973
	Lou Graham	(68-64-67)	1973
	Sandy Lyle	(68-63-68)	1988
Low 54	George Archer	199 (67-64-68)	1967
	Dave Stockton	(67-67-65)	1967
	Billy Casper	(67-64-68)	1973
	Lou Graham	(68-64-67)	1973
	Sandy Lyle	(68-63-68)	1988
Low 72	George Archer	267 (67-64-68-68)	1967
	Billy Casper	(65-67-69-66)	1968
	Chi Chi Rodriguez	(68-66-67-66)	1973
Highest winning score	Vic Ghezzi	286 (69-72-72-73)	1947
Largest winning margin	Ben Hogan (270)	9 strokes	1940
Largest 18-hole lead	Sam Snead (64)	3 strokes	1964
	Tom Weiskopf (64)		1975
Largest 36-hole lead	Sam Snead (135)	5 strokes	1956
	Tom Weiskopf (135)		1975
	Sandy Lyle (132)		1986
Largest 54-hole lead	Ben Hogan (203)	7 strokes	1940
Lowest start by winner	Gary Player	63	1970
Highest start by winner	Brian Allin	75	1971
Lowest finish by winner	Davis Love III	62	1992
Highest finish by winner	Dow Finsterwald	77	1959
Best final-round comeback	Steve Elkington	7 back	1990
	Mark Brooks		1991

Shell Houston Open

Record	Player(s)	Score	Year
Low 18	Ron Streck	62	1981
	Fred Funk	62	1992
Low first 36	Curtis Strange	129 (66-63)	1980
	Blaine McCallister	(64-65)	1993
Low 36	Curtis Strange	129 (66-63)	1980
	Blaine McCallister	(64-65)	1993
Low first 54	Curtis Strange	195 (66-63-66)	1980
Low 54	Curtis Strange	195 (66-63-66)	1980
Low 72	Curtis Strange	266 (66-63-66-71)	1980
Highest winning score	Cary Middlecoff	283	1953
Largest winning margin	Jack Burke Jr. (277)	6 strokes	1952
Largest 18-hole lead	Ed Furgol	2 strokes	1950
Largest 36-hole lead	Curtis Strange (129)	4 strokes	1980
	Mike Donald (134)		1989
	Jeff Maggert (130)		1991
Largest 54-hole lead	Curtis Strange (195)	6 strokes	1980
Lowest start by winner	Gary Player	64	1978
	Ed Sneed		1982
Highest start by winner	Mike Sullivan	76	1989
Lowest finish by winner	Ron Streck	62	1981
Highest finish by winner	Bill Collins	75	1960
Best final-round comeback	Mike Sullivan	7 back	1989
	Fulton Allem		1991
Lowest 36-hole cut score		140	1993
Highest 36-hole cut score		159	1947

BellSouth Classic

Record	Player(s)	Score	Year
Low 18	Andy Bean	61	1979
Low first 36	Larry Nelson	129 (63-66)	1988
Low 36	Andy Bean	128 (67-61)	1979 (rounds 2-3)
		(61-67)	(rounds 3-4)
Low first 54	Larry Nelson	195 (63-66-66)	1988
Low 54	Andy Bean	195 (67-61-67)	1979 (rounds 2-3-4)
	Larry Nelson	(63-66-66)	1988
Low 72	Andy Bean	265 (70-67-61-67)	1979
	Dave Barr	(66-68-66-65)	1987
Highest winning score	Bob Charles	284 (72-71-69-70)	1967
Largest winning margin	Andy Bean (265)	8 strokes	1979
Largest 18-hole lead	Mark Lye (63)	4 strokes	1979
Largest 36-hole lead	Jack Nicklaus (133)	4 strokes	1973
	Larry Nelson (129)		1988
Largest 54-hole lead	Jack Nicklaus (199)	6 strokes	1973
Lowest start by winner	Larry Nelson	63	1988
Highest start by winner	Bob Charles	72	1967
	Scott Simpson		1989
	Wayne Levi		1990
Lowest finish by winner	Calvin Peete	63*	1983
Highest finish by winner	Jack Nicklaus	73	1973
	Larry Nelson		1988
Best final-round comeback	Wayne Levi	4 back	1985*
	Bob Tway		1986
	Scott Simpson		1989
	Nolan Henke		1993
Lowest 36-hole cut score		141	1987
Highest 36-hole cut score		151	1967

* 54-hole tournament

GTE BYRON NELSON GOLF CLASSIC

Record	Player(s)	Score	Year
Low 18	Sam Snead	60	1957
Low first 36	John McMullin	129 (64-65)	1958
	Wayne Levi	129 (62-67)	1989
	Dan Forsman	129 (65-64)	1993
Low 36	Sam Snead	126 (60-66)	1957 (rounds 2-3)
Low first 54	Sam Snead	196 (70-60-66)	1957
	Fred Couples	(65-67-64)	1987
Low 54	Sam Snead	194 (60-66-68)	1957 (rounds 2-3-4)
Low 72	Sam Snead	264 (70-60-66-68)	1957
Highest winning score	Ben Hogan	284 (70-69-72-73)	1946
Largest winning margin	Byron Nelson (276)	10 strokes	1946
	Sam Snead (264)		1957
Lowest start by winner	Don January Tom Watson	64	1956 1979, 1980
Highest start by winner	Tom Watson	72	1975
Lowest finish by winner	Peter Thomson	63	1956
Highest finish by winner	Ben Hogan	73	1946
Best final-round comeback	Peter Thomson	7 back	1956
Lowest 36-hole cut score		137	1989
Highest 36-hole cut score		149	1970, 1984

MEMORIAL TOURNAMENT

Record	Player(s)	Score	Year
Low 18	Kenny Perry	63	1991
Low first 36	Scott Hoch	131 (67-64)	1987
Low 36	Scott Hoch	131 (67-64)	1987
	Denis Watson	(66-65)	1987 (rounds 2-3)
	Curtis Strange	(64-67)	1988 (rounds 3-4)
	Hale Irwin	(65-66)	1991 (rounds 3-4)
Low first 54	Scott Hoch	198 (67-64-67)	1987
Low 54	Scott Hoch	198 (67-64-67)	1987
Low 72	Hal Sutton	271 (68-69-66-68)	1986
Highest winning score	Roger Maltbie	288 (71-71-70-76)	1976
Largest winning margin	Hal Sutton (271)	4 strokes	1986
Largest 18-hole lead	Fred Couples (69)	4 strokes	1990
Largest 36-hole lead	Roger Maltbie (134)	6 strokes	1982

(Memorial Tournament continued / right column top)

Record	Player(s)	Score	Year
Largest 54-hole lead	Tom Watson (214)	4 strokes	1979
	Scott Hoch (198)		1987
Lowest start by winner	Jim Simons	68	1978
	Hale Irwin		1985
	Hal Sutton		1986
	Paul Azinger		1993
Highest start by winner	Raymond Floyd	74	1982
Lowest finish by winner	Curtis Strange David Edwards	67	1988 1992
Highest finish by winner	Roger Maltbie	76	1976
Best final-round comeback	David Edwards	5 back	1992
Lowest 36-hole cut score		145	1992, 1993
Highest 36-hole cut score		157	1976, 1979, 1990

COLONIAL NATIONAL INVITATION

Record	Player(s)	Score	Year
Low 18	Keith Clearwater Lee Janzen	61	1993 1993
Low first 36	Fulton Allem	129 (66-63)	1993
Low 36	Keith Clearwater	128 (64-64)	1987 (rounds 3-4)
	Greg Norman	(64-64)	1983 (rounds 2-3)
Low first 54	Fulton Allem	197 (66-63-68)	1993
	Greg Norman	(69-64-64)	1993
Low 54	Greg Norman	196 (64-64-68)	1993 (rounds 2-3-4)
Low 72	Fulton Allem	264 (66-63-68-67)	1993
Highest winning score	Ben Hogan	285 (69-67-77-72)	1959
Largest winning margin	Chandler Harper (276)	8 strokes	1955
Largest 18-hole lead	Dave Stockton (65)	2 strokes	1967
	Bruce Lietzke (63)		1980
Largest 36-hole lead	Chandler Harper (134)	7 strokes	1955
Largest 54-hole lead	Chandler Harper (204)	6 strokes	1955
Lowest start by winner	Bruce Lietzke	63	1980
Highest start by winner	Ben Hogan Mike Souchak	74	1952 1956
Lowest finish by winner	Keith Clearwater Tom Purtzer	64	1987 1991
Highest finish by winner	Arnold Palmer	76	1962
Best final-round comeback	Ben Hogan	6 back	1952
Lowest 36-hole cut score		141	1987
Highest 36-hole cut score		148	1971, 1973

KEMPER OPEN

Record	Player(s)	Score	Year
Low 18	Jerry McGee	61	1979
Low first 36	Craig Stadler	131 (62-69)	1979
	Hal Sutton	(66-65)	1991
Low 36	Billy Andrade	128 (64-64)	1991 (rounds 2-3)
	Jeff Sluman	(64-64)	1991 (rounds 2-3)
Low first 54	Hal Sutton	195 (66-65-64)	1991
Low 54	Jeff Sluman	193 (64-64-65)	1991 (rounds 2-3-4)
Low 72	Billy Andrade	263 (68-64-64-67)	1991
	Jeff Sluman	(70-64-64-65)	1991
Highest winning score	Fred Couples	287 (71-71-68-77)	1983
Largest winning margin	Craig Stadler (275)	7 strokes	1982
	Tom Kite (270)		1987
Largest 18-hole lead	George Burns (64)	4 strokes	1983
Largest 36-hole lead	Greg Norman (136)	4 strokes	1984
Largest 54-hole lead	Greg Norman (207)	7 strokes	1984
Lowest start by winner	Jerry McGee	61	1979
Highest start by winner	Dick Lotz	72	1970
	Andy Bean		1978
	Craig Stadler		1982
	Bill Glasson		1985
	Greg Norman		1986
Lowest finish by winner	Andy Bean	66	1978
	Bill Glasson		1985
	Greg Norman		1986
Highest finish by winner	Fred Couples	77	1983
Best final-round comeback	Bill Glasson	6 back	1985
Lowest 36-hole cut score		140	1991
Highest 36-hole cut score		150	1983, 1984

BUICK CLASSIC (WESTCHESTER)

Record	Player(s)	Score	Year
Low 18	Dan Sikes	62	1967
	Jimmy Wright		1976
	Peter Jacobsen		1982
Low first 36	Bob Gilder	127 (64-63)	1982
Low 36	Bob Gilder	127 (64-63)	1982
Low first 54	Bob Gilder	192 (64-63-65)	1982
Low 54	Bob Gilder	192 (64-63-65)	1982
Low 72	Bob Gilder	261 (64-63-65-69)	1982
Highest winning score	Vijay Singh	280 (72-68-74-66)	1993
Largest winning margin	David Frost (268)	8 strokes	1992
Largest 18-hole lead	Tom Weiskopf (64)	3 strokes	1973

Record	Player(s)	Score	Year
	David Graham (65)		1979
Largest 36-hole lead	Tom Weiskopf (129)	7 strokes	1975
Largest 54-hole lead	Bob Gilder (192)	6 strokes	1982
Lowest start by winner	David Graham	63	1976
Highest start by winner	Bob Tway	73	1986
Lowest finish by winner	Bobby Nichols	65	1973
	Scott Simpson		1984
Highest finish by winner	Wayne Grady	72	1989
Best final-round comeback	Bobby Nichols	5 back	1973
	Vijay Singh		1993
Lowest 36-hole cut score		141	1982
Highest 36-hole cut score		147	1983, 1993

CANON GREATER HARTFORD OPEN

Record	Player(s)	Score	Year
Low 18	Tommy Bolt	60	1954
Low first 36	Tim Norris	127 (63-64)	1982
Low 36	Tim Norris	127 (63-64)	1982
Low first 54	Tim Norris	193 (63-64-66)	1982
Low 54	Tim Norris	193 (63-64-66)	1982
Low 72	Tim Norris	259 (63-64-66-66)	1982
Highest winning score	Arnold Palmer	274	1956
	Billy Casper		1965
Largest winning margin	Sam Snead (269)	7 strokes	1955
Largest 18-hole lead	Several players	2 strokes	
Largest 36-hole lead	Skee Riegel (133)	4 strokes	1952
	Jack Burke Jr. (130)		1958
Largest 54-hole lead	Sam Snead (199)	5 strokes	1955
Lowest start by winner	Jack Burke Jr.	63	1958
	Tim Norris		1982
Highest start by winner	Phil Blackmar	72	1985
Lowest finish by winner	Mac O'Grady	62	1986
Highest finish by winner	Paul Azinger	72	1987
Best final-round comeback	Billy Casper	5 back	1963
	Mac O'Grady		1986
	Lanny Wadkins		1992
Lowest 36-hole cut score		139	1981, 1982, 1983
Highest 36-hole cut score		152	1958

MOTOROLA WESTERN OPEN

Record	Player(s)	Score	Year
Low 18	Cary Middlecoff	63	1955
	Jeff Sluman		1992
Low first 36	Hugh Royer	132 (67-65)	1970
Low 36	Hugh Royer	132 (67-65)	1970
Low first 54	Sam Snead	201 (69-67-65)	1949
Low 54	Sam Snead	199 (67-65-67)	1949
Low 72	Sam Snead	268 (69-67-65-67)	1949
	Chi Chi Rodriguez	(64-69-68-67)	1964
Highest winning score	Alex Smith	318	1903
Largest winning margin	Walter Hagen (279)	9 strokes	1927
Largest 18-hole lead	David Graham (65)	3 strokes	1975
Largest 36-hole lead	Bob Dickson (136)	6 strokes	1976
Largest 54-hole lead	Tom Weiskopf (212)	5 strokes	1974
	Bob Dickson (210)		1976
	Scott Simpson (209)		1980
Lowest start by winner	Chi Chi Rodriguez	64	1964
	Nick Price		1993
Highest start by winner	Robert Simpson	84	1907
Lowest finish by winner	Cary Middlecoff	63	1955
Highest finish by winner	Jock Hutchison	80	1920
Best final-round comeback	Tom Kite	7 back	1986
Lowest 36-hole cut score		144	1993
Highest 36-hole cut score		153	1974, 1976

ANHEUSER-BUSCH GOLF CLASSIC

Record	Player(s)	Score	Year
Low 18	Mike Sullivan	62	1990
	Ian Baker-Finch		1991
	Kenny Knox		1991
	Brian Claar		1991
	Tom Byrum		1993
	Dillard Pruitt		1993
Low first 36	Ian Baker-Finch	130 (62-68)	1991
	Mike Donald	(66-64)	1991
Low 36	Ronnie Black	129 (66-63)	1984 (rounds 3-4)
Low first 54	Dan Pohl	196 (64-67-65)	1991
Low 54	Dan Pohl	196 (64-67-65)	1991
Low 72	Lanny Wadkins	266 (65-66-67-68)	1990
	Mike Hulbert	(66-67-65-68)	1991
	Kenny Knox	(67-69-62-68)	1991
Highest winning score	John Mahaffey	276 (72-67-70-67)	1981
Largest winning margin	Lanny Wadkins (266)	5 strokes	1990
Largest 18-hole lead	Scott Simpson (64)	2 strokes	1983
	Willie Wood (63)		1984
	Lon Hinkle (64)		1985
Largest 36-hole lead	Hal Sutton (132)	6 strokes	1983
Largest 54-hole lead	Hal Sutton (201)	6 strokes	1983
Lowest start by winner	Mark McCumber	65	1987
	Lanny Wadkins		1990
Highest start by winner	John Mahaffey	72	1981
Lowest finish by winner	Ronnie Black	63	1984
Highest finish by winner	Mark Wiebe	70	1985
Best final-round comeback	Ronnie Black	7 back	1984
Lowest 36-hole cut score		140	1991
Highest 36-hole cut score		147	1983

NEW ENGLAND CLASSIC

Record	Player(s)	Score	Year
Low 18	Nick Price	62	1989
	David Peoples		1993
Low first 36	Don Pooley	131 (66-65)	1989
	Bruce Fleisher	(64-67)	1991
	Roger Maltbie	(65-66)	1992
Low 36	Mike McCullough	130 (64-66)	1982 (rounds 2-3)
Low first 54	Sam Randolph	199 (67-68-64)	1987*
Low 54	Sam Randolph	199 (67-68-64)	1987*
	Jay Delsing	199 (67-65-67)	1993 (rounds 2-3-4)
Low 72	George Burns	267 (67-66-68-66)	1985
Highest winning score	Tom Shaw	280 (68-68-67-77)	1969
Largest winning margin	George Archer (270)	6 strokes	1984
	George Burns (267)		1985
Largest 18-hole lead	Fred Marti (64)	3 strokes	1977
	Bobby Clampett (63)		1993
Largest 36-hole lead	Tom Shaw (136)	5 strokes	1969
Largest 54-hole lead	Tom Shaw (203)	7 strokes	1969
Lowest start by winner	Bruce Fleisher	64	1991
Highest start by winner	Roger Maltbie	72	1975
	Brian Allin		1976
Lowest finish by winner	Mark Lye	64	1983
	Sam Randolph		1987*
	Bruce Fleisher		1991
Best final-round comeback	Mark Lye	8 back	1983
Lowest 36-hole cut score		140	1991
Highest 36-hole cut score		150	1969

* 54-hole tournament

FEDERAL EXPRESS ST. JUDE CLASSIC

Record	Player(s)	Score	Year
Low 18	Al Geiberger	59	1977
Low first 36	Dan Forsman	130 (64-66)	1992
Low 36	Jay Haas	128 (64-64)	1992 (rounds 3-4)
Low first 54	Dan Forsman	198 (64-66-68)	1992
Low 54	Jay Haas	195 (67-64-64)	1992 (rounds 2-3-4)
Low 72	Jay Haas	263 (68-67-64-64)	1992
Highest winning score	Dave Hill	283 (68-69-74-72)	1973
Largest winning margin	Raymond Floyd (271)	6 strokes	1982
Largest 18-hole lead	Larry Silveira (62)	3 strokes	1990
Largest 36-hole lead	Al Geiberger (131)	6 strokes	1977
Largest 54-hole lead	Gene Littler (204)	5 strokes	1975
	Raymond Floyd (202)		1982
Lowest start by winner	Bert Yancey	63	1966
	Dave Hill		1970
Highest start by winner	Tommy Bolt	72	1960
	Al Geiberger		1977
	Gil Morgan		1979
	Tom Kite		1990
Lowest finish by winner	Jay Haas	64	1992
Highest finish by winner	Dave Hill	73	1967
Best final-round comeback	Hal Sutton	8 back	1985
Lowest 36-hole cut score		139	1992
Highest 36-hole cut score		150	1972, 1973, 1986

BUICK OPEN

Record	Player(s)	Score	Year
Low 18	Denis Watson	63	1984
	Robert Wrenn		1987
	Trevor Dodds		1987
	Hale Irwin		1990
	Ken Green		1990
	Scott Hoch		1991
Low first 36	Robert Wrenn	128 (65-63)	1987
Low 36	Robert Wrenn	128 (65-63)	1987
Low first 54	Robert Wrenn	195 (65-63-67)	1987
Low 54	Robert Wrenn	195 (65-63-67)	1987
Low 72	Robert Wrenn	262 (65-63-67-67)	1987
Highest winning score	Billy Casper	285	1958
Largest winning margin	Robert Wrenn (262)	7 strokes	1987
Largest 18-hole lead	Scott Hoch (63)	3 strokes	1991

Record	Player(s)	Score	Year
Largest 36-hole lead	Rex Caldwell (132)	5 strokes	1980
Largest 54-hole lead	Julius Boros (205)	6 strokes	1963
	Robert Wrenn (195)		1987
Lowest start by winner	Larry Mize	64	1993
Highest start by winner	Tom Weiskopf	73	1968
Lowest finish by winner	Lanny Wadkins	65	1982
	Wayne Levi		1983
	Chip Beck		1990
Highest finish by winner	Art Wall	72	1959
	Bill Collins		1972
	Hale Irwin		1981
Best final-round comeback	Chip Beck	8 back	1990
Lowest 36-hole cut score		141	1986, 1987, 1991
Highest 36-hole cut score		155	1958

THE INTERNATIONAL

No all-time tournament records because of Stableford scoring system.

NEC WORLD SERIES OF GOLF

Record	Player(s)	Score	Year
Low 18	José Maria Olazabal	61	1990
Low first 36	José Maria Olazabal	128 (61-67)	1990
Low 36	José Maria Olazabal	128 (61-67)	1990
Low first 54	José Maria Olazabal	195 (61-67-67)	1990
Low 54	José Maria Olazabal	195 (61-67-67)	1990
Low 72	José Maria Olazabal	262 (61-67-67-67)	1990
Highest winning score	Tom Purtzer	279 (72-69-67-71)	1991
Largest winning margin	José Maria Olazabal (262)	12 strokes	1990
Largest 18-hole lead	José Maria Olazabal (61)	4 strokes	1990
Largest 36-hole lead	José Maria Olazabal (128)	9 strokes	1990
Largest 54-hole lead	José Maria Olazabal (195)	8 strokes	1990
Lowest start by winner	José Maria Olazabal	61	1990
Highest start by winner	Tom Purtzer	72	1991
Lowest finish by winner	Fulton Allem	62	1993
Highest start by winner	Dan Pohl	71	1986
	Curtis Strange		1987
	Tom Purtzer		1991
Best final-round comeback	Craig Stadler	5 back	1982
No 36-hole cut score			

GREATER MILWAUKEE OPEN

Record	Player(s)	Score	Year
Low 18	Ken Green	61	1988
	Robert Gamez		1991
Low first 36	Robert Gamez	127 (61-66)	1991
Low 36	Robert Gamez	127 (61-66)	1991
Low first 54	Greg Norman	199 (64-69-66)	1989
Low 54	Ken Green	198 (69-61-68) (rounds 2-3-4)	1988
Low 72	Bill Kratzert	266 (67-66-67-66)	1980
Highest winning score	Dave Eichelberger	278 (71-68-69-70)	1977
Largest winning margin	Ken Green (268)	6 strokes	1988
Largest 18-hole lead	Ed Sneed (66)	2 strokes	1974
	Miller Barber (65)		1975
	Ken Still (64)		1976
	Jim Colbert (66)		1985
	Tommy Nakajima (62)		1987
	Robert Gamez (61)		1991
Largest 36-hole lead	Dave Stockton (132)	4 strokes	1973
Largest 54-hole lead	Dave Stockton (203)	6 strokes	1973
Lowest start by winner	Greg Norman	64	1989
Highest start by winner	Jim Thorpe	73	1985
Lowest finish by winner	Calvin Peete	65	1979
Highest finish by winner	Dave Stockton	73	1973
	Jay Haas		1981
Best final-round comeback	Jim Gallagher Jr.	5 strokes	1990
Lowest 36-hole cut score		140	1991
Highest 36-hole cut score		148	1974, 1977

CANADIAN OPEN

Record	Player(s)	Score	Year
Low 18	Leonard Thompson	62	1981
	Greg Norman		1986
Low first 36	Johnny Palmer	131 (66-65)	1952
	Arnold Palmer	(64-67)	1955
	Steve Jones	(67-64)	1989
	Jim Benepe	(64-67)	1991
Low 36	George Bayer	129 (64-65)	1958
	Doug Ford	(64-65)	1958
Low first 54	Arnold Palmer	195 (64-67-64)	1955
Low 54	Arnold Palmer	195 (64-67-64)	1955
Low 72	Johnny Palmer	263 (66-65-66-66)	1952
Highest winning score	Charles Murray	314	1911
Largest winning margin	J. Douglas Edgar (278)	16 strokes	1919
Largest 18-hole lead	Several players	2 strokes	
Largest 36-hole lead	Nick Price (134)	6 strokes	1984
Largest 54-hole lead	Johnny Palmer (197)	8 strokes	1952
Lowest start by winner	Arnold Palmer	64	1955
Highest start by winner	Bruce Lietzke	76	1978
Lowest finish by winner	Leo Diegel	66	1929
	Johnny Palmer		1952
	Nick Price		1991
Best final-round comeback	Nick Price	5 back	1991
Lowest 36-hole cut score		145	1952
Highest 36-hole cut score		175	1922, 1923

HARDEE'S GOLF CLASSIC

Record	Player(s)	Score	Year
Low 18	Mike Smith	61	1987
Low first 36	Scott Hoch	129 (63-66)	1980
	Brad Fabel	(64-65)	1987
	Leonard Thompson	(67-62)	1991
Low 36	Blaine McCallister	125 (62-63)	1988 (rounds 2-3)
Low first 54	Blaine McCallister	193 (68-62-63)	1988
Low 54	David Frost	191 (63-64-64)	1993 (rounds 2-3-4)
Low 72	David Frost	259 (68-63-64-64)	1993
Highest winning score	Roger Maltbie	275 (74-65-72-74)	1975
Largest winning margin	David Frost (259)	7 strokes	1993
Largest 18-hole lead	Scott Hoch (63)	2 strokes	1980
	Gene Sauers (62)		1988
	David Frost (62)		1992
	Jeff Woodland (63)		1993
Largest 36-hole lead	Dave Eichelberger	5 strokes	1975
Largest 54-hole lead	David Frost	5 strokes	1993
Lowest start by winner	David Frost	62	1993
Highest start by winner	Roger Maltbie	74	1975
Lowest finish by winner	Payne Stewart	63	1982
Highest finish by winner	David Frost	72	1992
Best final-round comeback	Roger Maltbie	7 back	1975
Lowest 36-hole cut score		138	1991, 1993
Highest 36-hole cut score		146	1975

B.C. OPEN

Record	Player(s)	Score	Year
Low 18	Fuzzy Zoeller	62	1982
	Jay Delsing		1985
	Steve Elkington		1989
Low first 36	Joey Sindelar	128 (65-63)	1987
Low 36	Calvin Peete	127 (63-64)	1982 (rounds 2-3)
Low first 54	Calvin Peete	196 (69-63-64)	1982
Low 54	Calvin Peete	196 (69-63-64)	1982
	Calvin Peete	(63-64-69)	(rounds 2-3-4)
Low 72	Calvin Peete	265 (69-63-64-69)	1982
Highest winning score	Wayne Levi	275 (67-71-71-66)	1984
Largest winning margin	Calvin Peete (265)	7 strokes	1982
Largest 18-hole lead	Calvin Peete (64)	3 strokes	1981
	Mark O'Meara (63)		1983
Largest 36-hole lead	Joey Sindelar (128)	7 strokes	1987
Largest 54-hole lead	Joey Sindelar (197)	8 strokes	1987
Lowest start by winner	Bob Wynn	65	1976
	Rick Fehr		1986
	Joey Sindelar		1987
Highest start by winner	Pat Lindsey	71	1983
Lowest finish by winner	Mike Hulbert	65	1989
Highest finish by winner	Bob Wynn	69	1976
	Gil Morgan		1977
	Jay Haas		1981
	Calvin Peete		1982
	Joey Sindelar		1987
	Bill Glasson		1988
Best final-round comeback	Wayne Levi	3 back	1984
	Mike Hulbert		1989
Lowest 36-hole cut score		141	1988
Highest 36-hole cut score		146	1984

BUICK SOUTHERN OPEN

Record	Player(s)	Score	Year
Low 18	Hale Irwin	61	1982
	Rod Curl		1986
	Dave Barr		1988
Low first 36	Tim Simpson	128 (64-64)	1985
Low 36	Tim Simpson	128 (64-64)	1985
	Tim Simpson	(65-63)	1989 (rounds 3-4)
Low first 54	Tim Simpson	197 (64-64-69)	1985
Low 54	Hubert Green	196 (66-66-64)	1975 (rounds 2-3-4)
	Kenny Knox	196 (62-68-66)	1990 (rounds 2-3-4)
Low 72	Hubert Green	264 (68-66-66-64)	1975
	Tim Simpson	(64-64-69-67)	1985
Highest winning score	John Inman	278 (71-73-64-70)	1993
Largest winning margin	Jerry Pate (266)	7 strokes	1977
	Ken Brown (266)		1987
Largest 18-hole lead	Jeff Sluman (63)	3 strokes	1988
Largest 36-hole lead	Jerry Pate (131)	4 strokes	1977
Largest 54-hole lead	Mike Sullivan (200)	5 strokes	1980
	Ken Brown (198)		1987
Lowest start by winner	Jerry Pate	64	1977
	Tim Simpson		1985
Highest start by winner	Mason Rudolph	75	1970
Lowest finish by winner	Mason Rudolph	64	1970
	Hubert Green		1975
	Bobby Clampett		1982
Highest finish by winner	DeWitt Weaver	72	1972
Best final-round comeback	Mason Rudolph	4 back	1970
Lowest 36-hole cut score		139	1990
Highest 36-hole cut score		148	1976

WALT DISNEY WORLD/OLDSMOBILE CLASSIC

Record	Player(s)	Score	Year
Low 18	Mark Lye	61	1984
	Bob Tway		1989
	Payne Stewart		1990
Low first 36	Tim Simpson	128 (64-64)	1990
Low 36	Tim Simpson	128 (64-64)	1990
	John Huston	(66-62)	1992 (rounds 3-4)
Low first 54	Tim Simpson	193 (64-64-65)	1990
Low 54	Tim Simpson	193 (64-64-65)	1990
Low 72	John Huston	262 (66-68-66-62)	1992
Highest winning score	Jack Nicklaus	275 (70-71-67-67)	1973
Largest winning margin	Jack Nicklaus (267)	9 strokes	1972
Largest 18-hole lead	Bob Tway (61)	4 strokes	1989
Largest 36-hole lead	Tim Simpson (128)	4 strokes	1990
Largest 54-hole lead	Tim Simpson (193)	6 strokes	1990
Lowest start by winner	Bob Lohr	62	1988
Highest start by winner	Hal Sutton	71	1982
Lowest finish by winner	John Huston	62	1992
Highest finish by winner	Raymond Floyd	71	1986
	Tim Simpson		1990
Best final-round comeback	Hal Sutton	5 back	1982
Lowest 54-hole cut score		208	1982
Highest 54-hole cut score		215	1986, 1989

Texas Open

Record	Player(s)	Score	Year
Low 18	Al Brosch	60	1951
	Ted Kroll		1954
	Mike Souchak		1955
Low first 36	Johnny Palmer	127 (65-62)	1954
Low 36	Ron Streck	125 (63-62)	1978 (rounds 3-4)
Low first 54	Johnny Palmer	191 (65-62-64)	1954
Low 54	Chandler Harper	189 (63-63-63)	1954
Low 72	Mike Souchak	257 (60-68-64-65)	1955
Highest winning score	Bill Mehlhorn	297	1928
Largest winning margin	Corey Pavin (259)	8 strokes	1988
Largest 18-hole lead	Several players	2 strokes	
Largest 36-hole lead	Jodie Mudd (129)	4 strokes	1985
	Tom Watson (131)		1987
	Blaine McCallister (130)		1991
Largest 54-hole lead	Corey Pavin (193)	5 strokes	1988
Lowest start by winner	Mike Souchak	60	1955
Highest start by winner	Ron Streck	73	1978
Lowest finish by winner	Ron Streck	62	1978
Highest finish by winner	Bill Mehlhorn	79	1928
Best final-round comeback	Bruce Crampton	6 back	1964
Lowest 36-hole cut score		137	1989
Highest 36-hole cut score		146	1962

Las Vegas Invitational

Record	Player(s)	Score	Year
Low 18	Chip Beck	59	1991
Low first 36	John Daly	129 (66-63)	1991
Low 36	Chip Beck	127 (59-68)	1991 (rounds 3-4)
Low first 54	Chip Beck	196 (65-72-59)	1991
	Bruce Lietzke	(68-63-65)	1991
	John Cook	(68-66-62)	1992
Low 54	D.A. Weibring	193 (64-65-64)	1991 (rounds 2-3-4)
Low first 72	Bruce Lietzke	263 (68-63-65-67)	1991
	Andrew Magee	(69-65-67-62)	1991
	Craig Stadler	(67-64-66-66)	1991
	D.A. Weibring	(70-64-65-64)	1991
Low 72	D.A. Weibring	259 (64-65-64-66)	1991 (rounds 2-3-4-5)
Low 90	Andrew Magee	329 (69-65-67-62-66)	1991
	D.A. Weibring	(70-64-65-64-66)	
Highest winning score	Denis Watson	341 (69-66-68-70-68)	1984
Largest winning margin	Davis Love III (331)	8 strokes	1993
Largest 18-hole lead	Bill Glasson (62)	3 strokes	1985
Largest 36-hole lead	Lon Hinkle (130)	3 strokes	1984
Largest 54-hole lead	John Cook (196)	5 strokes	1992
Largest 72-hole lead	Fuzzy Zoeller (267)	6 strokes	1983
	Davis Love III (265)		1993
Lowest start by winner	Fuzzy Zoeller	63	1983
Highest start by winner	Greg Norman	73	1986
Lowest finish by winner	Paul Azinger	64	1987
Highest finish by winner	Fuzzy Zoeller	73	1983
Best final-round comeback	Denis Watson	3 back	1984
	Gary Koch		1988
Lowest 54-hole cut score		207	1991
Highest 54-hole cut score		215	1988

Tour Championship

Record	Player(s)	Score	Year
Low 18	Wayne Levi	63	1989, 1990
	Jim Gallagher Jr.		1993
Low first 36	Tom Watson	131 (65-66)	1987
Low 36	Wayne Levi	130 (67-63)	1990
Low first 54	Tom Watson	200 (65-66-69)	1987
Low 54	Chip Beck	199 (67-68-64)	1987 (rounds 2-3-4)
Low 72	Tom Watson	268 (65-66-69-68)	1987
Highest winning score	Curtis Strange	279 (64-71-70-74)	1988
	Craig Stadler	279 (68-68-72-71)	1991
Largest winning margin	Paul Azinger (276)	3 strokes	1992
Largest 18-hole lead	Jim Gallagher Jr. (63)	5 strokes	1993
Largest 36-hole lead	Tom Watson (131)	4 strokes	1987
	Tom Kite (134)		1989
Largest 54-hole lead	Tom Watson (200)	4 strokes	1987
Lowest start by winner	Jim Gallagher Jr.	63	1993
Highest start by winner	Paul Azinger	70	1992
Lowest finish by winner	Tom Watson	68	1987
	Tom Kite		1989
	Jodie Mudd		1990
Highest finish by winner	Curtis Strange	74	1988
Best final-round comeback	Jim Gallagher Jr.	3 back	1993

No 36-hole cut

MERCEDES CHAMPIONSHIPS
(formerly Tournament of Champions)

Year	Winner	Score
	Tournament of Champions	
1953	Al Besselink	280
1954	Art Wall	278
1955	Gene Littler	280
1956	Gene Littler	281
1957	Gene Littler	285
1958	Stan Leonard	278
1959	Mike Souchak	281
1960	Jerry Barber	268
1961	Sam Snead	273
1962	Arnold Palmer	276
1963	Jack Nicklaus	273
1964	Jack Nicklaus	279
1965	Arnold Palmer	277
1966	*Arnold Palmer	283
1967	Frank Beard	278
1968	Don January	276
1969	Gary Player	284
1970	Frank Beard	278
1971	Jack Nicklaus	279
1972	*Bobby Mitchell	280
1973	Jack Nicklaus	276
1974	Johnny Miller	280
	MONY Tournament of Champions	
1975	*Al Geiberger	277
1976	Don January	277
1977	*Jack Nicklaus	281
1978	Gary Player	281
1979	Tom Watson	275
1980	Tom Watson	276
1981	Lee Trevino	273
1982	Lanny Wadkins	280
1983	Lanny Wadkins	280
1984	Tom Watson	274
1985	Tom Kite	275
1986	Calvin Peete	267
1987	Mac O'Grady	278
1988	Steve Pate	202
1989	Steve Jones	279
	Infiniti Tournament of Champions	
1990	Paul Azinger	272
1991	Tom Kite	272
1992	*Steve Elkington	279
1993	Davis Love III	272
1994	*Phil Mickelson	276

* Playoff

UNITED AIRLINES HAWAIIAN OPEN

Year	Winner	Score
	Hawaiian Open	
1965	Gay Brewer	281
1966	Ted Makalena	271
1967	*Dudley Wysong	284
1968	Lee Trevino	272
1969	Bruce Crampton	272
1970	No tournament	
1971	Tom Shaw	273
1972	*Grier Jones	274
1973	John Schlee	273
1974	Jack Nicklaus	271
1975	Gary Groh	274
1976	Ben Crenshaw	270
1977	Bruce Lietzke	273
1978	*Hubert Green	274
1979	Hubert Green	267
1980	Andy Bean	266
1981	Hale Irwin	265
1982	Wayne Levi	277
1983	Isao Aoki	268
1984	*Jack Renner	271
1985	Mark O'Meara	267
1986	Corey Pavin	272
1987	*Corey Pavin	270
1988	Lanny Wadkins	271
1989	#Gene Sauers	197
1990	David Ishii	279
	United Airlines Hawaiian Open	
1991	Lanny Wadkins	270
1992	John Cook	265
1993	Howard Twitty	269
1994	Brett Ogle	269

* Playoff
\# Rain-shortened

NORTHERN TELECOM OPEN (TUCSON)

Year	Winner	Score
	Tucson Open	
1945	Ray Mangrum	268
1946	Jimmy Demaret	268
1947	Jimmy Demaret	264
1948	Skip Alexander	264
1949	Lloyd Mangrum	263
1950	Chandler Harper	267
1951	Lloyd Mangrum	269
1952	Henry Williams	274
1953	Tommy Bolt	265
1954	No tournament	
1955	Tommy Bolt	265
1956	Ted Kroll	264
1957	Dow Finsterwald	269
1958	Lionel Hebert	265
1959	Gene Littler	266
1960	Don January	271
	Home of the Sun Open Invitational	
1961	*Dave Hill	269
1962	Phil Rodgers	263
1963	Don January	266
1964	Jacky Cupit	274
1965	Bob Charles	271
1966	*Joe Campbell	278
1967	Arnold Palmer	273
1968	George Knudson	273
1969	Lee Trevino	271
1970	*Lee Trevino	275
1971	J.C. Snead	273
1972	Miller Barber	273
	Dean Martin Tucson Open	
1973	Bruce Crampton	277
1974	Johnny Miller	272
1975	Johnny Miller	263
	NBC Tucson Open	
1976	Johnny Miller	274
	Joe Garagiola Tucson Open	
1977	*Bruce Lietzke	275
1978	Tom Watson	276
1979	Bruce Lietzke	265
1980	Jim Colbert	270
1981	Johnny Miller	265
1982	Craig Stadler	266
1983	*Gil Morgan	271
	Seiko-Tucson Match Play Championship	
1984	Tom Watson	2&1
1985	Jim Thorpe	4&3
1986	Jim Thorpe	67
	Seiko Tucson Open	
1987	Mike Reid	268
	Northern Telecom Tucson Open	
1988	David Frost	266
1989	No tournament	
1990	Robert Gamez	270
	Northern Telecom Open	
1991	aPhil Mickelson	272
1992	Lee Janzen	270
1993	Larry Mize	271
1994	Andrew Magee	270

* Playoff
a Amateur

PHOENIX OPEN

Year	Winner	Score
1932	Ralph Guldahl	285
1933	Harry Cooper	281
1934	No tournament	
1935	Ky Laffoon	281
1936–		
1938	No tournaments	
1939	Byron Nelson	198
1940	Porky Oliver	205
1941	Porky Oliver	275
1942	Herman Barron	276
1943	No tournament	
1944	*Jug McSpaden	273
1945	Byron Nelson	274
1946	*Ben Hogan	273
1947	Ben Hogan	270
1948	Bobby Locke	268
1949	*Jimmy Demaret	278
1950	Jimmy Demaret	269
1951	Lew Worsham	272
1952	Lloyd Mangrum	274
1953	Lloyd Mangrum	272
1954	*Ed Furgol	272
1955	Gene Littler	275
1956	Cary Middlecoff	276
1957	Billy Casper	271
1958	Ken Venturi	274
1959	Gene Littler	268
1960	*Jack Fleck	273
1961	*Arnold Palmer	270
1962	Arnold Palmer	269
1963	Arnold Palmer	273
1964	Jack Nicklaus	271
1965	Rod Funseth	274
1966	Dudley Wysong	278
1967	Julius Boros	272
1968	George Knudson	272
1969	Gene Littler	263
1970	Dale Douglass	271
1971	Miller Barber	261
1972	*Homero Blancas	273
1973	Bruce Crampton	268
1974	Johnny Miller	271
1975	Johnny Miller	260
1976	Bob Gilder	268
1977	*Jerry Pate	277
1978	Miller Barber	272
1979	#Ben Crenshaw	199
1980	Jeff Mitchell	272
1981	David Graham	268

Year	Winner	Score
1982	Lanny Wadkins	263
1983	*Bob Gilder	271
1984	Tom Purtzer	268
1985	Calvin Peete	270
1986	Hal Sutton	267
1987	Paul Azinger	268
1988	*Sandy Lyle	269
1989	Mark Calcavecchia	263
1990	Tommy Armour III	267
1991	Nolan Henke	268
1992	Mark Calcavecchia	264
1993	Lee Janzen	273
1994	Bill Glasson	268

* Playoff
# Rain-curtailed

AT&T PEBBLE BEACH NATIONAL PRO-AM

Year	Winner	Score
	Bing Crosby Pro-Am	
1937	Sam Snead	68
1938	Sam Snead	139
1939	Dutch Harrison	138
1940	Ed Oliver	135
1941	Sam Snead	136
1942	Tie–Lloyd Mangrum	
	Leland Gibson	133
1943–		
1946	No tournaments	
1947	Tie–Ed Furgol	
	George Fazio	213
1948	Lloyd Mangrum	205
1949	Ben Hogan	208
1950	Tie–Sam Snead	
	Jack Burke, Jr.	
	Smiley Quick	
	Dave Douglas	214
1951	Byron Nelson	209
1952	Jimmy Demaret	145
	Bing Crosby Pro-Am Invitational	
1953	Lloyd Mangrum	204
1954	Dutch Harrison	210
1955	Cary Middlecoff	209
	Bing Crosby Pro-Am Golf Championship	
1956	Cary Middlecoff	202
1957	Jay Hebert	213
1958	Billy Casper	277
	Bing Crosby National	
1959	Art Wall	279
1960	Ken Venturi	286
1961	Bob Rosburg	282
1962	*Doug Ford	286
1963	Billy Casper	285
	Bing Crosby National Pro-Am	
1964	Tony Lema	284
1965	Bruce Crampton	284
1966	Don Massengale	283
1967	Jack Nicklaus	284
1968	*Johnny Pott	285
1969	George Archer	283
1970	Bert Yancey	278
1971	Tom Shaw	278
1972	*Jack Nicklaus	284
1973	*Jack Nicklaus	282
1974	#Johnny Miller	208
1975	Gene Littler	280
1976	Ben Crenshaw	281
1977	Tom Watson	273
1978	*Tom Watson	280
1979	Lon Hinkle	284
1980	George Burns	280
1981	#*John Cook	209
1982	Jim Simons	274
1983	Tom Kite	276
1984	*Hale Irwin	278
1985	Mark O'Meara	283
	AT&T Pebble Beach National Pro-Am	
1986	#Fuzzy Zoeller	205
1987	Johnny Miller	278
1988	*Steve Jones	280
1989	Mark O'Meara	277
1990	Mark O'Meara	281
1991	Paul Azinger	274
1992	Mark O'Meara	275
1993	Brett Ogle	276
1994	Johnny Miller	281

* Playoff
# Rain-shortened

NISSAN LOS ANGELES OPEN

Year	Winner	Score
	Los Angeles Open	
1926	Harry Cooper	279
1927	Bobby Cruickshank	282
1928	Mac Smith	284
1929	Mac Smith	285
1930	Densmore Shute	296
1931	Ed Dudley	285
1932	Mac Smith	281
1933	Craig Wood	281
1934	Mac Smith	280
1935	*Vic Ghezzi	285
1936	Jimmy Hines	280
1937	Harry Cooper	274
1938	Jimmy Thomson	273
1939	Jimmy Demaret	274
1940	Lawson Little	282
1941	Johnny Bulla	281
1942	*Ben Hogan	282
1943	No tournament	
1944	Harold McSpaden	278
1945	Sam Snead	283
1946	Byron Nelson	284
1947	Ben Hogan	280
1948	Ben Hogan	275
1949	Lloyd Mangrum	284
1950	*Sam Snead	280
1951	Lloyd Mangrum	280
1952	Tommy Bolt	289
1953	Lloyd Mangrum	280
1954	Fred Wampler	281
1955	Gene Littler	276
1956	Lloyd Mangrum	272
1957	Doug Ford	280
1958	Frank Stranahan	275
1959	Ken Venturi	278
1960	Dow Finsterwald	280
1961	Bob Goalby	275
1962	Phil Rodgers	268
1963	Arnold Palmer	274
1964	Paul Harney	280
1965	Paul Harney	276
1966	Arnold Palmer	273
1967	Arnold Palmer	269
1968	Billy Casper	274
1969	*Charles Sifford	276
1970	*Billy Casper	276
	Glen Campbell Los Angeles Open	
1971	*Bob Lunn	274
1972	*George Archer	270
1973	Rod Funseth	276
1974	Dave Stockton	276
1975	Pat Fitzsimons	275
1976	Hale Irwin	272
1977	Tom Purtzer	273
1978	Gil Morgan	278
1979	Lanny Wadkins	276
1980	Tom Watson	276
1981	Johnny Miller	270
1982	*Tom Watson	271
1983	Gil Morgan	270
	Los Angeles Open	
1984	David Edwards	279
1985	Lanny Wadkins	264
1986	Doug Tewell	270
	Los Angeles Open Presented by Nissan	
1987	*Tze-Chung Chen	275
1988	Chip Beck	267
	Nissan Los Angeles Open	
1989	Mark Calcavecchia	272
1990	Fred Couples	266
1991	Ted Schulz	272
1992	*Fred Couples	269
1993	#Tom Kite	206
1994	Corey Pavin	271

* Playoff
# Rain-shortened

BOB HOPE CHRYSLER CLASSIC

Year	Winner	Score
	Palm Springs Golf Classic	
1960	Arnold Palmer	338
1961	Billy Maxwell	345
1962	Arnold Palmer	342
1963	*Jack Nicklaus	345
1964	Tommy Jacobs	348
	Bob Hope Desert Classic	
1965	Billy Casper	348
1966	*Doug Sanders	349
1967	Tom Nieporte	349
1968	*Arnold Palmer	348
1969	Billy Casper	345
1970	Bruce Devlin	339
1971	*Arnold Palmer	342
1972	Bob Rosburg	344
1973	Arnold Palmer	343
1974	Hubert Green	341
1975	Johnny Miller	339
1976	Johnny Miller	344
1977	Rik Massengale	337
1978	Bill Rogers	339
1979	John Mahaffey	343
1980	Craig Stadler	343
1981	Bruce Lietzke	335
1982	*Ed Fiori	335
1983	*Keith Fergus	335
	Bob Hope Classic	
1984	*John Mahaffey	340
1985	*Lanny Wadkins	333
	Bob Hope Chrysler Classic	
1986	Donnie Hammond	335
1987	Corey Pavin	341
1988	Jay Haas	338
1989	*Steve Jones	343
1990	Peter Jacobsen	339
1991	*Corey Pavin	331
1992	*John Cook	336
1993	Tom Kite	325
1994	Scott Hoch	334

* Playoff

BUICK INVITATIONAL OF CALIFORNIA

Year	Winner	Score
	San Diego Open	
1952	Ted Kroll	276
1953	Tommy Bolt	274
1954	[a]Gene Littler	274
	Convair San Diego Open	
1955	Tommy Bolt	274
1956	Bob Rosburg	270
	San Diego Open Invitational	
1957	Arnold Palmer	271
1958	No tournament	
1959	Marty Furgol	274
1960	Mike Souchak	269
1961	*Arnold Palmer	271
1962	*Tommy Jacobs	277
1963	Gary Player	270
1964	Art Wall	274
1965	*Wes Ellis	267
1966	Billy Casper	268
1967	Bob Goalby	269
	Andy Williams San Diego Open Invitational	
1968	Tom Weiskopf	273
1969	Jack Nicklaus	284
1970	Pete Brown	275
1971	George Archer	272
1972	Paul Harney	275
1973	Bob Dickson	278
1974	Bobby Nichols	275
1975	*J.C. Snead	279
1976	J.C. Snead	272
1977	Tom Watson	269
1978	Jay Haas	278
1979	Fuzzy Zoeller	279
1980	*Tom Watson	275
	Wickes/Andy Williams San Diego Open	
1981	*Bruce Lietzke	278
1982	Johnny Miller	270
	Isuzu Andy Williams San Diego Open	
1983	Gary Hallberg	271
1984	*Gary Koch	272
1985	*Woody Blackburn	269
	Shearson Lehman Brothers Andy Williams Open	
1986	*#Bob Tway	204
1987	George Burns	266
	Shearson Lehman Hutton Andy Williams Open	
1988	Steve Pate	269
	Shearson Lehman Hutton Open	
1989	Greg Twiggs	271
1990	Dan Forsman	275
	Shearson Lehman Brothers Open	
1991	Jay Don Blake	268
	Buick Invitational of California	
1992	#Steve Pate	200
1993	Phil Mickelson	278
1994	Craig Stadler	268

* Playoff
a Amateur
Rain-shortened

DORAL-RYDER OPEN

Year	Winner	Score
	Doral CC Open Invitational	
1962	Billy Casper	283
1963	Dan Sikes	283
1964	Billy Casper	277
1965	Doug Sanders	274
1966	Phil Rodgers	278
1967	Doug Sanders	275
1968	Gardner Dickinson	275
1969	Tom Shaw	276
	Doral-Eastern Open Invitational	
1970	Mike Hill	279
1971	J.C. Snead	275
1972	Jack Nicklaus	276
1973	Lee Trevino	276
1974	Brian Allin	274
1975	Jack Nicklaus	275
1976	Hubert Green	270
1977	Andy Bean	277
1978	Tom Weiskopf	272
1979	Mark McCumber	279
1980	*Raymond Floyd	279
1981	Raymond Floyd	273
1982	Andy Bean	278
1983	Gary Koch	271
1984	Tom Kite	272
1985	Mark McCumber	284
1986	*Andy Bean	276
	Doral Ryder Open	
1987	Lanny Wadkins	277
1988	Ben Crenshaw	274
1989	Bill Glasson	275
1990	*Greg Norman	273
1991	*Rocco Mediate	276
1992	Raymond Floyd	271
1993	Greg Norman	265
1994	John Huston	274

* Playoff

HONDA CLASSIC

Year	Winner	Score
	Jackie Gleason Inverrary Classic	
1972	Tom Weiskopf	276
	Jackie Gleason Inverrary National Airlines Classic	
1973	Lee Trevino	279
	Jackie Gleason Inverrary Classic	
1974	Leonard Thompson	278
1975	Bob Murphy	273
1976	Hosted Tournament	
	Players Championship	
1977	Jack Nicklaus	275
1978	Jack Nicklaus	276
1979	Larry Nelson	274
1980	Johnny Miller	274
	American Motors Inverrary Classic	
1981	Tom Kite	274
	Honda Inverrary Classic	
1982	Hale Irwin	269
1983	Johnny Miller	278
	Honda Classic	
1984	*Bruce Lietzke	280
1985	*Curtis Strange	275
1986	Kenny Knox	287
1987	Mark Calcavecchia	279
1988	Joey Sindelar	276
1989	Blaine McCallister	266
1990	John Huston	282
1991	Steve Pate	279
1992	*Corey Pavin	273
1993	#Fred Couples	207
1994	Nick Price	276

* Playoff
# Rain-shortened

NESTLÉ INVITATIONAL

Year	Winner	Score
	Florida Citrus Open Invitational	
1966	Lionel Hebert	279
1967	Julius Boros	274
1968	Dan Sikes	274
1969	Ken Still	278
1970	Bob Lunn	271
1971	Arnold Palmer	270
1972	Jerry Heard	276
1973	Brian Allin	265
1974	Jerry Heard	273
1975	Lee Trevino	276
1976	*Hale Irwin	270
1977	Gary Koch	274
1978	Mac McLendon	271
	Bay Hill Citrus Classic	
1979	*Bob Byman	278
	Bay Hill Classic	
1980	Dave Eichelberger	279
1981	Andy Bean	266
1982	*Tom Kite	278
1983	*Mike Nicolette	283
1984	*Gary Koch	272
	Hertz Bay Hill Classic	
1985	Fuzzy Zoeller	275
1986	#Dan Forsman	202
1987	Payne Stewart	264
1988	Paul Azinger	271
	The Nestlé Invitational	
1989	*Tom Kite	278
1990	Robert Gamez	274
1991	#Andrew Magee	203
1992	Fred Couples	269
1993	Ben Crenshaw	280
1994	Loren Roberts	275

* Playoff
# Rain-shortened

THE PLAYERS CHAMPIONSHIP

Year	Winner	Score
	Tournament Players Championship	
1974	Jack Nicklaus	272
1975	Al Geiberger	270
1976	Jack Nicklaus	269
1977	Mark Hayes	289
1978	Jack Nicklaus	289
1979	Lanny Wadkins	283
1980	Lee Trevino	278
1981	*Raymond Floyd	285
1982	Jerry Pate	280
1983	Hal Sutton	283
1984	Fred Couples	277
1985	Calvin Peete	274
1986	John Mahaffey	275
1987	*Sandy Lyle	274
	The Players Championship	
1988	Mark McCumber	273
1989	Tom Kite	279
1990	Jodie Mudd	278
1991	Steve Elkington	276
1992	Davis Love III	273
1993	Nick Price	270
1994	Greg Norman	264

* Playoff

FREEPORT-McMoRan Classic

Year	Winner	Score
	Greater New Orleans Open Invitational	
1938	Harry Cooper	285
1939	Henry Picard	284
1940	Jimmy Demaret	286
1941	Henry Picard	276
1942	Lloyd Mangrum	281
1943	No tournament	
1944	Sam Byrd	285
1945	*Byron Nelson	284
1946	Byron Nelson	277
1947	No tournament	
1948	Bob Hamilton	280
1949–		
1957	No tournaments	
1958	*Billy Casper	278
1959	Bill Collins	280
1960	Dow Finsterwald	270
1961	Doug Sanders	272
1962	Bo Wininger	281
1963	Bo Wininger	279
1964	Mason Rudolph	283
1965	Dick Mayer	273
1966	Frank Beard	276
1967	George Knudson	277
1968	George Archer	271
1969	*Larry Hinson	275
1970	*Miller Barber	278
1971	Frank Beard	276
1972	Gary Player	279
1973	*Jack Nicklaus	280
1974	Lee Trevino	267
	First NBC New Orleans Open	
1975	Billy Casper	271
1976	Larry Ziegler	274
1977	Jim Simons	273
1978	Lon Hinkle	271
1979	Hubert Green	273
	Greater New Orleans Open	
1980	Tom Watson	273
	USF&G New Orleans Open	
1981	Tom Watson	270
	USF&G Classic	
1982	#Scott Hoch	206
1983	Bill Rogers	274
1984	Bob Eastwood	272
1985	#Seve Ballesteros	205
1986	Calvin Peete	269
1987	Ben Crenshaw	268
1988	Chip Beck	262
1989	Tim Simpson	274
1990	David Frost	276
1991	*Ian Woosnam	275
	Freeport McMoRan Classic	
1992	Chip Beck	276
1993	Mike Standly	281
1994	Ben Crenshaw	273

* Playoff
\# Rain-shortened

THE MASTERS

Year	Winner	Score
1934	Horton Smith	284
1935	*Gene Sarazen	282
1936	Horton Smith	285
1937	Byron Nelson	283
1938	Henry Picard	285
1939	Ralph Guldahl	279
1940	Jimmy Demaret	280
1941	Craig Wood	280
1942	*Byron Nelson	280
1943–		
1945	No tournaments	
1946	Herman Keiser	282
1947	Jimmy Demaret	281
1948	Claude Harmon	279
1949	Sam Snead	282
1950	Jimmy Demaret	283
1951	Ben Hogan	280
1952	Sam Snead	286
1953	Ben Hogan	274
1954	*Sam Snead	289
1955	Cary Middlecoff	279
1956	Jack Burke, Jr.	289
1957	Doug Ford	282
1958	Arnold Palmer	284
1959	Art Wall, Jr.	284
1960	Arnold Palmer	282
1961	Gary Player	280
1962	*Arnold Palmer	280
1963	Jack Nicklaus	286
1964	Arnold Palmer	276
1965	Jack Nicklaus	271
1966	*Jack Nicklaus	288
1967	Gay Brewer, Jr.	280
1968	Bob Goalby	277
1969	George Archer	281
1970	*Billy Casper	279
1971	Charles Coody	279
1972	Jack Nicklaus	286
1973	Tommy Aaron	283
1974	Gary Player	278
1975	Jack Nicklaus	276
1976	Raymond Floyd	271
1977	Tom Watson	276
1978	Gary Player	277
1979	*Fuzzy Zoeller	280
1980	Seve Ballesteros	275
1981	Tom Watson	280
1982	*Craig Stadler	284
1983	Seve Ballesteros	280
1984	Ben Crenshaw	277
1985	Bernhard Langer	282
1986	Jack Nicklaus	279
1987	*Larry Mize	285
1988	Sandy Lyle	281
1989	*Nick Faldo	283
1990	*Nick Faldo	278
1991	Ian Woosnam	277
1992	Fred Couples	275
1993	Bernhard Langer	277
1994	José Maria Olazabal	279

* Playoff

DEPOSIT GUARANTY GOLF CLASSIC

Year	Winner	Score
	Magnolia State Classic	
1968	*B.R. McLendon	269
1969	Larry Mowry	272
1970	Chris Blocker	271
1971	Roy Pace	270
1972	Mike Morley	269
1973	Dwight Nevil	268
1974	Dwight Nevil	133
1975	Bob Wynn	270
1976	Dennis Meyer	271
1977	Mike McCullough	269
1978	Craig Stadler	268
1979	Bobby Walzel	272

Year	Winner	Score
1980	#*Roger Maltbie	65
1981	*Tom Jones	268
1982	Payne Stewart	270
1983	++#Russ Cochran	203
1984	++#*Lance Ten Broeck	201
1985	#*Jim Gallagher, Jr.	131
	Deposit Guaranty Golf Classic	
1986	Dan Halldorson	263
1987	David Ogrin	267
1988	Frank Conner	267
1989	#*Jim Booros	199
1990	Gene Sauers	268
1991	*Larry Silveira	266
1992	Richard Zokol	267
1993	Greg Kraft	267

* Playoff
\# Rain-shortened
++ Scheduled 54 holes

MCI HERITAGE CLASSIC

Year	Winner	Score
	Heritage Classic	
1969	Arnold Palmer	283
1970	Bob Goalby	280
	Sea Pines Heritage Classic	
1971	Hale Irwin	279
1972	Johnny Miller	281
1973	Hale Irwin	272
1974	Johnny Miller	276
1975	Jack Nicklaus	271
1976	Hubert Green	274
1977	Graham Marsh	273
1978	Hubert Green	277
1979	Tom Watson	270
1980	*Doug Tewell	280
1981	Bill Rogers	278
1982	*Tom Watson	280
1983	Fuzzy Zoeller	275
1984	Nick Faldo	270
1985	*Bernhard Langer	273
1986	Fuzzy Zoeller	276
	MCI Heritage Classic	
1987	Davis Love III	271
1988	Greg Norman	271
1989	Payne Stewart	268
1990	*Payne Stewart	276
1991	Davis Love III	271
1992	Davis Love III	269
1993	David Edwards	273
1994	Hale Irwin	266

* Playoff

KMART GREATER GREENSBORO OPEN

Year	Winner	Score
	Greater Greensboro Open	
1938	Sam Snead	272
1939	Ralph Guldahl	280
1940	Ben Hogan	270
1941	Byron Nelson	276
1942	Sam Byrd	279
1943–		
1944	No tournaments	
1945	Byron Nelson	271
1946	Sam Snead	270
1947	Vic Ghezzi	286

1948	Lloyd Mangrum	278
1949	*Sam Snead	276
1950	Sam Snead	269
1951	Art Doering	279
1952	Dave Douglas	277
1953	*Earl Stewart	275
1954	*Doug Ford	283
1955	Sam Snead	273
1956	*Sam Snead	279
1957	Stan Leonard	276
1958	Bob Goalby	273
1959	Dow Finsterwald	278
1960	Sam Snead	270
1961	Mike Souchak	276
1962	Billy Casper	275
1963	Doug Sanders	270
1964	*Julius Boros	277
1965	Sam Snead	273
1966	*Doug Sanders	276
1967	George Archer	267
1968	Billy Casper	267
1969	*Gene Littler	274
1970	Gary Player	271
1971	*Brian Allin	275
1972	*George Archer	267
1973	Chi Chi Rodriguez	267
1974	Bob Charles	270
1975	Tom Weiskopf	275
1976	Al Geiberger	268
1977	Danny Edwards	276
1978	Seve Ballesteros	282
1979	Raymond Floyd	282
1980	Craig Stadler	273
1981	*Larry Nelson	281
1982	Danny Edwards	285
1983	Lanny Wadkins	275
1984	Andy Bean	280
1985	Joey Sindelar	285
1986	Sandy Lyle	275
1987	Scott Simpson	282
Kmart Greater Greensboro Open		
1988	Sandy Lyle	271
1989	Ken Green	277
1990	Steve Elkington	282
1991	*Mark Brooks	275
1992	Davis Love III	272
1993	Rocco Mediate	281
1994	Mike Springer	275

* Playoff

SHELL HOUSTON OPEN

Year	Winner	Score
Tournament of Champions		
1946	Byron Nelson	274
1947	Bobby Locke	277
1948	No tournament	
1949	John Palmer	272
Houston Open		
1950	Cary Middlecoff	277
1951	Marty Furgol	277
1952	Jack Burke, Jr.	277
1953	*Cary Middlecoff	283
1954	Dave Douglas	277
1955	Mike Souchak	273
1956	Ted Kroll	277
1957	Arnold Palmer	279
1958	Ed Oliver	278
Houston Classic		
1959	*Jack Burke, Jr.	277
1960	*Bill Collins	280
1961	*Jay Hebert	276
1962	*Bobby Nichols	278

1963	Bob Charles	268
1964	Mike Souchak	278
1965	Bobby Nichols	273
Houston Champions International		
1966	Arnold Palmer	275
1967	Frank Beard	274
1968	Roberto De Vicenzo	274
1969	No tournament	
1970	*Gibby Gilbert	282
1971	*Hubert Green	280
Houston Open		
1972	Bruce Devlin	278
1973	Bruce Crampton	277
1974	Dave Hill	276
1975	Bruce Crampton	277
1976	Lee Elder	276
1977	Gene Littler	276
1978	Gary Player	270
1979	Wayne Levi	268
Michelob Houston Open		
1980	*Curtis Strange	266
1981	#Ron Streck	198
1982	*Ed Sneed	275
Houston Coca-Cola Open		
1983	David Graham	275
1984	Corey Pavin	274
Houston Open		
1985	Raymond Floyd	277
1986	*Curtis Strange	274
Big I Houston Open		
1987	*Jay Haas	276
Independent Insurance Open		
1988	*Curtis Strange	270
1989	Mike Sullivan	280
1990	#Tony Sills	204
1991	Fulton Allem	273
Shell Houston Open		
1992	Fred Funk	272
1993	#Jim McGovern	199
1994	Mike Heinen	272

* Playoff
# Rain-shortened

BELLSOUTH CLASSIC

Year	Winner	Score
Atlanta Classic		
1967	Bob Charles	284
1968	Bob Lunn	280
1969	*Bert Yancey	277
1970	Tommy Aaron	275
1971	*Gardner Dickinson	275
1972	Bob Lunn	275
1973	Jack Nicklaus	272
Hosted Players Championship		
1974		
1975	Hale Irwin	271
1976	No tournament	
1977	Hale Irwin	273
1978	Jerry Heard	269
1979	Andy Bean	265
1980	Larry Nelson	270
1981	*Tom Watson	277
Georgia-Pacific Atlanta Golf Classic		
1982	*Keith Fergus	273
1983	#Calvin Peete	206
1984	Tom Kite	269
1985	*Wayne Levi	273
1986	Bob Tway	269
1987	Dave Barr	265
1988	Larry Nelson	268
BellSouth Atlanta Golf Classic		
1989	*Scott Simpson	278
1990	Wayne Levi	275

1991	*Corey Pavin	272
BellSouth Classic		
1992	Tom Kite	272
1993	Nolan Henke	271
1994	John Daly	274

* Playoff
# Rain-shortened

GTE BYRON NELSON GOLF CLASSIC

Year	Winner	Score
Texas Victory Open		
1944	Byron Nelson	276
Dallas Open		
1945	Sam Snead	276
1946	Ben Hogan	284
1947–	No tournaments	
1955		
1956	Don January	268
1956A	*Peter Thomson	267
1957	Sam Snead	264
1958	*Sam Snead	272
1959	Julius Boros	274
1960	*Johnny Pott	275
1961	Earl Stewart, Jr.	278
1962	Billy Maxwell	277
1963	No tournament	
1964	Charles Coody	271
1965	No tournament	
1966	Roberto De Vicenzo	276
1967	Bert Yancey	274
Byron Nelson Golf Classic		
1968	Miller Barber	270
1969	Bruce Devlin	277
1970	*Jack Nicklaus	274
1971	Jack Nicklaus	274
1972	*Chi Chi Rodriguez	273
1973	*Lanny Wadkins	277
1974	Brian Allin	269
1975	Tom Watson	269
1976	Mark Hayes	273
1977	Raymond Floyd	276
1978	Tom Watson	272
1979	*Tom Watson	275
1980	Tom Watson	274
1981	*Bruce Lietzke	281
1982	Bob Gilder	266
1983	Ben Crenshaw	273
1984	Craig Stadler	276
1985	*Bob Eastwood	272
1986	Andy Bean	269
1987	*Fred Couples	266
GTE Byron Nelson Golf Classic		
1988	*Bruce Lietzke	271
1989	Jodie Mudd	265
1990	#Payne Stewart	202
1991	Nick Price	270
1992	#Billy Ray Brown	199
1993	Scott Simpson	270
1994	#*Neal Lancaster	132

* Playoff
# Rain-shortened

MEMORIAL TOURNAMENT

Year	Winner	Score
1976	*Roger Maltbie	288
1977	Jack Nicklaus	281

1978	Jim Simons	284
1979	Tom Watson	285
1980	David Graham	280
1981	Keith Fergus	284
1982	Raymond Floyd	281
1983	Hale Irwin	281
1984	*Jack Nicklaus	280
1985	Hale Irwin	281
1986	Hal Sutton	271
1987	Don Pooler	272
1988	Curtis Strange	274
1989	Bob Tway	277
1990	#Greg Norman	216
1991	*Kenny Perry	273
1992	*David Edwards	273
1993	Paul Azinger	274

* Playoff
# Rain-shortened

COLONIAL NATIONAL INVITATION

Year	Winner	Score
	Colonial National Invitation Tournament	
1946	Ben Hogan	279
1947	Ben Hogan	279
1948	Clayton Heafner	272
1949	No tournament	
1950	Sam Snead	277
1951	Cary Middlecoff	282
1952	Ben Hogan	279
1953	Ben Hogan	282
1954	Johnny Palmer	280
1955	Chandler Harper	276
1956	Mike Souchak	280
1957	Roberto De Vicenzo	284
1958	Tommy Bolt	282
1959	*Ben Hogan	285
1960	Julius Boros	280
1961	Doug Sanders	281
1962	*Arnold Palmer	281
1963	Julius Boros	279
1964	Billy Casper	279
1965	Bruce Crampton	276
1966	Bruce Devlin	280
1967	Dave Stockton	278
1968	Billy Casper	275
1969	Gardner Dickinson	278
1970	Homero Blancas	273
1971	Gene Littler	283
1972	Jerry Heard	275
1973	Tom Weiskopf	276
1974	Rod Curl	276
1975	*Al Geiberger	270
1976	Lee Trevino	273
1977	Ben Crenshaw	272
1978	Lee Trevino	268
1979	Al Geiberger	274
1980	Bruce Lietzke	271
1981	Fuzzy Zoeller	274
1982	Jack Nicklaus	273
1983	*Jim Colbert	278
1984	*Peter Jacobsen	270
1985	Corey Pavin	266
1986	#*Dan Pohl	205
1987	Keith Clearwater	266
1988	Lanny Wadkins	270
	Southwestern Bell Colonial	
1989	Ian Baker-Finch	270
1990	Ben Crenshaw	272
1991	Tom Purtzer	267
1992	*Bruce Lietzke	267
1993	Fulton Allem	264

* Playoff
# Rain-shortened

KEMPER OPEN

Year	Winner	Score
1968	Arnold Palmer	276
1969	Dale Douglass	274
1970	Dick Lotz	278
1971	*Tom Weiskopf	277
1972	Doug Sanders	275
1973	Tom Weiskopf	271
1974	*Bob Menne	270
1975	Raymond Floyd	278
1976	Joe Inman	277
1977	Tom Weiskopf	277
1978	Andy Bean	273
1979	Jerry McGee	272
1980	John Mahaffey	275
1981	Craig Stadler	270
1982	Craig Stadler	275
1983	*Fred Couples	287
1984	Greg Norman	280
1985	Bill Glasson	278
1986	*Greg Norman	277
1987	Tom Kite	270
1988	*Morris Hatalsky	274
1989	Tom Byrum	268
1990	Gil Morgan	274
1991	*Billy Andrade	263
1992	Bill Glasson	276
1993	Grant White	275

* Playoff

BUICK CLASSIC (WESTCHESTER)

Year	Winner	Score
	Westchester Classic	
1967	Jack Nicklaus	272
1968	Julius Boros	272
1969	Frank Beard	275
1970	Bruce Crampton	273
1971	Arnold Palmer	270
1972	Jack Nicklaus	270
1973	*Bobby Nichols	272
1974	Johnny Miller	269
1975	*Gene Littler	271
	American Express Westchester Classic	
1976	David Graham	272
1977	Andy North	272
1978	Lee Elder	274
	Manufacturers Hanover Westchester Classic	
1979	Jack Renner	277
1980	Curtis Strange	273
1981	Raymond Floyd	275
1982	Bob Gilder	261
1983	Seve Ballesteros	276
1984	Scott Simpson	269
1985	*Roger Maltbie	275
1986	Bob Tway	272
1987	*J.C. Snead	276
1988	*Seve Ballesteros	276
1989	*Wayne Grady	277
	Buick Classic	
1990	Hale Irwin	269
1991	Billy Andrade	273
1992	David Frost	268
1993	*Vijay Singh	280

* Playoff

CANON GREATER HARTFORD OPEN

Year	Winner	Score
	Insurance City Open	
1952	Ted Kroll	273
1953	Bob Toski	269
1954	*Tommy Bolt	271
1955	Sam Snead	269
1956	*Arnold Palmer	274
1957	Gardner Dickinson	272
1958	Jack Burke, Jr.	268
1959	Gene Littler	272
1960	*Arnold Palmer	270
1961	*Billy Maxwell	271
1962	*Bob Goalby	271
1963	Billy Casper	271
1964	Ken Venturi	273
1965	*Billy Casper	274
1966	Art Wall	266
	Greater Hartford Open Invitational	
1967	Charlie Sifford	272
1968	Billy Casper	266
1969	*Bob Lunn	268
1970	Bob Murphy	267
1971	*George Archer	268
1972	*Lee Trevino	269
	Sammy Davis Jr. Greater Hartford Open	
1973	Billy Casper	264
1974	Dave Stockton	268
1975	*Don Bies	267
1976	Rik Massengale	266
1977	Bill Kratzert	265
1978	Rod Funseth	264
1979	Jerry McGee	267
1980	*Howard Twitty	266
1981	Hubert Green	264
1982	Tim Norris	259
1983	Curtis Strange	268
1984	Peter Jacobsen	269
1985	*Phil Blackmar	271
	Canon Sammy Davis Jr. Greater Hartford Open	
1986	*Mac O'Grady	269
1987	Paul Azinger	269
	Canon Greater Hartford Open	
1988	*Mark Brooks	269
1989	Paul Azinger	267
1990	Wayne Levi	267
1991	*Billy Ray Brown	271
1992	Lanny Wadkins	274
1993	Nick Price	271

* Playoff

MOTOROLA WESTERN OPEN

Year	Winner	Score
	Western Open	
1899	*Willie Smith	156
1900	No tournament	
1901	Laurie Auchterlonie	160
1902	Willie Anderson	299
1903	Alex Smith	318
1904	Willie Anderson	304
1905	Arthur Smith	278
1906	Alex Smith	306
1907	Robert Simpson	307
1908	Willie Anderson	299
1909	Willie Anderson	288
1910	[a]Chick Evans, Jr.	6&5
1911	Robert Simpson	2&1

1912	Mac Smith	299
1913	John McDermott	295
1914	Jim Barnes	293
1915	Tom McNamara	304
1916	Walter Hagen	286
1917	Jim Barnes	283
1918	No tournament	
1919	Jim Barnes	283
1920	Jock Hutchinson	296
1921	Walter Hagen	287
1922	Mike Brady	291
1923	Jock Hutchinson	281
1924	Bill Mehlhorn	293
1925	Mac Smith	281
1926	Walter Hagen	279
1927	Walter Hagen	281
1928	Abe Espinosa	291
1929	Tommy Armour	273
1930	Gene Sarazen	278
1931	Ed Dudley	280
1932	Walter Hagen	287
1933	Mac Smith	282
1934	*Harry Cooper	274
1935	Johnny Revolta	290
1936	Ralph Guldahl	274
1937	*Ralph Guldahl	288
1938	Ralph Guldahl	279
1939	Byron Nelson	281
1940	*Jimmy Demaret	293
1941	Ed Oliver	275
1942	Herman Barron	276
1943–		
1945	No tournaments	
1946	Ben Hogan	271
1947	Johnny Palmer	270
1948	*Ben Hogan	281
1949	Sam Snead	268
1950	Sam Snead	282
1951	Marty Furgol	270
1952	Lloyd Mangrum	274
1953	Dutch Harrison	278
1954	*Lloyd Mangrum	277
1955	Cary Middlecoff	272
1956	*Mike Fetchick	284
1957	*Doug Ford	279
1958	Doug Sanders	275
1959	Mike Souchak	272
1960	*Stan Leonard	278
1961	Arnold Palmer	271
1962	Jacky Cupit	281
1963	*Arnold Palmer	280
1964	Chi Chi Rodriguez	268
1965	Billy Casper	270
1966	Bill Casper	283
1967	Jack Nicklaus	274
1968	Jack Nicklaus	273
1969	Billy Casper	276
1970	Hugh Royer	273
1971	Bruce Crampton	279
1972	Jim Jamieson	271
1973	Billy Casper	272
1974	Tom Watson	287
1975	Hale Irwin	283
1976	Al Geiberger	288
1977	Tom Watson	283
1978	*Andy Bean	282
1979	*Larry Nelson	286
1980	Scott Simpson	281
1981	Ed Fiori	277
1982	Tom Weiskopf	276
1983	Mark McCumber	284
1984	*Tom Watson	280
1985	aScott Verplank	279
1986	*Tom Kite	286
	Beatrice Western Open	

1987	#D.A. Weibring	207
1988	Jim Benepe	278
1989	*Mark McCumber	275
	Centel Western Open	
1990	Wayne Levi	275
1991	Russ Cochran	275
1992	Ben Crenshaw	276
1993	Nick Price	269

* Playoff
a Amateur
\# Rain-shortened

ANHEUSER-BUSCH GOLF CLASSIC

Year	Winner	Score
	Kaiser International Open Invitational	
1968	Kermit Zarley	273
1969	#Miller Barber	135
1969A	*Jack Nicklaus	273
1970	*Ken Still	278
1971	Billy Casper	269
1972	George Knudson	271
1973	*Ed Sneed	275
1974	Johnny Miller	271
1975	Johnny Miller	272
1976	J.C. Snead	274
	Anheuser-Busch Golf Classic	
1977	Miller Barber	272
1978	Tom Watson	270
1979	John Fought	277
1980	Ben Crenshaw	272
1981	John Mahaffey	276
1982	#Calvin Peete	203
1983	Calvin Peete	276
1984	Ronnie Black	267
1985	*Mark Wiebe	273
1986	Fuzzy Zoeller	274
1987	Mark McCumber	267
1988	*Tom Sieckmann	270
1989	Mike Donald	268
1990	Lanny Wadkins	266
1991	*Mike Hulbert	266
1992	David Peoples	271
1993	Jim Gallagher	269

* Playoff
\# Rain-shortened

NEW ENGLAND CLASSIC

Year	Winner	Score
	Carling World Open	
1965	Tony Lema	279
1966–		
1967	No tournament	
	Kemper Open	
1968	Arnold Palmer	276
	AVCO Golf Classic	
1969	Tom Shaw	280
1970	Billy Casper	277
	Massachusetts Classic	
1971	Dave Stockton	275
	USI Classic	
1972	Bruce Devlin	275
1973	Lanny Wadkins	279
	Pleasant Valley Classic	
1974	Victor Regalado	278
1975	Roger Maltbie	276
1976	Bud Allin	277
1977	Raymond Floyd	271

	American Optical Classic	
1978	John Mahaffey	270
1979	Lou Graham	275
	Pleasant Valley Jimmy Fund Classic	
1980	*Wayne Levi	273
1981	Jack Renner	273
	Bank of Boston Classic	
1982	Bob Gilder	271
1983	Mark Lye	273
1984	George Archer	270
1985	George Burns	267
1986	*Gene Sauers	274
1987	#Sam Randolph	199
1988	Mark Calcavecchia	284
1989	Blaine McCallister	271
1990	Morris Hatalsky	275
	New England Classic	
1991	*Bruce Fleisher	268
1992	Brad Faxon	268
1993		

* Playoff
\# Rain-shortened

FEDERAL EXPRESS ST. JUDE CLASSIC

Year	Winner	Score
	Memphis Invitational Open	
1958	Billy Maxwell	267
1959	*Don Whitt	272
1960	*Tommy Bolt	273
1961	Cary Middlecoff	266
1962	*Lionel Hebert	267
1963	*Tony Lema	270
1964	Mike Souchak	270
1965	*Jack Nicklaus	271
1966	Bert Yancey	265
1967	Dave Hill	272
1968	Bob Lunn	268
1969	Dave Hill	265
	Danny Thomas Memphis Classic	
1970	Dave Hill	267
1971	Lee Trevino	268
1972	Lee Trevino	281
1973	Dave Hill	283
1974	Gary Player	273
1975	Gene Littler	270
1976	Gibby Gilbert	273
1977	Al Geiberger	273
1978	*Andy Bean	277
1979	*Gil Morgan	278
1980	Lee Trevino	272
1981	Jerry Pate	274
1982	Raymond Floyd	271
1983	Larry Mize	274
1984	Bob Eastwood	280
	St. Jude Memphis Classic	
1985	*Hal Sutton	279
	Federal Express St. Jude Classic	
1986	Mike Hulbert	280
1987	Curtis Strange	275
1988	Jodie Mudd	273
1989	John Mahaffey	272
1990	*Tom Kite	269
1991	Fred Couples	269
1992	Jay Haas	263
1993	Nick Price	266

* Playoff

BUICK OPEN

Year	Winner	Score
	Buick Open Invitational	
1958	Billy Casper	285
1959	Art Wall	282
1960	Mike Souchak	282
1961	Jack Burke, Jr.	284
1962	Bill Collins	284
1963	*Julius Boros	274
1964	Tony Lema	277
1965	Tony Lema	280
1966	Phil Rodgers	284
1967	Julius Boros	283
1968	Tom Weiskopf	280
1969	Dave Hill	277
1970–		
1971	No tournament	
	Vern Parsell Buick Open	
1972	^Gary Groh	273
	Lake Michigan Classic	
1973	^Wilf Homenuik	215
	Flint Elks Open	
1974	^Bryan Abbott	135
1975	^Spike Kelley	208
1976	^Ed Sabo	279
1977	Bobby Cole	271
	Buick Goodwrench Open	
1978	*Jack Newton	280
1979	*John Fought	280
1980	Peter Jacobsen	276
	Buick Open	
1981	*Hale Irwin	277
1982	Lanny Wadkins	273
1983	Wayne Levi	272
1984	Denis Watson	271
1985	Ken Green	268
1986	Ben Crenshaw	270
1987	Robert Wrenn	262
1988	Scott Verplank	268
1989	Leonard Thompson	273
1990	Chip Beck	272
1991	*Brad Faxon	271
1992	*Dan Forsman	276
1993	Larry Mize	272

* Playoff
^ Second-tour event

THE INTERNATIONAL

Year	Winner	Score
1986	Ken Green	Plus 12*
1987	John Cook	Plus 11
1988	Joey Sindelar	Plus 17
1989	Greg Norman	Plus 13
1990	Davis Love III	Plus 14
1991	José Maria Olazabal	Plus 10
1992	Brad Faxon	Plus 14
1993	Phil Mickelson	Plus 45**

* Scoring is by points in modified Stableford System.
** Scoring cumulative for four rounds beginning in 1993. In prior years, winning score is final-round score.

NEC WORLD SERIES OF GOLF

Year	Winner	Score
1962	Jack Nicklaus	135
1963	Jack Nicklaus	140
1964	Tony Lema	138
1965	Gary Player	139
1966	Gene Littler	143
1967	Jack Nicklaus	144
1968	Gary Player	143
1969	Orville Moody	141
1970	Jack Nicklaus	136
1971	Charles Coody	141
1972	Gary Player	142
1973	Tom Weiskopf	137
1974	*Lee Trevino	139
1975	Tom Watson	140
1976	Jack Nicklaus	275
1977	Lanny Wadkins	267
1978	*Gil Morgan	278
1979	Lon Hinkle	272
1980	Tom Watson	270
1981	Bill Rogers	275**
1982	Craig Stadler	278
1983	Nick Price	270
1984	Denis Watson	271
1985	Roger Maltbie	268
1986	Dan Pohl	277
1987	Curtis Strange	275
1988	*Mike Reid	275
1989	*David Frost	276
1990	José Maria Olazabal	262
1991	Tom Purtzer	279
1992	Craig Stadler	273
1993	Fulton Allem	270

* Playoff
** 72-hole event beginning in 1976 (in prior years, a 36-hole exhibition)

GREATER MILWAUKEE OPEN

Year	Winner	Score
1968	Dave Stockton	275
1969	Ken Still	277
1970	Deane Beman	276
1971	Dave Eichelberger	270
1972	Jim Colbert	271
1973	Dave Stockton	276
1974	Ed Sneed	276
1975	Art Wall	271
1976	Dave Hill	270
1977	Dave Eichelberger	278
1978	*Lee Elder	275
1979	Calvin Peete	269
1980	Bill Kratzert	266
1981	Jay Haas	274
1982	Calvin Peete	274
1983	*Morris Hatalsky	275
1984	Mark O'Meara	272
1985	Jim Thorpe	274
1986	*Corey Pavin	272
1987	Gary Hallberg	269
1988	Ken Green	268
1989	Greg Norman	269
1990	*Jim Gallagher, Jr.	271
1991	Mark Brooks	270
1992	Richard Zokol	269
1993	*Billy Mayfair	270

* Playoff

CANADIAN OPEN

Year	Winner	Score
1904	J.H. Oke	156
1905	George Cumming	148
1906	Charles Murray	170
1907	Percy Barrett	306
1908	Albert Murray	300
1909	Karl Keffer	309
1910	Daniel Kenny	303
1911	Charles Murray	314
1912	George Sargent	299
1913	Albert Murray	295
1914	Karl Keffer	300
1915–		
1918	No tournaments	
1919	J. Douglas Edgar	278
1920	*J. Douglas Edgar	298
1921	W.H. Trovinger	293
1922	Al Watrous	303
1923	C.W. Hackney	295
1924	Leo Diegel	285
1925	Leo Diegel	295
1926	Mac Smith	283
1927	T.D. Armour	288
1928	Leo Diegel	282
1929	Leo Diegel	274
1930	*T.D. Armour	273
1931	*Walter Hagen	292
1932	Harry Cooper	290
1933	Joe Kirkwood	282
1934	T.D. Armour	287
1935	Gene Kunes	280
1936	Lawson Little	271
1937	Harry Cooper	285
1938	*Sam Snead	277
1939	H. McSpaden	282
1940	*Sam Snead	281
1941	Sam Snead	274
1942	Craig Wood	275
1943–		
1944	No tournaments	
1945	Byron Nelson	280
1946	*George Fazio	278
1947	Bobby Locke	268
1948	C.W. Congdon	280
1949	Dutch Harrison	271
1950	Jim Ferrier	271
1951	Jim Ferrier	273
1952	John Palmer	263
1953	Dave Douglas	273
1954	Pat Fletcher	280
1955	Arnold Palmer	265
1956	aDoug Sanders	273
1957	George Bayer	271
1958	Wes Ellis	267
1959	Doug Ford	276
1960	Art Wall, Jr.	269
1961	Jacky Cupit	270
1962	Ted Kroll	278
1963	Doug Ford	280
1964	Kel Nagle	277
1965	Gene Littler	273
1966	Don Massengale	280
1967	*Billy Casper	279
1968	Bob Charles	274
1969	*Tommy Aaron	275
1970	Kermit Zarley	279
1971	*Lee Trevino	275
1972	Gay Brewer	275
1973	Tom Weiskopf	278
1974	Bobby Nichols	270
1975	*Tom Weiskopf	274
1976	Jerry Pate	267

1977	Lee Trevino	280
1978	Bruce Lietzke	283
1979	Lee Trevino	281
1980	Bob Gilder	274
1981	Peter Oosterhuis	280
1982	Bruce Lietzke	277
1983	*John Cook	277
1984	Greg Norman	278
1985	Curtis Strange	279
1986	Bob Murphy	280
1987	Curtis Strange	276
1988	Ken Green	275
1989	Steve Jones	271
1990	Wayne Levi	278
1991	Nick Price	273
1992	*Greg Norman	280
1993	David Frost	279

* Playoff
a Amateur

HARDEE'S GOLF CLASSIC

Year	Winner	Score
	Quad Cities Open	
1972	Deane Beman	279
1973	Sam Adams	268
1974	Dave Stockton	271
	Ed McMahon–Jaycees Quad City Open	
1975	Roger Maltbie	275
1976	John Lister	268
1977	Mike Morley	267
1978	Victor Regalado	269
1979	D.A. Weibring	266
	Quad Cities Open	
1980	Scott Hoch	266
1981	*Dave Barr	270
	Miller High-Life Quad Cities Open	
1982	Payne Stewart	268
1983	*Danny Edwards	266
1984	Scott Hoch	266
	Lite Quad Cities Open	
1985	Dan Forsman	267
	Hardee's Golf Classic	
1986	Mark Wiebe	268
1987	Kenny Knox	265
1988	Blaine McCallister	261
1989	Curt Byrum	268
1990	*Joey Sindelar	268
1991	D.A. Weibring	267
1992	David Frost	266
1993	David Frost	259

* Playoff

B.C. OPEN

Year	Winner	Score
	Broome County Open	
1971	*Claude Harmon, Jr.	69
	B.C. Open	
1972	Bob Payne	136
1973	Hubert Green	266
1974	*Richie Karl	273
1975	Don Iverson	274
1976	Bob Wynn	271
1977	Gil Morgan	270
1978	Tom Kite	267
1979	Howard Twitty	270
1980	Don Pooley	271
1981	Jay Haas	270

1982	Calvin Peete	265
1983	Pat Lindsey	268
1984	Wayne Levi	275
1985	Joey Sindelar	274
1986	Rick Fehr	267
1987	Joey Sindelar	266
1988	Bill Glasson	268
1989	*Mike Hulbert	268
1990	Nolan Henke	268
1991	Fred Couples	269
1992	John Daly	266
1993	Blaine McCallister	217

* Playoff

BUICK SOUTHERN OPEN

Year	Winner	Score
	Green Island Open Invitational	
1970	Mason Rudolph	274
	Southern Open Invitational	
1971	Johnny Miller	267
1972	*DeWitt Weaver	276
1973	Gary Player	270
1974	Forrest Fezler	271
1975	Hubert Green	264
1976	Mac McLendon	274
1977	Jerry Pate	266
1978	Jerry Pate	269
1979	*Ed Fiori	274
1980	Mike Sullivan	269
1981	*J.C. Snead	271
1982	Bobby Clampett	266
1983	*Ronnie Black	271
1984	Hubert Green	265
1985	Tim Simpson	264
1986	Fred Wadsworth	269
1987	Ken Brown	266
1988	*David Frost	270
1989	Ted Schulz	266
	Buick Southern Open	
1990	*Kenny Knox	265
1991	David Peoples	276
1992	#Gary Hallberg	206
1993	*John Inman	278

* Playoff
# Rain-shortened

WALT DISNEY WORLD/OLDSMOBILE CLASSIC

Year	Winner	Score
	Walt Disney World Open Invitational	
1971	Jack Nicklaus	273
1972	Jack Nicklaus	267
1973	Jack Nicklaus	275
	Walt Disney World National Team Championship	
1974	Hubert Green/	255
	Mac McLendon	
1975	Jim Colbert/	252
	Dean Refram	
1976	*Woody Blackburn/	260
	Bill Kratzert	
1977	Gibby Gilbert/	253
	Grier Jones	
1978	Wayne Levi/	254
	Bob Mann	
1979	George Burns/	255
	Ben Crenshaw	

1980	Danny Edwards/	253
	David Edwards	
1981	Vance Heafner/	275
	Mike Holland	
	Walt Disney World Golf Classic	
1982	*Hal Sutton	269
1983	Payne Stewart	269
1984	Larry Nelson	266
	Walt Disney World/Oldsmobile Classic	
1985	Lanny Wadkins	267
1986	*Ray Floyd	275
1987	Larry Nelson	268
1988	*Bob Lohr	263
1989	Tim Simpson	272
1990	Tim Simpson	264
1991	Mark O'Meara	267
1992	John Huston	262
1993	Jeff Maggert	265

* Playoff

TEXAS OPEN

Year	Winner	Score
	Texas Open	
1922	Bob MacDonald	281
1923	Walter Hagen	279
1924	Joe Kirkwood	279
1925	Joe Turnesa	284
1926	Mac Smith	288
1927	Bobby Cruickshank	272
1928	Bill Mehlhorn	297
1929	Bill Mehlhorn	277
1930	Denny Shute	277
1931	Abe Espinosa	281
1932	Clarence Clark	287
1933	No tournament	
1934	Wiffy Cox	283
1935–	No tournament	
1938		
1939	Dutch Harrison	271
1940	Byron Nelson	271
1941	Lawson Little	273
1942	*Chick Harbert	272
1943	No tournament	
1944	Johnny Revolta	273
1945	Sam Byrd	268
1946	Ben Hogan	264
1947	Ed Oliver	265
1948	Sam Snead	264
1949	Dave Douglas	268
1950	Sam Snead	265
1951	*Dutch Harrison	265
1952	Jack Burke, Jr.	260
1953	Tony Holguin	264
1954	Chandler Harper	259
1955	Mike Souchak	257
1956	Gene Littler	276
1957	Jay Hebert	271
1958	Bill Johnston	274
1959	Wes Ellis	276
1960	Arnold Palmer	276
1961	Arnold Palmer	270
1962	Arnold Palmer	273
1963	Phil Rodgers	268
1964	Bruce Crampton	273
1965	Frank Beard	270
1966	Harold Henning	272
1967	Chi Chi Rodriguez	277
1968	No tournament	
1969	*Deane Beman	274
	San Antonio Texas Open	
1970	Ron Cerrudo	273

1971	No tournament	
1972	Mike Hill	273
1973	Ben Crenshaw	270
1974	Terry Diehl	269
1975	*Don January	275
1976	*Butch Baird	273
1977	Hale Irwin	266
1978	Ron Streck	265
1979	Lou Graham	268
1980	Lee Trevino	265
	Texas Open	
1981	*Bill Rogers	266
1982	Jay Haas	262
1983	Jim Colbert	261
1984	Calvin Peete	266
1985	*John Mahaffey	268
	Vantage Championship	
1986	#Ben Crenshaw	196
	Nabisco Championships of Golf	
1987	Tom Watson	268
	Texas Open Presented by Nabisco	
1988	Corey Pavin	259
1989	Donnie Hammond	258
	H.E.B. Texas Open	
1990	Mark O'Meara	261
1991	*Blaine McCallister	269
1992	*Nick Price	283
1993	*Jay Haas	263

* Playoff
# Rain-shortened

LAS VEGAS INVITATIONAL

Year	Winner	Score
	Panasonic Las Vegas Pro-Celebrity Classic	
1983	Fuzzy Zoeller	340
	Panasonic Las Vegas Invitational	
1984	Denis Watson	341
1985	Curtis Strange	338
1986	Greg Norman	333
1987	#Paul Azinger	271
1988	#Gary Koch	274
	Las Vegas Invitational	
1989	*Scott Hoch	336
1990	*Bob Tway	334
1991	*Andrew Magee	329
1992	John Cook	334
1993	Davis Love III	331

* Playoff
# Rain-shortened

TOUR CHAMPIONSHIP

Year	Winner	Site	Score
1986**	#Ben Crenshaw	Oak Hills CC	196
1987	Tom Watson	Oak Hills CC	268
1988	*Curtis Strange	Pebble Beach GL	279
1989	*Tom Kite	Harbour Town GL	276
1990	*Jodie Mudd	Champions GC	273
1991	*Craig Stadler	Pinehurst Number 2	279
1992	Paul Azinger	Pinehurst Number 2	276
1993	Jim Gallagher, Jr.	Olympic GC	277

* Playoff
** Vantage Championship (not counted in tournament records)

Unofficial Money Events

LINCOLN-MERCURY KAPALUA INTERNATIONAL

Year	Winner	Score
1983	Greg Norman	268
1984	Sandy Lyle	266
	Isuzu Kapalua International	
1985	Mark O'Meara	275
1986	Andy Bean	278
1987	Andy Bean	267
1988	Bob Gilder	266
1989	*Peter Jacobsen	270
1990	David Peoples	264
	Ping Kapalua International	
1991	*Mike Hulbert	276
	Lincoln-Mercury Kapalua International	
1992	Davis Love III	275
1993	Fred Couples	274

* Playoff

WORLD CUP OF GOLF

Year	Winning team	Winning Individual
1988	UNITED STATES	
	Ben Crenshaw, Mark McCumber	Ben Crenshaw, U.S.
1989	AUSTRALIA	
	Peter Fowler, Wayne Grady	Peter Fowler, Australia
1990	GERMANY	
	Bernhard Langer, Torsten Giedeon	Payne Stewart, U.S
1991	SWEDEN	
	Anders Forsbrand, Per-Ulrick Johansson	Ian Woosnam, Wales
1992	UNITED STATES	
	Fred Couples, Davis Love III	Brett Ogle, Australia
1993	UNITED STATES	
	Fred Couples, Davis Love III	Bernhard Langer, Germany

SKINS GAME

Year	Winner	Score
1983	Gary Player	$170,000
1984	Jack Nicklaus	$240,000
1985	Fuzzy Zoeller	$255,000
1986	Fuzzy Zoeller	$370,000
1987	Lee Trevino	$310,000
1988	Ray Floyd	$290,000
1989	Curtis Strange	$265,000
1990	Curtis Strange	$225,000
1991	Payne Stewart	$260,000
1992	Payne Stewart	$220,000
1993	Payne Stewart	$280,000

FRANKLIN FUNDS SHARK SHOOTOUT

Year	Winners	Score
	RMCC Invitational	
1989	Curtis Strange & Mark O'Meara	190
1990	Raymond Floyd & Fred Couples	182
	Shark Shootout Benefitting RMCC	
1991	Tom Purtzer & Lanny Wadkins	189
	Franklin Funds Shark Shootout	
1992	Davis Love III & Tom Kite	191
1993	Steve Elkington & Raymond Floyd	188

JC PENNEY CLASSIC

Year	Winners	Score
	Haig & Haig Scotch Foursome	
1960	*Jim Turnesa & Gloria Armstrong	139
1961	Dave Ragan & Mickey Wright	272
1962	Mason Rudolph & Kathy Whitworth	272
1963	Dave Ragan & Mickey Wright	273
1964	Sam Snead & Shirley Englehorn	272
1965	Gardner Dickinson & Ruth Jessen	281
1966	Jack Rule & Sandra Spuzich	276
1967– 1975	No tournaments	
	Pepsi-Cola Mixed Team	
1976	Chi Chi Rodriguez & JoAnn Washam	275
1977	Jerry Pate & Hollis Stacy	270
	JC Penney Classic	
1978	*Lon Hinkle & Pat Bradley	267
1979	Dave Eichelberger & Murle Breer	268
1980	Curtis Strange & Nancy Lopez	268
1981	Tom Kite & Beth Daniel	270
1982	John Mahaffey & JoAnne Carner	268
1983	Fred Couples & Jan Stephenson	264
1984	Mike Donald & Vicki Alvarez	270
1985	Larry Rinker & Laurie Rinker	267
1986	Tom Purtzer & Juli Inkster	267
1987	Steve Jones & Jane Crafter	268
1988	John Huston & Amy Benz	269
1989	*Bill Glasson & Pat Bradley	267
1990	Davis Love III & Beth Daniel	266
1991	*Billy Andrade & Kris Tschetter	266
1992	Dan Forsman & Dottie Mochrie	264
1993	Mike Springer & Melissa McNamara	265

* Playoff

ALL-TIME PGA TOUR RECORDS
All Information Based on Official PGA Tour Co-Sponsored or Approved Events

SCORING RECORDS
72 holes:
257— (60-68-64-65) by Mike Souchak, at Brackenridge Park Golf Course, San Antonio, Tex., in 1955 Texas Open (27 under par).
258— (65-64-65-64) by Donnie Hammond, at Oak Hills Country Club, SanAntonio, Tex., in 1989 Texas Open Presented by Nabisco (22 under par).
259— (62-68-63-66) by,Byron Nelson, at Broadmoor Golf Club, Seattle, Wash., in 1945 Seattle Open (21 under par).
259— (70-63-63-63) by Chandler Harper, at Brackenridge Park Golf Course, San Antonio, Tex., in 1954 Texas Open (25 under par).
259— (63-64-66-66) by Tim Norris, at Wethersfield Country Club, Hartford, Conn., in 1982 Sammy Davis Jr. Greater Hartford Open (25 under par).
259— (64-63-66-66) by Corey Pavin, at Oak Hills Country Club, San Antonio, Tex., in 1988 Texas Open (21 under par).
259— (68-63-64-64) by David Frost, at Oakwood Country Club, Coal Valley, Ill., in 1993 Hardee's Golf Classic (21 under par).
Consecutive rounds.
258— (67-64-65-62) by Tom Kite, at four courses, La Quinta, Cal., in last four rounds of 90-hole 1993 Bob Hope Chrysler Classic (30 under par).
259— (64-65-64-66) by D.A. Weibring, at three courses, Las Vegas, Nev., in last four rounds of 90-hole 1991 Las Vegas Invitational (29 under par).

90 holes:
325— (67-67-64-65-62) by Tom Kite, at four courses, La Quinta, Cal., in 1993 Bob Hope Chrysler Classic (35 under par).
329— (69-65-67-62-66) by Andrew Magee, at three courses, Las Vegas, Nev., in 1991 Las Vegas Invitational (31 under par).
329— (70-64-65-64-66) by D.A. Weibring, at three courses, Las Vegas, Nev., in 1991 Las Vegas Invitational (31 under par).

Most shots under par:
72 holes:
27— Mike Souchak in winning the 1955 Texas Open with 257.
27— Ben Hogan in winning the 1945 Portland Invitational with 261.
26— Gay Brewer in winning the 1967 Pensacola Open with 262.
26— Robert Wrenn in winning the 1987 Buick Open with 262.
26— Chip Beck in winning the 1988 USF&G Classic with 262.
26— John Huston in winning the 1992 Walt Disney World/Oldsmobile Classic with 262.

90 holes:
35— Tom Kite in winning the 1993 Bob Hope Chrysler Classic with 325.
31— Andrew Magee in winning the 1991 Las Vegas Invitational with 329.
31— D.A. Weibring in finishing second in the 1991 Las Vegas Invitational with 329 (lost playoff).

54 holes:
Opening rounds
191— (66-64-61) by Gay Brewer, at Pensacola Country Club, Pensacola, Fla., in 1967 Pensacola Open (22 under par).
192— (60-68-64) by Mike Souchak, at Brackenridge Park Golf Course, San Antonio, Tex., in 1955 Texas Open (21 under par).
192— (64-63-65) by Bob Gilder, at Westchester Country Club, Harrison, N.Y., in 1982 Manufacturers Hanover Westchester Classic (18 under par).
Consecutive rounds
189— (63-63-63) by Chandler Harper, at Brackenridge Park Golf Course, San Antonio, Tex., in last three rounds of 1954 Texas Open (24 under par).

36 holes:
Opening rounds
126— (64-62) by Tommy Bolt, at Cavalier Yacht & Country Club, Virginia Beach, Va., in 1954 Virginia Beach Open (12 under par).
126— (64-62) by Paul Azinger, at Oak Hills Country Club, San Antonio, Tex., in 1989 Texas Open Presented by Nabisco (14 under par).
Consecutive rounds
125— (64-61) by Gay Brewer, at Pensacola Country Club, Pensacola, Fla., in

middle two rounds of 1967 Pensacola Open (17 under par).
125— (63-62) by Ron Streck, at Oak Hills Country Club, San Antonio, Tex., in last two rounds of 1978 Texas Open (15 under par).
125— (62-63) by Blaine McCallister, at Oakwood Country Club, Coal Valley, Ill., in middle two rounds of 1988 Hardee's Golf Classic (15 under par).
126— (62-64) by Johnny Palmer, at El Rio Country Club, Tucson, Ariz., in last two rounds of 1948 Tucson Open (14 under par).
126— (63-63) by Sam Snead, at Brackenridge Park Golf Course, San Antonio, Tex., in last two rounds of 1950 Texas Open (16 under par).
126— (63-63) by Chandler Harper, at Brackenridge Park Golf Course, San Antonio, Tex., in middle two rounds and last two rounds of 1954 Texas Open (16 under par)
126— (60-66) by Sam Snead, at Glen Lakes Country Club, Dallas, Tex., in middle two rounds of 1957 Dallas Open (16 under par).
126— (61-65) by Jack Rule, Jr., at Keller Golf Club, St. Paul, Minn., in middle two rounds of 1963 St. Paul Open (18 under par).
126— (63-63) by Mark Pfeil, at Oak Hills Country Club, San Antonio, Tex., in middle two rounds of 1983 Texas Open (14 under par).
126— (65-61) by Mark Wiebe, at TPC at StarPass, Tucson, Ariz., in middle two rounds of 1988 Northern Telecom Tucson Open (18 under par).

18 holes:
59— by Al Geiberger, at Colonial Country Club, Memphis, Tenn., in second round of 1977 Danny Thomas Memphis Classic (13 under par).
59— by Chip Beck, at Sunrise Golf Club, Las Vegas, Nev., in third round of 1991 Las Vegas Invitational (13 under par).
60— by Al Brosch, at Brackenridge Park Golf Course, San Antonio, Tex., in third round of 1951 Texas Open (11 under par).
60— by Bill Nary, at El Paso Country Club, El Paso, Tex., in third round of 1952 El Paso Open (11 under par).
60— by Ted Kroll, at Brackenridge Park Golf Course, San Antonio, Tex,. in third round of 1954 Texas Open (11 under par).
60— by Wally Ulrich, at Cavalier Yacht & Country Club, Virginia Beach, Va., in second round of 1954 Virginia Beach Open (9 under par).
60— by Tommy Bolt, at Wethersfield Country Club, Hartford, Conn., in second round of 1954 Insurance City Open (11 under par).
60— by Mike Souchak, at Brackenridge Park Golf Course, San Antonio, Tex., in first round of 1955 Texas Open (11 under par).
60— by Sam Snead, at Glen Lakes Country Club, Dallas, Tex., in second round of 1957 Dallas Open (11 under par).
60— by David Frost, at Randolph Park Golf Course, Tucson, Ariz., in second round of 1990 Northern Telecom Tucson Open (12 under par).
60— by Davis Love III, at Waialae Country Club, Honolulu, Haw., in second round of 1994 United Airlines Hawaiian Open.
9 holes:
27— by Mike Souchak, at Brackenridge Park Golf Course, San Antonio, Tex., on par-35 second nine of first round in 1955 Texas Open.
27— by Andy North, at En-Joie Golf Club, Endicott, N.Y., on par-34 second nine of first round in 1975 B.C. Open.

Best Vardon Trophy scoring average:
69.23— Sam Snead in 1950 (6646 strokes, 96 rounds).
69.30— Ben Hogan in 1948 (5267 strokes, 76 rounds).
69.37— Sam Snead in 1949 (5064 strokes, 73 rounds).

Most consecutive rounds under 70:
19— Byron Nelson in 1945.

Most birdies in a row:
8— Bob Goalby, at Pasadena Golf Club, St. Petersburg, Fla., during fourth round of 1961 St. Petersburg Open.
8— Fuzzy Zoeller, at Oakwood Country Club, Coal Valley, Ill., during first round of 1976 Quad Cities Open.
8— Dewey Arnette, at Warwick Hills Golf and Country Club, Grand Blanc, Mich., during first round of 1987 Buick Open.

Best birdie-eagle streak:
6— birdies and 1 eagle by Al Geiberger at Colonial Country Club, Memphis, Tenn., during second round of 1977 Danny Thomas Memphis Classic.

Most birdies in a row to win:
5— by Jack Nicklaus to win 1978 Jackie Gleason Inverrary Classic (last five holes).

Fewest putts, one round:
18— Sam Trahan, at Whitemarsh Valley Country Club, in final round of 1979 IVB-Philadelphia Golf Classic.
18— Mike McGee, at Colonial Country Club, in first round of 1987 Federal Express St. Jude Classic.
18— Kenny Knox, at Harbour Town Golf Links, in first round of 1989 MCI Heritage Classic.
18— Andy North, at Kingsmill Golf Club, in second round of 1990 Anheuser-Busch Golf Classic.
18— Jim McGovern, at TPC at Southwind, in second round of 1992 Federal Express St. Jude Classic.

Fewest putts, four rounds:
93— Kenny Knox, at Harbour Town Golf Links, in 1989 MCI Heritage Classic.
94— George Archer, at Harbour Town Golf Links, in 1980 Sea Pines Heritage Classic.

Fewest putts, nine holes:
8— Jim Colbert, at the Deerwood Club, on front nine of last round in 1967 Greater Jacksonville Open.
8— Sam Trahan, at Whitemarsh Valley Country Club, on back nine of last round in 1979 IVB-Philadelphia Golf Classic.
8— Kenny Knox, at Harbour Town Golf Links, on back nine of first round in 1989 MCI Heritage Classic.

VICTORY RECORDS

Most victories during career (PGA Tour co-sponsored and/or approved events only):
81— Sam Snead
70— Jack Nicklaus
63— Ben Hogan
60— Arnold Palmer
52— Byron Nelson
51— Billy Casper

Most consecutive years winning at least one tournament:
17— Jack Nicklaus (1962-78)
17— Arnold Palmer (1955-71)
16— Billy Casper (1956-71)

Most consecutive victories:
11— Byron Nelson, from Miami Four Ball, March 8-11, 1945, through Canadian Open, August 2-4, 1945. Tournament site, dates, score, purse—Miami Four Ball, Miami Springs Course, Miami, Fla., March 8-11, won 8 & 6, $1,500; Charlotte Open, Myers Park Golf Club, Charlotte, N.C., March 16-19, 272, $2,000; Greensboro Open, Starmount Country Club, Greensboro, N.C., March 23-25, 271, $1,000; Durham Open, Hope Valley Country Club, Durham, N.C., March 30-April 1, 276, $1,000; Atlanta Open, Capital City Course, Atlanta, Ga., April 5-8, 263, $2,000; Montreal Open, Islemere Golf and Country Club, Montreal, Que., June 7-10, 268, $2,000; Philadelphia Inquirer Invitational, Llanerch Country Club, Philadelphia, Pa., June 14-17, 269, $3,000; Chicago Victory National Open, Calumet Country Club, Chicago, Ill., June 29-July 1, 275, $2,000; PGA Championship, Moraine Country Club, Dayton, Ohio, July 9-15, 4 & 3, $3,750; Tam O'Shanter Open, Tam O'Shanter Country Club, Chicago, Ill., July 26-29, 269, $10,000; Canadian Open, Thornhill Country Club, Toronto, Ont., August 2-4, 280, $2,000; Winnings for streak: $30,250. NOTE: Nelson won a 12th event in Spring Lake, N.J., which is not counted as official as its $2,500 purse was below the PGA $3,000 minimum.
4— Jack Burke, Jr., in 1952: From February 14 to March 9—Texas Open, Houston Open, Baton Rouge Open, St. Petersburg Open.
3— Byron Nelson in 1944, 1945-46; Sam Snead in 1945; Ben Hogan in 1946; Bobby Locke in 1947; Jim Ferrier in 1951; Billy Casper in 1960; Arnold Palmer in 1960, 1962; Johnny Miller in 1974; Hubert Green in 1976; Gary Player in 1978; Tom Watson in 1980; Nick Price in 1993.

Most victories in a single event:
8— Sam Snead, Greater Greensboro Open: 1938, 1946. 1949, 1950, 1955, 1956, 1960, 1965.
6— Sam Snead, Miami Open: 1937, 1939, 1946, 1950, 1951, 1955.
6— Jack Nicklaus, Masters: 1963, 1965, 1966, 1972, 1975, 1986.
5— Walter Hagen, PGA Championship: 1921, 1924, 1925, 1926, 1927.
5— Ben Hogan, Colonial NIT: 1946, 1947, 1952, 1953, 1959.
5— Arnold Palmer, Bob Hope Desert Classic: 1960, 1962, 1968, 1971, 1973.

5— Jack Nicklaus, Tournament of Champions: 1963, 1964, 1971, 1973, 1977.
5— Jack Nicklaus, PGA Championship: 1963, 1971, 1973, 1975, 1980.
5— Walter Hagen, Western Open: 1916, 1921, 1926, 1927, 1932.

Most consecutive victories in a single event:
4— Walter Hagen, PGA Championship, 1924-1927.
3— Willie Anderson, U.S. Open, 1903-1905.
3— Ralph Guldahl, Western Open, 1936-1938.
3— Gene Littler, Tournament of Champions, 1955-1957.
3— Billy Casper, Portland Open, 1959-1961.
3— Arnold Palmer, Texas Open, 1960-1962; Phoenix Open, 1961-1963.
3— Jack Nicklaus, Disney World Golf Classic, 1971-1973.
3— Johnny Miller, Tucson Open, 1974-1976.
3— Tom Watson, Byron Nelson Classic, 1978-1980.

Most victories in a calendar year:
18— Byron Nelson (1945)
13— Ben Hogan (1946)
11— Sam Snead (1950)
10— Ben Hogan (1948)
8— Sam Snead (1938)
8— Byron Nelson (1944)
8— Lloyd Mangrum (1948)
8— Arnold Palmer (1960)
8— Johnny Miller (1974)

Most years between victories:
13 by Howard Twitty (1980-1993)
12 by Leonard Thompson (1977-1989)

Most years from first victory to last:
29 by Ray Floyd (1963-1992)
29 by Sam Snead (1936-1965)
24 by Jack Nicklaus (1962-1986)
23 by Gene Littler (1954-1977)
23 by Johnny Miller (1971-1994)
22 by Art Wall (1953-1975)

Most first-time winners during one calendar year:
14— 1991

Youngest winners:
Johnny McDermott, 19 years and 10 months, 1911 U.S. Open.
Gene Sarazen, 20 years and 4 months, 1922 U.S. Open.
Horton Smith, 20 years and 5 months, 1928 Oklahoma City Open.
Ray Floyd, 20 years and 6 months, 1963 St. Petersburg Open.
Phil Mickelson, 20 years and 6 months, 1991 Northern Telecom Open.
Seve Ballesteros, 20 years and 11 months, 1978 Greater Greensboro Open.

Oldest winners:
Sam Snead, 52 years and 10 months, 1965 Greater Greensboro Open.
Art Wall, 51 years and 10 months, 1975 Greater Milwaukee Open.
John Barnum, 51 years and 1 month, 1962 Cajun Classic.
Jim Barnes, 50 years, 1937 Long Island Open.
Ray Floyd, 49 years and 6 months, 1992 Doral-Ryder Open.

MONEY-WINNING RECORDS

Most money won in a calendar year:
$1,478,557 by Nick Price in 1993.
$1,458,456 by Paul Azinger in 1993.
$1,395,278 by Tom Kite in 1989.
$1,359,653 by Greg Norman in 1993.

Most money won by a rookie:
$574,783 by John Daly in 1991.
$461,407 by Robert Gamez in 1990.
$337,374 by Brett Ogle in 1993.
$320,007 by Keith Clearwater in 1987.

Most consecutive events without missing cut:

113— Byron Nelson, during the 1940s.
105— Jack Nicklaus, from Sahara Open, November 1970, through World Series of Golf, September 1976 (missed cut in 1976 World Open).
86— Hale Irwin, from Tucson Open, February 1975, through conclusion of 1978 season.

Widest winning margin:

16 strokes—Bobby Locke, 1948 Chicago Victory National Championship.
14 strokes—Ben Hogan, 1945 Portland Invitational; Johnny Miller, 1975 Phoenix Open.
13 strokes—Byron Nelson, 1945 Seattle Open.
12 strokes—Arnold Palmer, 1962 Phoenix Open; José Maria Olazabal, 1990 NEC World Series of Golf.

Longest sudden-death playoffs:

11 holes—Cary Middlecoff and Lloyd Mangrum were declared co-winners by mutual agreement in the 1949 Motor City Open.
8 holes—Dick Hart defeated Phil Rodgers in the 1965 Azalea Open.
8 holes—Lee Elder defeated Lee Trevino in the 1978 Greater Milwaukee Open.
8 holes—Dave Barr defeated Woody Blackburn, Dan Halldorson, Frank Conner, and Victor Regalado in the 1981 Quad Cities Open.
8 holes—Bob Gilder defeated Rex Caldwell, Johnny Miller, and Mark O'Meara, in the 1983 Phoenix Open.

Youngest pro shooting age:

66— (4 under), Sam Snead (age 67), 1979 Quad Cities Open.

ALL-TIME TOUR WINNERS

1.	Sam Snead	81	Craig Wood	21
2.	Jack Nicklaus	70	Lanny Wadkins	21
3.	Ben Hogan	63	T30. James Barnes	20
4.	Arnold Palmer	60	Doug Sanders	20
5.	Byron Nelson	52	T32. Doug Ford	19
6.	Billy Casper	51	Hubert Green	19
T7.	Walter Hagen	40	Hale Irwin	19
	Cary Middlecoff	40	Tom Kite	19
9.	Gene Sarazen	38	T36. Julius Boros	18
10.	Lloyd Mangrum	36	Jim Ferrier	18
T11.	Horton Smith	32	Johnny Revolta	18
	Tom Watson	32	T39. Jack Burke, Jr.	17
T13.	Harry Cooper	31	Ben Crenshaw	17
	Jimmy Demaret	31	Bobby Cruickshank	17
15.	Leo Diegel	30	Harold McSpaden	17
T16.	Gene Littler	29	Curtis Strange	17
	Paul Runyan	29	44. Ralph Guldahl	16
18.	Lee Trevino	27	T45. Tommy Bolt	15
19.	Henry Picard	26	Ed Dudley	15
T20.	Tommy Armour	24	Denny Shute	15
	Macdonald Smith	24	Mike Souchak	15
	Johnny Miller	24	Tom Weiskopf	15
T23.	Johnny Farrell	22		
	Ray Floyd	22		
	Gary Player	22		
T26.	Willie Macfarlane	21		
	Bill Mehlhorn	21		

Course	Length	Par
Castle Pines GC	7559	72
TPC at Summerlin	7243	72
Magnolia GC	7190	72
Las Vegas CC	7164	72
Annandale GC	7157	72
Firestone CC	7149	70
Tucson National CC	7148	72
English Turn G&CC	7116	72
Bay Hill Club & Lodge	7114	72
Glen Abbey GC	7112	72
Desert Inn CC	7111	72
Pleasant Valley CC	7110	72
Warwick Hills G&CC	7105	72
Muirfield Village	7104	72
Cog Hill G&CC	7073	72
Weston Hills CC	7069	72
Callaway Gardens Resort	7057	72
TPC at The Woodlands	7042	72
La Costa CC	7022	72
Atlanta CC	7018	72
Colonial CC	7010	70
Starr Pass GC	7010	72
TPC at Southwind	7006	71
TPC at Avenel	7005	71
Torrey Pines GC (South)	7000	72
TPC of Scottsdale	6992	71
Waialae CC	6975	72
Palm GC	6967	72
En-Joie GC	6966	71
Forest Oaks GC	6958	72
Riviera CC	6946	71
Doral Resort & CC	6939	72
Bermuda Dunes CC	6927	72
Augusta National GC	6925	72
Harbour Town GL	6912	71
PGA West (Arnold Palmer)	6901	72
TPC at Sawgrass	6896	72
Tamarisk CC	6881	72
Poppy Hills GC	6865	72
La Quinta CC	6852	72
Lake Buena Vista CC	6829	72
TPC at River Highlands	6820	70
Spyglass Hill GC	6810	72
Pebble Beach GL	6799	72
Kingsmill GC	6797	71
Westchester CC	6779	71
Oakwood CC	6755	70
TPC at Las Colinas	6742	70
Brown Deer GC	6701	70
Oak Hills CC	6650	71
Torrey Pines GC (North)	6592	72
Indian Wells CC	6478	72

PGA TOUR TOUGHEST COURSES
1991–93

Rank	Course	Par	Ydg	Score	O/U Par	Egl	Bird	Pars	Bog	Dbl Bog	Tpl Bg+	Tournament Name
1	SPYGLASS HILL GC	72	6,810	73.957	1.957	25	1,385	6,109	1,911	242	30	AT&T Pebble Beach National Pro-Am
2	FIRESTONE CC	70	7,149	71.933	1.933	24	1,405	5,830	1,952	204	35	NEC World Series of Golf
3	WESTCHESTER CC	71	6,779	72.874	1.874	66	3,822	14,782	5,044	627	67	Buick Classic
4	ENGLISH TURN G&CC	72	7,116	73.632	1.632	56	3,840	14,292	4,636	564	102	Freeport-McMoRan Classic
5	TPC AT RIVER HIGHLANDS	70	6,820	71.542	1.542	27	3,584	16,044	4,402	524	97	Canon Greater Hartford Open
6	GLEN ABBEY GC	72	7,112	73.405	1.405	65	4,132	14,979	4,721	590	83	Canadian Open
7	BAY HILL CLUB	72	7,114	73.108	1.108	76	3,188	12,527	3,356	509	72	Nestlé Invitational
8	POPPY HILLS GC	72	6,865	73.061	1.061	53	1,556	6,170	1,693	210	38	AT&T Pebble Beach National Pro-Am
9	CALLAWAY GARDENS RESORT	72	7,057	72.976	.976	56	3,799	14,932	4,349	345	45	Buick Southern Open
10	EN-JOIE GC	71	6,966	71.802	.802	31	3,721	16,152	3,909	399	52	B.C. Open
11	HARBOUR TOWN GL	71	6,912	71.710	.710	60	3,419	13,862	3,376	416	53	MCI Heritage Classic
12	FOREST OAKS CC	72	6,958	72.677	.677	49	3,970	16,223	4,248	330	38	Kmart Greater Greensboro Open
13	TPC AT LAS COLINAS	70	6,742	70.648	.648	55	3,864	15,411	3,885	422	51	GTE Byron Nelson Golf Classic
14	TPC AT AVENEL	71	7,005	71.648	.648	91	4,370	15,584	3,973	564	96	Kemper Open
15	COG HILL CC	71	7,073	72.627	.627	72	4,328	16,050	4,247	462	59	Motorola Western Open
16	RIVIERA CC	71	6,946	71.578	.578	60	3,787	14,316	3,772	329	38	Nissan L.A. Open
17	PEBBLE BEACH GOLF LINKS	72	6,799	72.463	.463	57	2,302	8,514	2,168	250	29	AT&T Pebble Beach National Pro-Am
18	AUGUSTA NATIONAL GC	72	6,925	72.462	.462	91	2,853	9,745	2,797	258	42	The Masters
19	ATLANTA CC	72	7,018	72.387	.387	43	3,150	10,488	2,606	385	68	BellSouth Classic
20	WESTON HILLS CC	72	7,069	72.261	.261	43	2,614	9,214	2,079	308	52	Honda Classic
21	TPC AT SAWGRASS	72	6,896	72.214	.214	67	4,362	14,707	3,617	475	64	The Players Championship
22	STARR PASS GC	72	7,010	72.169	.169	58	2,212	6,727	1,775	232	48	Northern Telecom Open
23	TORREY PINES–SOUTH	72	7,000	72.134	.134	49	2,708	9,868	2,574	194	33	Buick Invitational of California
24	COLONIAL CC	70	7,010	70.054	.054	29	3,497	13,444	2,776	353	43	Southwestern Bell Colonial
25	MUIRFIELD VILLAGE GC	72	7,104	72.034	.034	78	3,855	12,492	3,063	401	55	The Memorial
26	PLEASANT VALLEY CC	71	7,110	70.984	.016-	52	4,358	16,018	3,515	373	56	New England Classic
27	KINGSMILL GC	71	6,797	70.915	.085-	79	4,692	16,033	3,831	369	52	Anheuser-Busch Classic
28	OAKWOOD CC	70	6,755	69.886	.114-	95	4,196	16,728	3,757	212	14	Hardee's Classic
29	DORAL RESORT & CC	72	6,939	71.865	.135-	66	4,383	15,550	3,588	313	40	Doral-Ryder Open
30	TPC AT SOUTHWIND	71	7,006	70.804	.196-	101	4,926	15,728	3,536	518	85	Federal Express St. Jude Classic
31	WARWICK HILLS G&CC	72	7,105	71.733	.267-	57	4,619	16,230	3,673	297	36	Buick Open
32	TORREY PINES–NORTH	72	6,592	71.631	.369-	45	1,582	5,320	1,260	98	11	Buick Invitational of California
33	LA COSTA CC	72	7,022	71.621	.379-	10	1,145	4,575	905	58	3	Mercedes Championships
34	WAIALAE CC	72	6,975	71.571	.429-	185	4,797	14,843	3,746	361	44	United Airlines Hawaiian Open
35	DESERT INN CC	72	7,111	71.511	.489-	36	947	3,586	723	68	4	Las Vegas Invitational
36	TPC OF SCOTTSDALE	71	6,992	70.486	.514-	96	4,489	14,863	3,321	294	31	Phoenix Open
37	TPC AT THE WOODLANDS	72	7,042	71.063	.937-	75	4,817	15,662	2,870	367	59	Shell Houston Open
38	OAK HILLS CC	71	6,650	70.004	.996-	84	3,636	10,191	2,327	241	27	H.E.B. Texas Open
39	TUCSON NAT'L GC	72	7,148	70.808	1.192-	73	2,952	8,973	1,662	209	27	Northern Telecom Open
40	TPC AT SUMMERLIN	72	7,243	70.659	1.141-	86	2,388	6,633	1,360	168	21	Las Vegas Invitational
41	PALMER COURSE/ PGA WEST	72	6,901	70.454	1.546-	40	1,975	5,098	952	141	20	Bob Hope Chrysler Classic
42	PALM GC	72	6,967	70.207	1.803-	36	1,528	4,691	747	65	7	Walt Disney World/Oldsmobile Classic
43	MAGNOLIA GC	72	7,190	70.105	1.895-	28	2,423	7,455	1,108	76	16	Walt Disney World/Oldsmobile Classic
44	LA QUINTA CC	72	6,852	70.103	1.897-	35	1,037	2,972	511	49	4	Bob Hope Chrysler Classic
45	LAS VEGAS CC	72	7,164	69.726	2.274-	23	632	1,593	301	23	2	Las Vegas Invitational
46	LAKE BUENA VISTA GC	72	6,829	69.643	2.357-	27	1,706	4,520	698	61	8	Walt Disney World/Oldsmobile Classic
47	BERMUDA DUNES CC	72	6,927	69.527	2.473-	28	1,931	5,405	721	62	7	Bob Hope Chrysler Classic
48	INDIAN WELLS CC	72	6,478	69.068	2.932-	69	2,190	5,058	775	88	10	Bob Hope Chrysler Classic
49	TAMARISK CC	72	6,881	68.905	3.095-	16	596	1,438	201	14	3	Bob Hope Chrysler Classic
		71.571			71.442	.129-						

PGA TOUR
TOUGHEST HOLES
1991–93

Rank	Course	Hole	Par	Ydg	Avg Score	O/U Par	Egl	Bird	Pars	Bog	Dbl Bog	Tpl Bg+	Tournament Name
1	ENGLISH TURN G&CC	18	4	471	4.493	.493	1	71	646	480	89	18	Freeport-McMoRan Classic
2	SPYGLASS HILL GC	08	4	395	4.419	.419	0	33	287	184	30	5	AT&T Pebble Beach National Pro-Am
3	SPYGLASS HILL GC	16	4	465	4.415	.415	1	25	297	188	24	4	AT&T Pebble Beach National Pro-Am
4	WESTCHESTER CC	12	4	476	4.411	.411	0	73	712	514	54	3	Buick Classic
5	BAY HILL CLUB	18	4	441	4.409	.409	0	101	597	272	105	21	Nestlé Invitational
6	FIRESTONE CC	04	4	458	4.387	.387	0	37	285	174	23	6	NEC World Series of Golf
7	WESTCHESTER CC	11	4	444	4.382	.382	0	74	778	425	72	7	Buick Classic
8	EN-JOIE GC	15	4	476	4.373	.373	0	89	748	442	57	12	B.C. Open
9	TPC AT SOUTHWIND	14	3	231	3.365	.365	0	137	751	377	98	20	Federal Express St. Jude Classic
10	COG HILL CC	18	4	452	4.360	.360	1	96	803	410	81	10	Motorola Western Open
11	OAKWOOD CC	04	4	495	4.350	.350	0	73	799	475	42	0	Hardee's Classic
12	WESTCHESTER CC	15	4	477	4.343	.343	1	82	787	429	50	7	Buick Classic
13	PEBBLE BCH GOLF LINK	09	4	464	4.338	.338	0	48	429	229	33	1	AT&T Pebble Beach National Pro-Am
14	COG HILL G&CC	13	4	446	4.333	.333	0	122	808	373	85	13	Motorola Western Open
15	TUCSON NAT'L GC	10	4	456	4.331	.331	1	73	437	208	45	8	Northern Telecom Open
16	TPC AT AVENEL	12	4	472	4.319	.319	0	133	794	338	92	14	Kemper Open
17	WESTCHESTER CC	08	4	455	4.319	.319	1	95	800	399	52	9	Buick Classic
18	TORREY PINES - NORTH	06	3	160	3.318	.318	0	39	261	141	19	2	Buick Invitational of California
19	WESTCHESTER CC	04	4	422	4.316	.316	1	118	785	366	75	11	Buick Classic
20	DORAL RESORT & CC	13	3	246	3.314	.314	0	64	806	439	20	1	Doral-Ryder Open
21	RIVIERA CC	02	4	460	4.307	.307	1	88	734	373	40	3	Nissan L.A. Open
22	WESTON HILLS CC	15	4	455	4.305	.305	1	63	501	166	53	11	Honda Classic
23	POPPY HILLS GC	03	4	406	4.305	.305	0	33	346	131	24	6	AT&T Pebble Beach National Pro-Am
24	TUCSON NAT'L GC	18	4	465	4.304	.304	0	62	490	164	45	11	Northern Telecom Open
25	SPYGLASS HILL GC	06	4	415	4.304	.304	0	43	309	170	14	3	AT&T Pebble Beach National Pro-Am
26	PALMER COURSE/ PGA WEST	10	4	455	4.304	.304	0	41	280	111	21	4	Bob Hope Chrysler Classic
27	PEBBLE BCH GOLF LINK	10	4	426	4.299	.299	0	68	430	202	34	6	AT&T Pebble Beach National Pro-Am
28	AUGUSTA NATIONAL GC	12	3	155	3.298	.298	0	102	530	159	65	21	The Masters
29	ATLANTA CC	15	4	452	4.296	.296	0	71	575	233	42	9	BellSouth Classic
30	GLEN ABBEY GC	14	4	426	4.294	.294	0	115	813	366	66	5	Canadian Open
31	TPC AT LAS COLINAS	03	4	460	4.294	.294	1	95	803	357	51	9	GTE Byron Nelson Golf Classic
32	TPC AT SAWGRASS	18	4	440	4.292	.292	0	113	788	309	74	10	The Players Championship
33	BAY HILL CLUB	01	4	441	4.285	.285	0	64	681	328	22	1	Nestlé Invitational
34	POPPY HILLS GC	16	4	439	4.283	.283	0	31	344	148	15	2	AT&T Pebble Beach National Pro-Am
35	SPYGLASS HILL GC	09	4	425	4.282	.282	0	35	332	157	15	0	AT&T Pebble Beach National Pro-Am
36	ATLANTA CC	09	4	421	4.281	.281	0	69	559	274	27	1	BellSouth Classic
37	WESTON HILLS CC	16	4	460	4.280	.280	0	75	491	173	47	9	Honda Classic
38	TORREY PINES - SOUTH	04	4	453	4.279	.279	0	64	520	248	20	5	Buick Invitational of California
39	FIRESTONE CC	09	4	470	4.278	.278	0	41	315	154	14	1	NEC World Series of Golf
40	DORAL RESORT & CC	18	4	425	4.277	.277	0	128	811	296	84	11	Doral-Ryder Open
41	STARR PASS GC	04	4	437	4.273	.273	0	61	373	154	21	5	Northern Telecom Open
42	TORREY PINES - SOUTH	01	4	447	4.271	.271	0	44	549	245	18	1	Buick Invitational of California
43	POPPY HILLS GC	01	4	413	4.268	.268	0	39	342	138	17	4	AT&T Pebble Beach National Pro-Am
44	STARR PASS GC	12	4	430	4.266	.266	0	81	339	152	36	6	Northern Telecom Open
45	TORREY PINES - SOUTH	07	4	453	4.265	.265	0	63	526	236	26	6	Buick Invitational of California
46	DORAL RESORT & CC	04	3	237	3.262	.262	0	95	853	327	48	7	Doral-Ryder Open
47	GLEN ABBEY GC	11	4	452	4.260	.260	0	182	778	305	75	25	Canadian Open
48	COLONIAL CC	05	4	459	4.256	.256	0	111	688	252	59	9	Southwestern Bell Colonial
49	MUIRFIELD VILLAGE GC	18	4	437	4.255	.255	0	98	682	283	39	6	The Memorial
50	TPC AT SUMMERLIN	08	3	239	3.253	.253	0	50	357	170	15	0	Las Vegas Invitational
51	RIVIERA CC	15	4	447	4.252	.252	0	93	784	324	37	1	Nissan L.A. Open
52	FOREST OAKS CC	03	4	409	4.251	.251	0	115	859	358	42	7	Kmart Greater Greensboro Open
53	HARBOUR TOWN GL	08	4	462	4.250	.250	0	105	744	267	53	8	MCI Heritage Classic
54	TPC AT RIVER HIGHLANDS	17	4	420	4.249	.249	0	167	813	289	89	13	Canon Greater Hartford Open
55	GLEN ABBEY GC	09	4	458	4.247	.247	0	141	848	283	83	10	Canadian Open
56	WARWICK HILLS G&CC	15	4	457	4.246	.246	1	115	860	365	36	7	Buick Open
57	LA COSTA CC	05	4	446	4.245	.245	0	31	229	101	11	0	Mercedes Championships
58	CALLAWAY GARDENS RESORT	09	4	427	4.242	.242	0	91	839	348	27	2	Buick Southern Open
59	FIRESTONE CC	06	4	469	4.241	.241	0	51	316	140	18	0	NEC World Series of Golf
60	WAIALAE CC	06	4	435	4.240	.240	1	116	826	345	39	5	United Airlines Hawaiian Open
61	TORREY PINES - SOUTH	12	4	468	4.239	.239	0	70	528	240	16	3	Buick Invitational of California
62	SPYGLASS HILL GC	18	4	405	4.239	.239	0	46	340	137	12	4	AT&T Pebble Beach National Pro-Am

Rank	Course	Hole	Par	Ydg	Avg Score	O/U Par	Egl	Bird	Pars	Bog	Dbl Bog	Tpl Bg+	Tournament Name
63	ENGLISH TURN G&CC	07	4	445	4.234	.234	1	142	749	376	35	2	Freeport-McMoRan Classic
64	TPC RIVER HIGLANDS	04	4	460	4.234	.234	0	103	882	353	28	5	Canon Greater Hartford Open
65	OAK HILLS CC	13	3	220	3.232	.232	0	75	605	191	42	4	H.E.B. Texas Open
66	COG HILL CC	04	4	416	4.232	.232	2	169	801	363	61	5	Motorola Western Open
67	WAIALAE CC	04	3	196	3.231	.231	0	111	847	333	37	4	United Airlines Hawaiian Open
68	HARBOUR TOWN GL	11	4	438	4.231	.231	1	95	742	310	28	1	MCI Heritage Classic
69	RIVIERA CC	04	3	238	3.229	.229	1	89	806	319	21	3	Nissan L.A. Open
70	CALLAWAY GARDENS RESORT	14	4	421	4.228	.228	0	117	823	328	29	10	Buick Southern Open
71	ATLANTA CC	06	3	190	3.227	.227	0	96	596	177	54	7	BellSouth Classic
72	FOREST OAKS CC	14	4	438	4.227	.227	0	142	827	371	38	3	Kmart GCO
73	GLEN ABBEY GC	17	4	436	4.226	.226	0	145	814	371	27	8	Canadian Open
74	GLEN ABBEY GC	10	4	443	4.226	.226	0	123	843	369	29	1	Canadian Open
75	PEBBLE BCH GOLF LINK	08	4	431	4.225	.225	0	72	457	185	24	2	AT&T Pebble Beach National Pro-Am
76	GLEN ABBEY GC	01	4	435	4.224	.224	0	144	812	369	40	0	Canadian Open
77	TPC AT LAS COLINAS	08	4	451	4.224	.224	2	132	782	374	24	2	GTE Byron Nelson Golf Classic
78	FOREST OAKS CC	04	3	190	3.218	.218	0	106	894	355	24	2	Kmart Greater Greensboro Open
79	GLEN ABBEY GC	12	3	187	3.218	.218	2	118	863	350	27	5	Canadian Open
80	PLEASANT VALLEY CC	10	4	467	4.218	.218	0	100	892	331	30	1	New England Classic
81	TPC AT AVENEL	07	4	461	4.216	.216	0	111	892	336	27	5	Kemper Open
82	WESTCHESTER CC	16	3	204	3.215	.215	0	126	850	345	32	3	Buick Classic
83	BAY HILL CLUB	17	3	219	3.215	.215	0	123	699	204	58	12	Nestlé Invitational
84	AUGUSTA NATIONAL GC	10	4	485	4.213	.213	0	74	560	224	19	0	The Masters
85	RIVIERA CC	18	4	447	4.213	.213	1	108	781	327	22	0	Nissan L.A. Open
86	AUGUSTA NATIONAL GC	04	3	205	3.212	.212	1	56	583	229	8	0	The Masters
87	TPC AT SAWGRASS	14	4	438	4.210	.210	0	138	795	315	43	3	The Players Championship
88	TPC AT RIVER HIGHLANDS	18	4	444	4.209	.209	2	144	842	337	43	3	Canon Greater Hartford Open
89	FIRESTONE CC	13	4	457	4.209	.209	0	45	335	136	8	1	NEC World Series of Golf
90	BAY HILL CLUB	08	4	424	4.208	.208	0	117	698	214	64	3	Nestlé Invitational
91	HARBOUR TOWN GL	04	3	198	3.208	.208	0	106	792	222	51	6	MCI Heritage Classic
92	TPC AT RIVER HIGHLANDS	10	4	462	4.205	.205	1	128	896	290	48	8	Canon Greater Hartford Open
93	WARWICK HILLS G&CC	18	4	435	4.204	.204	1	133	886	318	40	6	Buick Open
94	TPC AT LAS COLINAS	14	4	390	4.204	.204	1	194	740	300	74	7	GTE Byron Nelson Golf Classic
95	BAY HILL CLUB	09	4	467	4.203	.203	0	89	721	263	20	3	Nestlé Invitational
96	FIRESTONE CC	18	4	464	4.201	.201	1	54	323	134	13	0	NEC World Series of Golf
97	CALLAWAY GARDENS RESORT	18	4	432	4.199	.199	1	122	821	344	18	1	Buick Southern Open
98	FOREST OAKS CC	18	4	426	4.197	.197	1	137	865	348	26	4	Kmart Greater Greensboro Open
99	POPPY HILLS GC	13	4	393	4.196	.196	0	49	355	118	17	1	AT&T Pebble Beach National Pro-Am
100	ENGLISH TURN G&CC	05	4	463	4.195	.195	0	110	857	309	29	0	Freeport-McMoRan Classic
101	CALLAWAY GARDENS RSEORT	03	4	400	4.195	.195	1	131	831	302	38	4	Buick Southern Open
102	BAY HILL CLUB	11	4	428	4.194	.194	0	109	721	211	48	7	Nestlé Invitational
103	TPC AT AVENEL	15	4	467	4.194	.194	1	147	845	345	30	3	Kemper Open
104	BUENA VISTA GC	09	4	438	4.192	.192	0	42	252	80	11	5	Walt Disney World/Oldsmobile Classic
105	TORREY PINES - NORTH	07	4	400	4.191	.191	0	52	284	114	10	2	Buick Invitational of California
106	MUIRFIELD VILLAGE GC	02	4	452	4.191	.191	1	106	722	243	31	5	The Memorial
107	KINGSMILL GC	18	4	435	4.191	.191	1	150	902	271	58	10	Anheuser-Busch Classic
108	BAY HILL CLUB	02	3	218	3.190	.190	0	82	724	284	6	0	Nestlé Invitational
109	POPPY HILLS GC	11	3	214	3.190	.190	0	51	354	119	14	2	AT&T Pebble Beach National Pro-Am
110	ENGLISH TURN G&CC	17	3	207	3.189	.189	0	99	878	312	14	2	Freeport-McMoRan Classic
111	OAK HILLS CC	07	4	460	4.188	.188	1	77	604	219	16	0	H.E.B Texas Open
112	PALMER COURSE/ PGA WEST	09	4	456	4.187	.187	0	47	296	94	18	2	Bob Hope Chrysler Classic
113	ENGLISH TURN G&CC	14	4	469	4.187	.187	0	120	844	319	22	0	Freeport-McMoRan Classic
114	TPC AT AVENEL	18	4	444	4.186	.186	1	144	865	326	32	3	Kemper Open
115	BAY HILL CLUB	03	4	395	4.186	.186	1	126	691	226	48	4	Nestlé Invitational
116	ATLANTA CC	17	4	421	4.184	.184	0	111	583	195	36	5	BellSouth Classic
117	SPYGLASS HILL GC	13	4	440	4.184	.184	0	48	358	121	10	2	AT&T Pebble Beach National Pro-Am
118	COG HILL CC	06	3	213	3.183	.183	1	105	960	309	24	2	Motorola Western Open
119	WESTCHESTER CC	13	4	381	4.182	.182	1	151	858	298	42	6	Buick Classic
120	EN-JOIE GC	11	4	433	4.180	.180	0	111	902	316	19	0	B.C. Open
121	DESERT INN CC	07	3	205	3.179	.179	0	30	201	51	15	1	Las Vegas Invitational
122	TUCSON NAT'L GC	09	4	440	4.178	.178	0	83	497	173	19	0	Northern Telecom Open
123	TPC AT RIVER HIGHLANDS	05	3	223	3.177	.177	0	88	963	310	9	1	Canon Greater Hartford Open
124	ATLANTA CC	10	4	457	4.176	.176	0	96	595	219	19	1	BellSouth Classic

Rank	Course	Hole	Par	Ydg	Avg Score	O/U Par	Egl	Bird	Pars	Bog	Dbl Bog	Tpl Bg+	Tournament Name
125	WESTCHESTER CC	01	3	192	3.176	.176	0	119	906	305	25	1	Buick Classic
126	ENGLISH TURN G&CC	10	4	420	4.174	.174	1	149	818	302	29	6	Freeport-McMoRan Classic
127	AUGUSTA NATIONAL GC	05	4	435	4.174	.174	0	76	590	193	17	1	The Masters
128	CALLAWAY GARDENS RESORT	16	3	218	3.174	.174	1	117	867	302	17	3	Buick Southern Open
129	TPC AT RIVER HIGHLANDS	07	4	443	4.172	.172	1	118	924	302	24	2	Canon Greater Hartford Open
130	LA QUINTA CC	12	3	200	3.171	.171	0	22	173	57	3	1	Bob Hope Chrysler Classic
131	TPC AT SUMMERLIN	17	3	196	3.170	.170	0	74	381	106	27	4	Las Vegas Invitational
132	TPC AT SOUTHWIND	18	4	437	4.170	.170	0	167	880	273	59	4	Federal Express St. Jude Classic
133	TPC AT LAS COLINAS	09	4	406	4.170	.170	0	141	874	239	53	9	GTE Byron Nelson Golf Classic
134	PALM GOLF COURSE	18	4	454	4.170	.170	0	37	263	83	9	1	Walt Disney World/Oldsmobile Classic
135	KINGSMILL GC	08	4	413	4.169	.169	2	161	879	311	32	7	Anheuser-Busch Classic
136	INDIAN WELLS CC	10	4	446	4.169	.169	0	52	289	99	12	3	Bob Hope Chrysler Classic
137	GLEN ABBEY GC	08	4	433	4.168	.168	1	157	853	327	24	3	Canadian Open
138	WESTON HILLS CC	17	3	214	3.167	.167	1	67	541	171	12	3	Honda Classic
139	SPYGLASS HILL GC	05	3	180	3.167	.167	0	38	381	112	8	0	AT&T Pebble Beach National Pro-Am
140	POPPY HILLS GC	05	4	426	4.166	.166	0	54	367	98	17	4	AT&T Pebble Beach National Pro-Am
141	KINGSMILL GC	04	4	437	4.165	.165	1	154	893	308	31	5	Anheuser-Busch Classic
142	PALM GOLF COURSE	06	4	412	4.165	.165	0	48	263	57	19	6	Walt Disney World/Oldsmobile Classic
143	WESTON HILLS CC	09	4	435	4.164	.164	1	83	521	162	27	1	Honda Classic
144	DESERT INN CC	08	4	442	4.163	.163	0	32	194	64	8	0	Las Vegas Invitational
145	TPC OF SCOTTSDALE	12	3	195	3.163	.163	0	115	883	248	36	1	Phoenix Open
146	SPYGLASS HILL GC	10	4	400	4.163	.163	0	56	354	115	13	1	AT&T Pebble Beach National Pro-Am
147	ENGLISH TURN G&CC	03	3	200	3.162	.162	0	114	887	283	19	2	Freeport-McMoRan Classic
148	EN-JOIE GC	13	4	441	4.162	.162	0	114	914	308	11	1	B.C. Open
149	COLONIAL CC	03	4	476	4.162	.162	1	101	755	242	17	3	Southwestern Bell Colonial
150	TPC AT SAWGRASS	08	3	215	3.161	.161	0	121	859	300	13	1	The Players Championship
151	PEBBLE BCH GOLF LINK	12	3	202	3.160	.160	1	83	464	182	8	2	AT&T Pebble Beach National Pro-Am
152	CALLAWAY GARDENS RESORT	05	3	212	3.159	.159	0	122	873	293	19	0	Buick Southern Open
153	PLEASANT VALLEY CC	17	4	412	4.159	.159	0	162	909	209	59	15	New England Classic
154	TPC OF SCOTTSDALE	14	4	444	4.157	.157	1	134	848	271	26	3	Phoenix Open
155	PALM GOLF COURSE	10	4	450	4.157	.157	0	35	269	81	8	0	Walt Disney World/Oldsmobile Classic
156	WESTON HILLS CC	05	3	197	3.156	.156	0	102	516	140	32	5	Honda Classic
157	TPC AT RIVER HIGHLANDS	16	3	171	3.156	.156	2	157	907	250	45	10	Canon Greater Hartford Open
158	AUGUSTA NATIONAL GC	11	4	455	4.156	.156	0	91	586	175	21	4	The Masters
159	TPC AT SOUTHWIND	09	4	450	4.156	.156	0	189	867	260	58	9	Federal Express St. Jude Classic
160	ATLANTA CC	16	3	206	3.155	.155	2	100	592	224	12	0	BellSouth Classic
161	TORREY PINES - NORTH	11	4	437	4.154	.154	0	47	308	99	6	2	Buick Invitational of California
162	EN-JOIE GC	01	4	388	4.152	.152	0	180	832	294	37	5	B.C. Open
163	ENGLISH TURN G&CC	16	4	442	4.151	.151	1	151	825	307	18	3	Freeport-McMoRan Classic
164	LAS VEGAS CC	05	4	468	4.147	.147	0	12	99	31	1	0	Las Vegas Invitational
165	CALLAWAY GARDENS RESORT	06	4	432	4.147	.147	0	138	869	275	22	3	Buick Southern Open
166	EN-JOIE GC	14	3	212	3.147	.147	0	121	941	257	25	4	B.C. Open
167	LA COSTA CC	10	4	450	4.147	.147	0	39	247	78	8	0	Mercedes Championships
168	FIRESTONE CC	03	4	442	4.145	.145	0	80	331	84	21	9	NEC World Series of Golf
169	POPPY HILLS GC	06	3	181	3.144	.144	0	64	344	122	10	0	AT&T Pebble Beach National Pro-Am
170	WAIALAE CC	15	4	398	4.143	.143	1	153	870	273	33	2	United Airlines Hawaiian Open
171	AUGUSTA NATIONAL GC	06	3	180	3.142	.142	0	91	581	195	9	1	The Masters
172	STARR PASS GC	07	3	197	3.142	.142	0	51	439	113	8	3	Northern Telecom Open
173	TPC AT RIVER HIGHLANDS	12	4	411	4.141	.141	1	205	839	272	37	17	Canon Greater Hartford Open
174	FIRESTONE CC	15	3	221	3.141	.141	0	61	336	120	6	2	NEC World Series of Golf
175	TORREY PINES - SOUTH	11	3	207	3.140	.140	0	76	589	181	10	1	Buick Invitational of California
176	DESERT INN CC	03	4	414	4.139	.139	0	29	202	64	3	0	Las Vegas Invitational
177	POPPY HILLS GC	15	3	210	3.139	.139	1	62	351	115	10	1	AT&T Pebble Beach National Pro-Am
178	TPC AT SOUTHWIND	07	4	458	4.139	.139	0	120	970	276	15	2	Federal Express St. Jude Classic
179	POPPY HILLS GC	08	4	390	4.139	.139	0	68	344	114	13	1	AT&T Pebble Beach National Pro-Am
180	TPC AT LAS COLINAS	10	4	447	4.139	.139	1	140	865	290	16	4	GTE Byron Nelson Golf Classic
181	GLEN ABBEY GC	02	4	414	4.138	.138	0	180	847	312	23	3	Canadian Open
182	TPC AT RIVER HIGHLANDS	14	4	421	4.138	.138	1	167	880	288	33	2	Canon Greater Hartford Open
183	OAKWOOD CC	13	4	435	4.138	.138	0	142	936	289	22	0	Hardee's Classic
184	RIVIERA CC	12	4	413	4.138	.138	0	177	766	254	38	4	Nissan L.A. Open
185	TPC AT AVENEL	04	4	435	4.137	.137	1	181	881	257	44	7	Kemper Open
186	COG HILL CC	07	4	410	4.137	.137	2	165	897	313	24	0	Motorola Western Open
187	TPC AT THE WOODLANDS	14	3	195	3.136	.136	0	123	907	279	16	0	Shell Houston Open

Rank	Course	Hole	Par	Ydg	Avg Score	O/U Par	Egl	Bird	Pars	Bog	Dbl Bog	Tpl Bg+	Tournament Name
188	LA QUINTA CC	02	4	433	4.136	.136	0	23	180	48	5	0	Bob Hope Chrysler Classic
189	GLEN ABBEY GC	07	3	197	3.135	.135	1	143	933	250	35	3	Canadian Open
190	FIRESTONE CC	14	4	418	4.135	.135	0	73	325	112	12	3	NEC World Series of Golf
191	TPC OF SCOTTSDALE	07	3	215	3.134	.134	0	117	888	268	9	1	Phoenix Open
192	COG HILL CC	12	3	209	3.134	.134	0	155	945	266	30	5	Motorola Western Open
193	HARBOUR TOWN GL	12	4	413	4.133	.133	0	154	746	246	29	2	MCI Heritage Classic
194	WAIALAE CC	05	4	478	4.132	.132	1	143	889	278	19	2	United Airlines Hawaiian Open
195	CALLAWAY GARDENS RESORT	04	4	397	4.132	.132	0	167	832	283	21	4	Buick Southern Open
196	TPC AT SAWGRASS	05	4	454	4.129	.129	2	148	866	243	30	5	The Players Championship
197	MUIRFIELD VILLAGE GC	13	4	442	4.129	.129	0	136	722	223	26	1	The Memorial
198	PLEASANT VALLEY CC	16	3	200	3.129	.129	0	131	932	278	12	1	New England Classic
199	BERMUDA DUNES CC	17	3	212	3.127	.127	0	45	311	96	1	0	Bob Hope Chrysler Classic
200	PEBBLE BCH GOLF LINK	14	5	565	5.126	.126	1	126	425	158	28	2	AT&T Pebble Beach National Pro-Am
201	HARBOUR TOWN GL	10	4	436	4.126	.126	0	129	793	232	22	1	MCI Heritage Classic
202	TPC AT SOUTHWIND	17	4	464	4.126	.126	0	161	926	262	29	5	Federal Express St. Jude Classic
203	FIRESTONE CC	05	3	210	3.125	.125	0	63	339	118	4	1	NEC World Series of Golf
204	MUIRFIELD VILLAGE GC	14	4	363	4.125	.125	1	204	623	221	54	5	The Memorial
205	WAIALAE CC	07	3	182	3.124	.124	0	143	911	253	20	5	United Airlines Hawaiian Open
206	TPC AT LAS COLINAS	12	4	426	4.124	.124	0	184	825	271	33	3	GTE Byron Nelson Golf Classic
207	SPYGLASS HILL GC	02	4	350	4.124	.124	0	56	375	95	12	1	AT&T Pebble Beach National Pro-Am
208	STARR PASS GC	17	3	203	3.123	.123	0	49	447	110	7	1	Northern Telecom Open
209	AUGUSTA NATIONAL GC	18	4	405	4.121	.121	0	103	580	182	9	3	The Masters
210	OAKWOOD CC	14	4	446	4.119	.119	1	161	918	290	19	0	Hardee's Classic
211	PLEASANT VALLEY CC	06	4	430	4.119	.119	2	157	915	244	31	5	New England Classic
212	TPC AT LAS COLINAS	15	4	412	4.119	.119	0	132	909	262	13	0	GTE Byron Nelson Golf Classic
213	WARWICK HILLS G&CC	02	4	431	4.118	.118	0	141	961	263	15	4	Buick Open
214	WESTCHESTER CC	03	4	419	4.118	.118	0	167	891	269	28	1	Buick Classic
215	TPC AT AVENEL	17	3	195	3.118	.118	0	193	928	168	65	17	Kemper Open
216	ENGLISH TURN G&CC	08	3	176	3.118	.118	0	180	839	245	35	6	Freeport-McMoRan Classic
217	ENGLISH TURN G&CC	04	4	349	4.118	.118	3	244	779	184	77	18	Freeport-McMoRan Classic
218	TPC OF SCOTTSDALE	11	4	469	4.117	.117	0	138	890	224	29	2	Phoenix Open
219	FOREST OAKS CC	08	3	215	3.117	.117	0	114	998	262	7	0	Kmart Greater Greensboro Open
220	TPC AT AVENEL	03	3	239	3.116	.116	1	152	942	246	26	4	Kemper Open
221	TORREY PINES - NORTH	08	4	436	4.116	.116	0	54	309	93	4	2	Buick Invitational of California
222	PLEASANT VALLEY CC	08	4	455	4.116	.116	1	163	891	276	21	2	New England Classic
223	CALLAWAY GARDENS RESORT	01	4	412	4.116	.116	1	159	860	267	19	1	Buick Southern Open
224	WESTCHESTER CC	02	4	386	4.115	.115	0	170	888	271	26	1	Buick Classic
225	HARBOUR TOWN GL	01	4	414	4.115	.115	1	126	816	209	22	3	MCI Heritage Classic
226	OAKWOOD CC	03	4	435	4.114	.114	0	135	978	260	15	1	Hardee's Classic
227	SPYGLASS HILL GC	04	4	365	4.113	.113	2	94	308	115	17	3	AT&T Pebble Beach National Pro-Am
228	TPC AT RIVER HIGHLANDS	01	4	434	4.112	.112	0	183	882	278	25	3	Canon Greater Hartford Open
229	BAY HILL CLUB	14	3	206	3.111	.111	1	114	753	217	11	0	Nestlé Invitational
230	CALLAWAY GARDENS RESORT	17	4	408	4.111	.111	0	161	865	263	16	2	Buick Southern Open
231	TPC AT LAS COLINAS	17	3	196	3.111	.111	0	137	910	248	19	2	GTE Byron Nelson Golf Classic
232	WAIALAE CC	16	4	419	4.111	.111	0	166	884	256	21	5	United Airlines Hawaiian Open
233	COG HILL CC	08	4	378	4.111	.111	0	176	926	269	27	3	Motorola Western Open
234	TPC AT AVENEL	09	3	166	3.110	.110	0	176	925	223	39	8	Kemper Open
235	WAIALAE CC	12	4	446	4.110	.110	1	146	913	249	23	0	United Airlines Hawaiian Open
236	TPC AT SAWGRASS	15	4	426	4.110	.110	1	134	911	221	23	4	The Players Championship
237	WESTON HILLS CC	06	4	436	4.109	.109	0	122	500	149	20	4	Honda Classic
238	KINGSMILL GC	09	4	452	4.109	.109	1	184	894	292	18	3	Anheuser-Busch Classic
239	MAGNOLIA GC	17	4	427	4.109	.109	1	83	428	72	23	10	Walt Disney World/Oldsmobile Classic
240	FOREST OAKS CC	17	3	188	3.109	.109	0	145	957	261	18	0	Kmart Greater Greensboro Open
241	FIRESTONE CC	10	4	410	4.109	.109	0	61	360	88	16	0	NEC World Series of Golf
242	LA COSTA CC	16	4	423	4.108	.108	0	42	251	76	2	1	Mercedes Championships
243	TORREY PINES - NORTH	04	4	398	4.108	.108	0	51	317	87	7	0	Buick Invitational of California
244	WAIALAE CC	02	4	362	4.107	.107	3	182	849	266	31	1	United Airlines Hawaiian Open
245	ENGLISH TURN G&CC	09	4	370	4.107	.107	0	237	771	232	51	14	Freeport-McMoRan Classic
246	FIRESTONE CC	07	3	219	3.106	.106	0	64	345	114	2	0	NEC World Series of Golf
247	MAGNOLIA GC	18	4	455	4.106	.106	0	64	441	95	17	0	Walt Disney World/Oldsmobile Classic
248	TPC AT RIVER HIGHLANDS	08	3	202	3.106	.106	0	130	982	243	15	1	Canon Greater Hartford Open
249	PLEASANT VALLEY CC	11	4	480	4.104	.104	0	153	917	272	12	0	New England Classic

Rank	Course	Hole	Par	Ydg	Avg Score	O/U Par	Egl	Bird	Pars	Bog	Dbl Bog	Tpl Bg+	Tournament Name
250	COLONIAL CC	04	3	246	3.104	.104	0	110	788	216	5	0	Southwestern Bell Colonial
251	KINGSMILL GC	05	3	183	3.103	.103	1	161	947	261	20	2	Anheuser-Busch Classic
252	EN-JOIE GC	06	4	433	4.103	.103	2	134	953	243	13	3	B.C. Open
253	TPC AT SAWGRASS	13	3	172	3.102	.102	1	192	836	219	34	12	The Players Championship
254	KINGSMILL GC	02	3	204	3.101	.101	0	148	962	275	7	0	Anheuser-Busch Classic
255	TPC OF SCOTTSDALE	05	4	453	4.101	.101	0	157	880	211	30	5	Phoenix Open
256	TPC AT SAWGRASS	07	4	439	4.099	.099	0	173	860	228	29	4	The Players Championship
257	DORAL RESORT & CC	03	4	398	4.099	.099	2	200	835	259	29	5	Doral-Ryder Open
258	TPC AT SUMMERLIN	18	4	444	4.098	.098	0	89	388	91	18	6	Las Vegas Invitational
259	COLONIAL CC	12	4	433	4.098	.098	0	147	737	213	22	0	Southwestern Bell Colonial
260	EN-JOIE GC	04	3	221	3.098	.098	0	132	959	251	5	1	B.C. Open
261	LA QUINTA CC	14	4	436	4.097	.097	0	30	180	38	7	1	Bob Hope Chrysler Classic
262	WAIALAE CC	03	4	410	4.097	.097	0	186	877	228	35	6	United Airlines Hawaiian Open
263	CALLAWAY GARDENS RESORT	10	4	431	4.096	.096	1	168	866	256	16	0	Buick Southern Open
264	TORREY PINES - SOUTH	05	4	404	4.095	.095	0	94	592	154	14	3	Buick Invitational of California
265	TPC AT THE WOODLANDS	08	3	218	3.095	.095	0	129	950	235	11	0	Shell Houston Open
266	WAIALAE CC	14	4	412	4.095	.095	0	161	910	239	18	4	United Airlines Hawaiian Open
267	BUENA VISTA GC	03	3	197	3.095	.095	0	40	275	73	2	0	Walt Disney World/Oldsmobile Classic
268	STARR PASS GC	09	4	437	4.094	.094	1	90	396	112	11	4	Northern Telecom Open
269	STARR PASS GC	15	3	199	3.094	.094	0	76	421	104	11	2	Northern Telecom Open
270	EN-JOIE GC	07	3	200	3.093	.093	0	185	943	142	67	11	B.C. Open
271	MUIRFIELD VILLAGE GC	17	4	430	4.093	.093	0	161	714	205	26	2	The Memorial
272	FOREST OAKS CC	16	4	408	4.092	.092	0	165	939	263	11	3	Kmart Greater Greensboro Open
273	FOREST OAKS CC	10	4	393	4.092	.092	0	164	946	249	21	1	Kmart Greater Greensboro Open
274	DESERT INN CC	11	3	209	3.091	.091	0	36	203	56	2	1	Las Vegas Invitational
275	TORREY PINES - SOUTH	17	4	425	4.091	.091	0	115	575	147	16	4	Buick Invitational of California
276	FIRESTONE CC	17	4	392	4.091	.091	0	73	337	108	7	0	NEC World Series of Golf
277	CALLAWAY GARDENS RESORT	12	3	186	3.090	.090	0	161	894	224	23	5	Buick Southern Open
278	TPC AT THE WOODLANDS	18	4	445	4.090	.090	1	182	881	216	38	7	Shell Houston Open
279	HARBOUR TOWN GL	07	3	180	3.088	.088	1	140	801	224	10	1	MCI Heritage Classic
280	RIVIERA CC	09	4	418	4.088	.088	0	166	820	238	14	1	Nissan L.A. Open
281	HARBOUR TOWN GL	18	4	478	4.087	.087	0	157	778	226	15	1	MCI Heritage Classic
282	MUIRFIELD VILLAGE GC	04	3	204	3.087	.087	1	158	710	226	10	3	The Memorial
283	TPC AT AVENEL	16	4	415	4.086	.086	3	184	910	242	30	2	Kemper Open
284	INDIAN WELLS CC	11	4	398	4.086	.086	0	74	287	80	13	1	Bob Hope Chrysler Classic
285	STARR PASS GC	01	4	439	4.086	.086	0	83	408	114	6	3	Northern Telecom Open
286	PALM GOLF COURSE	04	4	422	4.086	.086	0	46	274	66	7	0	Walt Disney World/Oldsmobile Classic
287	FIRESTONE CC	01	4	399	4.086	.086	0	81	338	87	16	3	NEC World Series of Golf
288	DESERT INN CC	02	4	433	4.085	.085	0	40	199	53	6	0	Las Vegas Invitational
289	STARR PASS GC	18	4	454	4.085	.085	0	87	400	112	15	0	Northern Telecom Open
290	TPC OF SCOTTSDALE	08	4	470	4.084	.084	0	147	892	234	10	0	Phoenix Open
291	KINGSMILL GC	10	4	431	4.084	.084	0	177	938	261	15	1	Anheuser-Busch Classic
292	RIVIERA CC	13	4	420	4.084	.084	0	162	836	222	18	1	Nissan L.A. Open
293	PALMER COURSE/ PGA WEST	01	4	427	4.084	.084	0	63	306	85	2	1	Bob Hope Chrysler Classic
294	MUIRFIELD VILLAGE GC	16	3	204	3.084	.084	1	124	778	192	12	1	The Memorial
295	COG HILL CC	17	4	388	4.084	.084	1	187	934	255	20	4	Motorola Western Open
296	OAK HILLS CC	03	4	456	4.083	.083	0	135	590	177	10	5	H.E.B. Texas Open
297	DESERT INN CC	09	4	432	4.082	.082	1	39	201	50	6	1	Las Vegas Invitational
298	OAK HILLS CC	12	4	444	4.082	.082	1	132	600	158	26	0	H.E.B. Texas Open
299	EN-JOIE GC	18	4	406	4.082	.082	0	192	878	254	23	1	B.C. Open
300	WESTCHESTER CC	17	4	376	4.082	.082	0	194	895	231	34	2	Buick Classic
301	HARBOUR TOWN GL	13	4	378	4.082	.082	1	157	785	212	22	0	MCI Heritage Classic
302	EN-JOIE GC	16	3	182	3.082	.082	0	154	949	226	19	0	B.C. Open
303	OAKWOOD CC	17	3	214	3.081	.081	3	131	1,015	231	9	0	Hardee's Classic
304	TPC AT SOUTHWIND	10	4	447	4.080	.080	1	180	925	262	14	1	Federal Express St. Jude Classic
305	OAKWOOD CC	01	4	413	4.080	.080	1	144	1,003	225	15	1	Hardee's Classic
306	PLEASANT VALLEY CC	07	3	180	3.080	.080	0	197	935	154	56	12	New England Classic
307	RIVIERA CC	03	4	434	4.080	.080	1	160	829	239	10	0	Nissan L.A. Open
308	BUENA VISTA GC	02	4	442	4.080	.080	0	44	275	67	4	0	Walt Disney World/Oldsmobile Classic
309	OAK HILLS CC	04	4	389	4.079	.079	1	144	575	178	17	2	H.E.B. Texas Open
310	OAKWOOD CC	18	4	391	4.079	.079	2	194	932	224	31	6	Hardee's Classic
311	HARBOUR TOWN GL	17	3	192	3.079	.079	0	160	798	188	26	5	MCI Heritage Classic
312	WESTCHESTER CC	07	4	333	4.079	.079	1	269	766	268	45	7	Buick Classic

Rank	Course	Hole	Par	Ydg	Avg Score	O/U Par	Egl	Bird	Pars	Bog	Dbl Bog	Tpl Bg+	Tournament Name
313	PLEASANT VALLEY CC	14	3	230	3.079	.079	0	149	964	227	13	1	New England Classic
314	COG HILL CC	14	3	192	3.079	.079	4	179	930	280	7	1	Motorola Western Open
315	TPC AT SOUTHWIND	12	4	375	4.079	.079	1	264	818	236	55	9	Federal Express St. Jude Classic
316	LAS VEGAS CC	13	4	449	4.077	.077	0	20	97	23	1	2	Las Vegas Invitational
317	DESERT INN CC	13	4	407	4.077	.077	0	32	215	48	3	0	Las Vegas Invitational
318	FOREST OAKS CC	12	3	186	3.077	.077	1	178	935	247	19	1	Kmart Greater Greensboro Open
319	GLEN ABBEY GC	06	4	437	4.076	.076	2	176	926	239	21	1	Canadian Open
320	PLEASANT VALLEY CC	02	4	426	4.076	.076	2	195	888	238	30	1	New England Classic
321	ATLANTA CC	05	4	432	4.075	.075	0	141	597	174	17	1	BellSouth Classic
322	TORREY PINES - NORTH	10	4	416	4.074	.074	1	48	335	73	4	1	Buick Invitational of California
323	TPC AT SAWGRASS	17	3	132	3.074	.074	1	214	857	144	70	8	The Players Championship
324	PALMER COURSE/ PGA WEST	13	4	446	4.074	.074	0	76	294	76	9	2	Bob Hope Chrysler Classic
325	TORREY PINES - NORTH	12	3	190	3.073	.073	0	56	322	79	5	0	Buick Invitational of California
326	WARWICK HILLS G&CC	05	4	437	4.073	.073	0	177	945	246	15	1	Buick Open
327	HARBOUR TOWN GL	03	4	411	4.073	.073	1	145	809	212	9	1	MCI Heritage Classic
328	PLEASANT VALLEY CC	01	3	183	3.073	.073	0	184	907	244	18	1	New England Classic
329	WESTON HILLS CC	04	4	385	4.071	.071	0	114	527	141	12	1	Honda Classic
330	ENGLISH TURN G&CC	12	3	158	3.071	.071	1	204	827	248	23	2	Freeport-McMoRan Classic
331	CALLAWAY GARDENS RESORT	08	3	178	3.071	.071	1	163	901	228	13	1	Buick Southern Open
332	PALMER COURSE/ PGA WEST	05	3	207	3.070	.070	0	62	318	67	8	2	Bob Hope Chrysler Classic
333	BAY HILL CLUB	07	3	197	3.069	.069	0	117	785	188	6	0	Nestlé Invitational
334	AUGUSTA NATIONAL GC	01	4	400	4.069	.069	0	109	611	143	14	0	The Masters
335	POPPY HILLS GC	17	3	163	3.068	.068	0	73	375	79	10	3	AT&T Pebble Beach National Pro-Am
336	AUGUSTA NATIONAL GC	03	4	360	4.068	.068	2	133	555	177	10	0	The Masters
337	FIRESTONE CC	08	4	450	4.068	.068	1	88	317	113	6	0	NEC World Series of Golf
338	TORREY PINES - NORTH	13	4	421	4.067	.067	0	55	327	74	6	0	Buick Invitational of California
339	TORREY PINES - SOUTH	16	3	203	3.066	.066	0	96	600	157	4	0	Buick Invitational of California
340	KINGSMILL GC	16	4	427	4.066	.066	0	197	937	230	25	3	Anheuser-Busch Classic
341	PLEASANT VALLEY CC	13	4	394	4.066	.066	1	173	942	216	19	3	New England Classic
342	AUGUSTA NATIONAL GC	17	4	400	4.066	.066	0	110	603	160	4	0	The Masters
343	MAGNOLIA GC	15	3	203	3.065	.065	0	81	416	119	1	0	Walt Disney World/Oldsmobile Classic
344	DORAL RESORT & CC	06	4	427	4.065	.065	0	177	903	236	14	0	Doral-Ryder Open
345	TAMARISK CC	03	4	443	4.063	.063	0	17	86	21	2	0	Bob Hope Chrysler Classic
346	DESERT INN CC	14	4	411	4.063	.063	0	34	216	43	5	0	Las Vegas Invitational
347	AUGUSTA NATIONAL GC	09	4	435	4.063	.063	1	127	577	160	12	0	The Masters
348	TORREY PINES - SOUTH	14	4	398	4.062	.062	0	125	574	147	8	3	Buick Invitational of California
349	PEBBLE BCH GOLF LINK	07	3	107	3.062	.062	0	103	505	116	15	1	AT&T Pebble Beach National Pro-Am
350	TPC AT SAWGRASS	03	3	162	3.061	.061	0	167	893	222	11	1	The Players Championship
351	AUGUSTA NATIONAL GC	16	3	170	3.060	.060	1	124	588	151	10	3	The Masters
352	KINGSMILL GC	12	4	395	4.060	.060	1	238	869	252	27	5	Anheuser-Busch Classic
353	WARWICK HILLS G&CC	08	3	199	3.060	.060	0	169	976	226	13	0	Buick Open
354	TPC AT SUMMERLIN	12	4	442	4.059	.059	1	89	390	100	10	2	Las Vegas Invitational
355	PEBBLE BCH GOLF LINK	05	4	166	3.059	.059	0	116	478	133	12	1	AT&T Pebble Beach National Pro-Am
356	ENGLISH TURN G&CC	01	4	398	4.059	.059	2	190	865	228	18	2	Freeport-McMoRan Classic
357	TPC AT SUMMERLIN	05	3	197	3.058	.058	0	86	403	89	11	3	Las Vegas Invitational
358	WARWICK HILLS G&CC	09	4	413	4.058	.058	0	208	913	239	22	2	Buick Open
359	LA QUINTA CC	17	4	419	4.058	.058	0	35	174	44	3	0	Bob Hope Chrysler Classic
360	TPC AT SUMMERLIN	11	4	448	4.057	.057	0	77	411	98	5	1	Las Vegas Invitational
361	TAMARISK CC	05	3	199	3.056	.056	0	10	99	17	0	0	Bob Hope Chrysler Classic
362	TPC AT LAS COLINAS	04	4	428	4.056	.056	0	203	865	218	25	5	GTE Byron Nelson Golf Classic
363	GLEN ABBEY GC	03	3	156	3.055	.055	1	220	888	220	31	5	Canadian Open
364	PALMER COURSE/ PGA WEST	12	3	201	3.055	.055	0	58	330	65	4	0	Bob Hope Chrysler Classic
365	MUIRFIELD VILLAGE GC	03	4	392	4.055	.055	0	215	676	169	42	6	The Memorial
366	COLONIAL CC	09	4	391	4.053	.053	1	206	726	119	59	8	Southwestern Bell Colonial
367	RIVIERA CC	07	4	406	4.053	.053	1	200	811	195	25	7	Nissan L.A. Open
368	TPC AT RIVER HIGHLANDS	03	4	431	4.052	.052	2	176	968	206	13	6	Canon Greater Hartford Open
369	KINGSMILL GC	17	3	177	3.051	.051	0	184	977	208	21	2	Anheuser-Busch Classic
370	TPC OF SCOTTSDALE	18	4	438	4.051	.051	0	217	833	196	27	10	Phoenix Open
371	WAIALAE CC	17	3	187	3.051	.051	0	171	942	199	19	1	United Airlines Hawaiian Open
372	TPC AT SOUTHWIND	01	4	426	4.051	.051	1	194	947	217	23	1	Federal Express St. Jude Classic
373	STARR PASS GC	13	4	396	4.050	.050	0	77	443	81	12	1	Northern Telecom Open
374	MUIRFIELD VILLAGE GC	09	4	410	4.050	.050	0	181	736	157	27	7	The Memorial

Rank	Course	Hole	Par	Ydg	Avg Score	O/U Par	Egl	Bird	Pars	Bog	Dbl Bog	Tpl Bg+	Tournament Name
375	WESTON HILLS CC	11	3	178	3.049	.049	0	104	559	125	7	0	Honda Classic
376	EN-JOIE GC	09	4	425	4.049	.049	0	201	901	227	17	2	B.C. Open
377	FOREST OAKS CC	11	4	383	4.049	.049	0	200	935	223	23	0	Kmart Greater Greensboro Open
378	OAKWOOD CC	12	3	174	3.049	.049	0	151	1,021	215	2	0	Hardee's Classic
379	TAMARISK CC	15	4	423	4.048	.048	0	20	85	17	3	1	Bob Hope Chrysler Classic
380	TPC AT SUMMERLIN	02	4	469	4.047	.047	0	87	412	75	16	2	Las Vegas Invitational
381	FOREST OAKS CC	01	4	407	4.047	.047	1	188	944	238	10	0	Kmart Greater Greensboro Open
382	STARR PASS GC	02	4	427	4.047	.047	0	97	400	108	8	1	Northern Telecom Open
383	FIRESTONE CC	12	3	178	3.047	.047	0	77	352	90	5	1	NEC World Series of Golf
384	TORREY PINES - NORTH	05	4	371	4.046	.046	0	63	321	73	5	0	Buick Invitational of California
385	TPC AT SOUTHWIND	04	3	194	3.046	.046	2	195	960	196	24	6	Federal Express St. Jude Classic
386	TORREY PINES - SOUTH	03	3	173	3.045	.045	0	104	613	129	10	1	Buick Invitational of California
387	OAKWOOD CC	08	3	183	3.045	.045	0	189	963	223	13	1	Hardee's Classic
388	MAGNOLIA GC	05	4	448	4.045	.045	1	92	410	107	6	1	Walt Disney World/Oldsmobile Classic
389	MUIRFIELD VILLAGE GC	12	3	156	3.045	.045	0	192	733	134	41	8	The Memorial
390	TPC AT SAWGRASS	06	4	381	4.045	.045	0	202	868	188	35	1	The Players Championship
391	RIVIERA CC	05	4	426	4.044	.044	1	173	869	171	19	6	Nissan L.A. Open
392	TPC AT THE WOODLANDS	17	4	383	4.044	.044	0	223	886	155	49	12	Shell Houston Open
393	LA COSTA CC	18	4	421	4.043	.043	0	45	269	55	3	0	Mercedes Championships
394	COG HILL CC	02	3	177	3.043	.043	0	172	1,007	212	10	0	Motorola Western Open
395	TPC AT THE WOODLANDS	04	4	413	4.043	.043	0	219	883	170	46	7	Shell Houston Open
396	TPC AT AVENEL	08	4	453	4.042	.042	0	214	908	230	18	1	Kemper Open
397	OAKWOOD CC	09	4	436	4.042	.042	1	204	929	247	8	0	Hardee's Classic
398	BAY HILL CLUB	15	4	425	4.042	.042	0	156	751	173	15	1	Nestlé Invitational
399	PALMER COURSE/ PGA WEST	07	4	439	4.042	.042	0	71	306	71	9	0	Bob Hope Chrysler Classic
400	TUCSON NAT'L GC	07	3	202	3.042	.042	1	98	549	119	5	0	Northern Telecom Open
401	PEBBLE BCH GOLF LINK	01	4	373	4.042	.042	0	98	520	115	7	0	AT&T Pebble Beach National Pro-Am
402	INDIAN WELLS CC	13	3	197	3.041	.041	0	64	314	74	3	0	Bob Hope Chrysler Classic
403	COG HILL CC	16	4	409	4.041	.041	1	187	987	206	19	1	Motorola Western Open
404	POPPY HILLS GC	04	5	560	5.041	.041	2	74	371	86	7	0	AT&T Pebble Beach National Pro-Am
405	TPC AT SAWGRASS	10	4	395	4.040	.040	0	200	870	200	20	4	The Players Championship
406	STARR PASS GC	16	4	433	4.040	.040	0	129	353	115	15	2	Northern Telecom Open
407	FIRESTONE CC	16	5	625	5.040	.040	0	117	307	71	23	7	NEC World Series of Golf
408	MUIRFIELD VILLAGE GC	01	4	446	4.040	.040	1	145	775	183	4	0	The Memorial
409	ATLANTA CC	12	4	426	4.039	.039	1	139	632	140	17	1	BellSouth Classic
410	LA COSTA CC	03	3	187	3.039	.039	0	46	268	55	3	0	Mercedes Championships
411	WARWICK HILLS G&CC	03	3	187	3.039	.039	0	177	993	199	12	3	Buick Open
412	LA QUINTA CC	10	4	389	4.039	.039	0	35	180	37	4	0	Bob Hope Chrysler Classic
413	DORAL RESORT & CC	14	4	418	4.038	.038	0	178	940	200	8	4	Doral-Ryder Open
414	HARBOUR TOWN GL	06	4	419	4.038	.038	1	165	830	158	15	8	MCI Heritage Classic
415	OAK HILLS CC	18	3	198	3.037	.037	1	136	620	148	12	0	H.E.B. Texas Open
416	TPC AT THE WOODLANDS	07	4	413	4.035	.035	1	200	924	154	40	6	Shell Houston Open
417	BAY HILL CLUB	10	4	400	4.035	.035	0	162	750	171	10	3	Nestlé Invitational
418	TPC AT SAWGRASS	01	4	388	4.035	.035	0	202	857	223	11	1	The Players Championship
419	GLEN ABBEY GC	15	3	141	3.034	.034	0	199	936	214	16	0	Canadian Open
420	EN-JOIE GC	17	3	198	3.034	.034	1	182	951	200	13	1	B.C. Open
421	LA QUINTA CC	15	3	194	3.034	.034	0	33	182	40	1	0	Bob Hope Chrysler Classic
422	WESTON HILLS CC	14	4	391	4.033	.033	0	111	563	107	12	2	Honda Classic
423	WARWICK HILLS G&CC	11	3	190	3.033	.033	1	182	987	198	16	0	Buick Open
424	PEBBLE BCH GOLF LINK	16	4	402	4.033	.033	1	104	517	108	9	1	AT&T Pebble Beach National Pro-Am
425	TORREY PINES - SOUTH	15	4	356	4.031	.031	0	140	560	146	10	1	Buick Invitational of California
426	COLONIAL CC	18	4	427	4.031	.031	1	193	731	159	33	2	Southwestern Bell Colonial
427	AUGUSTA NATIONAL GC	07	4	360	4.031	.031	1	168	523	173	11	1	The Masters
428	MUIRFIELD VILLAGE GC	10	4	441	4.031	.031	2	162	754	180	10	0	The Memorial
429	SPYGLASS HILL GC	17	4	320	4.031	.031	1	70	385	78	4	1	AT&T Pebble Beach National Pro-Am
430	COLONIAL CC	15	4	430	4.030	.030	0	175	763	154	26	1	Southwestern Bell Colonial
431	SPYGLASS HILL GC	15	3	130	3.029	.029	0	97	352	70	18	2	AT&T Pebble Beach National Pro-Am
432	DORAL RESORT & CC	17	4	406	4.029	.029	1	201	900	216	10	2	Doral-Ryder Open
433	DESERT INN CC	12	4	420	4.028	.028	0	40	214	40	4	0	Las Vegas Invitational
434	WARWICK HILLS G&CC	04	4	401	4.028	.028	3	229	906	220	23	3	Buick Open
435	WAIALAE CC	11	3	181	3.028	.028	2	173	955	190	12	0	United Airlines Hawaiian Open
436	POPPY HILLS GC	07	4	388	4.028	.028	2	78	373	78	8	1	AT&T Pebble Beach National Pro-Am
437	OAK HILLS CC	16	4	385	4.027	.027	0	151	603	151	11	1	H.E.B. Texas Open
438	TPC OF SCOTTSDALE	10	4	403	4.027	.027	0	177	903	197	5	1	Phoenix Open
439	DESERT INN CC	18	4	432	4.026	.026	0	36	222	36	4	0	Las Vegas Invitational

Rank	Course	Hole	Par	Ydg	Avg Score	O/U Par	Egl	Bird	Pars	Bog	Dbl Bog	Tpl Bg+	Tournament Name
440	TPC AT SUMMERLIN	04	4	450	4.025	.025	1	97	388	98	8	0	Las Vegas Invitational
441	TPC AT AVENEL	01	4	393	4.025	.025	0	207	937	213	14	0	Kemper Open
442	TPC OF SCOTTSDALE	06	4	389	4.025	.025	2	233	803	224	19	2	Phoenix Open
443	LA COSTA CC	01	4	412	4.025	.025	0	54	261	52	4	1	Mercedes Championships
444	LA COSTA CC	14	3	204	3.025	.025	0	48	270	51	3	0	Mercedes Championships
445	TAMARISK CC	14	3	225	3.024	.024	0	19	85	22	0	0	Bob Hope Chrysler Classic
446	RIVIERA CC	14	3	180	3.024	.024	1	163	892	177	4	2	Nissan L.A. Open
447	TPC AT RIVER HIGHLANDS	13	5	523	5.023	.023	7	331	736	235	46	16	Canon Greater Hartford Open
448	WESTCHESTER CC	14	3	154	3.023	.023	1	212	922	196	25	0	Buick Classic
449	TPC AT THE WOODLANDS	09	4	427	4.023	.023	1	221	867	217	16	3	Shell Houston Open
450	TPC AT SOUTHWIND	11	3	146	3.022	.022	0	258	928	134	48	15	Federal Express St. Jude Classic
451	WARWICK HILLS G&CC	17	3	197	3.022	.022	0	197	968	209	10	0	Buick Open
452	SPYGLASS HILL GC	14	5	555	5.022	.022	0	98	353	67	20	1	AT&T Pebble Beach National Pro-Am
453	AUGUSTA NATIONAL GC	14	4	405	4.021	.021	1	144	579	143	9	1	The Masters
454	TPC AT SUMMERLIN	06	4	430	4.020	.020	0	102	392	82	16	0	Las Vegas Invitational
455	FOREST OAKS CC	06	4	386	4.020	.020	1	208	948	214	6	4	Kmart Greater Greensboro Open
456	LA QUINTA CC	04	4	397	4.020	.020	0	41	176	34	4	1	Bob Hope Chrysler Classic
457	POPPY HILLS GC	14	4	417	4.020	.020	1	82	369	82	5	1	AT&T Pebble Beach National Pro-Am
458	TUCSON NAT'L GC	04	3	170	3.019	.019	0	111	555	85	19	2	Northern Telecom Open
459	WARWICK HILLS G&CC	06	4	421	4.019	.019	0	236	909	217	20	2	Buick Open
460	COLONIAL CC	08	3	192	3.019	.019	0	158	793	156	12	0	Southwestern Bell Colonial
461	TORREY PINES - NORTH	17	3	172	3.018	.018	0	71	322	59	10	0	Buick Invitational of California
462	TPC AT LAS COLINAS	13	3	183	3.018	.018	0	173	952	180	11	0	GTE Byron Nelson Golf Classic
463	DESERT INN CC	16	3	173	3.016	.016	1	31	228	38	0	0	Las Vegas Invitational
464	OAK HILLS CC	06	4	352	4.015	.015	2	181	579	121	27	7	H.E.B. Texas Open
465	PEBBLE BCH GOLF LINK	17	3	209	3.015	.015	0	111	516	106	5	2	AT&T Pebble Beach National Pro-Am
466	TPC AT THE WOODLANDS	05	4	457	4.014	.014	0	216	896	197	12	4	Shell Houston Open
467	FOREST OAKS CC	05	4	415	4.014	.014	0	203	972	189	16	1	Kmart Greater Greensboro Open
468	EN-JOIE GC	02	4	363	4.013	.013	1	241	907	149	42	8	B.C. Open
469	INDIAN WELLS CC	04	3	162	3.013	.013	0	73	310	65	7	0	Bob Hope Chrysler Classic
470	BERMUDA DUNES CC	04	3	209	3.013	.013	0	62	324	65	2	0	Bob Hope Chrysler Classic
471	COLONIAL CC	14	4	426	4.012	.012	2	176	768	155	16	2	Southwestern Bell Colonial
472	PEBBLE BCH GOLF LINK	15	4	397	4.012	.012	0	110	525	92	12	1	AT&T Pebble Beach National Pro-Am
473	BERMUDA DUNES CC	16	4	451	4.012	.012	0	69	317	60	7	0	Bob Hope Chrysler Classic
474	WESTON HILLS CC	18	5	585	5.010	.010	2	141	541	77	28	6	Honda Classic
475	TPC AT LAS COLINAS	18	4	415	4.010	.010	0	180	945	186	5	0	GTE Byron Nelson Golf Classic
476	LAS VEGAS CC	03	3	199	3.007	.007	0	17	108	18	0	0	Las Vegas Invitational
477	TPC OF SCOTTSDALE	09	4	415	4.007	.007	0	219	857	190	16	1	Phoenix Open
478	FOREST OAKS CC	07	4	372	4.007	.007	2	222	942	196	18	1	Kmart Greater Greensboro Open
479	COLONIAL CC	16	3	188	3.007	.007	1	168	781	160	8	1	Southwestern Bell Colonial
480	MUIRFIELD VILLAGE GC	06	4	430	4.007	.007	0	183	757	147	19	2	The Memorial
481	OAKWOOD CC	15	4	409	4.007	.007	1	186	1,011	184	7	0	Hardee's Classic
482	WAIALAE CC	08	4	402	4.007	.007	0	213	912	193	12	2	United Airlines Hawaiian Open
483	BAY HILL CLUB	05	4	365	4.006	.006	0	154	783	154	5	0	Nestlé Invitational
484	PEBBLE BCH GOLF LINK	13	4	392	4.006	.006	3	113	509	107	7	1	AT&T Pebble Beach National Pro-Am
485	TPC OF SCOTTSDALE	16	3	162	3.005	.005	1	208	874	189	9	2	Phoenix Open
486	HARBOUR TOWN GL	14	3	165	3.005	.005	0	182	856	92	44	3	MCI Heritage Classic
487	PALM GOLF COURSE	12	3	199	3.005	.005	0	53	286	53	1	0	Walt Disney World/Oldsmobile Classic
488	MUIRFIELD VILLAGE GC	08	3	189	3.004	.004	0	180	749	173	6	0	The Memorial
489	DORAL RESORT & CC	09	3	163	3.004	.004	0	196	950	165	19	0	Doral-Ryder Open
490	WESTON HILLS CC	13	4	409	4.003	.003	0	138	542	100	12	3	Honda Classic
491	DESERT INN CC	06	4	424	4.002	.002	0	40	219	37	2	0	Las Vegas Invitational
492	SPYGLASS HILL GC	12	3	180	3.002	.002	1	96	362	63	16	1	AT&T Pebble Beach National Pro-Am
493	PLEASANT VALLEY CC	15	4	371	4.002	.002	1	260	873	184	27	9	New England Classic
494	LAS VEGAS CC	17	3	210	3.000	.000	0	21	102	19	1	0	Las Vegas Invitational
495	ATLANTA CC	04	4	427	4.000	.000	0	166	616	131	16	1	BellSouth Classic
496	RIVIERA CC	06	3	170	2.999	.000	1	214	822	195	7	0	Nissan L.A. Open
497	COLONIAL CC	10	4	404	3.999	.000	1	183	764	160	8	3	Southwestern Bell Colonial
498	ENGLISH TURN G&CC	13	4	380	4.000	.000	0	248	816	235	5	1	Freeport-McMoRan Classic
499	WARWICK HILLS G&CC	10	4	401	3.998	.001-	3	251	890	225	15	0	Buick Open
500	OAK HILLS CC	11	4	426	3.998	.001-	2	164	593	150	7	1	H.E.B. Texas Open
501	TPC AT SOUTHWIND	13	4	430	3.997	.002-	1	201	994	175	12	0	Federal Express St. Jude Classic
502	LA COSTA CC	07	3	188	2.997	.002-	1	56	260	53	2	0	Mercedes Championships
503	STARR PASS GC	05	3	155	2.996	.003-	2	107	411	84	10	0	Northern Telecom Open
504	TPC AT AVENEL	10	4	374	3.997	.003-	2	271	897	150	40	11	Kemper Open
505	COLONIAL CC	13	3	178	2.996	.004-	0	196	788	92	33	10	Southwestern Bell Colonial

Rank	Course	Hole	Par	Ydg	Avg Score	O/U Par	Egl	Bird	Pars	Bog	Dbl Bog	Tpl Bg+	Tournament Name
506	DORAL RESORT & CC	07	4	415	3.995	.004-	1	206	926	193	4	0	Doral-Ryder Open
507	TUCSON NAT'L GC	01	4	410	3.995	.004-	0	127	527	106	11	1	Northern Telecom Open
508	ATLANTA CC	14	4	335	3.996	.004-	1	214	568	98	37	12	BellSouth Classic
509	PALM GOLF COURSE	08	3	205	2.995	.005-	0	53	290	49	1	0	Walt Disney World/Oldsmobile Classic
510	TUCSON NAT'L GC	12	3	182	2.994	.005-	0	104	563	102	3	0	Northern Telecom Open
511	LA COSTA CC	04	4	386	3.993	.006-	0	59	261	49	2	1	Mercedes Championships
512	MAGNOLIA GC	09	4	431	3.993	.006-	1	83	454	77	2	0	Walt Disney World/Oldsmobile Classic
513	TPC AT LAS COLINAS	02	3	176	2.993	.006-	1	204	919	188	4	0	GTE Byron Nelson Golf Classic
514	TPC AT THE WOODLANDS	02	4	365	3.993	.007-	0	238	875	195	15	2	Shell Houston Open
515	COG HILL CC	01	4	420	3.993	.007-	0	233	952	210	5	1	Motorola Western Open
516	MAGNOLIA GC	01	4	428	3.992	.007-	0	96	437	78	5	1	Walt Disney World/Oldsmobile Classic
517	SPYGLASS HILL GC	01	5	600	4.992	.007-	0	104	348	75	11	1	AT&T Pebble Beach National Pro-Am
518	LA QUINTA CC	08	4	391	3.992	.007-	0	44	174	34	4	0	Bob Hope Chrysler Classic
519	LAS VEGAS CC	11	4	447	3.993	.007-	0	23	99	20	1	0	Las Vegas Invitational
520	ATLANTA CC	01	4	407	3.991	.008-	0	143	662	116	8	1	BellSouth Classic
521	SPYGLASS HILL GC	03	3	150	2.990	.009-	0	88	374	71	6	0	AT&T Pebble Beach National Pro-Am
522	TUCSON NAT'L GC	17	3	186	2.990	.009-	1	102	578	87	3	1	Northern Telecom Open
523	TPC OF SCOTTSDALE	02	4	416	3.991	.009-	0	221	871	176	13	2	Phoenix Open
524	BERMUDA DUNES CC	15	4	399	3.990	.009-	0	71	322	50	10	0	Bob Hope Chrysler Classic
525	EN-JOIE GC	10	4	360	3.990	.009-	1	241	909	166	29	2	B.C. Open
526	GLEN ABBEY GC	04	4	417	3.989	.010-	0	261	876	209	19	0	Canadian Open
527	KINGSMILL GC	13	3	179	2.989	.010-	1	229	958	193	10	1	Anheuser-Busch Classic
528	RIVIERA CC	16	3	168	2.988	.011-	1	226	823	170	19	0	Nissan L.A. Open
529	TPC AT AVENEL	11	3	165	2.989	.011-	0	257	912	171	26	5	Kemper Open
530	OAKWOOD CC	16	4	389	3.987	.012-	0	204	1,005	175	4	1	Hardee's Classic
531	PEBBLE BCH GOLF LINK	03	4	388	3.986	.013-	0	131	496	107	5	1	AT&T Pebble Beach National Pro-Am
532	KINGSMILL GC	11	4	396	3.986	.014-	1	225	968	189	9	0	Anheuser-Busch Classic
533	WESTON HILLS CC	08	4	419	3.986	.014-	0	126	562	104	3	0	Honda Classic
534	LAS VEGAS CC	07	3	179	2.986	.014-	0	25	96	21	1	0	Las Vegas Invitational
535	STARR PASS GC	06	4	350	3.984	.015-	1	134	375	79	20	5	Northern Telecom Open
536	WAIALAE CC	10	4	355	3.984	.015-	0	226	914	180	11	1	United Airlines Hawaiian Open
537	TPC AT THE WOODLANDS	10	4	428	3.984	.016-	1	219	921	173	10	1	Shell Houston Open
538	INDIAN WELLS CC	17	4	398	3.983	.017-	1	84	294	72	4	0	Bob Hope Chrysler Classic
539	WESTON HILLS CC	03	3	149	2.983	.017-	0	146	527	114	8	0	Honda Classic
540	TUCSON NAT'L GC	16	4	427	3.982	.018-	1	131	525	105	9	1	Northern Telecom Open
541	POPPY HILLS GC	02	3	162	2.981	.018-	0	87	381	68	3	1	AT&T Pebble Beach National Pro-Am
542	PALMER COURSE/ PGA WEST	15	3	155	2.981	.019-	0	93	307	34	21	2	Bob Hope Chrysler Classic
543	MAGNOLIA GC	02	4	417	3.980	.020-	1	110	414	86	5	1	Walt Disney World/Oldsmobile Classic
544	COLONIAL CC	07	4	420	3.978	.021-	1	203	743	165	6	1	Southwestern Bell Colonial
545	ATLANTA CC	13	3	156	2.978	.021-	0	180	622	104	20	4	BellSouth Classic
546	LAS VEGAS CC	01	4	435	3.979	.021-	0	24	99	19	1	0	Las Vegas Invitational
547	PALM GOLF COURSE	09	4	373	3.977	.022-	0	49	309	30	5	0	Walt Disney World/Oldsmobile Classic
548	ATLANTA CC	07	4	340	3.977	.022-	1	192	598	112	21	6	BellSouth Classic
549	TORREY PINES - SOUTH	10	4	373	3.976	.023-	0	142	583	126	6	0	Buick Invitational of California
550	TPC AT SOUTHWIND	08	3	169	2.976	.024-	0	227	972	175	9	0	Federal Express St. Jude Classic
551	TAMARISK CC	10	4	407	3.976	.024-	0	18	93	15	0	0	Bob Hope Chrysler Classic
552	TPC AT LAS COLINAS	11	4	341	3.973	.026-	1	248	883	150	31	3	GTE Byron Nelson Golf Classic
553	LA COSTA CC	08	4	398	3.974	.026-	1	63	256	48	4	0	Mercedes Championships
554	TPC AT SUMMERLIN	10	4	420	3.973	.027-	0	113	392	80	5	2	Las Vegas Invitational
555	LA QUINTA CC	03	3	186	2.972	.028-	0	47	173	32	4	0	Bob Hope Chrysler Classic
556	LAS VEGAS CC	15	4	430	3.972	.028-	0	25	98	19	1	0	Las Vegas Invitational
557	CALLAWAY GARDENS RESORT	15	5	539	4.970	.029-	4	286	803	180	30	4	Buick Southern Open
558	RIVIERA CC	08	4	368	3.970	.029-	4	233	818	166	17	1	Nissan L.A. Open
559	OAKWOOD CC	05	3	169	2.970	.029-	1	214	1,004	165	5	0	Hardee's Classic
560	LA COSTA CC	06	4	365	3.970	.029-	0	64	257	49	2	0	Mercedes Championships
561	ENGLISH TURN G&CC	06	5	557	4.970	.029-	7	324	722	209	38	5	Freeport-McMoRan Classic
562	PEBBLE BCH GOLF LINK	18	5	548	4.968	.031-	4	165	467	67	30	7	AT&T Pebble Beach National Pro-Am
563	TPC AT LAS COLINAS	06	4	396	3.969	.031-	1	219	933	148	14	1	GTE Byron Nelson Golf Classic
564	INDIAN WELLS CC	03	4	382	3.968	.031-	1	76	322	52	4	0	Bob Hope Chrysler Classic
565	TAMARISK CC	16	4	404	3.968	.032-	0	21	88	17	0	0	Bob Hope Chrysler Classic
566	TPC AT THE WOODLANDS	03	3	165	2.966	.033-	1	231	946	111	32	4	Shell Houston Open
567	OAK HILLS CC	01	4	349	3.967	.033-	0	203	556	145	12	1	H.E.B. Texas Open
568	BUENA VISTA GC	07	3	200	2.965	.034-	1	72	258	57	2	0	Walt Disney World/Oldsmobile Classic
569	BERMUDA DUNES CC	10	4	414	3.965	.034-	0	76	316	58	2	1	Bob Hope Chrysler Classic

Rank	Course	Hole	Par	Ydg	Avg Score	O/U Par	Egl	Bird	Pars	Bog	Dbl Bog	Tpl Bg+	Tournament Name
570	LA COSTA CC	13	4	410	3.964	.035-	1	59	267	42	3	0	Mercedes Championships
571	HARBOUR TOWN GL	09	4	337	3.960	.039-	2	230	772	160	11	2	MCI Heritage Classic
572	HARBOUR TOWN GL	16	4	376	3.959	.040-	1	212	820	125	16	3	MCI Heritage Classic
573	LA COSTA CC	17	5	569	4.959	.040-	0	73	243	53	3	0	Mercedes Championships
574	PALMER COURSE/ PGA WEST	04	4	395	3.958	.042-	1	106	287	50	9	4	Bob Hope Chrysler Classic
575	COG HILL CC	03	4	415	3.957	.042-	1	242	988	157	11	2	Motorola Western Open
576	LAS VEGAS CC	14	3	192	2.958	.042-	0	30	89	24	0	0	Las Vegas Invitational
577	TPC AT SOUTHWIND	06	4	427	3.956	.044-	0	219	1,013	144	7	0	Federal Express St. Jude Classic
578	WESTON HILLS CC	02	4	331	3.955	.044-	1	179	479	125	9	2	Honda Classic
579	TPC AT THE WOODLANDS	16	3	177	2.954	.045-	0	215	956	146	8	0	Shell Houston Open
580	LA COSTA CC	15	4	378	3.954	.045-	0	73	249	44	6	0	Mercedes Championships
581	INDIAN WELLS CC	09	4	398	3.954	.045-	0	88	317	37	11	2	Bob Hope Chrysler Classic
582	TORREY PINES - NORTH	03	3	121	2.954	.045-	1	78	331	48	2	2	Buick Invitational of California
583	KINGSMILL GC	14	4	383	3.953	.046-	2	258	952	166	12	2	Anheuser-Busch Classic
584	MAGNOLIA GC	06	3	195	2.953	.047-	1	87	473	52	4	0	Walt Disney World/Oldsmobile Classic
585	DESERT INN CC	04	3	191	2.953	.047-	0	45	224	27	2	0	Las Vegas Invitational
586	TUCSON NAT'L GC	13	4	406	3.951	.048-	0	146	532	87	6	1	Northern Telecom Open
587	BERMUDA DUNES CC	05	4	432	3.951	.048-	0	76	323	52	2	0	Bob Hope Chrysler Classic
588	FIRESTONE CC	11	4	370	3.952	.048-	3	110	329	76	7	0	NEC World Series of Golf
589	PEBBLE BCH GOLF LINK	11	4	384	3.951	.049-	2	123	527	85	3	0	AT&T Pebble Beach National Pro-Am
590	LAS VEGAS CC	16	4	447	3.951	.049-	0	26	99	17	1	0	Las Vegas Invitational
591	DORAL RESORT & CC	15	3	174	2.949	.050-	1	226	950	146	6	1	Doral-Ryder Open
592	ENGLISH TURN G&CC	15	5	542	4.950	.050-	8	341	749	146	43	18	Freeport-McMoRan Classic
593	TPC OF SCOTTSDALE	01	4	410	3.948	.051-	0	234	893	144	12	0	Phoenix Open
594	PALMER COURSE/ PGA WEST	16	4	364	3.949	.051-	1	109	277	57	12	1	Bob Hope Chrysler Classic
595	ATLANTA CC	03	3	188	2.948	.051-	1	161	655	111	2	0	BellSouth Classic
596	COG HILL CC	09	4	568	4.947	.052-	1	293	911	174	18	4	Motorola Western Open
597	CALLAWAY GARDENS RESORT	13	4	367	3.948	.052-	0	252	881	162	11	1	Buick Southern Open
598	OAKWOOD CC	02	4	400	3.945	.054-	0	255	965	160	7	2	Hardee's Classic
599	BERMUDA DUNES CC	07	3	176	2.945	.055-	0	59	360	34	0	0	Bob Hope Chrysler Classic
600	STARR PASS GC	10	4	380	3.944	.055-	2	137	383	84	8	0	Northern Telecom Open
601	TORREY PINES - NORTH	16	4	338	3.944	.055-	1	95	302	58	6	0	Buick Invitational of California
602	DORAL RESORT & CC	02	4	355	3.944	.056-	0	244	924	155	7	0	Doral-Ryder Open
603	TAMARISK CC	09	4	439	3.944	.056-	0	22	91	12	0	1	Bob Hope Chrysler Classic
604	PALMER COURSE/ PGA WEST	17	3	131	2.943	.057-	0	102	283	62	10	0	Bob Hope Chrysler Classic
605	LA QUINTA CC	07	3	174	2.941	.058-	0	38	195	23	0	0	Bob Hope Chrysler Classic
606	PALM GOLF COURSE	15	4	426	3.939	.061-	2	72	271	44	4	0	Walt Disney World/Oldsmobile Classic
607	BUENA VISTA GC	06	4	384	3.938	.061-	0	76	266	44	4	0	Walt Disney World/Oldsmobile Classic
608	PALM GOLF COURSE	02	4	389	3.938	.061-	0	79	263	47	4	0	Walt Disney World/Oldsmobile Classic
609	DESERT INN CC	17	4	395	3.937	.062-	0	53	213	30	2	0	Las Vegas Invitational
610	INDIAN WELLS CC	01	4	388	3.936	.063-	0	78	337	33	7	0	Bob Hope Chrysler Classic
611	LAS VEGAS CC	02	4	405	3.937	.063-	0	32	91	17	3	0	Las Vegas Invitational
612	LAS VEGAS CC	08	4	440	3.937	.063-	0	23	106	14	0	0	Las Vegas Invitational
613	DORAL RESORT & CC	05	4	371	3.936	.064-	1	261	898	163	6	1	Doral-Ryder Open
614	DORAL RESORT & CC	11	4	348	3.935	.065-	2	248	924	147	9	0	Doral-Ryder Open
615	OAKWOOD CC	11	4	386	3.935	.065-	2	256	969	155	6	1	Hardee's Classic
616	TPC AT SOUTHWIND	15	4	385	3.934	.065-	2	297	904	153	23	4	Federal Express St. Jude Classic
617	TPC AT RIVER HIGHLANDS	06	5	574	4.934	.065-	1	294	894	161	17	4	Canon Greater Hartford Open
618	WESTON HILLS CC	10	4	412	3.934	.066-	0	159	543	86	7	0	Honda Classic
619	BUENA VISTA GC	15	4	354	3.932	.067-	0	73	280	29	6	2	Walt Disney World/Oldsmobile Classic
620	TPC AT SAWGRASS	04	4	384	3.931	.069-	1	329	761	169	31	3	The Players Championship
621	COLONIAL CC	17	4	383	3.931	.069-	0	234	743	127	15	0	Southwestern Bell Colonial
622	LA QUINTA CC	16	4	411	3.930	.069-	0	49	178	27	2	0	Bob Hope Chrysler Classic
623	TPC AT LAS COLINAS	05	3	176	2.930	.070-	0	250	922	127	17	0	GTE Byron Nelson Golf Classic
624	PALMER COURSE/ PGA WEST	03	3	180	2.929	.070-	0	80	329	48	0	0	Bob Hope Chrysler Classic
625	TPC AT AVENEL	02	5	622	4.929	.070-	1	294	890	176	10	0	Kemper Open
626	KINGSMILL GC	01	4	360	3.928	.071-	1	301	900	178	11	1	Anheuser-Busch Classic
627	MAGNOLIA GC	12	3	169	2.928	.071-	0	113	439	61	4	0	Walt Disney World/Oldsmobile Classic
628	TORREY PINES - SOUTH	08	3	171	2.926	.073-	0	155	611	85	6	0	Buick Invitational of California
629	WESTCHESTER CC	10	4	314	3.926	.073-	4	329	811	191	17	4	Buick Classic
630	TORREY PINES - NORTH	15	4	397	3.923	.076-	0	91	316	54	1	0	Buick Invitational of California

Rank	Course	Hole	Par	Ydg	Avg Score	O/U Par	Egl	Bird	Pars	Bog	Dbl Bog	Tpl Bg+	Tournament Name
631	TPC AT THE WOODLANDS	11	4	421	3.923	.076-	0	253	934	125	12	1	Shell Houston Open
632	TPC AT RIVER HIGHLANDS	15	4	296	3.923	.077-	6	349	792	196	25	3	Canon Greater Hartford Open
633	FOREST OAKS CC	15	5	554	4.922	.077-	7	310	868	178	14	4	Kmart Greater Greensboro Open
634	HARBOUR TOWN GL	15	5	575	4.921	.078-	1	270	748	141	14	3	MCI Heritage Classic
635	PALM GOLF COURSE	17	4	397	3.921	.078-	1	78	266	47	1	0	Walt Disney World/Oldsmobile Classic
636	TPC AT RIVER HIGHLANDS	09	4	406	3.921	.078-	2	251	989	115	11	3	Canon Greater Hartford Open
637	DESERT INN CC	05	5	578	4.922	.078-	2	59	199	37	0	1	Las Vegas Invitational
638	COLONIAL CC	06	4	393	3.919	.080-	1	241	739	126	10	2	Southwestern Bell Colonial
639	GLEN ABBEY GC	13	5	529	4.918	.081-	13	331	808	186	24	3	Canadian Open
640	OAK HILLS CC	09	3	155	2.918	.081-	0	198	610	95	14	0	H.E.B. Texas Open
641	BAY HILL CLUB	12	5	570	4.916	.083-	0	236	726	120	12	2	Nestlé Invitational
642	TPC AT THE WOODLANDS	12	4	388	3.915	.084-	1	273	896	146	7	2	Shell Houston Open
643	LA COSTA CC	11	3	180	2.912	.087-	0	68	268	36	0	0	Mercedes Championships
644	BUENA VISTA GC	11	3	176	2.912	.087-	0	68	288	34	0	0	Walt Disney World/Oldsmobile Classic
645	TPC AT AVENEL	05	4	359	3.911	.088-	0	286	931	144	10	0	Kemper Open
646	COG HILL CC	10	4	372	3.912	.088-	2	323	892	166	16	2	Motorola Western Open
647	PALM GOLF COURSE	05	4	403	3.908	.091-	0	71	288	33	1	0	Walt Disney World/Oldsmobile Classic
648	DORAL RESORT & CC	12	5	591	4.909	.091-	5	287	871	159	8	0	Doral-Ryder Open
649	TORREY PINES - NORTH	02	4	326	3.908	.091-	1	98	308	53	2	0	Buick Invitational of California
650	PLEASANT VALLEY CC	12	4	377	3.908	.092-	3	275	943	112	19	2	New England Classic
651	BAY HILL CLUB	13	4	364	3.908	.092-	0	240	746	82	24	4	Nestlé Invitational
652	BERMUDA DUNES CC	14	4	385	3.907	.093-	0	117	276	45	15	0	Bob Hope Chrysler Classic
653	TPC OF SCOTTSDALE	04	3	150	2.906	.093-	2	253	900	119	9	0	Phoenix Open
654	PLEASANT VALLEY CC	03	4	386	3.907	.093-	1	303	887	153	8	2	New England Classic
655	OAK HILLS CC	02	3	175	2.905	.095-	0	179	648	88	2	0	H.E.B. Texas Open
656	TAMARISK CC	02	3	171	2.905	.095-	0	21	96	9	0	0	Bob Hope Chrysler Classic
657	TAMARISK CC	11	3	191	2.905	.095-	0	25	89	11	1	0	Bob Hope Chrysler Classic
658	DORAL RESORT & CC	10	5	563	4.904	.096-	5	325	825	149	21	5	Doral-Ryder Open
659	OAK HILLS CC	14	4	328	3.903	.097-	0	188	639	82	7	1	H.E.B. Texas Open
660	TPC AT SUMMERLIN	15	4	341	3.902	.098-	3	133	384	63	9	0	Las Vegas Invitational
661	INDIAN WELLS CC	07	4	338	3.899	.100-	0	96	312	41	5	1	Bob Hope Chrysler Classic
662	TPC AT RIVER HIGHLANDS	02	4	341	3.896	.103-	0	316	892	151	12	0	Canon Greater Hartford Open
663	PALM GOLF COURSE	16	3	172	2.895	.104-	0	72	290	31	0	0	Walt Disney World/Oldsmobile Classic
664	STARR PASS GC	14	5	506	4.894	.105-	9	206	281	94	18	6	Northern Telecom Open
665	TPC AT RIVER HIGHLANDS	11	3	158	2.894	.106-	1	277	963	126	4	0	Canon Greater Hartford Open
666	BERMUDA DUNES CC	11	4	382	3.894	.106-	0	93	319	37	4	0	Bob Hope Chrysler Classic
667	COLONIAL CC	02	4	400	3.892	.107-	1	242	760	109	6	1	Southwestern Bell Colonial
668	TUCSON NAT'L GC	14	4	405	3.891	.108-	0	162	543	61	6	0	Northern Telecom Open
669	BUENA VISTA GC	01	4	385	3.889	.110-	0	80	273	37	0	0	Walt Disney World/Oldsmobile Classic
670	PEBBLE BCH GOLF LINK	04	4	327	3.889	.110-	1	168	490	74	7	0	AT&T Pebble Beach National Pro-Am
671	BUENA VISTA GC	12	4	409	3.889	.110-	0	80	274	35	1	0	Walt Disney World/Oldsmobile Classic
672	DORAL RESORT & CC	16	4	360	3.888	.111-	1	310	861	152	6	0	Doral-Ryder Open
673	BUENA VISTA GC	14	4	390	3.884	.115-	0	77	283	28	2	0	Walt Disney World/Oldsmobile Classic
674	BAY HILL CLUB	06	5	543	4.884	.115-	4	298	664	92	29	9	Nestlé Invitational
675	INDIAN WELLS CC	15	3	163	2.883	.116-	0	102	308	43	2	0	Bob Hope Chrysler Classic
676	OAK HILLS CC	17	4	367	3.882	.118-	4	237	552	114	8	2	H.E.B. Texas Open
677	FOREST OAKS CC	09	5	574	4.878	.121-	8	341	870	140	18	4	Kmart Greater Greensboro Open
678	TPC AT LAS COLINAS	01	4	352	3.877	.122-	2	297	889	117	10	1	GTE Byron Nelson Golf Classic
679	TPC AT SAWGRASS	09	5	582	4.877	.122-	2	325	808	148	11	0	The Players Championship
680	ATLANTA CC	18	5	499	4.877	.122-	15	323	415	132	32	13	BellSouth Classic
681	WESTCHESTER CC	06	3	133	2.877	.123-	6	305	902	136	7	0	Buick Classic
682	EN-JOIE GC	08	5	553	4.875	.124-	4	301	907	131	5	0	B.C. Open
683	PALM GOLF COURSE	03	3	175	2.875	.124-	0	71	300	22	0	0	Walt Disney World/Oldsmobile Classic
684	OAKWOOD CC	07	4	350	3.875	.124-	1	319	928	136	4	1	Hardee's Classic
685	BUENA VISTA GC	04	4	397	3.874	.125-	0	90	260	39	1	0	Walt Disney World/Oldsmobile Classic
686	LA QUINTA CC	09	4	391	3.875	.125-	1	50	186	18	1	0	Bob Hope Chrysler Classic
687	BERMUDA DUNES CC	02	4	418	3.872	.128-	0	97	319	34	3	0	Bob Hope Chrysler Classic
688	WARWICK HILLS G&CC	01	5	567	4.866	.133-	3	361	858	142	19	1	Buick Open
689	PLEASANT VALLEY CC	09	4	383	3.865	.135-	1	304	930	115	4	0	New England Classic
690	TPC AT SUMMERLIN	01	4	408	3.865	.135-	1	132	407	50	2	0	Las Vegas Invitational
691	TUCSON NAT'L GC	06	4	426	3.864	.136-	1	177	519	70	5	0	Northern Telecom Open
692	MAGNOLIA GC	07	4	410	3.862	.137-	3	127	440	46	1	0	Walt Disney World/Oldsmobile Classic
693	TUCSON NAT'L GC	05	4	395	3.863	.137-	0	187	505	75	5	0	Northern Telecom Open
694	TORREY PINES - SOUTH	02	4	365	3.862	.137-	4	196	558	96	3	0	Buick Invitational of California
695	TPC AT SUMMERLIN	07	4	382	3.863	.137-	0	140	397	52	2	1	Las Vegas Invitational
696	RIVIERA CC	17	5	578	4.861	.139-	1	280	863	88	5	2	Nissan L.A. Open

Rank	Course	Hole	Par	Ydg	Avg Score	O/U Par	Egl	Bird	Pars	Bog	Dbl Bog	Tpl Bg+	Tournament Name
697	BERMUDA DUNES CC	09	4	389	3.860	.140-	0	102	317	33	0	1	Bob Hope Chrysler Classic
698	ATLANTA CC	08	5	550	4.860	.140-	1	234	605	76	12	2	BellSouth Classic
699	POPPY HILLS GC	12	5	531	4.859	.141-	6	153	314	52	10	5	AT&T Pebble Beach National Pro-Am
700	TPC AT SUMMERLIN	14	3	156	2.858	.141-	0	136	406	48	2	0	Las Vegas Invitational
701	MUIRFIELD VILLAGE GC	11	5	538	4.857	.143-	6	315	653	111	16	7	The Memorial
702	RIVIERA CC	11	5	561	4.856	.143-	8	326	761	132	12	0	Nissan L.A. Open
703	WESTCHESTER CC	05	5	573	4.856	.143-	10	384	783	153	22	4	Buick Classic
704	BERMUDA DUNES CC	12	3	160	2.857	.143-	0	90	335	28	0	0	Bob Hope Chrysler Classic
705	TAMARISK CC	08	4	393	3.857	.143-	0	25	95	5	1	0	Bob Hope Chrysler Classic
706	LA QUINTA CC	01	4	382	3.855	.144-	0	60	174	21	1	0	Bob Hope Chrysler Classic
707	LA QUINTA CC	18	4	396	3.855	.145-	0	61	171	24	0	0	Bob Hope Chrysler Classic
708	BUENA VISTA GC	18	4	448	3.853	.146-	0	97	256	34	3	0	Walt Disney World/Oldsmobile Classic
709	BUENA VISTA GC	16	3	157	2.851	.149-	0	94	267	22	7	0	Walt Disney World/Oldsmobile Classic
710	COLONIAL CC	11	5	599	4.848	.151-	2	281	734	89	13	0	Southwestern Bell Colonial
711	RIVIERA CC	10	4	311	3.848	.151-	5	325	777	120	9	3	Nissan L.A. Open
712	TPC AT SAWGRASS	11	5	529	4.848	.152-	7	370	752	146	16	3	The Players Championship
713	STARR PASS GC	08	5	543	4.848	.152-	2	192	347	53	13	7	Northern Telecom Open
714	MAGNOLIA GC	16	4	400	3.847	.153-	0	148	420	45	3	1	Walt Disney World/Oldsmobile Classic
715	BUENA VISTA GC	13	4	382	3.845	.154-	0	86	278	26	0	0	Walt Disney World/Oldsmobile Classic
716	LAS VEGAS CC	12	4	401	3.846	.154-	0	34	98	10	1	0	Las Vegas Invitational
717	MAGNOLIA GC	03	3	160	2.845	.155-	1	142	425	49	0	0	Walt Disney World/Oldsmobile Classic
718	TPC AT SOUTHWIND	02	4	387	3.844	.155-	1	356	893	123	10	0	Federal Express St. Jude Classic
719	TPC AT AVENEL	14	4	301	3.845	.155-	1	398	812	143	14	3	Kemper Open
720	KINGSMILL GC	06	4	365	3.842	.157-	3	345	916	124	4	0	Anheuser-Busch Classic
721	TUCSON NAT'L GC	03	4	377	3.838	.161-	0	181	537	48	6	0	Northern Telecom Open
722	TPC AT THE WOODLANDS	06	5	577	4.837	.162-	0	354	840	122	6	3	Shell Houston Open
723	INDIAN WELLS CC	02	4	355	3.833	.166-	0	121	295	34	4	1	Bob Hope Chrysler Classic
724	POPPY HILLS GC	10	5	515	4.833	.166-	12	175	271	60	19	3	AT&T Pebble Beach National Pro-Am
725	TAMARISK CC	06	4	375	3.833	.167-	0	32	83	11	0	0	Bob Hope Chrysler Classic
726	TAMARISK CC	13	4	417	3.833	.167-	0	27	93	6	0	0	Bob Hope Chrysler Classic
727	TPC AT SUMMERLIN	13	5	606	4.828	.172-	2	157	378	51	4	0	Las Vegas Invitational
728	PALMER COURSE/ PGA WEST	14	5	571	4.824	.175-	0	127	293	31	4	2	Bob Hope Chrysler Classic
729	BERMUDA DUNES CC	03	4	377	3.823	.177-	0	117	302	34	0	0	Bob Hope Chrysler Classic
730	BERMUDA DUNES CC	06	4	368	3.821	.178-	0	108	318	26	1	0	Bob Hope Chrysler Classic
731	MAGNOLIA GC	14	5	595	4.819	.181-	1	165	402	45	2	2	Walt Disney World/Oldsmobile Classic
732	PLEASANT VALLEY CC	05	5	606	4.818	.182-	3	361	877	106	7	0	New England Classic
733	EN-JOIE GC	05	5	565	4.816	.183-	6	343	896	98	5	0	B.C. Open
734	MAGNOLIA GC	11	4	385	3.816	.183-	0	150	431	35	1	0	Walt Disney World/Oldsmobile Classic
735	MAGNOLIA GC	08	5	614	4.816	.184-	0	159	412	46	0	0	Walt Disney World/Oldsmobile Classic
736	WARWICK HILLS G&CC	07	5	584	4.816	.184-	7	363	895	116	3	0	Buick Open
737	WESTCHESTER CC	09	5	505	4.808	.192-	21	401	768	151	14	1	Buick Classic
738	WARWICK HILLS G&CC	12	4	335	3.806	.193-	0	383	892	103	6	0	Buick Open
739	TPC AT THE WOODLANDS	13	5	525	4.806	.193-	14	403	772	98	32	6	Shell Houston Open
740	TPC AT SAWGRASS	12	4	336	3.806	.194-	5	351	832	104	1	1	The Players Championship
741	PALM GOLF COURSE	14	5	547	4.804	.196-	2	112	240	39	0	0	Walt Disney World/Oldsmobile Classic
742	TPC OF SCOTTSDALE	17	4	332	3.801	.198-	6	390	750	127	10	0	Phoenix Open
743	TUCSON NAT'L GC	11	5	515	4.797	.202-	5	227	466	70	4	0	Northern Telecom Open
744	OAK HILLS CC	08	4	309	3.795	.204-	5	269	562	72	8	1	H.E.B. Texas Open
745	EN-JOIE GC	03	5	554	4.794	.205-	6	384	845	107	5	1	B.C. Open
746	WARWICK HILLS G&CC	13	5	548	4.794	.205-	29	448	710	175	18	4	Buick Open
747	COG HILL CC	11	5	564	4.793	.206-	12	403	862	112	10	2	Motorola Western Open
748	TAMARISK CC	07	4	331	3.794	.206-	1	31	88	5	1	0	Bob Hope Chrysler Classic
749	TAMARISK CC	17	4	395	3.794	.206-	0	40	76	7	2	1	Bob Hope Chrysler Classic
750	INDIAN WELLS CC	16	4	354	3.791	.208-	1	130	294	28	2	0	Bob Hope Chrysler Classic
751	DORAL RESORT & CC	08	5	528	4.788	.211-	18	410	755	132	12	3	Doral-Ryder Open
752	GLEN ABBEY GC	18	5	508	4.788	.211-	22	493	651	162	29	8	Canadian Open
753	LA COSTA CC	09	5	538	4.786	.213-	2	97	251	22	0	0	Mercedes Championships
754	WARWICK HILLS G&CC	16	5	580	4.784	.215-	3	420	846	106	6	3	Buick Open
755	MAGNOLIA GC	13	4	375	3.784	.215-	0	182	386	49	0	0	Walt Disney World/Oldsmobile Classic
756	TPC AT AVENEL	13	5	524	4.779	.221-	16	460	737	131	23	4	Kemper Open
757	LA COSTA CC	02	5	526	4.773	.226-	3	104	240	24	1	0	Mercedes Championships
758	TORREY PINES - SOUTH	13	5	535	4.772	.227-	10	250	524	63	7	3	Buick Invitational of California
759	PALM GOLF COURSE	13	4	364	3.771	.229-	0	112	259	22	0	0	Walt Disney World/Oldsmobile Classic
760	BERMUDA DUNES CC	13	5	564	4.769	.230-	1	139	291	12	9	1	Bob Hope Chrysler Classic
761	WARWICK HILLS G&CC	14	4	322	3.769	.231-	6	429	835	106	8	0	Buick Open

Rank	Course	Hole	Par	Ydg	Avg Score	O/U Par	Egl	Bird	Pars	Bog	Dbl Bog	Tpl Bg+	Tournament Name
762	LAS VEGAS CC	04	4	365	3.769	.231-	0	47	83	12	1	0	Las Vegas Invitational
763	POPPY HILLS GC	18	5	500	4.766	.233-	6	183	292	51	7	1	AT&T Pebble Beach National Pro-Am
764	OAK HILLS CC	05	5	604	4.763	.237-	6	322	477	107	5	0	H.E.B. Texas Open
765	EN-JOIE GC	12	5	556	4.759	.240-	10	416	817	98	7	0	B.C. Open
766	TUCSON NAT'L GC	15	5	663	4.759	.241-	5	236	478	43	10	0	Northern Telecom Open
767	PALMER COURSE/ PGA WEST	08	4	358	3.758	.241-	1	132	297	25	2	0	Bob Hope Chrysler Classic
768	WESTON HILLS CC	07	5	535	4.759	.241-	5	260	468	51	8	3	Honda Classic
769	ENGLISH TURN G&CC	11	5	550	4.757	.243-	17	438	712	121	15	2	Freeport-McMoRan Classic
770	BAY HILL CLUB	04	5	530	4.756	.244-	18	352	616	96	14	0	Nestlé Invitational
771	TORREY PINES - NORTH	01	5	520	4.754	.245-	2	149	273	37	1	0	Buick Invitational of California
772	COG HILL CC	15	5	519	4.750	.250-	10	468	798	114	9	2	Motorola Western Open
773	AUGUSTA NATIONAL GC	08	5	535	4.748	.251-	9	281	509	78	0	0	The Masters
774	SPYGLASS HILL GC	07	5	515	4.747	.252-	15	162	312	44	5	1	AT&T Pebble Beach National Pro-Am
775	KINGSMILL GC	07	5	516	4.742	.257-	19	517	712	102	34	8	Anheuser-Busch Classic
776	FOREST OAKS CC	13	5	503	4.742	.258-	8	472	790	95	14	2	Kmart Greater Greensboro Open
777	HARBOUR TOWN GL	05	5	535	4.739	.260-	18	385	680	76	16	2	MCI Heritage Classic
778	GLEN ABBEY GC	05	5	527	4.739	.260-	11	450	796	102	5	1	Canadian Open
779	BUENA VISTA GC	08	5	526	4.739	.261-	4	148	198	27	12	1	Walt Disney World/Oldsmobile Classic
780	TPC AT SAWGRASS	02	5	526	4.738	.261-	17	433	726	110	6	2	The Players Championship
781	TAMARISK CC	12	5	550	4.738	.262-	0	46	69	9	2	0	Bob Hope Chrysler Classic
782	SPYGLASS HILL GC	11	5	520	4.734	.265-	5	196	282	49	7	0	AT&T Pebble Beach National Pro-Am
783	PEBBLE BCH GOLF LINK	06	5	516	4.734	.266-	13	254	397	69	7	0	AT&T Pebble Beach National Pro-Am
784	CALLAWAY GARDENS RESORT	11	5	546	4.733	.267-	11	442	746	103	4	1	Buick Southern Open
785	AUGUSTA NATIONAL GC	02	5	555	4.732	.268-	10	308	473	80	5	1	The Masters
786	CALLAWAY GARDENS RESORT	07	5	543	4.728	.271-	13	441	753	91	6	3	Buick Southern Open
787	TPC OF SCOTTSDALE	03	5	554	4.727	.272-	15	417	765	75	11	0	Phoenix Open
788	INDIAN WELLS CC	06	3	140	2.726	.274-	0	138	301	16	0	0	Bob Hope Chrysler Classic
789	PLEASANT VALLEY CC	18	5	583	4.725	.274-	9	466	775	96	7	1	New England Classic
790	INDIAN WELLS CC	12	4	343	3.724	.275-	1	142	288	24	0	0	Bob Hope Chrysler Classic
791	AUGUSTA NATIONAL GC	13	5	465	4.723	.276-	28	349	363	114	20	3	The Masters
792	TPC AT LAS COLINAS	07	5	533	4.721	.278-	29	442	722	111	9	3	GTE Byron Nelson Golf Classic
793	COLONIAL CC	01	5	565	4.719	.280-	17	372	643	82	5	0	Southwestern Bell Colonial
794	TPC AT LAS COLINAS	16	5	554	4.716	.283-	16	493	673	119	13	2	GTE Byron Nelson Golf Classic
795	TORREY PINES - SOUTH	06	5	535	4.716	.284-	2	315	471	57	12	0	Buick Invitational of California
796	MUIRFIELD VILLAGE GC	07	5	549	4.713	.286-	5	380	655	63	5	0	The Memorial
797	LA COSTA CC	12	5	541	4.707	.292-	2	124	228	17	1	0	Mercedes Championships
798	MUIRFIELD VILLAGE GC	05	5	531	4.706	.294-	13	406	594	85	10	0	The Memorial
799	WESTON HILLS CC	01	5	548	4.701	.298-	9	282	456	42	5	1	Honda Classic
800	ENGLISH TURN G&CC	02	5	519	4.697	.302-	14	478	708	100	4	1	Freeport-McMoRan Classic
801	KINGSMILL GC	03	5	538	4.695	.305-	22	516	735	101	18	0	Anheuser-Busch Classic
802	TORREY PINES - NORTH	14	5	507	4.689	.310-	14	169	230	46	3	0	Buick Invitational of California
803	KINGSMILL GC	15	5	506	4.681	.318-	23	547	694	109	17	2	Anheuser-Busch Classic
804	TORREY PINES - NORTH	09	5	497	4.681	.318-	7	181	232	38	4	0	Buick Invitational of California
805	TPC AT SOUTHWIND	03	5	525	4.674	.325-	34	535	679	120	13	2	Federal Express St. Jude Classic
806	TORREY PINES - SOUTH	09	5	536	4.673	.326-	15	317	445	75	4	1	Buick Invitational of California
807	GLEN ABBEY GC	16	5	516	4.670	.330-	12	554	694	87	16	2	Canadian Open
808	ATLANTA CC	11	5	548	4.667	.332-	10	365	493	52	8	2	BellSouth Classic
809	PALM GOLF COURSE	11	5	552	4.666	.333-	2	149	222	18	2	0	Walt Disney World/Oldsmobile Classic
810	ATLANTA CC	02	5	563	4.660	.340-	11	349	525	38	5	2	BellSouth Classic
811	TPC AT SAWGRASS	16	5	497	4.656	.343-	30	550	568	128	17	1	The Players Championship
812	TPC OF SCOTTSDALE	15	5	501	4.657	.343-	37	547	536	146	16	1	Phoenix Open
813	BUENA VISTA GC	17	5	524	4.656	.344-	7	156	196	26	5	0	Walt Disney World/Oldsmobile Classic
814	TPC AT AVENEL	06	5	520	4.649	.350-	64	562	578	134	24	9	Kemper Open
815	WESTCHESTER CC	18	5	535	4.646	.354-	19	553	680	97	7	0	Buick Classic
816	CALLAWAY GARDENS RESORT	02	5	508	4.637	.363-	22	561	608	100	16	0	Buick Southern Open
817	LA QUINTA CC	11	5	526	4.637	.363-	5	100	137	11	3	0	Bob Hope Chrysler Classic
818	TUCSON NAT'L GC	08	5	528	4.635	.364-	16	308	400	40	6	2	Northern Telecom Open
819	POPPY HILLS GC	09	5	557	4.635	.364-	23	200	277	34	4	2	AT&T Pebble Beach National Pro-Am
820	BERMUDA DUNES CC	08	5	540	4.628	.371-	4	189	241	16	1	2	Bob Hope Chrysler Classic
821	TPC AT THE WOODLANDS	15	5	530	4.628	.371-	26	538	674	79	7	1	Shell Houston Open
822	LAS VEGAS CC	18	5	525	4.629	.371-	7	57	64	12	3	0	Las Vegas Invitational

Rank	Course	Hole	Par	Ydg	Avg Score	O/U Par	Egl	Bird	Pars	Bog	Dbl Bog	Tpl Bg+	Tournament Name
823	PALMER COURSE/												
	PGA WEST	18	5	532	4.627	.372-	7	197	213	33	7	0	Bob Hope Chrysler Classic
824	TORREY PINES - SOUTH	18	5	498	4.625	.374-	18	342	450	42	4	1	Buick Invitational of California
825	TPC AT SUMMERLIN	09	5	563	4.625	.374-	13	240	297	40	2	0	Las Vegas Invitational
826	LAS VEGAS CC	10	5	552	4.622	.378-	1	63	69	9	1	0	Las Vegas Invitational
827	FOREST OAKS CC	02	5	511	4.618	.381-	20	560	734	61	5	1	Kmart Greater Greensboro Open
828	HARBOUR TOWN GL	02	5	505	4.615	.385-	32	501	552	76	13	3	MCI Heritage Classic
829	MAGNOLIA GC	04	5	552	4.613	.386-	2	258	334	22	1	0	Walt Disney World/Oldsmobile Classic
830	DESERT INN CC	15	5	512	4.613	.386-	11	125	132	28	2	0	Las Vegas Invitational
831	STARR PASS GC	11	5	522	4.612	.387-	25	276	241	59	11	2	Northern Telecom Open
832	TORREY PINES - NORTH	18	5	485	4.613	.387-	18	185	222	34	3	0	Buick Invitational of California
833	PALMER COURSE/												
	PGA WEST	06	5	560	4.608	.392-	4	185	255	12	1	0	Bob Hope Chrysler Classic
834	OAKWOOD CC	10	5	515	4.602	.397-	30	554	746	57	2	0	Hardee's Classic
835	TPC AT SOUTHWIND	05	5	527	4.601	.398-	34	589	669	79	11	1	Federal Express St. Jude Classic
836	WESTON HILLS CC	12	5	530	4.596	.404-	23	342	377	46	6	1	Honda Classic
837	TAMARISK CC	04	5	509	4.595	.405-	5	56	52	11	2	0	Bob Hope Chrysler Classic
838	STARR PASS GC	03	5	502	4.591	.409-	16	279	270	47	2	0	Northern Telecom Open
839	TPC OF SOUTHWIND	16	5	528	4.588	.412-	24	637	632	74	10	6	Federal Express St. Jude Classic
840	TPC OF SCOTTSDALE	13	5	576	4.585	.415-	32	565	597	82	7	0	Phoenix Open
841	WAIALAE CC	01	5	539	4.582	.417-	30	591	632	65	12	2	United Airlines Hawaiian Open
842	INDIAN WELLS CC	08	5	515	4.582	.417-	6	206	217	23	3	0	Bob Hope Chrysler Classic
843	TPC AT SUMMERLIN	16	5	560	4.581	.418-	15	268	268	32	9	0	Las Vegas Invitational
844	PALMER COURSE/												
	PGA WEST	02	5	512	4.580	.419-	16	189	228	21	3	0	Bob Hope Chrysler Classic
845	OAK HILLS CC	15	5	527	4.581	.419-	32	403	412	58	11	1	H.E.B. Texas Open
846	BERMUDA DUNES CC	01	5	538	4.580	.420-	7	192	238	15	1	0	Bob Hope Chrysler Classic
847	TPC AT THE WOODLANDS	01	5	515	4.577	.423-	29	580	654	52	10	0	Shell Houston Open
848	BUENA VISTA GC	10	5	514	4.574	.425-	6	181	177	25	1	0	Walt Disney World/Oldsmobile Classic
849	FIRESTONE CC	02	5	497	4.572	.427-	19	229	240	33	3	1	NEC World Series of Golf
850	LAS VEGAS CC	06	5	546	4.573	.427-	1	69	67	2	4	0	Las Vegas Invitational
851	DESERT INN CC	10	5	518	4.569	.430-	10	118	161	9	0	0	Las Vegas Invitational
852	AUGUSTA NATIONAL GC	15	5	500	4.565	.434-	37	407	354	61	15	3	The Masters
853	DESERT INN CC	01	5	515	4.566	.434-	11	128	143	12	4	0	Las Vegas Invitational
854	MUIRFIELD VILLAGE GC	15	5	490	4.562	.437-	47	509	459	68	23	2	The Memorial
855	INDIAN WELLS CC	18	5	501	4.563	.437-	24	201	197	23	8	2	Bob Hope Chrysler Classic
856	PEBBLE BCH GOLF LINK	02	5	502	4.558	.441-	31	309	362	33	4	1	AT&T Pebble Beach National Pro-Am
857	PALM GOLF COURSE	07	5	532	4.549	.450-	9	179	187	16	2	0	Walt Disney World/Oldsmobile Classic
858	WAIALAE CC	18	5	552	4.549	.450-	39	593	634	61	5	0	United Airlines Hawaiian Open
859	OAK HILLS CC	10	5	506	4.549	.450-	29	442	366	73	6	1	H.E.B. Texas Open
860	RIVIERA CC	01	5	501	4.544	.455-	33	604	524	62	12	4	Nissan L.A. Open
861	LA QUINTA CC	13	5	508	4.543	.457-	6	123	113	10	4	0	Bob Hope Chrysler Classic
862	WAIALAE CC	09	5	513	4.541	.458-	51	630	552	82	13	4	United Airlines Hawaiian Open
863	PLEASANT VALLEY CC	04	5	547	4.540	.459-	28	625	641	60	0	0	New England Classic
864	COG HILL G&CC	05	5	525	4.538	.462-	34	653	649	58	5	2	Motorola Western Open
865	MAGNOLIA GC	10	5	526	4.532	.467-	16	283	293	24	1	0	Walt Disney World/Oldsmobile Classic
866	LA QUINTA CC	05	5	498	4.531	.468-	11	109	127	7	2	0	Bob Hope Chrysler Classic
867	DORAL RESORT & CC	01	5	514	4.529	.471-	29	627	618	54	2	0	Doral-Ryder Open
868	BERMUDA DUNES CC	18	5	513	4.513	.487-	16	229	176	26	4	2	Bob Hope Chrysler Classic
869	BAY HILL CLUB	16	5	481	4.491	.508-	52	548	421	61	12	2	Nestlé Invitational
870	PALMER COURSE/												
	PGA WEST	11	5	512	4.481	.519-	10	237	199	10	1	0	Bob Hope Chrysler Classic
871	BUENA VISTA GC	05	5	506	4.475	.524-	9	202	164	15	0	0	Walt Disney World/Oldsmobile Classic
872	OAKWOOD CC	06	5	515	4.468	.532-	52	684	606	46	1	0	Hardee's Classic
873	INDIAN WELLS CC	05	5	517	4.467	.533-	16	238	177	21	3	0	Bob Hope Chrysler Classic
874	INDIAN WELLS CC	14	5	483	4.450	.549-	19	227	199	10	0	0	Bob Hope Chrysler Classic
875	WAIALAE CC	13	5	508	4.439	.560-	56	693	526	56	1	0	United Airlines Hawaiian Open
876	LA QUINTA CC	06	5	521	4.417	.582-	12	137	99	6	1	1	Bob Hope Chrysler Classic
877	TAMARISK CC	18	5	527	4.389	.611-	5	70	48	3	0	0	Bob Hope Chrysler Classic
878	PALM GOLF COURSE	01	5	495	4.386	.613-	20	212	151	9	1	0	Walt Disney World/Oldsmobile Classic
879	TPC AT SUMMERLIN	03	5	492	4.377	.623-	50	318	182	35	7	0	Las Vegas Invitational
880	TUCSON NAT'L GC	02	5	495	4.376	.624-	42	437	272	19	2	0	Northern Telecom Open
881	LAS VEGAS CC	09	5	474	4.343	.657-	14	84	29	14	2	0	Las Vegas Invitational
882	TAMARISK CC	01	5	482	4.183	.817-	5	96	22	3	0	0	Bob Hope Chrysler Classic

Acknowledgments

Since 1986, when the original edition of this book appeared, the landscape of the PGA Tour has changed substantially. New tournaments have joined the schedule, several long-standing events have moved to new courses, and many of the incumbent courses have undergone redesigns and updates. In all, nearly half of the Tour's playing field is different from what it was a decade ago. Thus, the book you're holding is more than an update or revision, it is a completely new edition of *Golf Courses of the PGA Tour*.

The most marked difference is in the photography. When we decided to redo the book, I was fearful we'd never be able to duplicate the photographic quality of the original edition. For that book, a team of three photographers crossed the country for nearly a year. This time, we opted to assign most of the work to just one photographer. How, I wondered, could he equal the work of three men?

He didn't—he did even better. This book marks the emergence of John Johnson as the next great golf course photographer. Not only did Johnson travel the same transcontinental routes as the original three photographers, he completed the work in half the time. Yet he never hurried, never settled for

John Johnson

a mediocre shot. When he ran into less than ideal weather, he waited hours—sometimes days—for the sun to appear. And when he got good weather, the results were magnificent. The majority of the scenic golf course photos herein are by John, and I'm extremely grateful for every one of them.

I will confess that Johnson wasn't my first choice—the job would have gone to Fred Vuich, had I not already chosen Fred for full-time work as the staff photographer for *GOLF Magazine*. However, these pages are blessed with several examples of Fred's work, including perhaps the single finest photo in the book, a shot of the eighth hole at Pebble Beach, taken from atop a cherry picker just before sunset.

Some of golf's most photogenic courses are those in the PGA Tour's network of Tournament Players Clubs, and the Tour chose wisely when it designated Mike Klemme as the man to photograph the TPC courses. I'm pleased that this book includes a number of his photos.

Of course, it's one thing to take scenic photos in solitude and quite another to take them in the midst of a PGA Tour event. The latter assignment fell to PGA Tour photographers Sam Greenwood, Pete Fontaine, and Jeff McBride, and I'm grateful to them for taking time from their duties to capture the action/scenics and the portraits of the Tour players.

I'm proud of the author's photo on the jacket flap because it was taken by one of the world's best photographers, but even prouder because that photographer happens to be a good and longtime friend, Leonard Kamsler, whose work has graced *GOLF Magazine* for over 30 years.

The attractive half of that photo belongs to my wife, Libby, as does much of the attractiveness of this book. When we did the original edition of *Golf Courses of the PGA Tour*, Libby had to audition to become the artist for the course maps. Back then, she was just beginning to make a transition from her training as a medical illustrator. Today, she is one of the most sought-after artists in golf. Her course maps, hole diagrams, and landscapes have appeared in numerous magazines and books and are featured regularly in network telecasts of golf events. As I write this, Libby has a list of commissions that will keep her busy for at least the next two years, yet our two sons and I surely will remain spoiled, since she always manages to give her best time to us.

Updating the text for this book involved the efforts of several people, and none was more important than *GOLF Magazine* Senior Editor David Barrett, golf statistician extraordinaire, who updated the tournament-by-tournament statistics, the scorecards for every course, the lists of past champions, and the all-time PGA Tour records for the extensive statistical section at the back of the book. I am grateful to David for this work, which I could never have done—at least not with his cheerfulness and accuracy.

This is the official guide to courses of the PGA Tour, and it could not have been completed without a great deal of official help, from the tournament directors at the various Tour sites and from the players who contributed instructional tips. At PGA Tour headquarters in Ponte Vedra, Florida, thanks are due to Vice President of Communications John Morris and Public Relations Director Sid Wilson for a variety of favors along the way and to Deane Beman, who retired recently after a remarkable twenty years as Commissioner, for his kind contribution of the Foreword.

Finally, my appreciation goes to my "team" at Harry N. Abrams, Inc. This is the fourth book I have done with Senior Vice President and Executive Editor Margaret L. Kaplan, a deft editor, an astute businesswoman, and a good friend. It was Margaret who first conceived the idea for a book about the courses of the pro tour, truly an inspiration given the fact that she herself is a confirmed non-golfer. It is also the fourth collaboration with Photo Editor John Crowley, Designer Bob McKee, and Production Director Shun Yamamoto. Harry N. Abrams, Inc., deserves its reputation as the world's preeminent publisher of elegant gift books, and these men are three of the main reasons.

The original edition of *Golf Courses of the PGA Tour* met with astonishing success, with some 240,000 copies now in print. This book may or may not have the same good fortune, but if not, it won't be for lack of effort by the people I have mentioned here. To each of them, I owe my sincerest thanks.

George Peper
Grandview, New York
January 1994

Photograph Credits

© David Bean: 20, 21 above

© James Blank: 65–66

Courtesy Annandale Country Club/© GilFord Photography: 110–11, 112–14

Courtesy Atlanta Country Club, photo Clate Sanders: 132–36

Courtesy TPC at The Woodlands/© Rowley Associates: 126–27, 128–30

© *GOLF Magazine:* 164 below

© *GOLF Magazine*/Fred Vuich: 2–3, 32–39, 41–44, 45 below, 47 left, 101, 102, 142–43, 144 above, 146, 147 below, 148, 168–69, 172 below

© John Johnson: 4–5, 6–7, 14–15, 16 below, 18, 19 below, 68–69, 72, 73 above, 74–75, 77 below, 79 right, 80–81, 82 above, 92–94, 95 above, 96–97, 122–23, 124 right, 125 below, 162–63, 165–66, 174–75, 178–79, 180 below, 181 below, 182–83, 185 below, 188–89, 190 below, 192–93, 194–96, 204–6, 207 below, 208 above, 210–11, 212 right, 214, 216, 217 below left and right, 218 below, 220–21, 222 above, 223, 224 above, 226 left, 228, 229 left, 230 below, 232–34, 240–41, 242 above, 243–44, 246–50

© Mike Klemme/Golfoto: endpapers, 1, 8–9, 10–11, 21 below right, 23 above, 24, 51–52, 58, 61 below, 84 left, 88 above, 90 below, 98–99, 103, 116–18, 119 below, 120, 138, 150–51, 152, 156, 158, 159 below, 160, 198, 200–1, 202, 253–54

All map paintings © Elizabeth Peper

Copyright PGA TOUR Archives: 11–12, 22, 40, 45 above, 48–49, 50, 55, 59 above, 62–63, 64 below, 70–71, 76 above, 78–79, 84–87, 89, 100, 104, 105–8, 115, 119 above, 124 left, 125, 137 below, 145, 170–71, 180 above, 184–85, 194 left, 207 above, 212 left, 226–27, 242 below, 252

Copyright PGA TOUR, photo Stan Badz: 13, 154, 159 above, 215, 217 above, 218 above, 229 right, 231, 236–37, 238 below, 251 below

Copyright PGA TOUR, photo Pete Fontaine: 90 above, 128, 172 above, 176, 213 below, 222 below, 224 below

Copyright PGA TOUR, photo Sam Greenwood: 16 above, 21 below left, 23 below, 26–27, 30, 47 right, 54, 56–57, 59 below, 64 above, 76 below, 82 below, 88 below, 97 right, 109 above, 112 left, 139–40, 144 below, 151 right, 153, 157, 164 above, 170 left, 185 above, 190 above, 191 below, 199, 201 right, 208 below, 235 below, 238 above, 255

Copyright PGA TOUR, photo Pete Marovich: 186

Copyright PGA TOUR, photo Jeff McBride: 16–17, 28–29, 147 above.